Lives of Faust

Lives of Faust

The Faust Theme in Literature
and Music

A Reader

Revised Edition

Edited by Lorna Fitzsimmons

Walter de Gruyter · Berlin · New York

♾ Printed on acid-free paper which falls within the guidelines
of the ANSI to ensure permanence and durability.

Library of Congress Cataloging-in-Publication Data

Lives of Faust : the Faust theme in literature and music : a reader / edited by
Lorna Fitzsimmons. – Rev. ed. p. cm. – (De Gruyter textbook)
Includes bibliographical references and index.
ISBN 978-3-11-019823-2 (alk. paper)
1. Faust, d. ca. 1540 – Fiction. 2. Faust, d. ca. 1540 – In literature. 3. Faust,
d. ca. 1540 – Songs and music. 4. Faust, d. ca. 1540 – Songs and music –
History and criticism. I. Fitzsimmons, Lorna, 1957 –
PN6071.F33L58 2008
809'.93351–dc22

ISBN 978-3-11-019823-2

Bibliographic information published by the Deutsche Nationalbibliothek

The Deutsche Nationalbibliothek lists this publication in the Deutsche
Nationalbibliografie; detailed bibliographic data are available in the Internet
at http://dnb.d-nb.de.

Printed in Germany
Typesetting: Dörlemann Satz, Lemförde
Cover design: deblik, Berlin
Printing and binding: AZ Druck und Datentechnik GmbH, Kempten

Contents

Acknowledgements

Every effort has been made to contact copyright holders. Permission to reproduce the following is gratefully acknowledged:

Peter Werres, "The Changing Faces of Dr. Faustus," *Doctor Faustus: Archetypal Subtext at the Millennium*, ed. Armand E. Singer and Jürgen Schlunk, Morgantown, West Virginia UP, 1999, 1–23.

Osman Durrani, *Faust: Icon of Modern Culture*, Helm Information, Mountfield, East Sussex, 2004, 25–28, 244, 351–352, 362–364, 379.

Philip Mason Palmer and Robert Pattison More, *Sources of the Faust Tradition*, New York, Haskell House, 1965, 82–126, 239–243.

Gerald Strauss, "How to Read a *Volksbuch*: The *Faust Book* of 1587," *Faust through Four Centuries*, ed. Peter Boerner and Sidney Johnson, Tübingen, Max Niemeyer Verlag, 1989, 27–39.

The Historie of the Damnable Life and Deserved Death of Doctor John Faustus, ed. William Rose, London, Routledge, 1925. Reprinted by permission of Taylor and Francis, Ltd., Abingdon.

Christopher Marlowe, *Doctor Faustus*, ed. David Wootton, Indianapolis, Hackett, 2005, xi, xiv-xxiv.

Klaus L. Berghahn, "Georg Johann Heinrich Faust: The Myth and Its History," *Our* Faust? *Roots and Ramifications of a Modern German Myth*, ed. Reinhold Grimm and Jost Hermand, Madison, U Wisconsin P, 1987, 3–21.

Gounod, *Faust*, Angel Records, Record Number SDL-3622.

Gounod, *Faust*, G. Schirmer Inc., London/New York, 1966, Scene I Act III, Scene I Act IV.

Steven R. Cerf, "The Faust Theme in Twentieth-Century Opera: Lyric Modernism," *Zeitschrift für Literaturwissenschaft und Linguistik* 66 (1987), 29–41.

Paul Valéry, "My Faust," *The Collected Works of Paul Valéry*, vol. 3, *Plays*, ed. Jackson Mathews, tr. David Paul and Robert Fitzgerald, Princeton, Princeton UP, 1960, 29–30, 36–41.

Karl Shapiro, "The Progress of Faust," *Selected Poems*, Random House, 1968, 121–122. Reprinted by permission of Harold Ober Associates, Inc., New York.

Paul M. Malone, "Faust as Rock Opera," in Durrani, op. cited, 263–275.

Preface

Lorna Fitzsimmons

Eric Bockstael edited the first edition of this book in 1976. Professor Bockstael's intent was to complement the television course *The Lives of Dr. Faust*, which he developed for Wayne State University's University Studies and Weekend College Program. The course on Faust had grown out of a course in Wayne State's experimental interdisciplinary general education program, partially funded by the Ford Foundation. Martin M. Herman, former Chair of Wayne State's Monteith College, recalls the original course well: "The original course attempted to survey humanity's view of itself: sometimes grandiose, monumental and noble – the magisterial view of mankind; at other times, insignificant, petty, and base – the worm's eye view of human activity. Central to the former category was a segment on the Faust legend: i.e., Marlowe, Goethe, Berlioz, Gounod, and Thomas Mann, plus art works by Michelangelo and Henry Moore. Included in the latter, were satirical works by Juvenal, Molière, Swift, Voltaire, Gilbert and Sullivan, Hogarth, and Daumier. The course's capstone was provided by Igor Stravinsky's *The Rake's Progress*, an opera with a libretto by W. H. Auden and Chester Kallman that incorporated and combined both Faustian and satirical elements." In his Preface, Bockstael explains why the segment on Faust was developed into a separate course: "Suffice it to say that the myth of Faust is one of the most outstanding expressions of Western man's search for knowledge, freedom, creation of his own existence and attempts not to succumb to the humdrum of life ..."

Today, over thirty years later, the number of universities offering courses centering on Faust discourse has grown significantly. Demand, both in and beyond the academe, remains high. The academic institutionalization of Faust studies is, of course, intricately enmeshed with the far-reaching commercialization of Faust discourse in the post-World War II period. Many students today are introduced to Faust themes as they listen to rock music, view video games, or shop for shoes, whether in the United States, Europe, Asia, or elsewhere. The popularity of Faust discourse is increasingly global, its audiences increasingly diverse, and its producers less rarely women.

In revising *Lives of Faust*, I have followed the first edition's aim of providing key texts by which to gain a broad understanding of the shifting contours and contexts of the Faust theme. Essays by Peter Werres,

Osman Durrani, Gerald Strauss, David Wootton, Klaus L. Berghahn, Henry Bacon, Steven R. Cerf, and Paul M. Malone bring the collection up-to-date.

I am appreciative of the support of Mrs. Julie Bockstael-Poll; Martin M. Herman, Professor Emeritus of Humanities, Wayne State University; Roslyn Schindler, Chair, Interdisciplinary Studies, Wayne State University; and Jane Hoehner, Director, Wayne State University Press.

Introduction

The Changing Faces of Dr. Faustus

Peter Werres

Is Faust the German tragedy, the dark German genius of high-flying dreams and Icarian crashes[1] *in nuce*, or is Faust more than just a German phenomenon? In 1939, Thomas Mann concluded that the occident has recognized the symbolic value of the Faust figure for its deepest essence.[2] Earlier this century, the conservative cultural philosopher Oswald Spengler (1880–1936) had discussed the Faustian in his controversial treatise known in the English-speaking world as *The Decline of the West*. He identifies the Faustian in the soul of the particular period of culture which we have inherited; our art, our morals, our science, our politics – all that the West has contributed to the history of civilization is Faustian culture, Spengler contends. He claims that Faustian aspiration is the key to all creative activities and personalities of post-medieval Western civilization.

* * *

The views of Spengler and Mann have prevailed: Together with a handful of other notorious dead white European males,[3] the figure of Dr. Faustus

---

[1] Especially in the aftermath of WWII, Germany has often been described as a country exhibiting a schizoid split, a place where idyll lives side by side with horror, where deep feeling and deep thought coexist with total coldness and goose-stepping – something Thomas Mann describes throughout his *Doctor Faustus*. The literary reference frequently employed in this context is Goethe's Faust moaning: "Zwei Seelen wohnen, ach, in meiner Brust,/ Die eine will sich von der andern trennen" ("Two souls, alas, are dwelling in my breast,/ and one is striving to be severed from the other" ll. 1112–13), a quote that has long become part of every German thesaurus.

[2] Remarks later published in the essay collection *Adel des Geistes* (1945).

[3] Out of the entire body of Western lliterature, Salvador de Madariaga selected four men – Faust, Hamlet, Don Juan, and Don Quixote – a composite of which would represent most of the Western experience: "Don Juan is one of the great Europeans of the spirit. With Faust, Hamlet and Don Quixote, he makes up the constellation of the four brightest stars of our European firmament .... [A]rtists are on even stronger ground [than philosophers and historians] ... in pointing to the world of European immortals as the highest, richest and brightest source of European consciousness and life" (*Don Juan as a European Figure*, Byron Foundation Lecture No. 22 [Nottingham: Univ. College, 1946]1).

is by now generally considered one of the archetypal manifestations of modern Western experience and has, beyond that, come to symbolize humankind's quest for ever greater knowledge and understanding.

It all started with the experience of the historical Dr. Faustus, excommunicated as a heretic, a victim of the political and religious tensions of his day, whose mysterious death contributed to the subsequent legends that have arisen surrounding his character. Over time, the changing faces of Faust have often shown bizarre distortions. Earlier this century, the Faustian drive for understanding and achieving gestalt in the physical and metaphysical context was first perverted by some literary scholars of the Nazi times and then wholeheartedly embraced by German politicians.

Archetypal Faust, of course, has all the elements of Western hubris and thus something of modern Western Everyman, who believes himself to have all the answers and often displays a coquettish attitude toward self-destruction – something that can also be sold to the modern consumer, from Mephisto footwear to Faust wine and Magic Cards. In 1958 even the quest for the long-elusive proof of a mathematical formula turned into a Faustian tale. An anthology entitled *Deals with the Devil*[4] contains a short story by Arthur Poges, "The Devil and Simon[5] Flag." Simon bets his soul on the devil's not being able to provide him with the answer to the question, "Is Fermat's Last Theorem correct?" After a day, the devil returns and admits defeat[6] – a rare occasion in a Faustian tale.

Over time, the Faust myth has simply become what an earlier age would have called "one of the literary bibles of the occident." Speaking of

---

[4] Ed. Mike Resnik et al. (New York: Ballantine, 1994 [reprint]).

[5] The very choice of the first name Simon is an allusion to signing one's soul away. Simon Magus was one of the numerous forerunners of the later Faust character. He had sought to buy the gift of the Holy Spirit by entering into a pact with the devil. From the Old to the New Testament, from Theophilus to Calderón's *Prodigious Magician*, we encounter "pre-Faustian" tales all sharing the same underlying phenomenon. Among the legends not yet discussed in literary scholarship is that of thirteenth-century Viking pirate Eustace the Monk, feared as the "Black Monk," who supposedly entered into a pact with the devil to make his ship invisible – something that apparently did not work all that well, as he was caught and beheaded at sea.

[6] Which comes as no surprise: In *The Last Problem* (Publications of the Mathematics Association of America, 1990), E. T. Bell had written that civilization would, most likely, come to an end before Fermat's Last Theorem could be solved. This Holy Grail of mathematics was actually uncovered only three years after Bell's prediction (356 years after Fermat's challenge) and, according to its discoverer, Princeton professor Andrew Wiles, without the devil's help.

bibles: some time ago, Jehovah's Witnesses were handing out *Watchtowers* with the headline "Beware the 'Faust Syndrome,'" Faust as universal man falling prey to evil temptations of all kinds? In 1991, and again in 1995, my interdisciplinary seminar on "Substance Abuse and Literature," which used the Faust myth as a metaphorical reference point, drew huge student crowds at George Washington University. In its May 1992 issue, the magazine *Musician* ran a cover story on "Drugs & Booze & Creativity: Dealing with the Devil." It also offered a Faustian interpretation of a self-indulgent life in the narcissistic fast lane as a sure one-way street to hell. The pact signed in blood is everywhere; whether musician, painter, or poet, whether American, French, Russian, or German, the image always fits. Case in point: The immortal Russian Sergej Jessenin, who seemed to have it all: the magic poetic touch, money, and one of the most beautiful women of his time, world-famous dancer and firebrand Isadora Duncan – had written himself a pact with a one-way ticket to alcoholic self-destruction; he penned his last poem – appropriately – with his own blood before hanging himself.

Just as is true for other archetypal Western figures,[7] the literature on the Faust figure is simply oceanic. Between 1900 and 1965 alone, Faust appeared as the subtext for more than two hundred literary creations. Not surprisingly, an MLA database search will yield, just for the years 1963 to the present, 1144 entries for items concerning themselves with modern Faust experiences. Needless to say, there are also numerous, virtually countless musical references to Faust, including works of such mainstream composers as Louis Spohr, Franz Liszt, Robert Schumann, Gustav Mahler, Charles-François Gounod, Hector Berlioz, Arrigo Boito, Edvard Hagerup Grieg,[8] and Ferrucio Busoni.[9] Film, the youngest of the media, now, at the millennium, looking back at its first century of existence, has been quick to embrace the Faust legend.

---

[7] As regards, for example, literature pertaining to one such archetypal figure, Don Juan, see Armand E. Singer, *The Don Juan Theme: An Annotated Bibliography of Versions, Analogues, Uses, and Adaptations* (Morgantown: West Virginia UP, 1993) with its over three thousand entries.

[8] Who set Ibsen's *Peer Gynt* to music.

[9] Even the grandmaster of musical drama, Richard Wagner, dabbled in Faustian material. While in the end no grand Faust opera was created, Wagner left us an often-performed Faust *Overture*, and it is also hard to overlook that topos and gestus of his *Rheingold*'s closing scene closely mirror the core of the last act of Goethe's *Faust II* (the old, godlike figure under the illusion that all has been accomplished, just when all is about to be lost).

One would be pressed for space were one to attempt, within the pages allotted here, merely to provide a list of the names of authors, composers, and other artists who created works inspired by the Faust legend. With regard to literature, an essay could, space permitting, criss-cross in and out of the Germanic literatures to follow the trail of Faust, from the original German folk book on Doctor Faustus (published by Spies in Frankfurt in 1587) and Christopher Marlowe's *Doctor Faustus* (already nine editions by 1640), to Johann Wolfgang von Goethe's *Faust*,[10] Friedrich Maximilian Klinger's Faust novel, Nicolaus Lenau's and Ernst August Friedrich Klingemann's Faust plays, Jakob Michael Reinhold Lenz's *The Judge from Hell*, Matthew G. Lewis's *The Monk*, Christian Dietrich Grabbe's *Don Juan and Faust*,[11] Wilhelm Hauff's "Cold Heart," Lord Byron's[12] *Manfred*, Henrik Ibsen's stage adaptation of a Norwegian folk tale, *Peer Gynt*, considered the "Nordic Faust," George Sand's *The Seven Strings of the Lyre*,[13] Victor Hugo's *Interior Voices*, Adalbert von Chamisso's *Faust* and *Peter Schlemihl*, Ivan Sergeyevich Turgenev's *Faust*, Gustave Flaubert's *The Temptation of Saint Anthony* (three versions),[14] Fyodor Dostoyevski's and Mikhail Lermontov's Faust-inspired oeuvre, Leo Tolstoy's "How Much Land Does a Man Need," Paul Valéry's *My Faust*, Stephen Vincent Benét's "The Devil and Daniel Webster," Joseph Conrad's *Victory*,[15] Hermann Hesse's "An

---

[10] Goethe's *Faust I* and *Faust II* are generally considered the greatest, if not the ultimate, Faust representation. E. M. Butler, in *The Fortunes of Faust* (London: Cambridge UP, 1952), ended up categorizing all post-Goethean Faust literature into either would-be-Goethean, non-Goethean, un-Goethean, or anti-Goethean.

[11] An interesting mix of the Faust and Don Juan characteristics. For a more recent attempt along these lines, see Albert Camus's plans to write "Don Faust et Dr. Juan."

[12] Byron himself was often referred to as "the son of Faust." As such, he was actually eulogized in Goethe's *Faust II* in the figure of Euphorion. Ibsen's entire *Peer Gynt* has also been interpreted as one monumental homage to the Faustian in Byron.

[13] In *Les sept cordes de la lyre* (1839), Sand examined her inner creative workings – Renan had referred to her as "la harpe éolienne de notre temps."

[14] In 1873, Turgenev (who, under the influence of Byron, had himself dabbled with a Faustian interpretation of the St. Anthony legend) wrote the introduction to the never-to-materialize Russian edition of this work, which portrays the protagonist's thirst for knowledge, for a perfect understanding of the nature of existence, and the metaphysical angst of his temptation.

[15] For a Faustian assessment, see Alice Raphael, *Goethe the Challenger* (New York: Jonathan Cape and Robert Ballon, 1932), especially the chapter "Joseph Conrad's Faust."

Evening with Doctor Faustus," J. R. R. Tolkien's "A Leaf by Niggle," Mikhail Bulgakov's *Master and Margarita*, and so many others.[16] Of interest for our purpose at hand are also Klaus Mann, troubled son of Thomas Mann, and his controversial 1936 novel *Mephisto*[17] (cinematic adaptation 1981), as well, of course, as Thomas Mann himself and one of the greatest novels of the last century before the millennium, his *Doctor Faustus*.[18]

As regard *Faust* the literary subtext, a more comprehensive, phenomenologically oriented *explication de textes* could focus on the following developments:

a) Changing representations of the actual pact, from a one-way ticket to hell (in the folk book and for Marlowe, Lenau, and Klingemann) to the possibility of redemption (Goethe: a bet, rather than a pact) and the more modern concept of the pact in which one is informed years after a "deal" that one has been "under contract" for some time (examples: Ibsen, Thomas Mann – we do not know we are in chains until the chains have become so strong that we can no longer break them on our own).

Chapter 6 of the original Faust Book left nothing to the imagination:

> I have written it with mine own hand and blood, being in perfect memory, and hereupon I subscribe to it with my name and title, calling all the infernal, middle, and supreme powers to witness of this my letter and subscription.
>
> John Faustus, approved in the elements,
and the spiritual doctor.[19]

---

[16] For a detailed analysis of Faust-related topics see the essay collection *Faust through Four Centuries: Retrospect and Analysis*, ed. Peter Boerner and Sidney Johnson (Tübingen: Niemeyer 1989) as well as the comprehensive annotated bibliographies of literature on the Faust theme by Hans Henning: *Faust Bibliographie* (Berlin-Weimar: Aufbau Verlag, 1966–76) and William E. Grim: *The Faust Legend in Music and Literature* (Lewiston, NY: Mellen, 1988–).

[17] Klaus Mann's stinging novel, subtitled "Roman einer Karriere," chastises the fictitious actor Höfgen for having compromised his conscience and his art in order to be a success under the Nazi regime. Höfgen and his pact – signed with the powers that be in the blood of millions of others – was widely understood as a portrayal of Gustav Gründgens, successful actor and director during *and after* the Nazi times, who was generally considered the ultimate performer of Goethe's Mephisto character.

[18] Even after half a century, by the close of the millennium, this novel is still a known entity, albeit not necessarily in a positive way: *"Doctor Faustus"* was the answer to a 1998 *Jeopardy* question: "What is the title of Thomas Mann's most unfinishable novel?"

[19] Quoted from the first English translation of the Faust Book, provided by P. F. Gent in 1592.

By contrast, and in what would appear only a hallucinatory encounter with the prince of darkness – echoing the devil's appearance in Dostoyevski's *The Brothers Karamazov* – Thomas Mann's Adrian Leverkühn is given the following explanation about the state of affairs:

> To be short, between us there needs no crosse way in the Spesser's Wood and no cercles. We are in league and business – with your blood you have affirmed it and promised yourself to us, and are baptized ours. This my visit concerns only the confirmation thereof. Time you have taken from us, a genius's time, high-flying time, full XXIV years *ab dato recessi*, which we set to you as the limit.[20]

b) changing forms of human affection, ranging from nearly complete lack thereof, a manifestation of self-indulgent, solipsistic drives (e.g., Grabbe, Ibsen), to a search for a soul mate with whom to share concerns at the depth of one's existence, capacity for compassion, and altruistic service and thus ultimate redemption (e.g., Goethe[21]) or condemnation (e.g., Grabbe, and virtually all Slavic Faust characters, where the focus tends to shift away from Faust to Mephisto, symptomatic of a schizoid, divided self) or a mix thereof (e.g., Ibsen and perhaps Thomas Mann). Mann, for instance, purposely stresses Adrian's persistent "avoidance of physical contact (220)" and explains:

> That he could have as many love-affairs as he chose seemed to satisfy him, it was as though he shrank from every connection with the actual because he saw therein a theft from the possible.   (169)

Along the same lines one could also, within a larger framework, describe the gradual transformations of Faust-figures not permitted to love altogether (folk book: love as undesirable competition for the diabolic) to modern Faust, who is often portrayed as incapable of loving (i.e., from external givens to internal ones). In chapter 9 of the folk book, entitled "How Doctor Faustus would have married, and how the Devil had

---

[20] *Doctor Faustus*, trans. H. T. Lowe-Porter (New York: Alfred A. Knopf, 1948) 248.

[21] At the end of *Faust II*, the creative moment is not supplied by the devil but by Faust himself, and not for solipsistic but for altruistic ends. This way, Faust would not be merely temporarily satisfied as in the past, but finally, in a lasting fashion, by satisfying others. And it is this moment of realization that Faust wants to *"last"* – the magic word, on account of which the Devil *thinks* he has won his bet.

almost killed him for it," Mephistopheles tries to persuade the obstinate doctor:

> "Sweet Faustus, think with what unquiet life, anger, strife, and debate thou shalt live in when thou takest a wife; therefore change thy mind." ... Faustus said unto him, "I am not able to resist nor bridle my fantasy; I must and will have a wife, and I pray thee give thy consent to it." Suddenly upon these words came such a whirlwind about the place that Faustus thought the whole house would come down; ... he was taken and thrown into the hall, that he was not able to stir hand nor foot. Then round about him ran a monstrous circle of fire, never standing still, that Faustus fried as he lay and thought there to have been burned."

Conversely, over the course of Adrian's aforementioned encounter, the devil confides:

> A general chilling of your life and your relations to men lies in the nature of things – rather it lies already in your nature; ... the fires of creation shall be hot enough to warm yourself in. Into them you will flee out of the cold of your life.   (249)

c) Changing concepts of condemnation (as the price for having selfishly enjoyed the privileges of Mephistophelian services). For the folk book and Marlowe's Doctor Faustus, for instance, punishment is external; it is perceived as concrete and physical. As a result, Marlowe's *Dr. Faustus* pleads to be dissolved into nothingness so that he does not have to pay the ultimate price for his "damnable life."

> (The clock strikes twelve.)
> It strikes, it strikes! Now body, turn to air,
> Or Lucifer will bear thee quick to hell!
> O soul, be changed into small water-drops
> And fall into the ocean, ne'er to be found.
> (Thunder, and enter the Devils.)   (5, ii)

This type of existential dissolution, disintegration, depersonalization, is exactly what Ibsen's Peer, as modern man, fears when his time comes. His punishment is internal: towards the end of act 5, "at a cross-roads," a "button moulder" with a huge casting-ladle intends to melt Peer down into the big depersonalized melting pot out of which new creations are to come.

> THE BUTTON MOULDER: Well, as you can see, I'm a moulder of buttons. You must go in my ladle.
> PEER GYNT: What becomes of me there?
> THE BUTTON MOULDER: You'll be melted down.

PEER GYNT: Melted? ... I'm certainly not an exceptional sinner.
THE BUTTON MOULDER: Ah, but, my friend, that's exactly the point; in
the strictest sense, you're no sinner at all. That's why you escape the ordeal of
the Pit and go, with the rest, in the casting-ladle.[22]

He explains that Peer was to have been a shining button on the waistcoat
of the world, yet this button had a flaw, its "hook" was not formed prop-
erly, so it could not permanently attach itself to its larger surroundings,
his *Mitwelt*,[23] could not take the step from "I" to "Thou" and "We." Peer's
self-centered, noncommittal attitudes (motto of his *Innenwelt*: "To Thine
Own Self Be Enough") robbed him (and those he encountered) of a truly
human experience, of the experience of non-solipsistic love and attempts
at altruistic service (as portrayed in Peer's unnamed counterpart/alter
ego, who appears briefly in acts 3 and 5, and, albeit ambiguously, in the
fifth act of Goethe's *Faust II*).

In intertextual play, a), b), and c) are frequently intertwined in presen-
tations of the archetypal Faust theme. One such, also one of the most recent literary manifestations of Faust as a literary subtext, can be found in
Vaclav Havel's *Temptation* (1987), where Foustka (alias Faust) meets world
history, and the death throes of a perverted Real Socialism end up foreshadowing a crisis of reason altogether. In philosophical terms, the original Dr. Faustus of the folk book, who stood at the threshold to the age of
reason, is no longer such a distant character at the turn of the millennium,
with its often-conjured up notions about the end of the age of reason,
if not of history altogether.[24] Havel gives us a taste of the Heisenberg
Uncertainty Principle:

FISTULA [Mephistopheles]: My dear sir, the truth isn't merely what we believe,
after all, but also why and to whom and under what circumstances we say it.[25]

A detailed study of the changing artistic frameworks available for Faustian settings would also reveal a circular motion: From the folk books and
puppet plays on Dr. Faustus in the sixteenth and seventeenth centuries to

---

22 Henrik Ibsen, *Peer Gynt: A Dramatic Poem*, trans. Peter Watts (Harmondsworth,
   Middlesex, England: Penguin, 1970) 197. This, and the later quoted p. 217,
   echoes Dante's *Inferno*: In the Vestibule of Hell we find all the fence-sitters,
   mealy-mouthed, non-committal characters, being eternally tortured by wasps.
23 To use the terminology of Swiss analyst Ludwig Binswanger, who defined different realms of existence with compounds ending in *-welt*.
24 See Francis Fukuyama, *The End of History and the Last Man* (New York: The Free
   Press, 1992) 55–142.
25 *Temptation*, trans. Marie Winn (New York: Grove/Atlantic, 1989) 60.

the highbrow literary achievements of the nineteenth and the early twentieth century and, subsequently, to the multimedia avenues of our times,
i.e., a return to popular genres that helped communicate the story of the
archetypal figure at the time of its original conception.

So, the legend of the white European male known as Dr. Faustus is certainly widespread in the West, but how alive as a subtext is it in today's
world? To answer this question we first have to take a hard look at the
changing faces of literature itself, i.e., we have to face up to the changing
recognition of the respective genres which in our days may prove capable
of acting as a medium for the legendary figure.

It has often been observed that contemporary culture is experiencing
the "gradual end of the classical age of reading,"[26] that it no longer has
any use for conspiratory literary codes, for the cryptography that charac-
terizes much of mainstream recent literature, especially German literature. In a world that shows less and less interest not only in the written
word but in words altogether (often preferring icons or other visual images instead), new, and in some cases very ancient, forms of communicating messages have emerged or reemerged. Popular literature has been
taking over (and in some cases has, as is the case with the Faust legend,
actually taken back) much of the terrain slowly abandoned by so-called
highbrow literature. Even when dealing with emotionally troublesome
legacies, popular culture genres may manage to turn what is difficult to
express, even the supposedly unspeakable,[27] into something to be com-
municated – including scary aspects of the Faust myth. Two examples:

Faust, a story that started as a folk-book and puppet show in the sixteenth century and later came to fascinate much of intellectual Europe,
has recently resurfaced in prime time as an episode of the funny social
satire[28] *The Simpsons*, an American TV series (also aired in Germany) with
great popular appeal to the young and the young at heart. Although

---

[26] Alvin Kernan, *The Death of Literature* (New Haven: Yale UP, 1990) 134.

[27] See, for instance, for our times, Art Spiegelman's award-winning 1986 comic
series on the holocaust, *Maus I* and *II*. Shocking, yet not new: following sixteenth-century German *Bänkelsang* tradition, some of the earliest German and
Dutch Faust books had a comic-book appearance.

[28] As early as 1862, brainy satires on Faustian literature began to surface: See,
for instance *Faust: Der Tragödie dritter Teil*, for which a Deutobold Symbolizetti
Allegoriowitsch Mystifizinsky took tongue-in-cheek credit, ridiculing the deep
gloom-and-doom mood among the post-Goethean German Faust disciples of
the time. (This Goethe parody was actually penned by the well-known Tübingen scholar Friedrich Theodor Vischer.)

mainly aimed at teenagers, the particularly brainy episode in question, "The Devil and Homer Simpson," was created by some brilliant satirists,[29] and its inspired lunacy appeals to even the most seasoned Faust aficionado. With the concept of the jury from hell, we encounter the Faust myth filtered through Benét's intertext, "The Devil and Daniel Webster." In this most popular American Faust tale, the focus appropriately shifts away from the Faust character to what once was considered America's most glamorous profession, the law. In an earlier American period, it was the lawyer Daniel Webster who got Jabeth Stone off the devil's hook by arguing his case before a jury of the dead. In our more enlightened times of lawyer bashing, the legal counsel botches his case and steals away – he literally bails out through the bathroom window – leaving it to the very unlikely eternal female Marge (short for Margaret, i.e., Goethe's Gretchen?) to save a beleaguered Homer Simpson – all of this in good Faust tradition: even legally speaking, Homer's soul is the property of his wife Marge.

Lawyer-bashing (all in character: the original Faust was, after all, Herr Doktor Jurisprudentiae, unhappy with his profession) and redeeming love also characterize an earlier filmic tongue-in-cheek reference to the Faust myth, the 1967 British film *Bedazzled*, a brainy British comedy supposedly with no higher inspirations than entertainment. Here we find the Faust theme intertwined with the myth of King Midas[30]: the Devil, as usual, gives people what they want, or rather, what they ask for. (Beware of what you wish for.) In *Bedazzled*,[31] Stanley Moon, an unlikely Faust character who, like Goethe's Faust, has a vial with poison on his shelf but who prefers – unsuccessfully – to attempt suicide by hanging himself, subsequently, under the Devil's guidance, fails to capitalize on any of his seven wishes and self-destructs under the weight of the seven deadly sins. Again lawyer bashing, *Bedazzled* provides an attorney as the living antithesis to the Faustian drive, allegorically represented by one of the seven deadly sins, sloth; the attorney ends up falling back into a drunken stupor while witnessing the damned man's signature. For convenience's sake, the

---

[29] The producer of *The Simpsons*, Matt Groening, incidentally, is of German descent and his series often portrays a fascination with German contradictions.

[30] In a twisted way, King Midas was a precursor to the Faust character: human hubris testing the territories beyond sensible human wishes and desires, something that also echoes through numerous European fairy tales, i.e., The Grimm Brothers' "Der süße Brei."

[31] Directed by Stanley Donen, screenplay by Peter Cook, music by Dudley Moore, with Raquel Welsh as "Lust" and a Devil with business cards.

Devil, who, as usual, has all the best lines, signs the contract with blood drawn from the lawyer.

Seeking the saving grace of the eternal female, Stanley Moon yearns to be united with his co-worker at the fast-food-place, yet the devil drags him through all the deadly sins, assuring him: "We'll get to that later." "That" is the object of the un-hero's desire, Margaret Spencer: whether play, novel, or comic, some aspects of the Faust myth never change – two hundred years earlier, Goethe's Faust suffered the same diversionary tactics at the hands of Mephisto. Yet even lowly Homer's Marge and Margaret Spencer understand that whoever is capable of giving his soul to another human being cannot possibly sell it to the devil. That is why all Mephisto characters attempt to spoil any gratifying moment of connectedness in their efforts to hold the "eternal female," the natural corrective of goodness, at bay – see "b" above. And only the Faust figures not self-absorbed and forever in love with themselves are capable of such giving in the first place – see "c" above.

With the reemergence of Satanic cults among the young at the close of the millennium, recent years have, again, seen a virtual explosion of Faust-inspired artistic creations, especially in the more popular genres. In the *Dead End Kids*[32] (in which five Mephistos request five signatures from Faust with five different Pens), several other American avantgarde plays, and recent American movies (mostly without any stated literary ambitions), including *Pale Rider*, *Oh God, You Devil*, *Needful Things*,[33] and *Tombstone* (in which the cast is watching Goethe's *Faust*), the Faust myth is alive, as it is in *The Jersey Devil* (now available as a video game) and *Angel Heart*, a Faustian tale with heavy bloodletting, describing a private eye's descent into hell in pursuit of a missing person who opted out of a pact with the devil. Even the blockbuster *Jurassic Park* offers obvious Faustian connotations, as, in the ultimate loss of gestalt,[34] the instinctual, primordial meets the high-tech world. And in the 1997 thriller *Devil's Advocate*, souls are lost (to the devil) as cases are won by a powerful New York City law firm.

Faust and classical music are a well-known entity. Two recent examples: In 1952, Brecht composer Hanns Eisler enraged the East Ger-

---

[32] Produced by the Theatre Morgan in 1983.

[33] Based on Stephen King's novel of the same title.

[34] The two faces of the dia-bolic appear throughout: primordial intoxication and icy, remote matter-of-factness. (In Nietzschean terms, this reflects a loss of gestalt, where the Dionysian does not join forces, but conflicts, with the Apollonian.)

man cultural bureaucracy with his *Johann Faustus* libretto (his opera was not performed until 1974), and German/Russian composer Alfred Schnittke's semi-atonal *Historia von D. Fausten*, based on the Hamburg Faust Book, premiered in early 1998, just months prior to the composer's death.

But what about contemporary popular music? In *Crossroads*, a guitarist sells his soul to the devil to become the perfect blues guitar player. The Charlie Daniels Band's "The Devil Went Down to Georgia" pitches a fiddler against the prince of darkness. Musically as well, the Faust myth reappears in ever new forms: in 1997, for instance, Washington's Kennedy Center presented "Faust in Africa," a three-day KenCen festival featuring, among others, South Africa's Handspring Puppet Company with life-sized wooden figures and deafening rap, presenting Faust as a jaded administrator and his devilish advocate as a weasely bureaucratic clerk. In what may well amount to the ultimate merging so far of genres and media, the French group Friches Théâtre Urbain invited audiences on a world tour from Washington to Perth, Australia, to follow the hair-raising journey of Faust, as Mephistopheles and fellow devils lead him to destruction. This roving street procession, entitled *Mephistomania*, featured outrageously exotic costumes, mostly paralyzing though at times inspiring music, and colorful pyrotechnics (mainly, erratic fireworks accentuated by blinding distress flares). In this internet-advertised 1997 street-theater happening, five towering characters on stilts were flailing three-meter-long heavy bamboo poles, supposedly for support, growling noisy and largely incomprehensible dialogue, merging, as it seemed, Artaud's Theater of Cruelty with Primal Scream Therapy. Faust appeared lost in all the extravaganza.[35]

Too extravagant for most of us? What about Faust and sports? In *Damn Yankees*,[36] a musical romp based on the Faust theme, a desperate fan strikes a deal with the devil to interfere with the fortunes of a failing baseball team, the New York Yankees. Recently there was a considerably less diabolic spin-off (with a happy ending – no parental guidance required): *Angels in the Outfield*.[37]

---

[35] On-line criticism provided by Mar Bucknell in *The Western Review* (westrev@ iinet.net.au) concluded that "hell is a place where bad French actors shout a lot."

[36] The 1958 film version was directed by George Abbott.

[37] Faust and politics? Hardly a week goes by without some reference – the most recent journalistic one, as of this writing, George F. Will's "Faustian Deal in California" (*The Washington Post* 24 May 1998: C7).

Yet how alive is Faust presently in so-called highbrow literature? Very much so. Havel's above-quoted play *Temptation* is but *one* example of many. To show that Faust is, indeed, very much alive as a subtext of literature in the more traditional sense, I will follow the trail of Faust's pact with the devil into the latter part of our century to two telling examples of texts embedded with Faustian markers. One example concerns itself with what has been perceived as *the* Faustian pact of our times, technology-driven progress as part of a diabolic design[38] to destroy our planet's equilibrium (the ecosystems upon which human life depends for its existence). The other example mixes these concerns with gender issues, observations on the male/female dichotomy: how male is the Faustian drive per se (in the eyes of a female writer) and how and where does the eternal female feature today? The two novels to be discussed are products of German-speaking Europe (one from Switzerland, the other from the former German Democratic Republic), yet they both aspire to transcend the Germanic realm. Toward the end of our millennium, these two literary works portray some of the most ponderous dilemmas of our times.

In Max Frisch's modern classic *Homo Faber* ("Man the Maker"), terminally ill without being aware of it, the hero builds dams against elemental forces, erects lifeless barriers against the flow of life, just as Goethe's Faust did toward the end of his life. As was typical for Faber's 1950s generation of robotic technocrats, who had signed their pact with technology with the blood of others,[39] he insists on being the creator from scratch, on starting with a tabula rasa, thus, in ruthless Faustian hubris and in a self-defeating way, destroying nature by working against rather than with it.[40]

The novel begins where Goethe's *Faust II*, act 5, left off (prior to the latter's often criticized apotheosis). It shows the protagonist, with his ex-

---

[38] The editor of the magazine *The Futurist*, Edward Cornish, once used the Faust analogy to describe humankind's love affair with technology. He contended that when the Industrial Revolution arrived, man entered into a Faustian bargain with the machine.

[39] Already in Goethe's *Faust II*, act 5, the price for unconditional progress is paid not by Faust, the architect of great schemes, but by simple people like Philemon and Baucis and, very tellingly, by a stranger who found refuge in their hut after being shipwrecked at sea – having escaped the wrath of the elements, he burns to death in the supposed safe haven in a man-made blaze.

[40] The old view – Faber's view – saw economic development and free-market principles as incompatible with environmental concerns. Yet with the hands on the clock moving toward the fateful hour, much of humankind has by now recognized that development and environmental stewardship simply must go hand in hand.

clusively quantitative approaches[41] relying on soulless technology, as the
destroyer of all that he touches; the devil always gives people what they
ask for, literally. One is not only reminded of Faust, but again, as noted in
an earlier context, of King Midas, himself tricked by a supernatural offer
he did not think through. It is inevitable that "Man the Maker," advoca-
ting, in the absence of truly utopian vision, nothing but shortsighted tech-
nological progress, will over time end up destroying the future of the
people in supposedly developing areas of the globe whom he claims to be
helping. His building of dead things to suppress the forces of life destroys,
in a perverted Faustian drive, the future of others, just as Faust's visionary
designs of progress in Goethe's *Faust II* destroy the existence of Philemon
and Baucis, who lived in peace and in harmony with nature.[42]

More immediately, Faber ends up destroying his own personal future
by causing the death of the only living thing he ever created: his daughter.
Again, parallels to Goethe's driven, solipsistic Faust character abound,
from Faber's Walpurgis Nights in Cuba to his damming of natural flow
patterns, which may also be interpreted as blockage of natural generational flows (a father's love affair with his daughter), resulting in a stag-
nant, sterile life. Just as Faber sold his soul to the lifeless technology
he helped create, so his heart is captured by the sight of his own flesh,
his daughter.[43] The shockingly young age of fifty-year-old Faber's lover –
who not only *could* be his daughter but actually *is*, without his knowing it –
reminds us of doomed young Gretchen in Goethe's *Faust*. With Gretchen, Faust attempts to turn the clock back, seemingly allowed to start
anew. He fails and ends up blinded, like Oedipus. Similarly, Faber's falling
in love with a child-woman less than half his age may also be seen as a
futile effort to regain his own youth. It constitutes in itself a narcissistic
act, a manifestation of a solipsistic relationship (see "b" and "c" above),
of being blindly in love with oneself, especially with a projected image of
one's own younger self: Goethe's Faust first encounters Gretchen when
looking in a mirror. Destructive Homo Faber (in his blind hubris, both

---

[41] Faber has a hard time realizing that not everything that counts can be counted.
     Again, parallels to Goethe's *Faust* are obvious.
[42] Both Faust and Faber fight nature, supposedly to help others. In both cases,
     they deal with the power of water.
[43] Earlier, Faber had committed a truly solipsistic act, when, in a love embrace, he
     ended up kissing his own arm by mistake. His relationship with his daughter,
     whom patriarchal Faber insists on renaming "Sabeth," constitutes the ultimate
     manifestation, on one level at least, of his viewing women as sex objects to be
     molded, reflecting his own brilliance.

life-giver and life-taker, responsible for large-scale environmental destruction and the death of his daughter) sees his young counter-image (as if in a mirror) right in front of him. In order to stay in character, he subconsciously *has* to eliminate his only live creation, hence he destroys what could have saved him. The laconic remark that the father destroyed everything, his lover, his daughter, and thus his future, constitutes the very last entry in Faber's diary and the last words of a novel which is, after all, entitled *Homo faber*, i.e., *constructive* man. In terms of classical mythology, Faber is thus to be equated not with gods that create but with the god of the dead, of the underworld, with Hades, or, as regards his attempts at god-likeness, in Christian terms, with Lucifer. Faustian Faber is thus, in a schizoid way, also Mephistopheles.

Not only does Goethe's *Faust*, again, come to mind, but also, ultimately, the melding of the Faust and Mephisto characters in much of modern representation[44]: in Mikhail Lermontov's *A Hero of Our Time*, the protagonist Pechorin is a schizoid character; one of his personalities is Faust-like, the other Mephistophelian, and the latter comes to dominate. Brecht's *Good Person of Szechwan* constitutes a more modern representation of the same phenomenon:

> Yes, it is me. Shui Ta and Shen Teh, I am both of them.
> Your original order
> To be good while yet surviving
> Split me like lightning in two people.[45]

The same duality also permeates, as mentioned earlier, much of Dostoyevski's work, from *Crime and Punishment*, to his *Devils* and his *Brothers Karamazov.* In the latter, the focus shifts away from Faust to his opponent/alter ego Mephisto: the devil appears to speak with thoughts out of the Protagonists' own minds. In a curious reversal of Genesis, one of the protagonists concludes: "I think if the devil does not exist, and man has created him, he has created him in his own image" (part I, book 2, ch. 6). In *Crime and Punishment*, the split nature of Raskolnikov is apparent from

---

[44] This also holds true for the arts: see, for instance, the illustration entitled *Circle Limit IV* by popular graphic artist M. C. Escher.

[45] Bertolt Brecht, *The Good Person of Szechwan*, trans. John Willet, ed. John Willet and Ralph Manheim (New York: Arcade, 1994) 105. The schizoid Faustian element is also evident in Brecht's earlier *Saint Joan of the Stockyards*, where cutthroat but doomed meat-packing boss Mauler yearns for his better half in the Salvation Army girl Joan. (Entire sections of this play, incidentally, parody rhythm and diction of Goethe's *Faust.*)

his very name: connecting the prefix *Ras* meaning "asunder," "torn to parts" to *kolot* (meaning "to split") renders the Russian equivalent of the Greek "schizo," "to split," "to be divided."[46]

While Faust appears only in palimpsest fashion in Frisch's *Homo Faber*, Christa Wolf's *Accident* is replete not only with Faustian allusions but actually refers to Faust himself throughout.[47] In her 1987 novel, Wolf delves back into the world of mythological images and fairy tales to get to the bottom of what she perceives as the Faustian in Western society gone awry: "I'll have to reconsider the destinies and decisions of modern Faust."[48] The novel could well be subtitled "Therapeutic Approaches to the Faust Syndrome," as Wolf puts a new spin on things: No longer is the Faustian seen as a genius's striving for greater insight and deeper connectedness. According to Wolf, plain and simple, something is wrong with the male brain,[49] literally: the author's "day's news" is a parallel account of the removal of her brother's brain tumor in a far-away hospital and emerging news about the Chernobyl nuclear disaster.

Wolf attempts to delineate a causal connection between male obsessive thought and its inhuman products such as nuclear and thermonuclear weaponry and technology,[50] with their potential for global destruction. Gazing at the sky which is, after the nuclear accident, no longer the harbinger of life and growth but of doom, the author ponders:

---

[46] See introductory remarks on Faust as perhaps more than just a German phenomenon.

[47] Over a dozen times total.

[48] *Accident: A Day's News*, trans. Heike Schwarzbauer and Rick Takvorian (New York: Farrar, 1989) 93.

[49] "At which crossroads did evolution possibly go so wrong!" (Wolf 65). "Highly gifted, very young men who – driven, I fear, by the hyperactivity in certain centers of the brain – have not signed a pact with the devil (oh brother! the good old devil! would that he still existed!), but rather with the fascination with a technical problem" (62). "Like the rats ... continuously pressing the 'desire button.' Where is the center of desire in the brains of those scientists?" (47).

[50] "Such catastrophes do not break in from heaven or hell, but overspecialization in technology and science seems to develop, almost without fail, into dystopia" (Ute Brandes, "Probing the Blind Spot: Utopia and Dystopia in Christa Wolf's *Störfall*," *New German Studies* 18.2 [1990]: 106). At the same time, Wolf, as the first-person narrator, is, ironically, relying on advanced laser technology for her brother's brain surgery and on the blessings of the computerized telephone system to keep in contact with the hospital in question.

How strange that a-tom in Greek means the same as in-dividuum in Latin: un-splittable. The inventors of these words knew neither nuclear fission nor schi-zophrenia. Whence the modern compulsion to split into ever smaller parts, to split off entire parts of the personality from that ancient being once thought indivisible.   (29)

In her novel, Wolf juxtaposes insular male knowledge and productivity as exhibited by Faber and his peers[51] – with the perceived superiority of the female (motherly/sisterly) mode of intuition and productivity (compare, for instance, the above-mentioned Mother Gaia cult in Grece, now the basis of feminist Gaia Theory) which, for some time now, has in the eyes of *some* feminists constituted the most essential emancipatory female claim.[52]

Faustian men are in usually abusive denial about their being violent agents of a destructive Mephistophelian paradigm bent on destroying the saving grace of love:

> Deep down, everybody knows that if the gratification of their deepest desire is not granted, does not succeed, or is denied, then they … create substitute gra-tification and cling to a substitute life, a substitute for life, the entire breathlessly expanding monstrous technological creation, a substitute for love.   (Wolf 32)

For Wolf, Faust is not a German phenomenon; it is a universal male phe-nomenon.[53] Through history, the writer contends, women have not en-tered into the Faustian bargain – the ruthless Faustian quest is the mani-festation of a fear-based, uncentered, schizoid personality, a solipsistic male aberration, a male "blind spot." In leitmotif fashion, Wolf, through-out her novel, refers to the German folk tale of "Little Brother and Little

---

[51]   In this regard, Wolf's novel echoes the anti-Faustian, Cassandra conclusion of act 2 of Friedrich Dürrenmatt's 1962 play *The Physicists*: "Our science has become horrible, our research dangerous, our knowledge fatal" (*Cassandra* also happens to be the title of an earlier Wolf novel). In Dürrenmatt's play, every-thing simply runs its course – from murders to nuclear proliferation.

[52]   For details, see Alexander Kluge and Oskar Negt, *Öffentlichkeit und Erfahrung: Zur Organisationsanalyse von bürgerlicher und proletarischer Öffentlichkeit* (Frankfurt/ Main: Suhrkamp, 1972) 50. As regards Christa Wolf herself, see Christiane Zehl Romero, "Remembrance of Things Future': On Establishing a Female Tradi-tion," and Karin McPherson, "Female Subjectivity as an Impulse for Renewal in Literature," both in *Responses to Christa Wolf*, ed. Marilyn Sibley Fries (Detroit: Wayne State UP, 1989) 108–27 and 149–61, respectively.

[53]   Hard to overlook is the fact that virtually all Faust authors and their protagon-ists are, after all, male – Emma Tennant's 1993 novel *Faustine* being one notable contemporary exception.

Sister." Men are like "little brother," who was bewitched and turned into a vulnerable buck deer[54] that now instinctively follows the call of the hunting bugle, seeking out danger, forever returning wounded from the hellbent chase, to be tended by "little sister."

In Wolf's eyes, women ("little sister") may show, out of an understanding, non-egotizing, *constructive*, nurturing sense of "social motherhood" based on feminine knowledge, the way for men to free themselves from the curse of being forever egomaniacal, critical, and controlling in their fight to keep their alienated position in the world. Wolf thus juxataposes the potentially *destructive* nature of a self-centered, yet splintered male self with the creative energies of the self-enclosed, harmonizing female world.

The destructive and self-destructive protagonist of Frisch's *Homo Faber* was, figuratively speaking, an accident waiting to happen. Wolf's *Accident* constitutes an after-the-fact assessment. Both novels serve as powerful reminders that, at the millennium, Faust as a subtext is as alive in highbrow literature as he presently is in popular literature.

Forever changing, Faust has always demanded our attention in the German-speaking and the whole of the modern Western world, in traditional literature and fringe genres, in earlier centuries and at the millennium. For all the diverse artistic representations of the Faustian, for all the morphing faces of Faust, Heraclitus's axiom holds: "Nothing endures like change" – yet with a corollary: The more the Faust myth changes, the more it endures. It is our myth, and we must go on confronting it.

---

[54] The original and several later Faust books, as well as Marlowe's *Doctor Faustus*, can be considered intertexts of this very Grimm fairy tale: they include an episode where Mephistopheles's magic turns a character into a deer and others into hounds to chase him down.

I The Historical Faustus

Osman Durrani

The story of Faustus is rooted in a climate of transition from naive faith in redemption to increasing focus on sinfulness that required hard work if it was to be overcome. In these turbulent times, the legendary doctor's life cannot be satisfactorily mapped or reconstructed. His itinerary is a confusing one that criss-crosses Germany and resembles that of a travelling huckster, fortune-teller and lowly apothecary. Many scholars have attempted to inquire into his biography and examine the possibility that there may be specific and verifiable events at the root of the tradition. Could there have been a single individual on whom the Faust legend was largely or exclusively based? This is an intriguing question that has been answered in many different ways; Hans Henning's bibliography lists 183 articles and books purporting to give information about the historical figure. Two groups of scholars believe that Faust's identity can be pinned down: those who follow Günther Mahal in locating his birthplace in the south-western town of Knittlingen in 1480, and those who, with Frank Baron, take it to have been Helmstadt near Heidelberg some fifteen years earlier. The name of Knittlingen, sometimes spelt 'Kundling', occurs in manuscripts by Johann Mennel [also Manlius] and Johann Wier [also Wierus, Piscinarius], as well as in Philip Melanchthon's table-talk; these date from the 1560s (Meek, 36–40). By contrast, the literary Faust Book has him see the light of the world in the eastern province of Saxony, but without hinting at his dates. It is probable that stories about many different savants and magicians, including Johannes Tritheim, Georg Helmstetter, and Cornelius Agrippa, had some effect on the content of the later chapbook. One critic actually suggests that they must have been a team or a family business, a hypothesis that neatly gets round the two names (Johann and Georg) and incompatible dates. That there were father-and-son teams of this type operating in the field of 'alternative therapy' is easily proven (Peukert, 55–74).

If there was a single Faustus, this person must have been widely travelled and have laid claim to an array of different skills, given the contradictory material that has been recorded. The sixteenth-century documents that refer to him vary in scope and reliability. To judge by the picture they convey, one or several figures were touring Europe under the name of 'Faustus' between 1500 and 1540. It has proved impossible to pin him down to a single individual with a recognisable biography. He is 'the classic outsider, rootless, a will o' the wisp, passing, like Socrates and

Jesus Christ, without a personally written legacy to assert his true identity'
(Jones, 3). All the evidence we have is in the form of isolated snippets,
Faustsplitter or 'splinters'. The incomplete and contradictory records were
first collected in large numbers by Alexander Tille in a compilation entitled *Die Faustsplitter in der Literatur des sechzehnten bis achtzehnten Jahrhunderts*
('The Faust fragments in the literature of the sixteenth to eighteenth century'), a portion of which was translated into English by Philip Palmer
and Robert More. The 'evidence' that is advanced by several German
towns (Simmern, Heidelberg, Knittlingen, Roda, Wittenberg, Leipzig,
Staufen) that they were the magician's birthplace or temporary domicile
must remain suspect, though later authorities have used such contradictory data to provide a stimulus to the local tourist industry. A largish
number of locations (Nuremberg, Ingolstadt, Erfurt, Bad Kreuznach,
Gelnhausen, Rebdorf) rely on manuscript references to support their
claims to have been visited by him. An association with the University of
Heidelberg, where one 'Georg Faust' matriculated in 1505, is unreliable.
The name was entered in the records, but there is nothing to suggest that
this individual was identical with the magician. The literary text on which
later Faust traditions are based gives a birthplace (Roda) and names a university (Wittenberg), yet there are no references in the chronicles of either
to the magician's birth or employment there. Marlowe turns Roda into
'Rhodes', which led Victor Hugo to assume the Mediterranean island to
have been his birthplace (Meek, 63).

What remains is a multitude of short, strangely unconnected and incompatible statements that provide tantalising glimpses of an itinerant
charlatan's reception in various German towns, castles and monasteries.
Baron regards eight of these as authentic, Mahal seven; both scholars use
them to support conflicting theories as to the man's provenance. Yet ultimately, 'There can be no coherent biography of the historical Faust. The
image we have of him is a colourful mosaic, patched together from the
incidental and sharply contradictory statements of his contemporaries.
Here, it often happens that legend and reality are closely intertwined'
(Reske, 10). It is a short step to the contention, first put forward in 1808
by Joseph Görres and later taken up by Friedrich Engels, that the Faust
stories were the invention of the common people, the *Volk*, and that the
chapbook (*Volksbuch* or 'folk-book') was like a folksong in that it had no
individual author. Just as in Britain stories about various outlaws were as-
similated into the 'iconic' figure of Robin Hood, Faust has a stereotypical
dimension that shows the influence of magicians and tricksters like Friar
Bacon and Till Eulenspiegel. What is clear is that, from its inception, the
legend incorporates many incongruous beliefs and prejudices typical of

the age through a kind of 'montage technique' (Baron (1989), 13 f; Burke, 171; Allen, 583). It also shows how people imagined progress to be achievable by diabolical intervention.

Works Cited

Marguerite de Huszar Allen, 'The Reception of the *Historia von D. Johann Fausten*', *German Quarterly* 59 (1986), 582–94.

Frank Baron, *Doctor Faustus from History to Legend*. Munich: Wilhelm Fink, 1978.

– *Faustus on Trial. The Origins of Johann Spies's 'Historia' in an Age of Witch Hunting*. Tübingen: Niemeyer, 1992.

– 'Der historische Faustus im Spiegel der Quellen des 16. Jahrhunderts. Von der Astrologie zum Teufelspakt', in Baron/Auernheimer, 84–107.

– 'Georg Lukács on the Origins of the Faust Legend', in Boerner/Johnson, 13–25.

Frank Baron and Richard Auernheimer (eds.), *War Dr Faustus in Kreuznach? Realität und Fiktion im Faust-Bild des Abtes Johannes Trithemius*. Alzey: Verlag der Rheinhessischen Druckwerkstätte, 2003.

Peter Boerner and Sidney Johnson (eds), *Faust through Four Centuries. Retrospect and Analysis. Vierhundert Jahre Faust. Rückblick und Analyse*. Tübingen: Niemeyer, 1989.

Peter Burke, *Popular Culture in Early Modern Europe*. London: Temple Smith, 1978.

John Henry Jones (ed.), *The English Faust Book. A critical edition based on the text of 1592*. Cambridge: University Press, 1994.

Günther Mahal (ed.), *Der historische Faust. Ein wissenschaftliches Symposium*. Knittlingen: Faust Archiv, 1982.

– *Faust starb in Staufen. Nachforschungen über ein verschwiegenes Faktum*. Vaihingen: Wilfried Melchior, 1986.

– *Faust. Die Spuren eines geheimnisvollen Lebens*. Reinbek: Rowohlt, 1995.

Harold Meek, *Johann Faust. The Man and the Myth*. London: Oxford University Press, 1930.

Philip Mason Palmer and Robert Pattison More. *The Sources of the Faust Tradition from Simon Magus to Lessing*. New York: Oxford University Press, 1936. Rptd New York: Octagon, 1966.

Will-Erich Peukert, 'Dr Faustus', *Zeitschrift für deutsche Philologie* 70 (1947), 55–74.

Hermann Reske, *Faust: eine Einführung*. Stuttgart: Kohlhammer, 1971.

Documents

Letter of Johannes Tritheim[1] to Johannes Virdung.[2]

The man of whom you wrote me, George Sabellicus, who has presumed to call himself the prince of necromancers, is a vagabond, a babbler and a rogue, who deserves to be thrashed so that he may not henceforth rashly venture to profess in public things so execrable and so hostile to the holy church. For what, other than symptoms of a very foolish and insane mind, are the titles assumed by this man, who shows himself to be a fool and not a philosopher? For thus he has formulated the title befitting him: Master George Sabellicus, the younger Faust, the chief of necromancers, astrologer, the second magus, palmist, diviner with earth and fire, second in the art of divination with water. Behold the foolish temerity of the man, the madness by which he is possessed, in that he dares to call himself the source of necromany, when in truth, in his ignorance of all good letters, he ought to call himself a fool rather than a master. But his wickedness is not hidden from me. When I was returning last year from the Mark Brandenburg, I happened upon this same man in the town of Gelnhausen, and many silly things were told me about him at the inn, – things promised by him with great rashness on his part. As soon as he heard that I was there, he fled from the inn and could not be persuaded to come into my presence. The description of his folly, such as he gave to you and which we have mentioned, he also sent to me through a certain citizen. Certain priests in the same town told me that he had said, in the presence of many people, that he had acquired such knowledge of all wisdom and such a memory, that if all the books of Plato and Aristotle, together with their whole philosophy, had totally passed from the memory of man, he himself, through his own genius, like another Hebrew Ezra,[3] would be able to

---

[1] Johannes Tritheim (1462–1516), physicist, humanist, writer. Abbot of the monastery at Sponheim near Kreuznach from 1485 to 1506. Then, after a short stay in Berlin, abbot of the monastery of St. James at Würzburg. Tritheim combined great learning with an inclination to the fantastic, which led to a considerable reputation as a magician.

[2] Johannes Virdung of Hasfurt was mathematician and astrologer to the Elector of the Palatinate, and a professor at Heidelberg.

[3] Cf. Eusebius, *Ecclesiastical History*, tr. by K. Lane, London, 1926. Vol. I, V, viii, 461: "– for when the Scriptures had been destroyed in the captivity of the people in the days of Nebuchadnezzer, and the Jews had gone back to their country after seventy years, then in the time of Artaxerxes, the king of the Per-

restore them all with increased beauty. Afterwards, while I was at Speyer, he came to Würzburg and, impelled by the same vanity, is reported to have said in the presence of many that the miracles of Christ the Saviour were not so wonderful, that he himself could do all the things which Christ had done, as often and whenever he wished. Towards the end of Lent of the present year he came to Kreuznach and with like folly and boastfulness made great promises, saying that in alchemy he was the most learned man of all times and that by his knowledge and ability, he could do whatever anyone might wish. In the meantime there was vacant in the same town the position of schoolmaster, to which he was appointed through the influence of Franz von Sickingen,[4] the magistrate of your prince and a man very fond of mystical lore. Then he began to indulge in the most dastardly kind of lewdness with the boys and when this was suddenly discovered, he avoided by flight the punishment that awaited him. These are the things which I know through very definite evidence concerning the man whose coming you await with such anticipation. When he comes to you, you will find him to be not a philosopher but a fool with an overabundance of rashness. – Wurzburg, the 20th day of August. A.D. 1507.

Letter of Conrad Mutianus Rufus[5] to Heinrich Urbanus.[6]

Eight days ago there came to Erfurt a certain soothsayer by the name of George Faust, the demigod of Heidelberg, a mere braggart and fool. His claims, like those of all diviners, are idle and such physiognomy has no more weight than a water spider. The ignorant marvel at him. Let the theologians rise against him and not try to destroy the philosopher

---

sians, he (God) inspired Ezra, the priest of the tribe of Levi, to restore all the sayings of the prophets who had gone before, and to restore to the people the law given by Moses." Quoted by Eusebius from Irenaeus.

[4] Franz von Sickingen (1481–1523), imperial counsellor, chamberlain and general, greatest of the "free knights," friend of Ulrich von Hutten and by him interested in humanism. Supporter of the Reformation.

[5] Conrad Mutianus Rufus (1417–1526). Canon of the Church of St. Mary's at Gotha. His real name was Konrad Muth. He led a studious life as a humanist and philosopher and was ranked by the humanists with Erasmus and Reuchlin, despite the fact that he never published any of his writings.

[6] Heinrich Urbanus, student and later friend of Mutianus Rufus, and through him interested in humanism. From about 1505 he was steward of the Cistercian cloister Georgenthal at Erfurt.

Reuchlin.[7] I heard him babbling at an inn, but I did not reprove his boastfulness. What is the foolishness of other people to me? – October 3, 1513.

From the Account Book of the Bishop of Bamberg,[8] 1519–1520.

The annual accounts of Hans Muller, chamberlain, from Walpurgis[9] 1519 to Walpurgis 1520.

Entry on February 12, 1520, under the heading "Miscellaneous."

10 gulden given and presented as a testimonial to Doctor Faust, the philosopher, who made for my master a horoscope or prognostication. Paid on the Sunday after Saint Scholastica's Day[10] by the order of his reverence.

From the Journal of Kiliam Lieb,[11] July 1528.

George Faust of Helmstet said on the fifth of June that when the sun and Jupiter are in the same constellation prophets are born (presumably such as he). He asserted that he was the commander or preceptor of the order of the Knights of St. John at a place called Hallestein[12] on the border of Carinthia.

From the Records of the City of Ingolstadt.

(a) Minutes on the actions of the city council in Ingolstadt.

Today, the Wednesday after St. Vitus' Day, 1528. The soothsayer shall be ordered to leave the city and to spend his penny elsewhere.

---

[7] Johann Reuchlin (1455–1522). Capnio was the Greek form of his name. He was learned in jurisprudence and languages (especially Greek and Hebrew). For many years he was in the service successively of Count Eberhard of Württemberg, Johann von Dalberg at Heidelberg, and Duke Ulrich of Württemberg. In 1519 he became Professor of Greek and Hebrew at Ingolstadt and from 1521 held the same chair at Tübingen. In 1511 he was involved in a bitter quarrel with the theological faculty at Cologne.

[8] George III Schenk of Limburg was Bishop of Bamberg from 1502 to 1522.

[9] i.e. May 1st.

[10] Saint Scholastica's Day fell on Friday, February 10, 1520.

[11] Kilian Leib was the prior of Rebdorf in Bavaria.

[12] Hallestein. According to Schottenloher this is probably Heilenstein in Styria which at one time was the seat of the Knights of St. John.

(b) Record of those banished from Ingolstadt.

On Wednesday after St. Vitus' Day, 1528, a certain man who called himself Dr. George Faust of Heidelberg was told to spend his penny elsewhere and he pledged himself not to take vengeance on or make fools of the authorities for this order.

Entry in the Records of the City Council of Nuremberg, May 10, 1532.

Safe conduct to Doctor Faust, the great sodomite and necromancer, at Fürth refused.

The junior Burgomaster.

From the Waldeck Chronicle.

Francis I by the grace of God, son of Philip II (Count of Waldeck) by his second marriage, Bishop of Münster, on June 25, 1535, invested the city of Münster which had been occupied by the Anabaptists and captured it with the aid of princes of the Empire under the leadership of Hensel Hochstraten. John of Leyden,[13] the boastful pretender, who called himself King of Israel and Zion, was executed together with Knipperdollinck and Krechting, their bodies being torn with red-hot pincers, enclosed in iron cages and suspended from the tower of St. Lambert's Church and the 23rd of January, 1536. It was at this time that the famous necromancer Dr. Faust, coming on the same day from Corbach,[14] prophesied that the city of Münster would surely be captured by the bishop on that very night.

---

[13] John of Leyden, originally a tailor, became a leader of the Anabaptist movement in Münster and set up there the "Kingdom of Zion" proclaiming himself king. Krechting was his chancellor. Knipperdollinck was mayor of Münster during the Anabaptist regime.

[14] A small town in the principality of Waldeck, about eighty miles southeast of Münster.

Letter of Joachim Camerarius[15] to Daniel Stibar.[16]

I owe to your friend Faust the pleasure of discussing these affairs with you. I wish he had taught you something of this sort rather than puffed you up with the wind of silly superstition or held you in suspense with I know not what juggler's trick. But what does he tell us, pray? For I know that you have questioned him diligently about all things. Is the emperor victorious?* That is the way you should go about it. – Tübingen, the 13th of August, 1536.

From the Tischreden of Martin Luther.[17]

God's word alone overcomes the fiery arrows of the devil and all his temptations.

When one evening at the table a sorcerer named Faust was mentioned, Doctor Martin said in a serious tone: "The devil does not make use of the services of sorcerers against me. If he had been able to do me any harm he would have done it long since. To be sure he has often had me by the head but he had to let me go again."

From the Tischreden of Martin Luther.

Mention was made of magicians and the magic art, and how Satan blinded men. Much was said about Faust, who called the devil his brother-in-law, and the remark was made: "If I, Martin Luther, had given him even a

---

[15] Joachim Camerarius (1500–1574). His real name was Joachim Liebhard. 1518, a teacher of Greek at Erfurt. 1521, he went to Wittenberg where he became a friend of Melanchthon. 1526, became teacher of Greek at the Gymnasium in Nuremberg. 1535, was called to Tübingen to reform the university. 1541, called to Leipzig for the same purpose. Camerarius' importance is beyond dispute. He was the best philologist of his time; and he wrote many works, mostly in the field of philology, but also of history and biography. He enjoyed an international reputation.

[16] Daniel Stibarus was a city councilman of Würzburg.

[17] Martin Luther (1483–1546), reformer and founder of the Protestant church. The *Tischreden* were published in Eisleben by Aurifaber in 1566. They give the comments and discussions of Luther in the informal circle of his family, friends, and acquaintances, as they had been recorded by Aurifaber himself and by numerous other intimates of Luther. The passage quoted is found in Chap. I, § 47 of the Aurifaber edition of 1566.

* Ed. note: war between the Emperor Charles V and King of France, François I.

hand, he would have destroyed me; but I would not have been afraid of him, – with God as my protector, I would have given him my hand in the name of the Lord."

From the Index Sanitatis of Philipp Begardi.[18]

There is another well-known and important man whom I would not have mentioned were it not for the fact that he himself had no desire to remain in obscurity and unknown. For some years ago he traveled through almost all countries, principalities and kingdoms, and himself made his name known to everybody and bragged much about his great skill not only in medicine but also in chiromancy, nigromancy *(necromancy)*, physiognomy, crystal gazing, and the like arts. And he not only bragged but confessed and signed himself as a famous and experienced master. He himself avowed and did not deny that he was and was called Faust and in addition signed himself "The philosopher of philosophers." The number of those who complained to me that they were cheated by him was very great. Now his promises were great like those of Thessalus;[19] likewise his fame as that of Theophrastus.[20] But his deeds, as I hear, were very petty and fraudulent. But in taking or – to speak more accurately – in receiving money he was not slow. And afterwards also, on his departure, as I have been informed, he left many to whistle for their money. But what is to be done about it? What's gone is gone. I will drop the subject here. Anything further is your affair.

---

[18] Philipp Begardi was city physician in Worms. The *Index Sanitatis* is of the year 1539.

[19] Thessalus was a Greek physician of the first century A.D. He lived in Rome during the reign of Nero and was buried there. He considered himself superior to his predecessors but Galen, while often mentioning him, always does so in terms of contempt.

[20] Theophrastus, i.e., Philippus Aureolus Paracelsus Theophrastus Bombastus von Hohenheim (1493–1541), physician and chemist. Bombastic in fact as well as by name, inclined to charlatanism, suspected of supernatural powers and himself promoting the suspicion, he is nevertheless credited by modern scholarship with genuine service in the fields of medicine, chemistry, and pharmacy.

Letter from Philipp von Hutten[21] to His Brother Moritz von Hutten.

Here you have a little about all the provinces so that you may see that we are not the only ones who have been unfortunate in Venezuela up to this time; that all the abovementioned expeditions which left Sevilla before and after us perished within three months. Therefore I must confess that the philosopher Faust hit the nail on the head, for we struck a very bad year. But God be praised, things went better for us than for any of the others. God willing I shall write you again before we leave here. Take good care of our dear old mother. Give my greetings to all our neighbours and friends, especially Balthasar Rabensteiner and George von Libra, William von Hessberg and all my good comrades. Pay my respects to Herr N of Thüngen, my master's brother. Done in Coro in the Province of Venezuela on January 16th, 1540.

From the Sermones Convivales of Johannes Gast.[22]

Concerning the Necromancer Faust

He puts up at night at a certain very rich monastery, intending to spend the night there. A brother places before him some ordinary wine of indifferent quality and without flavor. Faust requests that he draw from another cask a better wine which it was the custom to give to nobles. Then the brother said: "I do not have the keys, the prior is sleeping, and it is a sin to awaken him." Faust said: "The keys are lying in that corner. Take them and open that cask on the left and give me a drink." The brother objected that he had no orders from the prior to place any other wine before guests. When Faust heard this he became very angry and said: "In a short time you shall see marvels, you inhospitable brother." Burning with rage he left early in the morning without saying farewell and sent a certain raging devil who made a great stir in the monastery by day and by night and moved things about both in the church and in cells of the monks, so that they could not get any rest, no matter what they did. Finally they deliberated whether they should leave the monastery or destroy it altogether. And so they wrote to the Count Palatine concerning the misfortune in

---

[21] Philipp von Hutten (1511–1546) was one of the leaders of the Welser troops in Venezuela, where he met his death. The letter would seem to indicate that Faust had made predictions concerning the fortunes of the expedition in Venezuela.

[22] Johannes Gast († 1572) was a Protestant clergyman at Basle. His *Sermones Convivales* were very popular. The quotation is from the second volume, published in 1548.

which they were involved. He took the monastery under his own protection and ejected the monks to whom he furnishes supplies from year to year and uses what is left for himself. It is said that to this very day, if monks enter the monastery, such great disturbances arise that those who live there can have no peace. This the devil was able to bring to pass.

Another Story about Faust

At Basle I dined with him in the great college and he gave to the cook various kinds of birds to roast. I do not know where he bought them or who gave them to him, since there were none on sale at the time. Moreover I never saw any like them in our regions. He had with him a dog and a horse which I believe to have been demons and which were ready for any service. I was told that the dog at times assumed the form of a servant and served the food. However, the wretch was destined to come to a deplorable end, for he was strangled by the devil and his body on its bier kept turning face downward even though it was five times turned on its back. God preserve us lest we become slaves of the devil.

From the Explicationes Melanchthoniae,[23] Pars. II.

There [in the presence of Nero] Simon Magus tried to fly to heaven, but Peter prayed that he might fall. I believe that the Apostles had great struggles although not all are recorded. Faust also tried this at Venice. But he was sorely dashed to the ground.

From the Explicationes Melanchthoniae, Pars. IV.

The devil is a marvellous craftsman, for he is able by some device to accomplish things which are (natural) but which we do not understand. For he can do more than man. Thus many strange feats of magic are recounted such as I have related elsewhere concerning the girl at Bologna.

---

[23] Philipp Melanchthon (Greek for Schwarzert) (1497–1560) was a co-worker of Luther and after him the most important figure in the German Reformation. From 1518 on he was professor of the Greek language and literature at Wittenberg. After Luther's death he became the head of the Protestant church.

The *Explicationes Melanchthoniae*, or *Postilla Melanthoniana*, as they were called in the Bretschneider and Bindseil edition of Melanchthon's works, were published by Christopher Pezelius, a former student of Melanchthon, in 1594 ff., and they reproduced Melanchthon's commentaries on the Scriptures, delivered between 1549 and 1560.

In like manner Faust, the magician, devoured at Vienna another magician who was discovered a few days later in a certain cave. The devil can perform many miracles; nevertheless the church has its own miracles.

From the Epistolae Medicinales of Conrad Gesner.[24]
Letter from Gesner to Johannes Crato[25] of Krafftheim.

Oporinus of Basle, formerly a disciple and companion of Theophrastus, narrates some wonderful things concerning the latter's dealings with demons. Such men practice vain astrology, geomancy, necromancy, and similar prohibited arts. I suspect indeed that they derive from the Druids who among the ancient Celts were for some years taught by demons in underground places. This has been practiced at Salamanca in Spain down to our own day. From that school came those commonly called "wandering scholars," among whom a certain Faust, who died not long since, is very celebrated.

From the Locorum Communium Collectanea of Johannes Manlius.[26]

I knew a certain man by the name of Faust from Kundling,[27] which is a small town near my birthplace. When he was a student at Cracow he studied magic, for there was formerly much practice of the art in that city and in that place too there were public lectures on this art. He wandered about everywhere and talked of many mysterious things. When he wished to provide a spectacle at Venice he said he would fly to heaven. So the devil raised him up and then cast him down so that he was dashed to the ground and almost killed. However he did not die.

---

[24] Conrad Gesner (1516–1565), a Swiss teacher, physician, and scholar. His scholarly activity was enormous. His main fields were zoology and botany, but he did tremendous work also in medicine, in philology, and in the editing and translating of Greek and Latin writers. His writings in these fields were encyclopedic.

   The letter is dated Zurich, August 16, 1561.

[25] Johannes Crato was Physician in Ordinary of the Emperor, Ferdinand I.

[26] Johannes Manlius (Mennel) of Ansbach was at one time a student under Melanchthon. In the *Locorum Communium Collectanea* (1563), Manlius gives extracts and quotations "from the lectures of D. Philipp Melanchthon and accounts of other most learned men." The passages cited are quoted from Melanchthon.

[27] i.e. Knittlingen, not far from Bretten, Melanchthon's birthplace.

A few years ago this same John Faust, on the day before his end, sat very downcast in a certain village in the Duchy of Württemberg. The host asked him why, contrary to his custom and habit, he was so downcast (he was otherwise a most shameful scoundrel who led a very wicked life, so that he was again and again nigh to being killed because of his dissolute habits). Then he said to the host in the village: "don't be frightened to-night." In the middle of the night the house was shaken. When Faust did not get up in the morning and when it was almost noon, the host with several others went into his bedroom and found him lying near the bed with his face turned toward his back. Thus the devil had killed him. While he was alive he had with him a dog which was the devil, just as the scoundrel[28] who wrote "De vanitate artium" likewise had a dog that ran about with him and was the devil. The same Faust escaped in this town of Wittenberg when the good prince Duke John had given orders to arrest him. Likewise in Nuremberg he escaped. He was just beginning to dine when he became restless and immediately rose and paid the host what he owed. He had hardly got outside the gate when the bailiffs came and inquired about him.

The same magician Faust, a vile beast and a sink of many devils, falsely boasted that all the victories which the emperor's armies have won in Italy had been gained by him through his magic. This was an absolute lie. I mention this for the sake of the young that they may not readily give ear to such lying men.

From the Zimmerische Chronik.[29]

That the practice of such art [soothsaying] is not only godless but in the highest degree dangerous is undeniable, for experience proves it and we know what happened to the notorious sorcerer Faust. After he had practiced during his lifetime many marvels about which a special treatise could be written, he was finally killed at a ripe old age by the evil one in the seigniory of Staufen in Breisgau.

---

[28] i.e. Cornelius Heinrich Agrippa von Nettesheim (1486–1535), author, physician, and philosopher. He, like so many others, was also suspected of being a sorcerer.

[29] The *Zimmerische Chronik* is a Swabian chronicle of the 16th century. The authors were Count Froben Christoph von Zimmern († 1566 or 1567) and his secretary Hans Müller († ca. 1600). The work centers about the history of the Swabian noblemen who later became the Counts of Zimmern. It contains an invaluable store of legends and folklore.

(After 1539). About this time also Faust died in or not far from the town of Staufen in Breisgau. In his day he was as remarkable a sorcerer as could be found in German lands in our times. He had so many strange experiences at various times that he will not easily be forgotten for many years. He became an old man and, as it is said, died miserably. From all sorts of reports and conjectures many have thought that the evil one, whom in his lifetime he used to call his brother-in-law, had killed him. The books which he left behind fell into the hands of the Count of Staufen in whose territory he died. Afterwards many people tried to get these books and in doing so in my opinion were seeking a dangerous and unlucky treasure and gift. He sent a spirit into the monastery of the monks at Lux-heim[30] in the Vosges mountains which they could not get rid of for years and which bothered them tremendously, – and this for no other reason than that once upon a time they did not wish to put him up over night. For this reason he sent them the restless guest. In like manner, it is said, a similar spirit was summoned and attached to the former abbot of St. Die-senberg by an envious wandering scholar.

From the De Praestigiis Daemonum of Johannes Wier.[31]

John Faust was born in the little town Kundling and studied magic in Cra-cow, where it was formerly taught openly; and for a few years previous to 1540 he practiced his art in various places in Germany with many lies and much fraud, to the marvel of many. There was nothing he could not do with his inane boasting and his promises. I will give one example of his art on the condition that the reader will first promise not to imitate him. This wretch, taken prisoner at Batenburg on the Maas, near the border of Gel-dern, while the Baron Hermann was away, was treated rather leniently by his chaplain, Dr. Johannes Dorstenius, because he promised the man, who was good but not shrewd, knowledge of many things and various arts. Hence he kept drawing him wine, by which Faust was very much exhilarated, until the vessel was empty. When Faust learned this, and the

---

[30] Compare the story cited above from Johannes Gast.

[31] Johannes Wier (1515–1588) was a Dutch physician and particularly known as an opponent of the prosecution of witches. The *Praestigiis Daemonum* (1st ed. 1563) was an appeal to the emperor and princes in Wier's campaign against superstition. The passages relating to Faust appear from the first time in the fourth edition (1568). For a study of the historical value of what Wier has to say, see the introduction to van't Hooft, *Das Holländische Volksbuch vom Doktor Faust.* Hague, 1926.

chaplain told him that he was going to Grave, that he might have his beard shaved, Faust promised him another unusual art by which his beard might be removed without the use of a razor, if he would provide more wine. When this condition was accepted, he told him to rub his beard vigorously with arsenic, but without any mention of its preparation. When the salve had been applied, there followed such an inflammation that not only the hair but also the skin and the flesh was burned off. The chaplain himself told me of this piece of villainy more than once with much indignation. When another acquaintance of mine, whose beard was black and whose face was rather dark and showed signs of melancholy (for he was splenetic), approached Faust, the latter exclaimed: "I surely thought you were my brother-in-law and therefore I looked at your feet to see whether long curved claws projected from them": thus comparing him to the devil whom he thought to be entering and whom he used to call his brother-in-law. He was finally found dead near his bed in a certain town in the Duchy of Württemberg, with his face turned towards his back; and it is reported that during the middle of the night preceding, the house was shaken.

From the Von Gespänsten of Ludwig Lavater.[32]

To this very day there are sorcerers who boast that they can saddle a horse on which they can in a short time make great journeys. The devil will give them all their reward[33] in the long run. What wonders is the notorious sorcerer Faust said to have done in our own times.

From the Chronica von Thüringen und der Stadt Erffurth of Zacharias Hogel.[34]

a) It was also probably about his time [1550] that those strange things happened which are said to have taken place in Erfurt in the case of the

---

[32] Ludwig Lavater (1527–1586), for many years preacher and finally head of the Protestant church in Zurich. His work *Von Gespänsten* (1569) was very popular and was also translated into French and Italian.

[33] Literally: pay for course and steed, and money for shoeing and saddle.

[34] Hogel's chronicle was written in the 17th century. Its source, however, is the Reichmann-Wambach chronicle of the middle of the 16th century. This latter work is now lost. The parts relating to Faust were entered in the chronicle by Wolf Wambach, who continued the work which had been begun by his brother-in-law Reichmann. The story of the efforts of the monk Klinge to convert Faust probably came to Wambach fairly directly.

notorious sorcerer and desperate brand of hell, Dr. Faust. Although he lived in Wittenberg, yet, just as his restless spirit in other instances drove him about in the world, so he also came to the university at Erfurt, rented quarters near the large Collegium, and through his boasting brought it to pass that he was allowed to lecture publicly and to explain the Greek poet Homer to the students. When, in this connection, he had occasion to mention the king of Troy, Priam, and the heroes of the Trojan war, Hector, Ajax, Ulysses, Agamemnon, and others, he described them each as they had appeared. He was asked (for there are always inquisitive fellows and there was no question as to what Faust was) to bring it to pass through his art, that these heroes should appear and show themselves as he had just described them. He consented to this and appointed the time when they should next come to the auditorium. And when the hour had come and more students than before had appeared before him, he said in the midst of his lecture that they could now get to see the ancient Greek heroes. And immediately he called in one after the other and as soon as one was gone another came in to them, looked at them and shook his head as though he were still in action on the field before Troy. The last of them all was the giant Polyphemus, who had only a single terrible big eye in the middle of his forehead. He wore a fiery red beard and was devouring a fellow, one of whose legs was dangling out of his mouth. The sight of him scared them so that their hair stood on end and when Dr. Faust motioned him to go out, he acted as though he did not understand but wanted to grasp a couple of them too with his teeth. And he hammered on the floor with his great iron spear so that the whole Collegium shook, and then he went away.

Not long afterward the commencement for masters was held and (at the banquet given in connection therewith), in the presence of the members of the theological faculty and of delegates from the council, the comedies of the ancient poets Plautus and Terence were discussed and regret was expressed that so many of them had been lost in times gone by, for if they were available, they could be used to good advantage in the schools. Dr. Faust listened to this and he also began to speak about the two poets and cited several quotations which were supposed to be in their lost comedies. And he offered, if it would not be held against him, and if the theologians had no objections, to bring to light again all the lost comedies and to put them at their disposal for several hours, during which time they would have to be copied quickly by a goodly number of students or clerks, if they wanted to have them. After that they would be able to use them as they pleased. The theologians and councilmen, however, did not take kindly to the proposal: for they said the devil might interpolate all sorts of offensive things into such newly found comedies. And after all, one could, even without them, learn enough good Latin from those which still existed. The conjurer accordingly could not exhibit one of his masterpieces in this connection.

He was accustomed to spend a good deal of his time while he was in Erfurt at the Anchor House of Squire N. in the Schlössergasse, entertaining him and his guests with his adventures. Once, when he had gone to Prague in Bohemia, a group of such guests gathered at the inn and, because they desired to have him present, begged mine host to tell them where he was. And one of the guests jokingly called Faust by name and begged him not to desert them. At that instant someone in the street knocks at the door. The servant runs to the window, looks out and asks who is there. And behold, there, before the door, stands Dr. Faust, holding his horse as though he had just dismounted, and says: "Don't you know me? I am he whom they have just called." The servant runs into the room and reports. The host refuses to believe it, saying that Dr. Faust was in Prague. In the meantime he knocks again at the door and master and servant again run to the window, see him, and open the door, and he is given a cordial welcome and immediately led in to the guests. The host's son takes his horse, saying that he will give it plenty of feed, and leads it into the the stable.

The squire immediately asks Dr. Faust how he had returned so quickly. "That's what my horse is for," says Dr. Faust. "Because the guests desired me so much and called me, I wanted to oblige them and to appear, although I have to be back in Prague before morning." Thereupon they drink to his health in copious draughts, and when he asks them whether they would also like to drink a foreign wine, they answer: "Yes." He asks whether it shall be Reinfal,[35] Malmsey, Spanish, or French wine. And when one of them says: "They are all good," he asks for an auger and with it makes four holes in the table and closes them with plugs. Then he takes fresh glasses and taps from the table that kind of wine which he names and continues to drink merrily with them. In the meantime the son runs into the room and says: "Doctor, your horse eats as though he were mad; he has already devoured several bushels of oats and continually stands and looks for more. But I will give him some more until he has enough." "Have done," says the doctor, "he has had enough; he would eat all the feed in your loft before he was full." But at midnight the horse utters a shrill neigh so that it is heard throughout the entire house.

---

[35] An Istrian wine highly esteemed in Germany in the middle ages.

"I must go," says the doctor, but tarries a little until the horse neighs a second and finally a third time. Thereupon he goes, takes his leave of them outside, mounts his horse and rides up the Schlössergasse. But the horse in plain sight rises quickly into the air and takes him back through the air to Prague. After several weeks he comes again from Prague to Erfurt with splendid gifts which had been given to him there, and invites the same company to be his guests at St. Michael's. They come and stand there in the rooms but there is no sign of any preparation. But he knocks with a knife on the table. Soon someone enters and says: "Sir, what do you wish?" Faust asks, "How quick are you?" The other answers: "As an arrow." "No," says Dr. Faust, "you shall not serve me. Go back to where you came from." Then he knocks again and when another servant enters and asks the same question, he says: "How quick are you?" "As the wind,", says he. "That is something," says Dr. Faust, but sends him out again too. But when he knocked a third time, another entered and, when he was asked the same question, said he was as quick as the thoughts of man. "Good," said Dr. Faust, "you'll do." And he went out with him, told him what he should do, and returned again to his guests and had them wash their hands and sit down. Soon the servant with two others brought in three covered dishes each, and this happened four times. Thirty six courses or dishes were served, therefore, with game, fowl, veg- etables, meat pies and other meats, not to mention the fruit, confections, cakes, etc. All the beakers, glasses, and mugs were put on the table empty. Soon Dr. Faust asked each one what he wished to drink in the way of beer and wine and then put the cups outside of the window and soon took them back again, full of just that fresh drink which each one wanted to have. The music which one of his servants played was so charming that his guests had never heard the like, and so wonderful as if several were playing in harmony or harmoniums, fifes, cornets, lutes, harps, trumpets, etc. So they made merry until broad daylight. What was to be the outcome? The man played so many tricks that the city and country began to talk about him and many of the nobility of the country came to Erfurt to him. People began to worry lest the devil might lead the tender youth and other simpletons astray, so that they also might show a leaning towards the black art and might regard it as only a clever thing to do. Since the sorcerer attached himself to the squire in the Anchor House, who was a papist, therefore the suggestion was made that the neighbor- ing monk, Dr. Klinge, should make an effort to tear him from the devil and convert him. The Franciscan did so, visited him and spoke to him, at first kindly, then sternly; explained to him God's wrath and the eternal damnation which must follow on such doings; said that he was a well educated man and could support himself without this in a godly and honorable way: therefore he should stop such frivolity, to which he had perhaps been persuaded by the devil in his youth, and should beg God for forgiveness of his sins, and should hope in this way to obtain that forgiveness of his sins which God had never yet denied anyone. Dr. Faust said: "My dear sir, I realize that you wish me well; I know all that, too, which you have just told me. But I have ventured so far, and with my own blood have contracted with the devil to be forever his, with body and soul: how can I now retract? or how can I be helped?" Dr. Klinge said: "That is quite possible, if you earnestly call on God for grace and mercy, show true repentance and do penance, refrain from sorcery and community with the devil, and neither harm nor seduce any one. We will hold mass for you in our cloister so that you will without a doubt get rid of the devil." "Mass here, mass here," said Dr. Faust. "My pledge binds me too absolutely. I have wantonly despised God and become perjured and faithless towards Him, and believed and trusted more in the devil than in Him. Therefore I can neither come to Him again nor obtain any comfort from His grace which I have forfeited. Besides, it would not be honest nor would it redound to my honor to have it said that I had violated my bond and seal, which I had made with my own blood. The devil has honestly kept the promise that he made to me, therefore I will honestly keep the pledge that I made and contracted with him." "Well," says the monk, "then go to, you cursed child of the devil, if you will not be helped, and will not have it otherwise." Thereupon he went to his Magnificence, the Rector, and reported it to him. The council was also informed and took steps so that Dr. Faust had to leave. So Erfurt got rid of the wicked man.

However, this affair with the aforesaid sorcerer probably took place in this year or shortly before or afterwards, during the lifetime of Dr. Klinge.

b) Also the Lord God afflicted Dr. Klinge, the above mentioned obdurate monk and abbot in the Franciscan cloister in Erfurt, so that he despaired of his life. But he recovered again and, because it was reported to him that they said of him in the city that he had become Lutheran, he wrote and published his book called *Catechismus Catholicus*, printed in 1570 in Cologne. And in the introduction he bore witness that he would remain in the doctrine which he had preached in Erfurt for thirty-six years. And this was the monk who wanted to turn and convert the notorious Dr. Faust from his evil life. Dr. Klinge however died in the year 1556 on the Tuesday after Oculi,[36] on which Sunday he had still preached in the

---

[36] 'Oculi' is the fourth Sunday before Easter.

church of Our Lady. And he lies buried in that church opposite the chancel, where his epitaph may be seen.

From the Christlich Bedencken of Augustin Lercheimer.[37]

He was born in a little place called Knittlingen, situated in Württemberg near the border of the Palatinate. For a time he was a schoolmaster in Kreuznach under Franz von Sickingen: he had to flee from there because he was guilty of sodomy. After that he travelled about the country with his devil; studied the black art at the university in Cracow; came to Wittenberg and was allowed to stay there for a time, until he carried things so far that they were on the point of arresting him, when he fled. He had neither house nor home in Wittenberg or elsewhere; in fact he had no permanent abode anywhere, but lived like a vagabond, was a parasite, drunkard, and gourmand, and supported himself by his quakery. How could he have a property at the outer gate in the Scheergasse in Wittenberg, when there never was any suburb there, and therefore also no outer gate? nor was there any Scheergasse there.

* * *

He was choked to death by the devil in a village in Württemberg, not at Kimlich near Wittenberg, since there is no village by that name. For he was never allowed to return to Wittenberg after he had fled from there to avoid arrest.

* * *

I do not touch upon other trival, false, and nasty things in the book. I have pointed out these particular things because it has vexed and grieved me greatly, as it has many other honest people, to see the honorable and famous institution together with Luther, Melanchthon, and others of sainted memory so libelled. I myself was a student there, once upon a time. At that time the doings of this magician were still remembered by many there.

* * *

---

[37] Augustin Lercheimer von Steinfelden (1522–1603) was professor of Greek at Heidelberg from 1563 to 1579. From 1579 to 1584 he held the same chair at Neustadt on the Hardt. From 1584 to his death he was again at Heidelberg as professor of mathematics.

The lewd, devilish fellow Faust stayed for a time in Wittenberg, as I stated before. He came at times to the house of Melanchthon, who gave him a good lecture, rebuked and warned him that he should reform in time, lest he come to an evil end, as finally happened. But he paid no attention to it. Now one day about ten o'clock Melanchthon left his study to go down to eat. With him was Faust, whom he had vigorously rebuked. Faust replied: Sir, you continually rebuke me with abusive words. One of these days, when you go to the table, I will bring it about that all the pots in your kitchen will fly out of the chimney, so that you and your guests will have nothing to eat. To this Melanchthon replied: you had better not. Hang you and your tricks. Nor did Faust carry out his threat: the devil could not rob the kitchen of the saintly man, as he had done to the wedding guests of whom mention was made before.

From the Operae Horarum Subcisivarum of Philipp Camerarius.[38]

We know, moreover, (not to mention Scymus of Terentum, Philistes of Syracuse, Heraclitus of Mytilene, who as we read were very distinguished and accomplished sorcerers in the time of Alexander the Great) that among the jugglers and magicians who became famous within the memory of our own fathers, John Faust of Kundling, who studied magic at Cracow where it was formerly publicly taught, acquired through his wonderful tricks and diabolical enchantments such a celebrated name that among the common people there can hardly be found anyone who is not able to recount some instance of his art. The same conjurer's tricks are ascribed to him as we have just related of the Bohemian magician.[39] Just as the lives of these magicians were similar, so each ended his life in a horrible manner. For Faust, it is said, and this is told by Wier, was found in a village in the Duchy of Württemberg lying dead alongside his bed with his head twisted round. And in the middle of the preceding night the house was shaken. The other, as we mentioned a little while ago, was carried off by his master while he was still alive. These were the fitting rewards of an impious and criminal curiosity. But to come back to Faust. From those in truth, who knew this imposter well, I have heard many things which show him to have been a master of the magic art (if indeed it is an art and not

---

[38] Philipp Camerarius (1537–1624) was the son of the Joachim Camerarius previously mentioned. He was trained in law at Leipzig, Tübingen, Strassburg, Basle, and in Italy. From 1581 to his death he was prorector of the university at Altdorf.

[39] The magician referred to is Zyto.

the jugglery of a fool). Among other deeds which he performed there is told one in particular which may seem ridiculous but which is truly diabolical. For from it may be seen how subtly and yet seriously, even in things which seem to us ridiculous, that arch conjurer, the devil, undermines the well being and safety of mankind ... It is reported that Faust's deception was of this kind. Once upon a time when he was staying with some friends who had heard much about his magician's tricks, they besought him that he should show them some sample of his magic. He refused for a long time, but finally, yielding to the importunity of the company, which was by no means sober, he promised to show them whatever they might wish. With one accord therefore they besought him that he should show them a full grown vine with ripe grapes. For they thought that on account of the unsuitable time of the year (for it was toward the end of December) he would by no means be able to accomplish this. Faust assented and promised that they should immediately see on the table what they wished but with this condition: they should all wait without moving and in absolute silence until he should order them to cut the grapes. If they should do otherwise they would be in danger of their lives. When they had promised to do this, then by his tricks he so befuddled the eyes and senses of this drunken crowd that there appeared to them on a beautiful vine as many bunches of grapes of marvellous size and plumpness as there were people present. Made greedy by the novelty of the thing and athirst from too much wine, they took their knives and awaited his orders to cut off the grapes. Finally, when Faust had held these triflers in suspense for some time in their silly error, suddenly the vine with its grapes disappeared in smoke and they were seen, each holding, not the grapes which each thought he had seized, but his own nose with his knife suspended over it so that if anyone had been unmindful of the directions given and had wished to cut the grapes without orders, he would have cut off his own nose. And it would have served them right and they would have deserved other mutilation, since, with intolerable curiosity, they occupied themselves as spectators and participants in the illusions of the devil, which no Christian may be interested in without great danger or rather sin.

II The Faust Books

How to Read a *Volksbuch*: The *Faust Book* of 1587

Gerald Strauss

How we see a subject depends first and foremost on how we have framed it. When the subject is a text of little intrinsic depth, frame is everything. It is not to disparage a prominent item in the German literary canon to say that in the *Faust Book* of 1587 we have such a text. This is a fact established by its acknowledged identity as a *Volksbuch* aimed by its makers at a particular class of consumers and intended to serve objectives in part commercial and in part educational (cf. Burke; Muchembled, *Popular Culture*; Bollème). If we are to discover the book's meaning, or point, we must look for it in these objectives. In its peculiar combination of episodic construction, shrewd catering to common tastes, and preachy censoriousness, the anonymous *Historia von D. Johann Fausten* is the very paradigm of a late medieval-early modern *Volksbuch*, a user-friendly article, attractively packaged, designed to grab and hold attention, and capable of leaving some sort of enduring mark on the mind of the targeted reader. Obviously, popular literature should entertain. It has long been understood that it was also intended to uplift, or at least to instruct. But to what purpose? And in whose interest? Reflecting what trends in the cultural and social processes of its time? These questions have not often been put to the products of the early printing press in Germany. I think a review of some current historical thinking on early modern Germany can help us in developing suitable attitudes toward the *Faust Book* itself, and toward the whole literature of sorcery, witchcraft, and devilry of which it is the foremost example.

Frame, to repeat, is everything. As the time frame within which the *Faust Book* must be read, Renaissance and Reformation have exerted a determining influence on our understanding, for they function not merely as chronological labels but also as conceptual tags of great suggestive power. Not so very long ago, "Renaissance" stood for the victory of individuality over collectivism and the triumph of creative innovation over tradition and conformity, while "Reformation" was synonymous with deliverance from spiritual subjugation and a turning away from religious superstition. No longer. We do not nowadays set Middle Ages and Renaissance in such drastic opposition to one another. On the contrary: the weight of scholarship has decisively tipped the scales against the old notion that in the fifteenth century a burst of inventiveness broke the stranglehold of a long period of inertia and stagnation. And as for the Reformation: only the most denominationally committed scholar would now speak of the age of state churches and orthodoxy as a time of religious emancipation. As a result, we have been gaining very different sight lines on the period's personalities, events, and cultural products. Faustus and his book are examples. To portray him as a prefiguration of the Enlightenment, a titanic intellectual rebel, is to misread a text distorted by the wrong historical frame. Barbara Könneker argued this twenty years ago in a fine article on what she saw as a coherent central conception at work in the *Faust Book*. But more can be said toward an interpretation adequate to the intention of the book's producers; above all, there is a more appropriate historical setting to be brought into focus.

What preoccupied the sixteenth century, in Europe generally and in Germany in particular, was not the philosophical or aesthetic challenge of Rome and Greece or the promise contained in the rediscovered gospel. It was a much more concrete phenomenon in the lives of people: the all-pervasiveness of political aggrandizement. Saying this is only to repeat the observation of scores of contemporaries, many of them made uneasy by the apparently inexorable drift of events. This drift was speeding the processes of judicial and administrative consolidation in cities and states, vastly strengthening central authorities and the bureaucracies they were putting into place. The Reformation in particular created unprecedented opportunities – in Catholic no less than in Protestant parts – for concentration of powers in the hands of princes and magistrates, for these powers now included oversight of ecclesiastical as well as of secular institutions. In the aftermath of the abortive uprisings of the 1520s, state and church authorities resolved to prevent a repetition of these frightening events by drawing the reins of law and government even tighter. There can be no doubt that life for all but the most inaccessibly situated men and women in urban and rural Germany became more rule-bound, more closely surveyed, and more rigorously directed in the sixteenth century than it had been at any time in the recent or distant medieval past.

All this is quite well understood. What has not been so well established is the linkage between these developments and a contemporaneous effort on the part of Europe's ruling groups to undermine, and ultimately to replace, the expressions of popular culture. Again, it was the religious shakeup of the sixteenth century that created opportunities for what has been called "a systematic attempt by some of the educated … to change the attitudes and values of the rest of the population" (Burke 207). To give

this endeavor some chance of success, Lutheran and Reformed establish-
ments, and the leaders of the Counter Reformation in Catholic regions,
felt it incumbent upon them to accustom or – to use a term sometimes
given now to this attempt at cultural subversion and substitution – to ac-
culturate the masses to habits of thought and codes of behavior thought
fitting and proper by the elites (cf. Muchembled, "Lay Judges"; Wirth).

Fitting and proper in what respects? A small number of mutually rein-
forcing principles turn up in official pronouncements justifying the in-
roads being made on popular ways. These principles are, first, order, then
reason, next the orderly and reasonable conditions of uniformity and orthodoxy and the authority of the written word, finally, and underlying all
of these, an unquestioned faith in the objective existence of truth coupled
with the conviction that this truth can be known and can be formulated as
laws of belief and conduct. Seen from the eminence of these lofty principles, ordinary life looked chaotic indeed. Its apparently ungovernable
profusion of indigenous folkways violated all canons of order and coherence. Most offensive among these motley habits were the religious practices of ordinary folk. They were superstitious, licentious, disorderly,
irrational; they blended the sacred with the profane. In every respect they
violated the reformers' elitist ethic of "decency, diligence, gravity, modesty, orderliness, prudence, reason, self-control, sobriety, and thrift" – to
quote a list of sanctioned virtues offered by Peter Burke (213).

Wherever Lutheran regimes established themselves from the late
1520s onward, they therefore made the achievement of orthodoxy and
order a matter of the most urgent priority. But this was an endeavor in
which, as they discovered, not much headway was being made. Even half
a century after the victory of the Reformation, people seemed stuck in
their old habits, paying little heed to the improving doctrines preached to
them from above. There is much documentary evidence to allow us to
reach this conclusion. It was collected by Reformation authorities themselves in the course of their annual parish visitations. As observers of the
contemporary scene, they never failed to deplore the apparent indifference of people to the saving message, and to lament the helplessness of
authorities in the face of public apathy. Even after fifty years of evangeli-
cal preaching and catechization, says one such observer, Augustin Lercheimer, people still live like heathens, and the pastorate does, or can do,
little about it. "Is it any wonder, then," Lercheimer concludes, "that the
Devil has won a place among these people and has taught them superstition and sorcery?" (323) Identical litanies were heard in every part of the
country. They sound as plaintive toward the end of the sixteenth century
as at its beginning. People are mired in their superstitions. They would

rather cast a spell than say a prayer, consult a soothsayer or faith healer than go to church. They are closer to Satan than to God.

Was this rhetoric or description? Did men like Lercheimer really believe that there was a devil-saturated culture of sorcery out there, indifferent to, and heedless of, gospel, doctrine, law, and civility? There can be no doubt that they did. Lercheimer himself was a partisan of a minority position that doubted the reality of magic, attributing its apparent effects instead to deception practiced by the devil. But by far the greater number of commentators maintained the objective existence not only of the devil – no one denied this – but also of acts of sorcery carried out by his human agents. Luther's full acceptance of this view is well known. The depth of his involvement with the devil has been brought out most poignantly in Heiko Oberman's biography, the subtitle of which is "A Man between God and Devil." "In no sense is it true," writes Oberman, "that Luther overcame the medieval belief in the Devil. On the contrary, he deepened it and made it more acute" (109). Most contemporary intellectuals were in the same camp. For every Lercheimer, Plantsch, Weyer, Gödelmann, and Loos who thought that conjuring and necromancing were merely sleight-of-hand or devilish tricks, there were a hundred – and they included the author and publisher of the *Faust Book* – to whom these acts were real phenomena accomplished by real sorcerers with real powers. Both factions, in any case, were in full agreement on the role, the resourcefulness, and the long-term goal of the devil (cf. Hondorff; Russell 35; Midelfort 10–14). In their view, every blameworthy action was a deed done in the service of Satan.

To demonstrate that this was so, German printers issued a host of cautionary books in which – to quote the dedication of the *Faust Book*, which is one of them – [the devil] is shown to be the root cause of every ill done or suffered in the world. These so-called *Teufelsbücher*, of which it has been estimated that a quarter of a million copies were circulating in the second half of the sixteenth century (Roos 108–09), are by no means the jolly entertainments they are often made out to be. Deadly serious in their objectives, they set out to brand every deviation as an act of apostasy, ultimately a denial of Christ. It has been pretty well established in the recent literature on these matters that the late-sixteenth- and seventeenth-century fixation on the devil did not originate as a popular notion deep in the grassroots of society. Instead, it was a position developed by the educated and spread by them to the populace, mostly through preaching, literature, and, probably most effectively, litigation. Germany was not the only country to experience this phenomenon. Robert Mandrou has shown how French judges, theologians, and other intellectuals became preoccupied with the devil in the 1580s and 1590s, fully embracing the whole catalogue of satanic atrocities: pacts, marks, sabbats, werewolves, and all the rest (137–52). And Carlo Ginzburg has demonstrated that inquisitors reshaped popular mythic material into accounts of repulsive rituals (39–57).

This sounds like madness to us. But there was method in it. Without doubting that these men believed what they professed, we can see that devilry was of great practical use to them as well. Bedeviling the world was a way of polarizing in the most radical way the options open to every individual in his or her walk of life. There was no such thing as a trivial decision: you must either choose the devil or choose Christ (*Theatrum diabolorum*, Fii v.). Loaf at work, and you are acting like a follower of the devil. Rebel against your superior, stay away from catechism class, and you have declared yourself a loyalist of Satan. It is easy to see the practical value of this linkage. It allowed early modern opinion makers to brand every infraction as, literally, devilish. It facilitated social control and strengthened authorities in their endeavor to bring people into line with the abstract, written, urban, civilized, academic, legal, and theological norms of the great tradition (Delumeau 487). Whatever term we use to characterize this cleansing operation – reform, acculturation, or christianization (and no label has so far gained general acceptance) – it had two essential aims, one ideological, the other political. The former was to root out plebeian folkways and replace them with an approved popular culture congenial to the educated and issuing from their sermons, catechisms, and church hymns, and from an edifying literature of improving instruction. The latter, the political goal, was to eliminate altogether the sprawling network of cunning folk, spell-casters, and fortune-tellers whose activities had, apparently, been competing successfully with the services offered by the ministers of the established church and state. The great problem facing sixteenth-century reformers was to detach people from what was seen as, to all effects and purposes, an alternative religion, and to bond them firmly to the elite-determined obligations of church, court, doctrine, parish, law book, and catechism (Bossy 51–70).

I hope enough has been said to enable us to see the *Faust Book* framed by this comprehensive reforming impulse. It remains to support the argument by considering the text itself. First, its publisher, Johann Spies was anything but a pureyor of best sellers to the masses. Despite his location in Frankfurt, which became in the second half of the sixteenth century a center for the printing of *Volksbücher*, he had other things at heart. In the early 1580s Spies belonged to the orthodox wing of German Lutheranism, which at that time was embroiled in a vehement battle

against moderate, that is to say compromise-oriented, followers of Melanchthon. Spies supported the conservative position by publishing, first
in Heidelberg, then, after 1585, in Frankfurt, works by its leading theologians and controversialists, also sermons, jurisprudence, and official
documents, including the text of the Book of Concordance. The rigorous brand of Lutheranism espoused by his authors, with its polemics
against Philippism on the one side and Calvinism on the other, was evi-
dently what Spies regarded as the correct position on matters of religion.
He continued to publish heavy theology into the next century, occasionally lightening his program with some books of spiritual advice. But he
brought out no reprints and no trendy crowd pleasers, except one: the
History of Dr. Johann Faustus, the World-Famous Sorcerer and Black Magician,
How He Contracted Himself to the Devil for a Certain Time, What Strange
Adventures He Saw and Pursued during This Time, Until in the End He Received
His Just Reward, Compiled and Printed, Mostly from His Own Writings, as a
Dreadful Example, Ghastly Case Study, and Faithful Warning to All Ambitious,
Curious, and Godless Men.

Read in the context of the late-sixteenth-century Lutheran world view,
these are not the conventional phrases they now seem at first sight. The
devil *is* mankind's sworn enemy, as the "Preface to the Christian Reader"
assures us (Henning edition 7). Sorcery *is*, to quote the preface again,
"without any doubt the greatest and most serious sin against God." Every
approach to magic and the other black arts *was* a willful violation of the
admonition from James 4, given on the title page: "Submit yourselves
therefore to God. Resist the Devil." Even Mephistophiles, when asked by
Faustus what he would do if he were a human creature, confesses:
"I would bow down before the Lord ... that I might not move him to
anger against me ... and that I might know that, after death, eternal joy,
glory, and bliss await me" (chap. 17). Just how vital and timely a message
this was for the still godless masses out there in the lands monitored by
Lutheran clerics, only these clerics, deeply imbued as they were with the
reforming mentality of late-sixteenth-century Protestantism, could know.
The *Faust Book* was no aberration on Spies's list. Far from a mere pot-
boiler to bring in money for printing more low-profit theology and jurisprudence, it was a product of rigorous Lutheranism and, more broadly, an
instrument in his beleaguered fellow Lutherans' reformist assault on folk
occultism as part of their large-scale push for cultural reform.

Everything we learn about the protagonist of the *Faust Book* links him
with the deplored scene of common occult dabbling. He craves wealth
and the freedom to enjoy it. He wants someone to do his bidding. He likes
to have his questions answered. Conjuring can satisfy these wishes, and

so – like many others – he conjures, thus initiating the progression leading to the satanic compact. Georg Gödelmann, a contemporary diabologist, comments: "The excessive desire to know future and hidden things (by which our first parents, too, were led astray) is the foremost reason why those who practice the black arts tie themselves to the Devil" (Ci v.– Cii r.). The *Faust Book*, too, reproaches its hero for being a "speculator," for being "eager to search for all the causes in the heavens and on the earth" (chap. 2). But when read in context, this characterization describes not the protoscientist of the Renaissance, but rather the would-be adept of occult cunning setting out to make a profitable career for himself among the guillible. The point here is that Faustus's world, though described as that of a man of learning, is in all respects the world of ordinary folk as it was observed and denounced by those who were most eager to reconstruct it. Like everyone else, Faustus was brought to his undoing by the damnable trait of *Sicherheit*, that sense of smug self-sufficiency against which every pastor railed from his pulpit. *Sicherheit* was, like magic, a form of superstition. It was placing one's confidence not in God, but in one's own wit and reason, or in idols. *Sicherheit*, magic, and the devil were therefore linked in inexorable sequence, as the preface to the *Faust Book* states explicitly when it asserts that: "Where [the devil] finds a self-assured person [*wo er einen sicheren menschen antrifft*] … there he enters and makes himself at home."

There is much in the *Faust Book* that is ideologically Lutheran in a specifically late-sixteenth-century way. The 1570s and 1580s were a tumultuous time in the internal affairs of denominational Lutheranism, a crisis phase in the long conflict among several opposing camps over the correct interpretation of Luther's theology. The issue came to a head in Saxony in 1575 when the elector August, taking the side of the so-called Gnesio – or orthodox – Lutherans, suppressed the rival Philippist, or Crypto-Calvinist, faction by imprisoning its leaders. This group, which was centered at the University of Wittenberg, held positions on free will, on good works, and on adiaphora that were obnoxious to the orthodox. Here, by the way, we have the explanation for the *Faust Book*'s insistent association of its hero with Wittenberg, a connection not found in earlier stories about the magician related by Luther, Johannes Manlius, and Hondorff. To the orthodox, who looked to the universities of Leipzig and Jena for doctrinal authority, Wittenberg was a hotbed of heterodoxy, and Faustus's alleged professorship there must have been intended to bring the place into disrepute.

And there was a particular reason why the orthodox might wish to do this in the late 1580s. In 1586 the situation in Saxony had suddenly changed. August's successor, Christian I, had abandoned his father's crusade against Philippism and moved toward a compromise on the theological points in dispute. This outraged the orthodox, but their battle lines were now redrawn over the adoption of the Book of Concord, which had been printed, after heated debates and long delays, in 1580. Johann Spies published it when he lived and worked in Heidelberg. He did not move from there to Frankfurt until that city accepted the Formula of Concord in 1585. He was very much on the side of the *Concordia*'s anti-Calvinist, anti-synergist slant, and his *Faust Book* is as much an expression of this inclination as are all the other titles on his list. Why did Faustus fall? Faustus himself admits it was the result of "my stubborn, stiff-necked and godless will." The postlapsarian corruption of the human will was a basic article of faith. Lutheran preachers had been trying to drill this lesson into their hearers' minds for more than half a century.

But other things also had to be taught if the book was to do its job as a reforming tract, and, indeed, the *Faust Book* does impart a great deal of conventional wisdom: about the cosmos on the approved Ptolemaic-Neoplatonic model, for example (chaps. 21, 25), and about the influence of the stars on people's lives (chaps. 28, 31, 32). Readers were given the correct line on Catholicism and the papacy, including a picturesquely detailed, very long chapter on the excesses rampant at the Roman court. Marriage and the work ethic, the twin fundaments of civic virtue, are legitimized by the devil's antipathy to them as Faustus learns from him to scorn the domestic state (chap. 10), and as Faustus's life of enjoying rewards without having to work for them is shown to be antithetical to Lutheran social morality (chap. 9). To those who were obdurate to these and similar counsels, the book offered a vivid description of hell (chap. 16). Stern Protestantism permitted no escape or reprieve for sinners guilty of collusion with Satan. For Faustus, no alternative exists but despair; understanding has come too late for him. For the book's audience, on the other hand, not yet contracted to the forces of evil, there was still hope. "Always struggle against the Devil," the sad and sorry Faustus urges near the end of the book, "and never stop trying to defeat him" (chap. 68). This was the chief moral lesson to be learned, a simple one, surely, but to the reformers of the 1580s a most fateful piece of advice.

The point is reinforced by the observation that the *Faust Book*'s didactic thrust is enormously intensified in the several augmentations of the text published at the very end of the sixteenth century. Georg Rudolf Widmann, for instance, comments at great length in his version on the arguments heard in his day against marriage, and shows why these arguments are wrong (112 ff.). For every example of an objectionable trait or act given in the *Faust Book*, Widmann and Johann Nikolaus Pfitzer, who wrote a further amplification in the seventeenth century, offer a dozen additional cases suitable for pointing socially valuable lessens. The sequel to the *Faust Book* supposedly written by Faustus's disciple Christoph Wagner takes an insistently modernist stand by contrasting superstition with the procedures of science, reason, and the practical skills. "If you would cure a disease," argues Wagner, "go and study medical books …. Do you want to prophesy? Turn to mathematics, geometry, astronomy and astrology, navigation, and optics …." We do not, in other words, need the devil to help us with our problems ("Anderer Teil" 176–85). Wagner's expatiations, and the unbearably prolix commentaries of Widmann and Pfitzer, give us some idea of how the *Faust Book* may have been used by preachers and other advice givers to drive home the points of an approved moral code. No doubt it made for enjoyable reading as well, for author and publisher, practicing a kind of ideological double standard, pandered to tastes of which they sternly disapproved by describing in alluring detail what on nearly every page they admonished their readers to abhor. It is this ambiguous stance of censorious titillation that has obscured for most modern readers the *Faust Book*'s true intention. But in its own time, too, the book probably worked against itself. Emphatic as it is in its declarations of disapproval, these condemnations are embroidered with such rich anecdotal detail that what remains in the memory is an entertaining story, not a grave and salutary caution.

This leaves open the question of who was reading the book, and why. Certainly the *Faust Book* was a favorite with the public. Three additional printings came out in various places during the remaining months of 1587 following the original Frankfurt publication of September of that year. There was also an illicit reprint that same winter, and Spies himself reissued the book in 1588. Twenty-two printings have been counted in all, plus a sequel, adaptations, and translations. Such success was predictable. Books about the devil had been good sellers in Germany for at least half a century, and they must have whetted the public's appetite for more of the same. It seems obvious that the *Faust Book* was aimed at an urban public, whose reading ability, judging by the little impressionistic evidence we can gather about it, increased markedly in the century after 1500 (cf. Burke 251–54; Gawthrop). My own work in the educational history of Reformation Germany has persuaded me that reading skills were on the rise also in the villages and market towns of the countryside, at least among the better-off peasants who made up the leadership of rural society. I do not believe that this growth of literacy had much to do with religion, with any desire, that is, on the part of plain folk to read the gospel unaided by interpreters. Most people had practical reasons for wishing to read, and governments responded by providing basic reading instruction in a host of elementary schools set up in towns and villages. Needless to say, state and church authorities had their own agenda in promoting literacy: they expected it to be of help in their effort to reform public thought and behavior. To nourish the newly stimulated taste for reading, a steady supply of wholesome literary materials was needed, utilizing themes and topics from the chiefly oral popular culture, but subjecting these themes to a process of taste modification in which they were brought into line with the more elevated culture of the elite.

In this way, reading, learning, schooling, and religion worked together as a comprehensive program of acculturation. The *Historia von D. Fausten* is a case in point of this program. By the time the *Faust Book* came off the press in 1587, a large potential readership had been created and rendered receptive to its message, a message which – it was hoped – would strip the crudeness and inconstancy from the lives of common people, and raise them to a condition of willing and obedient Christian subjects.

Works Cited

Anderer Teil D. Johannis Fausti Historien, darin beschrieben ist Christophori Wagners Pact mit dem Teufel (1593). In *Doctor Fausti Weheklag,* ed. Helmut Wiemken, pp. 137–310. Bremen: Carl Schünemann, 1961.

Bollème, Geneviève. *La bibliothèque bleue*. Paris: Julliard, 1971.

– *Les contes bleus*. Paris: Montalba, 1983.

Bossy, John. "The Counter-Reformation and the People of Catholic Europe." *Past and Present* 47 (1970): 51–70.

Burke, Peter. *Popular Culture in Early Modern Europe*. New York: New York University Press, 1978.

Delumeau, Jean. "Les réformateurs et la superstition." In *Actes du colloque L'Amiral de Coligny et son temps*. Paris: Société de l'histoire du Protestantisme français, 1974.

Gawthrop, Richard. "Literacy Drives in Preindustrial Germany, 1500–1800." In *National Literacy Campaigns in Historical and Comparative Perspective*, ed. Harvey J. Graff and Robert F. Arnove. New York: Plenum Press, 1987.

Ginzburg, Carlo. "The Witches' Sabbat: Popular Cult or Inquisitorial Stereotype?" In *Understanding Popular Culture*, ed. Steven L. Kaplan, pp. 39–51. Berlin: Mouton Publishers, 1984.

Gödelmann, Georg. *Von Zauberern, Hexen und Unholden* .... Frankfurt am Main, 1592.

Historia von D. Johann Fausten. Neudruck des Faust-Buches von 1587, ed. Hans Henning. Halle: Sprache und Literatur, 1963.

Hondorff, Andreas. *Promptuarium exemplorum*. Leipzig, 1568.

Könneker, Barbara. "Faust-Konzeption und Teufelspakt im Volksbuch von 1587." In *Festschrift Gottfried Weber*, ed. H. O. Burger and K. von See, pp. 159–213. Bad Homburg: Gehlen, 1967.

Lercheimer, Augustin. *Christlich Bedenken und Erinnerung von Zauberey ..., wie diesem Laster zu wehren ...* (1585). In J. Scheible, *Das Kloster*, vol. 5, pp. 263–348. Stuttgart, 1847.

Mandrou, Robert. *Magistrats et sorciers en France au XVIIe siècle*. Paris: Plon, 1968.

Manlius, Johannes, *Locorum communium collectanea*. Basel, 1563.

Midelfort, H. C. Erik. *Witch Hunting in Southwestern Germany, 1562–1684*. Stanford, 1972.

Muchembled, Robert. "Lay Judges and the Acculturation of the Masses." In *Religion and Society in Early Modern Europe, 1500–1800*, ed. Kaspar von Greyerz, pp. 56–65. London: German Historical Institute, 1984.

– *Popular Culture and Elite Culture in France, 1400–1750*. Baton Rouge: Louisiana State University Press, 1985.

Oberman, Heiko. *Luther. Mensch zwischen Gott und Teufel*. 2nd edition. Berlin: Severin und Siedler, 1983.

Pfitzer, Johann Nikolaus. *Das ärgerliche Leben und schreckliche Ende ...* (see Widmann, Georg Rudolf, below).

Roos, Keith L. *The Devil in Sixteenth-Century German Literature*. Bern: Herbert Lang, 1972.

Russell, Jeffrey Burton, *Mephistopheles: The Devil in the Modern World*. Ithaca: Cornell University Press, 1986.

Theatrum diabolorum. Frankfurt am Main, 1569.

Widmann, Georg Rudolf. *Das ärgerliche Leben und schreckliche Ende dess viel-berüchtigten Ertz-Schwartzkünstlers Johannis Fausti ...*, ed. Adelbert von Keller. In *Bibliothek des litterarischen Vereins in Stuttgart*, vol. 146. Tübingen, 1880.

Wirth, Jean. "Against the Acculturation Thesis." In *Religion and Society in Early Modern Europe, 1500–1800*, ed. Kaspar von Greyerz, pp. 66–78. London: German Historical Institute, 1984.

Zarncke, Friedrich. "Johann Spies, der Herausgeber des Faustbuches, und sein Verlag." In *Kleine Schriften*, vol. 1, pp. 289–99. Leipzig: E. Avenarius, 1897.

THE HISTORIE

of the damnable

life, and deserued death of
Doctor Iohn Faustus,

Newly imprinted, and in conueni-
ent places *imperfect matter amended:*
according to the true Copie printed
at Franckfort, *and ·translated into*
English by P. F. *Gent.*

Seene and allowed.

Imprinted at London by Thomas Orwin, and are to be
solde by Edward White, dwelling at the little North
doore of Paules, at the signe of the Gun. 1592.

Here followeth the contents of this Book

A Discourse of the most famous Doctor John Faustus of Wittenberg in Germanie, Coniurer, and Necromancer: wherein is declared many strange things that he himselfe hath seene, and done in the earth and in the Ayre, with his bringing vp, his trauailes, studies, and last end

Chapter I

Of his Parentage and Birth

JOHN FAUSTUS, born in the town of Rhode, lying in the province of Weimer in Germanie, his father a poor husbandman, and not able well to bring him up: but having an uncle at Wittenberg, a rich man, and without issue, took this J. Faustus from his father, and made him his heir, in so much that his father was no more toubled with him, for he remained with his uncle at Wittenberg, where he was kept at the University in the same city of study Divinity. But Faustus being of a naughty mind and otherwise addicted, applied not his studies, but took himself to other exercises: the which his uncle often-times hearing, rebuked him for it, as Eli oft-times rebuked his children for sinning against the Lord: even so this good man laboured to have Faustus apply his study of Divinity, that he might come to the knowledge of God and his laws. But it is manifest that many virtuous parents have wicked children, as Cain, Ruben, Absolom, and such-like have been to their parents: so this Faustus having godly parents, and seeing him to be of a toward wit, were very desirous to bring him up in those virtuous studies, namely, of Divinity: but he gave himself secretly to study Necromancy and Conjuration, in so much that few or none could perceive his profession.

But to the purpose: Faustus continued at study in the University, and was by the Rectors and sixteen Masters afterwards examined how he had profited in his studies; and being found by them, that none for his time were able to argue with him in Divinity, or for the excellency of his wisdom to compare with him, with one consent they made him Doctor of Divinity. But Doctor Faustus within short time after he had obtained his degree, fell into such fantasies and deep cogitations, that he was marked of many, and of the most part of the Students was called the Speculator; and sometime he would throw the Scriptures from him as though he had no care of his former profession: so that he began a very ungodly life, as hereafter more at large may appear; for the old proverb saith, Who can hold that will away? so, who can hold Faustus from the Devil, that seeks after him with all his endeavour? For he accompanied himself with divers that were seen in those Devilish Arts, and that had the Chaldean, Persian, Hebrew, Arabian, and Greek tongues, using Figures, Characters, Conjurations, Incantations, with many other ceremonies belonging to these infernal Arts, as Necromancy, Charms, Soothsaying, Witchcraft, Enchantment, being delighted with their books, words, and names so well, that he studied day and night therein: in so much that he could not abide to be called Doctor of Divinity, but waxed a worldly man, and named himself an Astrologian, and a Mathematician: and for a shadow sometimes a Physician, and did great cures, namely, with herbs, roots, waters, drinks, receipts, and clysters. And without doubt he was passing wise, and excellent perfect in the holy scriptures: but he that knoweth his master's will and doth it not, is worthy to be beaten with many stripes. It is written, no man can serve two masters: and, thou shalt not tempt the Lord thy God: but Faustus threw all this in the wind, and made his soul of no estimation, regarding more his worldly pleasure than the joys to come: therefore at the day of judgment there is no hope of his redemption.

Chapter II

How Doctor Faustus began to practise in his Devilish Art, and how he conjured the Devil, making him to appear and meet him on the morrow at his own house

YOU have heard before, that all Faustus' mind was set to study the arts of Necromancy and Conjuration, the which exercise he followed day and night: and taking to him the wings of an Eagle, thought to fly over the whole world, and to know the secrets of heaven and earth; for his Speculation was so wonderful, being expert in using his Vocabula, Figures, Characters, Conjurations, and other Ceremonial actions, that in all the haste he put in practice to bring the Devil before him. And taking his way to a thick Wood near to Wittenberg, called in the German tongue Spisser Waldt: that is in English the Spissers Wood (as Faustus would often-times boast of it among his crew being in his jollity), he came into the same wood towards evening into a cross way, where he made with a wand a Circle in the dust, and within that many more Circles and Characters: and thus he passed away the time, until it was nine or ten of the clock in the night, then began Doctor Faustus to call for Mephostophiles the Spirit, and to charge him in the name of Beelzebub to appear there personally without any long stay: then presently the Devil began so great a rumour in the Wood, as if heaven and earth would have come together with wind, the trees bowing their tops to the ground, then fell the Devil to blare as if the whole Wood had been full of Lions, and suddenly about the Circle ran the Devil as if a thousand Wagons had been running together on paved stones. After this at the four corners of the Wood it thundered horribly, with such lightnings as if the whole world, to his seeming, had been on fire. Faustus all this while half amazed at the Devil's so long tarrying, and doubting whether he were best to abide any more such horrible Conjurings, thought to leave his Circle and depart; whereupon the Devil made him such music of all sorts, as if the Nymphs themselves had been in place: whereat Faustus was revived and stood stoutly in his circle aspecting his purpose, and began again to conjure the Spirit Mephostophiles in the name of the Prince of Devils to appear in his likeness: whereat suddenly over his head hanged hovering in the air a mighty Dragon: then calls Faustus again after his Devilish manner, at which there was a monstrous cry in the Wood, as if Hell had been open, and all the tormented souls crying to God for mercy; presently not three fathoms above his head fell a flame in manner of a lightning, and changed itself into a Globe: yet Faustus feared it not, but did persuade himself that the Devil should give him his request before he would leave: Often-times after to his companions he would boast, that he had the stoutest head (under the cope of heaven) at commandment: whereat they answered, they knew none stouter than the Pope or Emperor: but Doctor Faustus said, the head that is my servant is above all on earth, and repeated certain words out of Saint Paul to the Ephesians to make his argument good: The Prince of this world is upon earth and under heaven. Well, let us come again to his Conjuration where we left him at his fiery Globe: Faustus vexed at the Spirit's so long tarrying, used his Charms with full purpose not to depart before he had his intent, and crying on Mephostophiles the Spirit; suddenly the Globe opened and sprang up in height of a man: so burning a time, in the end it converted to the shape of a fiery man. This pleasant beast ran about the Circle a great while, and lastly appeared in manner of a gray Friar, asking Faustus what was his request. Faustus commanded that the next morning at twelve of the clock he should appear to him at his house; but the Devil would in no wise grant. Faustus began again to conjure him in the name of Beelzebub, that he should fulfil his request: whereupon the Spirit agreed, and so they departed each one his way.

Chapter III

The conference of Doctor Faustus with the Spirit Mephostophiles the morning following at his own house

DOCTOR FAUSTUS having commanded the Spirit to be with him, at his hour appointed he came and appeared in his chamber, demanding of Faustus what his desire was: then began Doctor Faustus anew with him to conjure him that he should be obedient unto him, and to answer him certain Articles, and to fulfil them in all points.

1. That the Spirit should serve him and be obedient unto him in all things that he asked of him from that hour until the hour of his death.

2. Farther, anything that he desired of him he should bring it to him.

3. Also, that in all Faustus his demands or Interrogations, the Spirit should tell him nothing but that which is true.

Hereupon the Spirit answered and laid his case forth, that he had no such power of himself, until he had first given his Prince (that was ruler over him) to understand thereof, and to know if he could obtain so much of his Lord: therefore speak farther that I may do thy whole desire to my Prince: for it is not in my power to fulfil without his leave. Shew me the cause why (said Faustus). The Spirit answered: Faustus, thou shalt understand, that with us it is even as well a kingdom, as with you on earth: yea, we have our rulers and servants, as I my self am one, and we name our whole number the Legion: for although that Lucifer is thrust and fallen out of heaven through his pride and high mind, yet he hath notwithstanding a Legion of Devils at his commandment, that we call the Oriental Princes; for his power is great and infinite. Also there is an host in Meridie, in Septentrio, in Occidente: and for that Lucifer hath his kingdom under heaven, we must change and give ourselves unto men to serve them at their pleasure. It is also certain, we have never as yet opened unto any man the truth of our dwelling, neither of our ruling, neither what our power is, neither have we given any man any gift, or learned him anything, except he promise to be ours.

Doctor Faustus upon this arose where he sat,[1] and said, I will have my request, and yet I will not be damned. The Spirit answered, Then shalt thou want thy desire, and yet art thou mine notwithstanding: if any man would detain thee it is in vain, for thine infidelity hath confounded thee.

---

[1] A mistranslation of the German text, "entsetzt sich darob," i.e. "was terrified at this."

Hereupon spake Faustus: Get thee hence from me, and take Saint Valentine's farewell and Crisam[2] with thee, yet I conjure thee that thou be here at evening, and bethink thyself on that I have asked thee, and ask thy Prince's counsel therein. Mephostophiles the Spirit, thus answered, vanished away, leaving Faustus in his study, where he sat pondering with himself how he might obtain his request of the Devil without loss of his soul: yet fully he was resolved in himself, rather than to want his pleasure, to do whatsoever the Spirit and his Lord should condition upon.

Chapter IV

The second time of the Spirit's appearing to Faustus in his house, and of their parley

FAUSTUS continuing in his Devilish cogitations, never moving out of the place where the Spirit left him (such was his fervent love to the Devil) the night approaching, this swift flying Spirit appeared to Faustus, offering himself with all submission to his service, with full authority from his Prince to do whatsoever he would request, if so be Faustus would promise to be his: this answer I bring thee, and an answer must thou make by me again, yet will I hear what is thy desire, because thou hast sworn me to be here at this time. Doctor Faustus gave him this answer, though faintly (for his soul's sake), That his request was none other but to become a Devil, or at the least a limb of him, and that the Spirit should agree unto these Articles as followeth.

1. That he might be a Spirit in shape and quality.
2. That Mephostophiles should be his servant, and at his commandment.
3. That Mephostophiles should bring him anything, and do for him whatsoever.
4. That at all times he should be in his house, invisible to all men, except only to himself, and at his commandment to shew himself.
5. Lastly, that Mephostophiles should at all times appear at his command, in what form or shape soever he would.

Upon these points the Spirit answered Doctor Faustus, that all this should be granted him and fulfilled, and more if he would agree unto him upon certain Articles as followeth.

First, that Doctor Faustus should give himself to his Lord Lucifer, body and soul.

---

[2] Saint Valentine's sickness is epilepsy.
Crisam is Gk. *chrisma*, a composition of oil and balm.

Secondly, for confirmation of the same, he should make him a writing, written with his own blood.

Thirdly, that he would be an enemy to all Christian people.

Fourthly, that he would deny his Christian belief.

Fifthly, that he let not any man change his opinion, if so be any man should go about to dissuade, or withdraw him from it.

Further, the Spirit promised Faustus to give him certain years to live in health and pleasure, and when such years were expired, that then Faustus should be fetched away, and if he should hold these Articles and conditions, that then he should have all whatsoever his heart would wish or desire; and that Faustus should quickly perceive himself to be a Spirit in all manner of actions whatsoever. Hereupon Doctor Faustus his mind was so inflamed, that he forgot his soul, and promised Mephostophiles to hold all things as he had mentioned them: he thought the Devil was not so black as they used to paint him, nor Hell so hot as the people say, *etc.*

Chapter V

The third parley between Doctor Faustus and Mephostophiles about a conclusion

AFTER Doctor Faustus had made his promise to the Devil, in the morning betimes he called the Spirit before him and commanded him that he should always come to him like a Friar, after the order of Saint Francis, with a bell in his hand like Saint Anthony, and to ring it once or twice before he appeared, that he might know of his certain coming: Then Faustus demanded the Spirit, what was his name? The Spirit answered, my name is as thou sayest, Mephostophiles, and I am a prince, but servant to Lucifer: and all the circuit from Septentrio to the Meridian, I rule under him. Even at these words was this wicked wretch Faustus inflamed, to hear himself to have gotten so great a Potentate to be his servant, forgot the Lord his maker, and Christ his redeemer, became an enemy unto all mankind, yea, worse than the Giants whom the Poets feign to climb the hills to make war with the Gods: not unlike that enemy of God and his Christ, that for his pride was cast into Hell: so likewise Faustus forgot that the high climbers catch the greatest falls, and that the sweetest meat requires the sourest sauce.

After a while, Faustus promised Mephostophiles to write and make his Obligation, with full assurance of the Articles in the Chapter before rehearsed. A pitiful case, (Christian Reader), for certainly this Letter or Obligation was found in his house after his most lamentable end, with all the rest of his damnable practices used in his whole life. Therefore I wish all Christians to take an example by this wicked Faustus, and to be comforted in Christ, contenting themselves with that vocation whereunto it hath pleased God to call them, and not to esteem the vain delights of this life, as did this unhappy Faustus, in giving his Soul to the Devil: and to confirm it the more assuredly, he took a small penknife, and pricked a vein in his left hand, and for certainty thereupon, were seen on his hand these words written, as if they had been written with blood, ò HOMO FUGE: whereat the Spirit vanished, but Faustus continued in his damnable mind, and made his writing as followeth.

Chapter VI

How Doctor Faustus set his blood in a saucer on warm ashes, and writ as followeth

I, JOHANNES FAUSTUS, Doctor, do openly acknowledge with mine own hand, to the greater force and strengthening of this Letter, that siththence I began to study and speculate the course and order of the Elements, I have not found through the gift that is given me from above, any such learning and wisdom, that can bring me to my desires: and for that I find, that men are unable to instruct me any farther in the matter, now have I Doctor John Faustus, unto the hellish prince of Orient and his messenger Mephostophiles, given both body and soul, upon such condition, that they shall learn me, and fulfil my desire in all things, as they have promised and vowed unto me, with due obedience unto me, according unto the Articles mentioned between us.

Further, I covenant and grant with them by these presents, that at the end of twenty-four years next ensuing the date of this present Letter, they being expired, and I in the meantime, during the said years be served of them at my will, they accomplishing my desires to the full in all points as we are agreed, that then I give them full power to do with me at their pleasure, to rule, to send, fetch, or carry me or mine, be it either body, soul, flesh, blood, or goods, into their habitation, be it wheresoever: and hereupon, I defy God and his Christ, all the host of heaven, and all living creatures that bear the shape of God, yea all that lives; and again I say it, and it shall be so. And to the more strengthening of this writing, I have written it with mine own hand and blood, being in perfect memory, and hereupon I subscribe to it with my name and title, calling all the infernal, middle, and supreme powers to witness of this my Letter and subscription.

John Faustus, Approved in the Elements,
and the spiritual Doctor.

Chapter VII

How Mephostophiles came for his writing, and in what manner he appeared, and his
sights he shewed him: and how he caused him to keep a copy of his own writing

DOCTOR FAUSTUS sitting pensive, having but one only boy with him,
suddenly there appeared his Spirit Mephostophiles, in likeness of a fiery
man, from whom issued most horrible fiery flames, in so much that
the boy was afraid, but being hardened by his master, he bade him stand
still and he should have no harm: the Spirit began to blare as in a singing
manner. This pretty sport pleased Doctor Faustus well, but he would not
call his Spirit into his Counting house, until he had seen more: anon was
heard a rushing of armed men, and trampling of horses: this ceasing,
came a kennel of hounds, and they chased a great Hart in the hall, and
there the Hart was slain. Faustus took heart, came forth, and looked upon
the Hart, but presently before him there was a Lion and a Dragon
together fighting, so fiercely, that Faustus thought they would have
brought down the house, but the Dragon overcame the Lion, and so they
vanished.

After this, came in a Peacock, with a Peahen, the cock brustling of
his tail, and turning to the female, beat her, and so vanished. Afterward
followed a furious Bull, that with a full fierceness ran upon Faustus, but
coming near him, vanished away. Afterward followed a great old Ape, this
Ape offered Faustus the hand, but he refused: so the Ape ran out of the
hall again. Hereupon fell a mist in the hall, that Faustus saw no light, but it
lasted not, and so soon as it was gone, there lay before Faustus two great
sacks, one full of gold, the other full of silver.

Lastly, was heard by Faustus all manner Instruments of music, as
Organs, Clarigolds,[3] Lutes, Viols, Citterns,[4] Waits,[5] Hornpipes, Flutes,
Anomes,[6] Harps, and all manner of other Instruments, the which so
ravished his mind, that he thought he had been in another world, forgot
both body and soul, in so much that he was minded never to change his
opinion concerning that which he had done. Hereat, came Mephostophiles into the Hall to Faustus, in apparel like unto a Friar, to whom Faustus spake, thou hast done me a wonderful pleasure in shewing me this
pastime, if you continue as thou hast begun, thou shalt win me heart and
soul, yea and have it. Mephostophiles answered, this is nothing, I will

---

[3] A stringed musical instrument, or clarichord.
[4] A kind of guitar.
[5] A wind instrument.
[6] This instrument is unknown.

please thee better: yet that thou mayest know my power and all, ask what thou wilt request of me, that shalt thou have, conditionally hold thy promise, and give me thy handwriting: at which words, the wretch thrust forth his hand, saying, hold thee, there hast thou my promise: Mephostophiles took the writing, and willing Faustus to take a copy of it, with that the perverse Faustus being resolute in his damnation, wrote a copy thereof, and gave the Devil the one, and kept in store the other. Thus the Spirit and Faustus were agreed, and dwelt together: no doubt there was a virtuous housekeeping.

Chapter VIII

The manner how Faustus proceeded with his damnable life, and of the diligent service Mephostophiles used towards him

DOCTOR FAUSTUS having given his soul to the Devil, renouncing all the powers of heaven, confirming this lamentable action with his own blood, and having already delivered his writing now into the Devil's hand, the which so puffed up his heart, that he had forgot the mind of a man, and thought rather himself to be a spirit. This Faustus dwelt in his uncle's house at Wittenberg, who died, and bequeathed it in his Testament to his Cousin Faustus. Faustus kept a boy with him that was his scholar, an unhappy wag, called Christopher Wagner, to whom this sport and life that he saw his master follow seemed pleasant. Faustus loved the boy well, hoping to make him as good or better seen in his Devilish exercise than himself; and he was fellow with Mephostophiles: otherwise Faustus had no more company in his house; but himself, his boy and his Spirit, that ever was diligent at Faustus' command, going about the house, clothed like a Friar, with a little bell in his hand, seen of none but Faustus. For his victual and other necessaries, Mephostophiles brought him at his pleasure from the Duke of Saxon, the Duke of Bavaria, and the Bishop of Saltzburg: for they had many times their best wine stolen out of their cellars by Mephostophile: Likewise their provision for their own table, such meat as Faustus wished for, his Spirit brought him in: besides that, Faustus himself was come so cunning, that when he opened his window, what fowl soever he wished for, it came presently flying into his house, were it never so dainty. Moreover, Faustus and his boy went in sumptuous apparel, the which Mephostophiles stole from the Mercers at Norenberg, Auspurg, Franckeford, and Liptzig: for it was hard for them to find a lock to keep out such a thief. All their maintenance was but stolen and borrowed ware: and thus they lived an odious life in the sight of God, though as yet the world were unacquainted with their wickedness. It must be so, for their fruits be none other: as Christ saith through John, were he calls the Devil a thief, and a murderer: and that found Faustus, for he stole him away both body and soul.

Chapter IX

How Doctor Faustus would have married, and how the Devil had almost killed him
  for it

DOCTOR FAUSTUS continued thus in his Epicurish life day and night, and believed not that there was a God, hell, or Devil: he thought that body and soul died together, and had quite forgotten Divinity or the immortality of his soul, but stood in his damnable heresy day and night. And bethinking himself of a wife, called Mephostophiles to counsel; which would in no wise agree: demanding of him if he would break the covenant made with him, or if he had forgot it. Hast not thou (quoth Mephostophiles) sworn thyself an enemy to God and all creatures? To this I answer thee, thou canst not marry; thou canst not serve two masters, God, and my Prince: for wedlock is a chief institution ordained of God, and that hast thou promised to defy, as we do all, and that hast thou also done: and moreover thou hast confirmed it with thy blood: persuade thyself, that what thou dost in contempt of wedlock, it is all to thine own delight. Therefore Faustus, look well about thee, and bethink thyself better, and I wish thee to change thy mind: for if thou keep not what thou hast promised in thy writing, we will tear thee in pieces like the dust under thy feet. Therefore sweet Faustus, think with what unquiet life, anger, strife, and debate thou shalt live in when thou takest a wife: therefore change thy mind.

Doctor Faustus was with these speeches in despair: and as all that have forsaken the Lord, can build upon no good foundation: so this wretched Faustus having forsook the rock, fell in despair with himself, fearing if he should motion Matrimony any more, that the Devil would tear him in pieces. For this time (quoth he to Mephostophiles) I am not minded to marry. Then you do well, answered his Spirit. But shortly and that within two hours after, Faustus called his Spirit, which came in his old manner like a Friar. Then Faustus said unto him, I am not able to resist nor bridle my fantasy, I must and will have a wife, and I pray thee give thy consent to it. Suddenly upon these words came such a whirlwind about the place, that Faustus thought the whole house would come down, all the doors in the house flew off the hooks: after all this, his house was full of smoke,

The journey to the witches' sabbath
After P. Cornelius

and the floor covered over with ashes: which when Doctor Faust perceived, he would have gone up the stairs: and flying up, he was taken and
thrown into the hall, that he was not able to stir hand nor foot: then round
about him ran a monstrous circle of fire, never standing still, that Faustus
fried as he lay, and thought there to have been burned. Then cried he out
to his Spirit Mephostophiles for help, promising him he would live in all
things as he had vowed in his handwriting. Hereupon appeared unto him
an ugly Devil, so fearful and monstrous to behold, that Faustus durst
not look on him. The Devil said, what wouldst thou have Faustus? how
likest thou thy wedding? what mind art thou in now? Faustus answered,

he had forgot his promise, desiring him of pardon, and he would talk no more of such things. The Devil answered, thou were best so to do, and so vanished.

After appeared unto him his Friar Mephostophiles with a bell in his hand, and spake to Faustus: It is no jesting with us, hold thou that which thou hast vowed, and we will perform as we have promised: and more than that, thou shalt have thy heart's desire of what women soever thou wilt, be she alive or dead, and so long as thou wilt, thou shalt keep her by thee.

These words pleased Faustus wonderful well, and repented himself that he was so foolish to wish himself married, that might have any woman in the whole City brought to him at his command; the which he practised and persevered in a long time.

Chapter X

Questions put forth by Doctor Faustus unto his Spirit Mephostophiles

DOCTOR FAUSTUS living in all manner of pleasure that his heart could desire, continuing in his amorous drifts, his delicate fare, and costly apparel, called on a time his Mephostophiles to him: which being come, brought with him a book in his hand of all manner of Devilish and enchanted arts, the which he gave Faustus, saying: hold my Faustus, work now thy heart's desire: The copy of this enchanting book was afterward found by his servant Christopher Wagner. Well (quoth Faustus to his Spirit) I have called thee to know what thou canst do if I have need of thy help. Then answered Mephostophiles and said, my Lord Faustus, I am a flying spirit: yea, so swift as thought can think, to do whatsoever. Here Faustus said: but how came thy Lord and master Lucifer to have so great a fall from heaven? Mephostophiles answered: My Lord Lucifer was a fair Angel, created of God as immortal, and being placed in the Seraphims, which are above the Cherubims, he would have presumed unto the Throne of God, with intent to have thrust God out of his seat. Upon this presumption the Lord cast him down headlong, and where before he was an Angel of light, now dwells he in darkness, not able to come near his first place, without God send for him to appear before him as Raphael: but unto the lower degree of Angels that have their conversation with men he was come, but not unto the second degree of Heavens that is kept by the Archangels, namely, Michael and Gabriel, for these are called Angels of God's wonders: yet are these far inferior places to that from whence my Lord and Master Lucifer fell. And thus far Faustus, because thou art one of the beloved children of my Lord Lucifer, following and feeding thy mind in manner as he did his, I have shortly resolved thy request, and more I will do for thee at thy pleasure. I thank thee Mephostophiles (quoth Faustus) come let us now go rest, for it is night: upon this they left their communication.

Chapter XI

How Doctor Faustus dreamed that he had seen hell in his sleep, and how he questioned with his Spirit of matters as concerning hell, with the Spirit's answer

THE night following, after Faustus his communication had with Mephostophiles, as concerning the fall of Lucifer, Doctor Faustus dreamed that he had seen a part of hell: but in what manner it was, or in what place he knew not: whereupon he was greatly troubled in mind, and called unto him Mephostophiles his Spirit, saying to him, my Mephostophiles, I pray thee resolve me in this doubt: what is hell, what substance is it of, in what place stands it, and when was it made? Mephostophiles answered: my Faustus, thou shalt know, that before the fall of my Lord Lucifer there was no hell, but even then was hell ordained: it is of no substance, but a confused thing: for I tell thee, that before all Elements were made, and the earth seen, the Spirit of God moved on the waters, and darkness was over all: but when God said, let it be light, it was so at his word, and the light was on God's right hand, and God praised the light. Judge thou further: God stood in the middle, the darkness was on his left hand, in the which my Lord was bound in chains until the day of judgment: in this confused hell is nought to find but a filthy, Sulphurish, fiery, stinking mist or fog. Further, we Devils know not what substance it is of, but a confused thing. For as a bubble of water flieth before the wind, so doth hell before the breath of God. Further, we Devils know not how God hath laid the foundation of our hell, nor whereof it is: but to be short with thee Faustus, we know that hell hath neither bottom nor end.

Chapter XII

The second question put forth by Doctor Faustus to his Spirit, what Kingdoms there were in hell, how many, and what were their rulers' names

FAUSTUS spake again to Mephostophiles, saying: thou speakest of wonderful things, I pray thee now tell me what Kingdoms is there in your hell, how many are there, what are they called, and who rules them: the Spirit answered him: my Faustus, know that hell is as thou wouldst think with thyself another world, in the which we have our being, under the earth, and above the earth, even to the Heavens; within the circumference whereof are contained ten Kingdoms, namely:

1. Lacus mortis.	6. Gehenna.
2. Stagnum ignis.	7. Herebus.
3. Terra tenebrosa.	8. Barathrum.
4. Tartarus.	9. Styx.
5. Terra oblivionis.	10. Acheron.

The which Kingdoms are govered by five kings, that is, Lucifer in the Orient, Beelzebub in Septentrio, Belial in Meridie, Astaroth in Occidente, and Phlegeton in the middest of them all: whose rule and dominions have none end until the day of Doom. And thus far Faustus, hast thou heard of our rule and Kingdoms.

Chapter XIII

Another question put forth by Doctor Faustus to his Spirit concerning his Lord Lucifer, with the sorrow that Faustus fell afterwards into

DOCTOR FAUSTUS began again to reason with Mephostophiles, requiring him to tell him in what form and shape, and in what estimation his Lord Lucifer was when he was in favour with God. Wereupon his Spirit required of him three days' respite, which Faustus granted. The three days being expired, Mephostophiles gave him this answer: Faustus, my Lord Lucifer (so called now, for that he was banished out of the clear light of heaven) was at the first an Angel of God, he sat on the Cherubims, and saw all the wonderful works of God, yea he was so of God ordained, for shape, pomp, authority, worthiness, and dwelling, that he far exceeded all other the creatures of God, yea our gold and precious stones: and so illuminated, that he far surpassed the brightness of the Sun and all other Stars: wherefore God placed him on the Cherubims, where he had a kingly office, and was always before God's seat, to the end he might be the more perfect in all his beings: but when he began to be high-minded, proud, and so presumptuous that he would usurp the seat of his Majesty, then was he banished out from amongst the heavenly powers, separated from their abiding into the manner of a fiery stone, that no water is able to quench, but continually burneth until the end of the world.

Doctos Faustus, when he had heard the words of his Spirit, began to consider with himself, having diverse and sundry opinions in his head:

and very pensively (saying nothing unto his Spirit) he went into his chamber, and laid him on his bed, recording the words of Mephostophiles; which so pierced his heart, that he fell into sighing and great lamentation, crying out: alas, ah, woe is me! what have I done? Even so shall it come to pass with me: am not I also a creature of God's making, bearing his own Image and similitude, into whom he hath breathed the Spirit of life and immortality, unto whom he hath made all things living subject: but woe is me, mine haughty mind, proud aspiring stomach, and filthy flesh, hath brought my soul into perpetual damnation; yea, pride hath abused my understanding, in so much that I have forgot my maker, the Spirit of God is departed from me. I have promised the Devil my Soul: and therefore it is but a folly for me to hope for grace, but it must be even with me as with Lucifer, thrown into perpetual burning fire: ah, woe is me that ever I was born. In this perplexity lay this miserable Doctor Faustus, having quite forgot his faith in Christ, never falling to repentance truly, thereby to attain the grace and holy Spirit of God again, the which would have been able to have resisted the strong assaults of Satan: for although he had made him a promise, yet he might have remembered through true repentance sinners come again into the favour of God; which faith the faithful firmly hold, knowing they that kill the body, are not able to hurt the soul: but he was in all his opinions doubtful, without faith or hope, and so he continued.

Chapter XIV

Another disputation betwixt Doctor Faustus and his Spirit, of the power of the Devil, and of his envy to mankind

AFTER Doctor Faustus had a while pondered and sorrowed with himself of his wretched estate, he called again Mephostophiles unto him, commanding him to tell him the judgment, rule, power, attempts, tyranny and temptation of the Devil, and why he was moved to such kind of living: whereupon the Spirit answered, this question that thou demandst of me, will turn thee to no small discontentment: therefore thou shouldst not have desired me of such matters, for it toucheth the secrets of our Kingdom, although I cannot deny to resolve thy request. Therefore know thou Faustus, that so soon as my Lord Lucifer fell from heaven, he became a mortal enemy both to God and man, and hath used (as now he doth) all manner of tyranny to the destruction of man, as is manifest by divers examples, one falling suddenly dead, another hangs himself, another drowns himself, others stab themselves, others unfaithfully despair, and so come to utter confusion: the first man Adam that was made perfect to the similitude of God, was by my Lord his policy, the whole decay of man: yea, Faustus, in him was the beginning and first tyranny of my Lord Lucifer used to man: the like did he with Cain, the same with the children of Israel, when they worshipped strange Gods, and fell to whoredom with strange women: the like with Saul: so did he by the seven husbands of her that after was the wife of Tobias: likewise Dagon our fellow brought to destruction thirty thousand men, whereupon the Ark of God was stolen: and Belial made David to number his men, whereupon were slain sixty thousand, also he deceived King Solomon that worshipped the Gods of the heathen: and there are such Spirits innumerable that can come by men and tempt them, drive them to sin, weaken their belief: for we rule the hearts of Kings and Princes, stirring them up to war and bloodshed; and to this intent do we spread ourselves throughout all the world, as the utter enemies of God, and his Son Christ, yea and all those that worship them: and that thou knowest by thyself Faustus, how we have dealt with thee. To this answered Faustus, why then thou didst also beguile me. Yea (quoth Mephostophiles) why should not we help thee forwards: for so soon as we saw thy heart, how thou didst despise thy degree taken in Divinity, and didst study to search and know the secrets of our Kingdom; even then did we enter into thee, giving thee divers foul and filthy cogitations, pricking thee forward in thine intent, and persuading thee that thou couldst never attain to thy desire, until thou hast the help of some Devil: and when thou wast delighted with this, then took we root in thee; and so firmly, that thou gavest thyself unto us, both body and soul the which thou (Faustus) canst not deny. Hereat answered Faustus, Thou sayest true Mephostophiles, I cannot deny it: Ah, woe is me miserable Faustus; how have I been deceived? had not I desired to know so much, I had not been in this case: for having studied the lives of the holy Saints and Prophets, and thereby thought myself to understand sufficient in heavenly matters, I thought myself not worthy to be called Doctor Faustus, if I should not also know the secrets of hell, and be associated with the furious Fiend thereof; now therefore must I be rewarded accordingly. Which speeches being uttered, Faustus went very sorrowfully away from Mephostophiles.

Chapter XV

*How Doctor Faustus desired again of his Spirit to know the secrets and pains of hell;
and whether those damned Devils and their company might ever come into the favour
of God again or not?*

DOCTOR FAUSTUS was ever pondering with himself how he might get loose
from so damnable an end as he had given himself unto, both of body and
soul: but his repentance was like to that of Cain and Judas, he thought his
sins greater than God could forgive, hereupon rested his mind: he looked
up to heaven, but saw nothing therein; for his heart was so possessed with
the Devil, that he could think of nought else but of hell, and the pains
thereof. Wherefore in all the haste he calleth unto him his Spirit Mephostophiles, desiring him to tell him some more of the secrets of hell, what
pains the damned were in, and how they were tormented, and whether
the damned souls might get again the favour of God, and so be released
out of their torments or not: whereupon the Spirit answered, my Faustus,
thou mayest well leave to question any more of such matters, for they will
but disquiet thy mind, I pray thee what meanest thou? Thinkest thou
through these thy fantasies to escape us? No, for if thou shouldst climb
up to heaven, there to hide thyself, yet would I thrust thee down again; for
thou art mine, and thou belongest unto our society: therefore sweet Faustus, thou wilt repent this thy foolish demand, except thou be content that
I shall tell thee nothing. Quoth Faustus ragingly, I will know, or I will not
live, wherefore dispatch and tell me: to whom Mephostophiles answered,
Faustus, it is no trouble unto me at all to tell thee, and therefore sith thou
forcest me thereto, I will tell thee things to the terror of thy soul, if thou
wilt abide the hearing. Thou wilt have me tell thee of the secrets of hell,
and of the pains thereof: know Faustus, that hell hath many figures, sem-
blances, and names, but it cannot be named nor figured in such sort unto
the living that are damned, as it is unto those that are dead, and do both
see and feel the torments thereof: for hell is said to be deadly, out of the
which came never any to life again but one, but he is as nothing for thee to
reckon upon, hell is bloodthirsty, and is never satisfied; hell is a valley, into
the which the damned souls fall: for so soon as the soul is out of man's
body, it would gladly go to the place from whence it came, and climbeth
up above the highest hills, even to the heavens; where being by the Angels
of the first Mobile denied entertainment (in consideration of their evil life
spent on the earth) they fall into the deepest pit of valley which hath no
bottom, into a perpetual fire, which shall never be quenched: for like as
the Flint thrown into the water, loseth not his virtue, neither is his fire extinguished; even so the hellish fire is unquenchable: and even as the Flint

stone in the fire being burned is red hot, and yet consumeth not: so like-wise the damned souls in our hellish fire are ever burning, but their pains never diminishing. Therefore is hell called the everlasting pain, in which is neither hope nor mercy: So is it called utter darkness, in which we see neither the light of Sun, Moon, nor Star: and were our darkness like the darkness of the night, yet were there hope of mercy, but ours is perpetual darkness, clean exempt from the face of God. Hell hath also a place within it called Chasma, out of the which issueth all manner of thunders, lightnings, with such horrible shriekings and wailings, that oft-times the very Devils themselves stand in fear thereof: for one while it sendeth forth winds with exceeding snow, hail, and rain congealing the water into ice; with the which the damned are frozen, gnash their teeth, howl and cry, and yet cannot die. Otherwhiles, it sendeth forth most horrible hot mists or fogs, with flashing flames of fire and brimstone, wherein the sor-rowful souls of the damned lie broiling in their reiterated torments: yea Faustus, hell is called a prison wherein the damned lie continually bound; it is also called Pernicies, and Exitium, death, destruction, hurtfulness, mischief, a mischance, a pitiful and an evil thing, world without end. We have also with us in hell a ladder, reaching of an exceeding height, as though it would touch the heavens, on which the damned ascend to seek the blessing of God; but through their infidelity, when they are at the very highest degree, they fall down again into their former miseries, complain-ing of the heat of that unquenchable fire: yea sweet Faustus, so must thou understand of hell, the while thou art so desirous to know the secrets of our Kingdom. And mark Faustus, hell is the nurse of death, the heat of all fire, the shadow of heaven and earth, the oblivion of all goodness, the pains unspeakable, the griefs unremovable, the dwelling of Devils, Dragons, Serpents, Adders, Toads, Crocodiles, and all manner of venom-ous creatures, the puddle of sin, the stinking fog ascending from the Styg-ian lake, Brimstone, Pitch, and all manner of unclean metals, the perpetual and unquenchable fire, the end of whose miseries was never purposed by God: yea, yea Faustus, thou sayest, I shall, I must, nay I will tell thee the secrets of our Kingdom, for thou buyest it dearly, and thou must and shalt be partaker of our torments, that (as the Lord God said) never shall cease: for hell, the woman's belly, and the earth are never satisfied; there shalt thou abide horrible torments, trembling, gnashing of teeth, howling, crying, burning, freezing, melting, swimming in a labyrinth of miseries, scalding, burning, smoking in thine eyes, stinking in thy nose, hoarseness of thy speech, deafness of thine ears, trembling of thy hands, biting thine own tongue with pain, thy heart crushed as in a press, thy bones broken, the Devils tossing firebrands upon thee, yea thy whole carcass tossed upon muckforks from one Devil to another, yea Faustus, then wilt thou wish for death, and he will fly from thee, thine unspeakable torments shall be every day augmented more and more, for the greater the sin, the greater is the punishment: how likest thou this, my Faustus, a resolution answerable to thy request?

Lastly, thou wilt have me tell thee that which belongeth only to God, which is, if it be possible for the damned to come again into the favour of God, or not: why Faustus, thou knowest that this is against thy promise, for what shouldst thou desire to know that, having already given thy soul to the Devil to have the pleasure of this world, and to know the secrets of hell? therefore art thou damned, and how canst thou then come again to the favour of God? Wherefore I directly answer, no; for whomsoever God hath forsaken and thrown into hell, must there abide his wrath and indignation in that unquenchable fire, where is no hope nor mercy to be looked for, but abiding in perpetual pains world without end: for even as much it availeth thee Faustus, to hope for the favour of God again, as Lucifer himself, who indeed although he and we all have a hope, yet is it to small avail, and taketh none effect, for out of that place God will neither hear crying nor sighing; if he do, thou shalt have as little remorse, as Dives, Cain, or Judas had: what helpeth the Emperor, King, Prince, Duke, Earl, Baron, Lord, Knight, Squire or Gentleman, to cry for mercy being there? Nothing: for if on the earth they would not be Tyrants, and selfwilled, rich with covetousness; proud with pomp, gluttons, drunkards, whoremongers, backbiters, robbers, murderers, blasphemers, and suchlike, then were there some hope to be looked for: therefore my Faustus, as thou comest to hell with these qualities, thou must say with Cain, My sins are greater than can be forgiven, go hang thyself with Judas: and lastly, be content to suffer torments with Dives. Therefore know Faustus, that the damned have neither end nor time appointed in the which they may hope to be released, for if there were any such hope, that they but by throwing one drop of water out of the Sea in a day, until it were all dry: or if there were an heap of sand as high as from the earth to the heavens, that a bird carrying away but one corn in a day, at the end of this so long labour; that yet they might hope at the last, God would have mercy on them, they would be comforted: but now there is no hope that God once thinks upon them, or that their howlings shall never be heard; yea, so impossible, as it is for thee to hide thyself from God, or impossible for thee to remove the mountains, or to empty the sea, or to tell the number of the drops of rain that have fallen from Heaven until this day, or to tell what there is most of in the world, yea and for a Camel to go through the eye of a needle: even so impossible it is for thee Faustus, and the rest of the damned, to come again into the favour of God. And thus Faustus hast thou heard my last sentence, and I pray thee how dost thou like it? But know this, that I counsel thee to let me be unmolested hereafter with such disputations, or else I will vex thee every limb, to thy small contentment. Doctor Faustus departed from his Spirit very pensive and sorrowful, laid him on his bed, altogether doubtful of the grace and favour of God, wherefore he fell into fantastical cogitations: fain he would have had his soul at liberty again, but the Devil had so blinded him, and taken such deep root in his heart, that he could never think to crave God's mercy, or if by chance he had any good motion, straightways the Devil would thrust him a fair Lady into his chamber, which fell to kissing and dalliance with him, through which means, he threw his godly motions in the wind, going forward still in his wicked practices, to the utter ruin both of his body and soul.

Chapter XVI

Another question put forth by Doctor Faustus to his Spirit Mephostophiles of his own estate

DOCTOR FAUSTUS, being yet desirous to hear more strange things, called his Spirit unto him, saying: My Mephostophiles, I have yet another suit unto thee, which I pray thee deny not to resolve me of. Faustus (quoth the Spirit) I am loth to reason with thee any further, for thou art never satisfied in thy mind, but always bringest me a new. Yet I pray thee this once (quoth Faustus) do me so much favour, as to tell me the truth in this matter, and hereafter I will be no more so earnest with thee. The Spirit was altogether against it, but yet once more he would abide him: well (said the Spirit to Faustus), what demandest thou of me? Faustus said, I would gladly know of thee, if thou wert a man in manner and form as I am; what wouldest thou do to please both God and man? Whereat the Spirit smiled saying: my Faustus, if I were a man as thou art, and that God had adorned me with those gifts of nature as thou once haddest; even so long as the breath of God were by, and within me, would I humble myself unto his Majesty, endeavouring in all that I could to keep his Commandments, praise him, glorify him, that I might continue in his favour, so were I sure to enjoy the eternal joy and felicity of his Kingdom. Faustus said, but that have not I done. No, thou sayest true (quoth Mephostophiles) thou hast not done it, but thou hast denied thy Lord and maker, which gave thee the breath of life, speech, hearing, sight, and all other thy reasonable senses that thou mightest understand his will and pleasure, to live to the glory and honour of his name, and to the advancement of thy body and soul, him I say being thy maker hast thou denied and defied, yea wickedly thou hast applied that excellent gift of thine understanding, and given thy soul to the Devil: therefore give none the blame but thine own self-will, thy proud and aspiring mind, which hath brought thee into the wrath of God and utter damnation. This is most true (quoth Faustus), but tell me Mephostophiles, wouldst thou be in my case as I am now? Yea, saith the Spirit (and with that fetched a great sigh) for yet would I so humble myself, that I would win the favour of God. Then (said Doctor Faustus) it were time enough for me if I amended. True (said Mephostophiles), if it were not for thy great sins, which are so odious and detestable in the sight of God, that it is too late for thee, for the wrath of God resteth upon thee. Leave off (quoth Faustus) and tell me my question to my greater comfort.

Chapter XVII

Here followeth the second part of Doctor Faustus his life, and practices, until his end

DOCTOR FAUSTUS having received denial of his Spirit, to be resolved any more in such-like questions propounded; forgot all good works, and fell to be a Calendar maker by help of his Spirit; and also in short time to be a good Astronomer or Astrologian: he had learned so perfectly of his Spirit the course of the Sun, Moon, and Stars, that he had the most famous name of all the Mathematicks[7] that lived in his time; as may well appear by his works dedicated unto sundry Dukes and Lords: for he did nothing without the advice of his Spirit, which learned him to presage of matters to come, which have come to pass since his death. The like praise won he with his Calendars, and Almanacs making, for when he presaged upon any change, Operation, or alteration of the weather, or Elements; as wind, rain, fogs, snow, hail, moist, dry, warm, cold, thunder, lightning: it fell so duly out, as if an Angel of heaven had forewarned it. He did not like the unskilful Astronomers of our time, that set in Winter cold, moist, airy, frosty; and in the Dog-days, hot, dry, thunder, fire, and such-like: but he set in all his works, day and hour, when, where, and how it should happen. If anything wonderful were at hand, as death, famine, plague, or wars, he would set the time and place in true and just order, when it should come to pass.

---

[7] i.e. Mathematicians.

Chapter XVIII

A question put forth by Doctor Faustus to his Spirit concerning Astronomy

DOCTOR FAUSTUS falling to practice, and making his Prognostications, he was doubtful in many points: wherefore he called unto him Mephostophiles his Spirit, saying: I find the ground of this science very difficult to attain unto: for that when I confer Astronomia and Astrologia, as the Mathematicians and ancient writers have left in memory, I find them to vary and very much to disagree: wherefore I pray thee to teach me the truth in this matter. To whom his Spirit answered, Faustus, thou shalt know that the practitioners or speculators, or at least the first inventors of these Arts, have done nothing of themselves certain, whereupon thou mayest attain to the true prognosticating or presaging of things concerning the heavens, or of the influence of the Planets: for if by chance some one Mathematician or Astronomer hath left behind him anything worthy of memory: they have so blinded it with Enigmatical words, blind Characters, and such obscure figures; that it is impossible for an earthly man to attain unto the knowledge thereof, without the aid of some Spirit, or else the special gift of God; for such are the hidden works of God from men: yet do we Spirits that fly and fleet in all Elements, know such, and there is nothing to be done, or by the Heavens pretended, but we know it, except only the day of Doom. Wherefore (Faustus) learn of me, I will teach thee the course and recourse of ♄. ♃. ♂. ☉. ♀. ☿ and ☾.[8] the cause of winter and summer, the exaltation and declination of the Sun, the eclipse of the Moon, the distance and height of the Poles, and every fixed Star, the nature and operation of the elements, fire, air, water, and earth, and all that is contained in them, yea herein there is nothing hidden from me, but only the fifth essence, which once thou hadst Faustus at liberty, but now Faustus thou hast lost it past recovery; wherefore leaving that which will not be again had, learn now of me to make thunder, lightning, hail, snow, and rain: the clouds to rend, the earth and craggy rocks to shake and split in sunder, the Seas to swell, and roar, and over-run their marks. Knowest not thou that the deeper the Sun shines, the hotter he pierces? so, the more thy Art is famous whilst thou art here, the greater shall be thy name when thou art gone. Knowest not thou that the earth is frozen cold and dry; the water running, cold and moist; the air flying, hot and moist; the fire consuming, hot and dry? Yea Faustus, so must thy heart be enflamed like the fire to mount on high: learn, Faustus, to fly like myself, as swift as thought

---

[8] The symbols of Saturn, Jupiter, Mars, the Sun, Venus, Mercury, and the Moon.

from one kingdom to another, to sit at princes' tables, to eat their daintiest fare, to have thy pleasure of their fair Ladies, wives and concubines, to use their jewels, and costly robes as things belonging to thee, and not unto them: learn of me, Faustus, to run through walls, doors, and gates of stone and iron, to creep into the earth like a worm, to swim in the water like a fish, to fly in the air like a bird, and to live and nourish thyself in the fire like a Salamander; so shalt thou be famous, renowned, far-spoken of, and extolled for thy skill: going on knives, not hurting thy feet; carrying fire in thy bosom, and not burning thy shirt; seeing through the heavens as through a Crystal, wherein is placed the Planets, with all the rest of the presaging Comets, the whole circuit of the world from the East to the West, North and South: there shalt thou know, Faustus, wherefore the fiery sphere above ♄ and the signs of the Zodiac doth not burn and consume the whole face of the earth, being hindered by placing the two moist elements between them, the airy clouds and the wavering waves of water: yea, Faustus, I will learn thee the secrets of nature, what the causes that the Sun in summer being at the highest, giveth all his heat downwards on the earth; and being in winter at the lowest, giveth all his heat upward into the heavens: that the snow should be of so great virtue, as the honey; and the Lady Saturnia ♓[9] in Occulto more hotter than the Sun in Manifesto. Come on my Faustus, I will make thee as perfect in these things as myself, I will learn thee to go invisible, to find out the mines of gold and silver, the fodines[10] of precious stones, as the Carbuncle, the Diamond, Sapphire, Emerald, Ruby, Topaz, Jacinth, Garnet, Jasper, Amethyst, use all these at thy pleasure, take thy heart's desire: thy time Faustus weareth away, then why wilt thou not take thy pleasure of the world? Come up, we will go visit Kings at their own courts, and at their most sumptuous banquets be their guests, if willingly they invite us not, then perforce we will serve our own turn with their best meat and daintiest wine: Agreed, quoth Faustus; but let me pause a while upon this thou hast even now declared unto me.

---

[9] The symbol of Pisces in the Zodiac.
[10] Mines.

Chapter XIX

How Doctor Faustus fell into despair with himself, for having put forth a question unto his Spirit, they fell at variance, whereupon the whole route of Devils appeared unto him, threatening him sharply

DOCTOR FAUSTUS revolving with himself the speeches of his Spirit, he became so woeful and sorrowful in his cogitations, that he thought himself already frying in the hottest flames of hell, and lying in his muse, suddenly there appeared unto him his Spirit, demanding what thing so grieved and troubled his conscience, whereat Doctor Faustus gave no answer: yet the Spirit very earnestly lay upon him to know the cause; and if it were possible, he would find remedy for his grief, and ease him of his sorrows. To whom Faustus answered, I have taken thee unto me as a servant to do me service, and thy service will be very dear unto me; yet I cannot have any diligence of thee farther than thou list thyself, neither dost thou in anything as it becometh thee. The Spirit replied, my Faustus, thou knowest that I was never against thy commandments as yet, but ready to serve and resolve thy questions, although I am not bound unto thee in such respects as concern the hurt of our Kingdom, yet was I always willing to answer thee, and so I am still: therefore my Faustus say on boldly, what is thy will and pleasure? At which words, the Spirit stole away the heart of Faustus, who spake in this sort, Mephostophiles, tell me how and after what sort God made the world, and all the creatures in them, and why man was made after the Image of God?

The Spirit hearing this, answered, Faustus thou knowest that all this is in vain for thee to ask, I know that thou art sorry for that thou hast done, but it availeth thee not, for I will tear thee in thousands of pieces, if thou change not thine opinions, and hereat he vanished away. Whereat Faustus all sorrowful for that he had put forth such a question, fell to weeping and to howling bitterly, not for his sins towards God, but for that the Devil was departed from him so suddenly, and in such a rage. And being in this perplexity, he was suddenly taken in such an extreme cold, as if he should have frozen in the place where he sat, in which, the greatest Devil in hell appeared unto him, with certain of his hideous and infernal company in the most ugliest shapes that it was possible to think upon, and traversing the chamber round about where Faustus sat, Faustus thought to himself, now are they come for me though my time be not come, and that because I have asked such questions of my servant Mephostophiles: at whose cogitations, the chiefest Devil which was his Lord, unto whom he gave his soul, that was Lucifer, spake in this sort: Faustus, I have seen thy thoughts, which are not as thou hast vowed unto me, by virtue of this letter, and shewed him the Obligation that he had written with his own blood, wherefore I am come to visit thee and to shew thee some of our hellish pastimes, in hope that will draw and confirm thy mind a little more sted-fast unto us. Content quoth Faustus, go to, let me see what pastime you can make. At which words, the great Devil in his likeness sat him down by Faustus, commanding the rest of the Devils to appear in their form, as if they were in hell: first entered Belial in form of a Bear, with curled black hair to the ground, his ears standing upright: within the ear was as red as blood, out of which issued flames of fire, his teeth were a foot at least long, as white as snow, with a tail three ells long (at the least) having two wings, one behind each arm, and thus one after another they appeared to Faustus in form as they were in hell. Lucifer himself sat in manner of a man, all hairy, but of a brown colour like a Squirrel, curled, and his tail turning upwards on his back as the Squirrels use, I think he could crack nuts too like a Squirrel. After him came Beelzebub in curled hair of horse-flesh colour, his head like the head of a Bull, with a mighty pair of horns, and two long ears down to the ground, and two wings on his back, with pricking stings like thorns: out of his wings issued flames of fire, his tail was like a Cow. Then came Astaroth in form of a worm, going upright on his tail; he had no feet, but a tail like a slow-worm: under his chaps grew two short hands, and his back was coal black, his belly thick in the middle, and yellow like gold, having many bristles on his back like a Hedgehog. After him came Chamagosta, being white and gray mixed, exceeding curled and hairy: he had a head like the head of an Ass, the tail like a Cat, and Claws like an Ox, lacking nothing of an ell broad. Then came Anobis; this Devil had a head like a Dog, white and black hair in shape of a Hog, saving that he had but two feet, one under his throat, the other at his tail: he was four ells long, with hanging ears like a Bloodhound. After him came Dythycan, he was a short thief in form of a Pheasant, with shining feathers, and four feet: his neck was green, his body red, and his feet black. The last was called Brachus, with four short feet like an Hedgehog, yellow and green: the upper side of his body was brown, and the belly like blue flames of fire; the tail red, like the tail of a Monkey. The rest of the Devils were in form of insensible beasts, as Swine, Harts, Bears, Wolves, Apes, Buffs, Goats, Antelopes, Elephants, Dragons, Horses, Asses, Lions, Cats Snakes, Toads, and all manner of ugly odious Serpents and Worms: yet came in such sort, that every one at his entry into the Hall, made their reverence unto Lucifer, and so took their places, standing in order as they came, until they had filled the whole Hall: wherewith suddenly fell a most horrible thunder-clap, that the house shook as though it would have fallen to the ground, upon which every monster had a muck-fork in his hand, holding them towards Faustus as though they would have run a tilt at him: which when Faustus perceived, he thought upon the words of Mephostophiles, when he told him how the souls in hell were tormented, being cast from Devil to Devil upon muck-forks, he thought verily to have been tormented there of them in like sort. But Lucifer perceiving his thought, spake to him, my Faustus, how likest thou this crew of mine? Quoth Faustus, why came you not in another manner of shape? Lucifer replied, we cannot change our hellish form, we have shewed ourselves here, as we are there; yet can we blind men's eyes in such sort, that when we will we repair unto them, as if we were men or Angels of light, although our dwelling be in darkness. Then said Faustus, I like not so many of you together, whereupon Lucifer commanded them to depart, except seven of the principal forthwith they presently vanished, which Faustus perceiving, he was somewhat better comforted, and spake to Lucifer, where is my servant Mephostophiles, let me see if he can do the like, whereupon came a fierce Dragon, flying and spitting fire round about the house, and coming towards Lucifer, made reverence, and then changed himself to the form of a Friar, saying, Faustus, what wilt thou? Saith Faustus, I will that thou teach me to transform myself in like sort as thou and the rest have done: then Lucifer put forth his Paw, and gave Faustus a book, saying hold, do what thou wilt, which he looking upon, straightways changed himself into a Hog, then into a Worm, then into a Dragon, and finding this for his purpose, it liked him well. Quoth he to Lucifer, and how cometh it that all these filthy forms are in the world? Lucifer answered, they are ordained of God as plagues unto men, and so shalt thou be plagued (quoth he) whereupon, came Scorpions, Wasps, Emmets, Bees, and Gnats, which fell to stinging and biting him, and all the whole house was filled with a most horrible stinking fog, in so much, that Faustus saw nothing, but still was tormented; wherefore he cried for help saying, Mephostophiles my faithful servant, where art thou, help, help, I pray thee: hereat his Spirit answered nothing, but Lucifer himself said, ho ho ho Faustus, how likest thou the creation of the world, and incontinent it was clear again, and the Devils and all the filthy Cattle were vanished, only Faustus was left alone; seeing nothing, but hearing the sweetest music that ever he heard before, at which he was so ravished with delight, that he forgot the fears he was in before: and it repented him that he had seen no more of their pastime.

Chapter XX

How Doctor Faustus desired to see hell, and of the manner how he was used therein

DOCTOR FAUSTUS bethinking how his time went away, and how he had spent eight years thereof, he meant to spend the rest to his better contentment, intending quite to forget any such motions as might offend the Devil any more: wherefore on a time he called his Spirit Mephostophiles, and said unto him, bring thou hither unto me thy Lord Lucifer, or Belial: he brought him (notwithstanding) one that was called Beelzebub, the which asked Faustus his pleasure. Quoth Faustus, I would know of thee if I may see hell and take a view thereof? That thou shalt (said the Devil) and at midnight I will fetch thee. Well, night being come, Doctor Faustus awaited very diligently for the coming of the Devil to fetch him, and thinking that he tarried all too long, he went to the window, where he pulled open a casement, and looking into the Element, he saw a cloud in the North more black, dark, and obscure, than all the rest of the Sky, from whence the wind blew most horrible right into Faustus his chamber, filled the whole house with smoke, that Faustus was almost smothered: hereat fell an exceeding thunderclap, and withal came a great rugged black Bear, all curled, and upon his back a chair of beaten gold, and spake to Faustus, saying, sit up and away with me: and Doctor Faustus that had so long abode the smoke, wished rather to be in hell than there, got on the Devil, and so they went together. But mark how the Devil blinded him, and made him believe that he carried him into hell, for he carried him into the air, where Faustus fell into a sound sleep, as if he had sat in a warm water or bath: at last they came to a place which burneth continually with flashing flames of fire and brimstone, whereout issued an exceeding mighty clap of thunder, with so horrible a noise, that Faustus awaked, but the Devil went forth on his way and carried Faustus thereinto, yet notwithstanding, howsoever it burnt, Doctor Faustus felt no more heat, than as it were the glimpse of the Sun in May: there heard he all manner of music to welcome him, but saw none playing on them; it pleased him well, but he durst not ask, for he was forbidden it before. To meet the Devil and the guest that came with him, came three other ugly Devils, the which ran back again before the Bear to make them way, against whom there came running an exceeding great Hart, which would have thrust Faustus out of his chair, but being defended by the other three Devils, the Hart was put to the repulse: thence going on their way Faustus looked, and behold there was nothing but Snakes, and all manner of venomous beasts about him, which were exceeding great, unto the which Snakes came many Storks, and swallowed up all the whole multitude of Snakes, that they left

not one: which when Faustus saw, he marvelled greatly: but proceeding further on their hellish voyage, there came forth of a hollow cliff an exceeding great flying Bull, the which with such a force hit Faustus his chair with his head and horns, that he turned Faustus and his Bear over and over, so that the Bear vanished away, whereat Faustus began to cry: oh, woe is me that ever I came here: for he thought there to have been beguiled of the Devil, and to make his end before his time appointed or conditioned of the Devil: but shortly came unto him a monstrous Ape, bidding Faustus be of good cheer, and said, get upon me; all the fire in hell seemed to Faustus to have been put out, whereupon followed a monstrous thick fog, that he saw nothing, but shortly it seemed to him to wax clear, where he saw two great Dragons fastened to a waggon, into the which the Ape ascended and set Faustus therein; forth flew the Dragons into an exceeding dark cloud, where Faustus saw neither Dragon nor Chariot wherein he sat, and such were the cries of tormented souls, with mighty thunder-claps and flashing lightnings about his ears, that poor Faustus shook for fear. Upon this came they to a water, stinking and filthy, thick like mud, into the which ran the Dragons, sinking under with waggon and all; but Faustus felt no water but as it were a small mist, saving that the waves beat so sore upon him, that he saw nothing under and over him but only water, in the which he lost his Dragons, Ape, and waggon; and sinking yet deeper and deeper, he came at last as it were upon an high Rock, where the waters parted and left him thereon: but when the water was gone, it seemed to him he should there have ended his life, for he saw no way but death: the Rock was as high from the bottom as Heaven is from the earth: there sat he, seeing nor hearing any man, and looked ever upon the Rock; at length he saw a little hole, out of the which issued fire; thought he, how shall I now do? I am forsaken of the Devils, and they that brought me hither, here must I either fall to the bottom, or burn in the fire, or sit still in despair: with that in his madness he gave a leap into the fiery hole, saying: hold you infernal Hags, take here this sacrifice as my last end; the which I justly have deserved: upon this he was entered, and finding himself as yet unburned or touched of the fire, he was the better appayed,[11] but there was so great a noise as he never heard the like before, it passed all the thunder that ever he had heard; and coming down further to the bottom of the Rock, he saw a fire, wherein were many worthy and noble personages, as Emperors, Kings, Dukes, and Lords, and many thousands more of tormented souls, at the edge of which fire ran a most pleasant, clear, and cool water to behold, into the which many tormented souls sprang out of the fire to cool themselves; but being so freezing cold, they were constrained to return again into the fire, and thus wearied themselves and spent their endless torments out of one labyrinth into another, one while in heat, another while in cold: but Faustus standing thus all this while gazing on them were thus tormented, he saw one leaping out of the fire and screeching horribly, whom he thought to have known, wherefore he would fain have spoken unto him, but remembering that he was forbidden, he refrained speaking. Then this Devil that brought him in, came to him again in likeness of a Bear, with the chair on his back, and bade him sit up, for it was time to depart: so Faustus got up, and the Devil carried him out into the air, where he had so sweet music that he fell asleep by the way. His boy Christopher being all this while at home, and missing his master so long, thought his master would have tarried and dwelt with the Devil for ever: but whilst his boy was in these cogitations, his master came home, for the Devil brought him home fast asleep as he sat in his chair, and so he threw him on his bed, where (being thus left of the Devil) he lay until day. When he awaked, he was amazed, like a man that had been in a dark dungeon; musing with himself if it were true or false that he had seen hell, or whether he was blinded or not: but he rather persuaded himself that he had been there than otherwise, because he had seen such wonderful things: wherefore he most carefully took pen and ink, and wrote those things in order as he had seen: the which writing was afterwards found by his boy in his study; which afterwards was published to the whole city of Wittenberg in open print, for example to all Christians.

---

[11] i.e. pleased.

Chapter XXI

How Doctor Faustus was carried through the air up to the heavens to see the world, and how the Sky and Planets ruled: after the which he wrote one letter to his friend of the same to Liptzig, how he went about the world in eight days

THIS letter was found by a freeman and Citizen of Wittenberg, written with his own hand, and sent to his friend at Liptzig a Physician, named John Victor, the contents of which were as followeth.

Amongst other things (my loving friend and brother) I remember yet the former friendship had together, when we were schoolfellows and students in the University at Wittenberg, whereas you first studied Physic, Astronomy, Astrology, Geometry, and Cosmography; I to the contrary (you know) studied Divinity: notwithstanding now in any of your own studies I am seen (I am persuaded) further then your self: for sithence I began I have never erred, for (might I speak it without affecting my own praise) my Calendars and other practices have not only the commendations of the common sort, but also of the chiefest Lords and Nobles of this our Dutch Nation: because (which is chiefly to be noted) I write and presaged of matters to come, which all accord and fall out so right, as if they had been already seen before. And for that (my beloved Victori) you write to know my voyage which I made into the Heavens, the which (as you certify me you have had some suspicion of, although you partly persuaded, yourself, that it is a thing impossible) no matter for that, it is as it is, and let it be as it will, once it was done, in such manner as now according unto your request I give you here to understand.

I being once laid on my bed, and could not sleep for thinking on my Calendar and practice, I marvelled with myself how it were possible that the Firmament should be known and so largely written of men, or whether they write true or false, by their own opinions, or supposition, or by due observations and true course of the heavens. Behold, being in these my muses, suddenly I heard a great noise, in so much that I thought my house would have been blown down, so that all my doors and chests flew open, whereat I was not a little astonied, for withal I heard a groaning voice which said, get up, the desire of thy heart, mind, and thought shalt thou see: at the which I answered, what my heart desireth, that would I fain see, and to make proof, if I shall see I will away with thee. Why then (quoth he) look out at thy window, there cometh a messenger for thee, that did I, and behold, there stood a Waggon, with two Dragons before it to draw the same, and all the Waggon was of a light burning fire, and for that the Moon shone, I was the willinger at that time to depart: but the voice spake again, sit up and let us away: I will, said I, go with thee, but

upon this condition, that I may ask after all things that I see, hear, or think
on: the voice answered, I am content for this time. Hereupon I got me
into the Waggon, so that the Dragons carried me upright into the air. The
Waggon had also four wheels the which rattled so, and made such a noise
as if we had been all this while running on the stones: and round about us
flew out flames of fire, and the higher that I came, the more the earth
seemed to be darkened, so that methought I came out of a dungeon, and
looking down from Heaven, behold, Mephostophiles my Spirit and servant was behind me, and when he perceived that I saw him, he came and
sat by me, to whom I said, I pray thee Mephostophiles whither shall I go
now? Let not that trouble thy mind, said he, and yet they carried us
higher up. And now will I tell thee good friend and schoolfellow, what
things I have seen and proved; for on the Tuesday went I out, and on
Tuesday seven-nights following I came home again, that is, eight days, in
which time I slept not, no not one wink came in mine eyes, and we went
invisible of any man: and as the day began to appear, after our first night's
journey, I said to my Spirit Mephostophiles, I pray thee how far have we
now ridden, I am sure thou knowest: for methinks that we are ridden exceeding far, the World seemeth so little: Mephostophiles answered me,
my Faustus believe me, that from the place from whence thou camest,
unto this place where we are now, is already forty-seven leagues right in
height, and as the day increased, I looked down upon the World, there
saw I many kingdoms and provinces, likewise the whole world, Asia, Eu-
ropa, and Africa, I had a sight of: and being so high, quoth I to my Spirit,
tell me now how these Kingdoms lie, and what they are called, the which
he denied not, saying, see this on our left hand is Hungaria, this is also
Prussia on our left hand, and Poland, Muscovia, Tartascelesia,[12] Bohemia,
Saxony: and here on our right hand, Spain, Portugal, France, England,
and Scotland: then right out before us lie the Kingdoms of Persia, India,
Arabia, the King of Alchar, and the great Cham: now are we come to
Wittenberg, and are right over the town of Weim in Austria, and ere long
will we be at Constantinople, Tripolie, and Jerusalem, and after will we
pierce the frozen Zone, and shortly touch the Horizon, and the Zenith of
Wittenberg. There looked I on the Ocean Sea, and beheld a great many
of ships and Galleys ready to the battle, one against another: and thus
I spent my journey, now cast I my eyes here, now there, toward South,
North, East, and West, I have been in one place where it rained and
hailed, and in another where the Sun shone excellent fair, and so I think

---

[12] Probably a corruption of Tartary and Silesia.

that I saw the most things in and about the world, with great admiration that in one place it rained, and in another hail and snow, on this side the Sun shone bright, some hills covered with snow never consuming, others were so hot that grass and trees were burned and consumed therewith. Then looked I up to the heavens, and behold, they went so swift, that I thought they would have sprung in thousands. Likewise it was so clear and so hot, that I could not long gaze into it, it so dimmed my sight: and had not my Spirit Mephostophiles covered me as it were with a shadowing cloud, I had been burnt with the extreme heat thereof, for the Sky the which we behold here when we look up from the earth, is so fast and thick as a wall, clear and shining bright as a Crystal, in the which is placed the Sun, which casteth forth his rays or beams over the universal world, to the uttermost confines of the earth. But we think that the Sun is very little: no, it is altogether as big as the world. Indeed the body substantial is but little in compass, but the rays or stream that it casteth forth, by reason of the thing wherein it is placed, maketh him to extend and shew himself over the whole world: and we think that the Sun runneth his course, and that the heavens stand still: no, it is the heavens that move his course, and the Sun abideth perpetually in his place, he is permanent, and fixed in his place, and although we see him beginning to ascend in the Orient or East, at the highest in the Meridian or South, setting in the Occident or West, yet is he at the lowest in Septentrio or North, and yet he moveth not. It is the axle of the heavens that moveth the whole firmament, being a Chaos or confused thing, and for that proof, I will shew thee this example, like as thou seest a bubble made of water and soap blown forth of a quill, is in form of a confused mass or Chaos, and being in this form, is moved at pleasure of the wind, which runneth round about that Chaos, and moveth him also round: even so is the whole firmament or Chaos, wherein are placed the sun, and the rest of the Planets turned and carried at the pleasure of the Spirit of God, which is wind. Yea Christian Reader, to the glory of God, and for the profit of thy soul, I will open unto thee the divine opinion touching the ruling of this confused Chaos, far more than any rude German Author, being possessed with the Devil, was able to utter; and to prove some of my sentence before to be true, look into Genesis unto the works of God, at the creation of the world, there shalt thou find, that the Spirit of God moved upon the waters before heaven and earth were made. Mark how he made it, and how by his word every element took his place: these were not his works, but his words; for all the words he used before, he concluded afterwards in one work, which was in making man: mark reader with patience for thy soul's health, see into all that was done by the word and work of God, light and darkness was, the firmament stood, and their great ⊙ and little light ☽ in it: the moist waters were in one place, the earth was dry, and every element brought forth according to the word of God: now followeth his works he made man like his own image, how? out of the earth? The earth will shape no image without water, there was one of the elements. But all this while where was wind? all elements were at the word of God, man was made, and in a form by the work of God, yet moved not that work, before God breathed the Spirit of life into his nostrils, and made him a living soul, here was the first wind and Spirit of God out of his own mouth, which we have likewise from the same seed which was only planted by God in Adam, which wind, breath, or spirit, when he had received, he was living and moving on earth, for it was ordained of God for his habitation, but the heavens are the habitation of the Lord: and like as I shewed before of the bubble or confused Chaos made of water and soap, through the wind and breath of man is turned round, and carried with every wind; even so the firmament wherein the Sun and the rest of the Planets are fixed, moved, turned, and carried with the wind, breath, or Spirit of God, for the heavens and firmament are movable as the Chaos, but the Sun is fixed in the firmament. And farther my good schoolfellow, I was thus nigh the heavens, where methought every Planet was but as half the earth, and under the firmament ruled the Spirits in the air, and as I came down I looked upon the world and the heavens, and methought that the earth was enclosed in comparison within the firmament, as the yolk of an egg within the white, and methought that the whole length of the earth was not a span long, and the water was as if it had been twice as broad and long as the earth, even thus at the eight days end came I home again, and fell asleep, and so I continued sleeping three days and three nights together: and the first hour that I waked, I fell fresh again to my Calendar, and have made them in right ample manner as you know, and to satisfy your request, for that you writ unto me, I have in consideration of our old friendship had at the University of Wittenberg, declared unto you my heavenly voyage, wishing no worse unto you, than unto myself, that is, that your mind were as mine in all respects. Dixi.

Doctor Faustus the Astrologian.

Chapter XXII

How Doctor Faustus made his journey through the principal and most famous lands in the world

DOCTOR FAUSTUS having overrun fifteen years of his appointed time, he took upon him a journey, with full pretence to see the whole world: and calling his spirit Mephostophiles unto him, he said: thou knowest that thou art bound unto me upon conditions, to perform and fulfil my desire in all things, wherefore my pretence is to visit the whole face of the earth visible and invisible when it pleaseth me: wherefore, I enjoin and command thee to the same. Whereupon Mephostophiles answered, I am ready my Lord at thy command and forthwith the Spirit changed himself unto the likeness of a flying horse, saying, Faustus sit up, I am ready. Doctor Faustus loftily sat upon him, and forward they went: Faustus came through many a land and Province; as Pannonia, Austria, Germania, Bohemia, Slesia, Saxony, Missene, During, Francklandt, Shawblandt, Beyerlandt, Stiria, Carinthia, Poland, Litaw, Liefland, Prussia, Denmarke, Muscovia, Tartaria, Turkie, Persia, Cathai, Alexandria, Barbaria, Ginnie, Peru, the straits of Magelanes, India, all about the frozen Zone, and Terra Incognita, Nova Hispaniola, the Isles of Terzera, Mederi, S. Michael's, the Canaries, and the Tenorrifocie, into Spaine, the Mayne Land, Portugall, Italie, Campania, the Kingdom of Naples, the Isles of Sicilia, Malta, Majoria, Minoria, to the Knights of the Rhodes, Candie, or Creete, Ciprus, Corinth, Switzerland, France, Freesland, Westphalia, Zeland, Holland, Brabant, and all the seventeen Provinces in Netherland, England, Scotland, Ireland, all America, and Island, the out Isles of Scotland, the Orchades, Norway, the Bishopric of Breame, and so home again: all these Kingdoms, Provinces, and Countries he passed in twenty-five days, in which time he saw very little that delighted his mind: wherefore he took a little rest at home, and burning in desire to see more at large, and to behold the secrets of each Kingdom, he set forward again on his journey upon his swift horse Mephostophiles, and came to Treir, for that he chiefly desired to see this town, and the monuments thereof; but there he saw not many wonders, except one fair Palace that belonged unto the Bishop, and also a mighty large Castle that was built of brick, with three walls and three great trenches, so strong, that it was impossible for any prince's power to win it; then he saw a Church, wherein was buried Simeon, and the Bishop Popo: their Tombs are of most sumptuous large Marble stone, closed and joined together with great bars of iron: from whence he departed to Paris, where he liked well the Academy; and what place or Kingdom soever fell in his mind, the same he visited. He came

The ride past the gallows
After P. Cornelius

from Paris to Mentz, where the river of Mayne falls into the Rhine; notwithstanding he tarried not long there, but went to Campania in the Kingdom of Neapolis, in which he saw an innumerable sort of Cloisters, Nunneries, and Churches, great and high houses of stone, the streets fair and large, and straight forth from one end of the town to the other as a line, and all the pavement of the City was of brick, and the more it rained in the town, the fairer the streets were; there saw he the Tomb of Virgil; and the highway that he cut through that mighty hill of stone in one night, the whole length of an English mile: then he saw the number of Galleys, and Argosies that lay there at the City head, the Windmill that stood in the water, the Castle in the water, and the houses above the water where under the Galleys might ride most safely from rain or wind; then he saw the Castle on the hill over the town, and many monuments within: also the hill called Vesuvius, whereon groweth all the Greekish wine, and most pleasant sweet Olives. From thence he came to Venice, whereat he wondered not a little to see a City so famously built standing in the Sea: where, through every street the water ran in such largeness, that great Ships and Barks might pass from one street to another, having yet a way on both sides the water, whereon men and horse might pass; he marvelled also how it was possible for so much victual to be found in the town and so good cheap, considering that for a whole league off nothing grew near the same. He wondered not a little at the fairness of Saint Mark's place, and the sumptuous Church standing therein called Saint Mark's; how all the pavement was set with coloured stones, and all the rood or loft of the Church double gilded over. Leaving this, he came to Padoa, beholding the manner of their Academy, which is called the mother or nurse of Christendom, there he heard the Doctors, and saw the most monuments in the town, entered his name into the University of the German nation, and wrote himself Doctor Faustus the insatiable Speculator: then saw he the worthiest monument in the world for a Church, named S. Anthony's Cloister, which for the pinnacles thereof and the contriving of the Church, hath not the like in Christendom. This town is fenced about with three mighty walls of stone and earth, betwixt the which runneth goodly ditches of water: twice every twenty-four hours passeth boats betwixt Padoa and Venice with passengers, as they do here betwixt London and Gravesend, and even so far they differ in distance: Faustus beheld likewise the Council house and the Castle with no small wonder. Well, forward he went to Rome, which lay, and doth yet lie, on the river Tybris, the which divideth the City in two parts: over the river are four great stone bridges, and upon the one bridge called Ponte S. Angelo is the Castle of S. Angelo, wherein are so many great cast pieces as there are days in a year, and such Pieces that will shoot seven bullets off with one fire, to this Castle cometh a privy vault from the Church and Palace of Saint Peter, through the which the Pope (if any danger be) passeth from his Palace to the Castle for safeguard; the City hath eleven gates, and a hill called Vaticinium,[13] whereon S. Peter's Church is built: in that Church the holy Fathers will hear no confession, without the penitent bring money in his hand. Adjoining to this Church, is the Campo Santo, the which Carolus Magnus built, where every day thirteen Pilgrims have their dinners served of the best: that is to say, Christ and his Twelve Apostles. Hard by this he visited the Church yard of S. Peter's, where he saw the Pyramid that Julius Cæsar brought out of Africa: it stood in Faustus his time leaning against the Church wall of Saint Peter's, but now Papa Sixtus hath erected it in the middle of S. Peter's Church yard; it is twenty-four fathoms long and at the lower end six fathoms four square, and so forth smaller upwards, on the top is a Crucifix of beaten gold, the stone standeth on four Lions of brass. Then he visited the seven Churches of Rome, that were S. Peter's, S. Paul's,

---

[13] A mistake for *Vaticanum.*

S. Sebastian's, S. John Lateran, S. Laurence, S. Mary Magdalen, and
S. Marie Majora: then went he without the town, where he saw the con-
duits of water that run level through hill and dale, bringing water into the
town fifteen Italian miles off: other monuments he saw, too many to re-
cite, but amongst the rest he was desirous to see the Pope's Palace, and his
manner of service at his table, wherefore he and his Spirit made themselves invisible, and came into the Pope's Court, and privy chamber where
he was, there saw he many servants attendant on his holiness, with many a
flattering Sycophant carrying of his meat, and there he marked the Pope
and the manner of his service, which he seeing to be so unmeasurable
and sumptuous; fie (quoth Faustus), why had not the Devil made a Pope
of me? Faustus saw notwithstanding in that place those that were like to
himself, proud, stout, wilful, gluttons, drunkards, whoremongers, break-
ers of wedlock, and followers of all manner of ungodly exercises: wherefore he said to his Spirit, I thought that I had been alone a hog, or pork of
the devil's, but he must bear with me yet a little longer, for these hogs of
Rome are already fattened, and fitted to make his roast-meat, the Devil
might do well now to spit them all and have them to the fire, and let him
summon the Nuns to turn the spits: for as none must confess the Nun
but the Friar, so none should turn the roasting Friar but the Nun. Thus
continued Faustus three days in the Pope's Palace, and yet had no lust to
his meat, but stood still in the Pope's chamber, and saw everything whatsoever it was: on a time the Pope would have a feast prepared for the Cardinal of Pavia, and for his first welcome the Cardinal was bidden to
dinner : and as he sat at meat, the Pope would ever be blessing and crossing over his mouth; Faustus could suffer it no longer, but up with his fist
and smote the Pope on the face, and withal he laughed that the whole
house might hear him, yet none of them saw him nor knew where he was:
the Pope persuaded his company that it was a damned soul, commanding
a Mass presently to be said for his delivery out of Purgatory, which was
done: the Pope sat still at meat, but when the latter mess came in to the
Pope's board, Doctor Faustus laid hands thereon saying; this is mine: and
so he took both dish and meat and fled unto the Capitol or Campadolia,
calling his Spirit unto him and said: come let us be merry, for thou must
fetch me some wine, and the cup that the Pope drinks of, and hereupon
Monte Caval will we make good cheer in spite of the Pope and all his fat
abbey lubbers. His Spirit hearing this, departed towards the Pope's
chamber, were he found them yet sitting and quaffing: wherefore he took
from before the Pope the fairest piece of plate or drinking goblet, and a
flagon of wine, and brought it to Faustus; but when the Pope and the rest
of his crew perceived they were robbed, and knew not after what sort,

The seven chief churches of Rome
Second Half of the 16th Century

they persuaded themselves that it was the damned soul that before had vexed the Pope so, and that smote him on the face, wherefore he sent commandment through all the whole City of Rome, that they should say Mass in every Church, and ring all the bells for to lay the walking Spirit, and to curse him with Bell, Book, and Candle, that so invisibly had misused the Pope's holiness, with the Cardinal of Pavia, and the rest of their company: but Faustus notwithstanding made good cheer with that which he had beguiled the Pope of, and in the midst of the order of Saint Barnard's bare-footed Friars, as they were going on Procession through the market place, called Campa de fiore, he let fall his plate dishes and cup, and withal for a farewell he made such a thunder-clap and a storm of rain, as though Heaven and earth should have met together, and so he left Rome, and came to Millain in Italie, near the Alps or borders of Switzerland, where he praised much to his Spirit the pleasantness of the place, the City being founded in so brave a plain, by the which ran most pleasant rivers on every side of the same, having besides within the compass or circuit of seven miles, seven small Seas: he saw also therein many fair Palaces and goodly buildings, the Duke's Palace, and the mighty strong Castle, which is in manner half the bigness of the town. Moreover, it liked him well to see the Hospital of Saint Mary's, with divers other things. He did nothing there worthy of memory, but he departed back again towards Bolognia, and from thence to Florence, where he was well pleased to see the pleasant walk of Merchants, the goodly vaults of the City, for that almost the whole City is vaulted, and the houses themselves are built outwardly, in such sort that the people may go under them as under a vault: then he perused the sumptuous Church in the Duke's Castle called Nostra Donna, our Lady's Church, in which he saw many monuments, as a Marble door most huge to look upon: the gate of the castle was Bell metal, wherein are graven the holy Patriarchs, with Christ and his twelve Apostles, and divers other histories out of the old and new Testament. Then went he to Sena, where he highly praised the church and Hospital of Santa Maria Formosa, with the goodly buildings, and especially the fairness and greatness of the City, and beautiful women. Then came he to Lyons in France, where he marked the situation of the City, which lay between two hills, environed with two waters: one worthy monument in the City pleased him well, that was the great Church with the Image therein; he commended the City highly for the great resort that it had unto it of strangers. From thence he went to Cullin, which lieth upon the River of Rhine, wherein he saw one of the ancientest monuments of the world, the which was the Tomb of the three Kings that came by the Angel of God, and their knowledge they had in the star, to worship Christ: which when

Faustus saw, he spake in this manner. Ah, alas good men how have you erred and lost your way, you should have gone to Palestina and Bethelem in Judea, how came you hither? or belike after your death you were thrown into Mare Mediterraneum about Tripolis in Syria; and so you fleeted out of the Straits of Giblaterra into the Ocean Sea, and so into the bay of Portugal; and not finding any rest you were driven along the coast of Galicia, Biskay, and France, and into the narrow Seas, then from thence into Mare Germanicum, and so I think taken up about the town of Dort in Holland, you were brought to Cullin to be buried: or else I think you came more easily with a whirlwind over the Alps, and being thrown into the River of Rhine, it conveyed you to this place, where you are kept as a monument? There saw he the Church of S. Ursula, where remains a monument of the thousand Virgins: it pleased him also to see the beauty of the women. Not far from Cullin lieth the town of Ach, where he saw the gorgeous Temple that the Emperor Carolus Quartus[14] built of Marble stone for a remembrance of him, to the end that all his successors should there be crowned. From Cullin and Ach, he went to Geuf, a City in Savoy, lying near Switzerland: it is a town of great traffic, the Lord thereof is a Bishop, whose Wine-cellar Faustus, and his Spirit visited for the love of his good wine. From thence he went to Strasburg, where he beheld the fairest steeple that ever he had seen in his life before, for on each side thereof he might see through it, even from the covering of the Minster to the top of the Pinnacle, and it is named one of the wonders of the world: wherefore he demanded why it was called Strasburg: his Spirit answered, because it hath so many high ways coming to it on every side, for Stras in Dutch is a high way, and hereof came the name, yea (said Mephostophiles) the Church which thou so wonderest at, hath more revenues belonging to it, then the twelve Dukes of Slesia are worth, for there pertain unto this Church fifty-five Towns, and four hundred and sixty-three Villages besides many houses in the Town. From hence went Faustus to Basile in Switzerland, whereat the River of Rhine runneth through the town, parting the same as the River of Thames doth London: in this town of Basile he saw many rich Monuments, the town walled with brick, and round about without it goeth a great trench: no Church pleased him but the Jesuits' Church, which was so sumptuously builded, and beset full of Alabaster pillars. Faustus demanded of his Spirit, how it took the name of Basyl: his Spirit made answer and said, that before this City was founded, there used a Basiliscus, a kind of Serpent, this Serpent killed as

---

[14] This should be Carolus Magnus.

many men, women, and children, as it took a sight of: but there was a
Knight that made himself a cover of Crystal to come over his head, and so
down to the ground, and being first covered with a black cloth, over that
he put the Crystal, and so boldly went to see the Basiliscus, and finding
the place where he haunted, he expected his coming, even before the
mouth of her cave: where standing a while, the Basylike came forth, who,
when she saw her own venomous shadow in the Crystal, she split in a
thousand pieces; wherefore the Knight was richly rewarded of the Emperor: after the which the Knight founded this Town upon the place
where he had slain the Serpent, and gave it the name of Basyl, in remembrance of his deed.

From Basyl Faustus went to Costuitz[15] in Sweitz, at the head of the
Rhine, where is a most sumptuous Bridge, that goeth over the Rhine,
even from the gates of the Town unto the other side of the stream: at the
head of the River of Rhine, is a small Sea, called of the Switzers the black[16]
Sea, twenty thousand paces long, and fifty hundred paces broad. The
town Costuitz took the name of this; the Emperor gave it to a Clown
for expounding of his riddle, wherefore the Clowne named the Town
Costuitz, that is in English, cost nothing. From Costuitz he came to Ulme,
where he saw the sumptuous town-house built by two and fifty of the
ancient Senators of the City, it took the name of Ulma, for that the whole
lands thereabout are full of Elms: but Faustus minding to depart from
thence, his Spirit said unto him: Faustus think on the town as thou wilt, it
hath three Dukedoms belonging to it, the which they have bought with
ready money. From Ulme, he came to Wartzburg the chiefest town in
Frankelandt, wherein the Bishop all together keepeth his Court, through
the which Town passeth the River of Mayne that runs into the Rhine:
thereabout groweth strong and pleasant wine, the which Faustus well
proved. The Castle standeth on a hill on the North side of the Town, at
the foot whereof runneth the River: this Town is full of beggarly Friars,
Nuns, Priests, and Jesuits: for there are five sorts of Begging Friars, besides three Cloisters of Nuns. At the foot of the Castle stands a Church, in
the which there is an Altar, where are engraven all the four Elements, and
all the orders and degrees in Heaven, that any man of understanding whosoever that hath a sight thereof, will say that it is the artificiallest thing that
ever he beheld. From thence he went to Norenberg, whither as he went
by the way, his Spirit informed him that the Town was named of Claudius

---

[15] i.e. Constance, which, however, is not in Switzerland.
[16] A mistranslation of the German *Bodensee.*

Tiberius the Son of Nero the Tyrant. In the Town are two famous Cathedral Churches, the one called Saint Sabolt, the other Saint Laurence; in which Church hangeth all the reliques of Carolus Magnus, that is his cloak, his hose and doublet, his sword and Crown, his Sceptre, and his Apple. It hath a very gorgeous gilden Conduit in the market of Saint Laurence, in which Conduit, is the spear that thrust our Saviour into the side, and a piece of the holy Cross; the wall is called the fair wall of Norenberg, and hath five hundred and twenty-eight streets, one hundred and sixty wells, four great, and two small clocks, six great gates, and two small doors, eleven stone bridges, twelve small hills, ten appointed market places, thirteen common hothouses,[17] ten Churches, within the Town are thirty wheels of watermills; it hath one hundred and thirty-two tall ships,[18] two mighty Town walls of hewn stone and earth, with very deep trenches. The walls have one hundred and eighty Towers about them, and four fair platforms, ten Apothecaries, ten Doctors of the common law, fourteen Doctors of Physic. From Norenberg, he went to Auspurg, where at the break of the day, he demanded of his Spirit whereupon the Town took his name: this Town (saith he) hath had many names, when it was first built, it was called Vindelica: secondly, it was called Zizaria, the iron bridge: lastly by the Emperor Octavius Augustus, it was called Augusta, and by corruption of language the Germans have named it Auspurg. Now for because that Faustus had been there before, he departed without visiting their monuments to Ravenspurg, where his Spirit certified him that the City had had seven names, the first Tyberia, the second Quadratis, the third Hyaspalis, the fourth Reginopolis, the fifth Imbripolis, the sixth Ratisbona, lastly Ravenspurg. The situation of the City pleased Faustus well, also the strong and sumptuous buildings: by the wall thereof runneth the River of Danubia, in Dutch called Donow, into the which not far from the compass of the City, falleth nearhand threescore other small Rivers and fresh waters. Faustus also liked the sumptuous stone bridge over the same water, with the Church standing thereon, the which was founded 1115, the name whereof is called S. Remedian: in this town Faustus went into the cellar of an Innholder, and let out all the Wine and Beer that was in his cellar. After the which feat he returned unto Mentz[19] in Bavaria, a right princely Town, the town appeared as if it were new, with great streets therein, both of breadth and length: from Mentz to Saltzburg, where the

---

[17] i.e. hot baths.

[18] Probably a mistranslation of a German word ending in -*schaft*.

[19] A mistake for Menchen (Munich).

Bishop is always resident: here saw he all the commodities that were possible to be seen, for at the hill he saw the form of Abel[20] made in Crystal, an
huge thing to look upon, that every year groweth bigger and bigger, by
reason of the freezing cold. From hence, he went to Vienna, in Austria:
this Town is of so great antiquity, that it is not possible to find the like: in
this Town (said the Spirit) is more Wine than water, for all under the
Town are wells, the which are filled every year with Wine, and all the water
that they have, runneth by the Town, that is the River Danubia. From
hence, he went unto Prage, the chief City in Bohemia, this is divided into
three parts, that is, old Prage, new Prage, and little Prage. Little Prage is
the place where the Emperor's Court is placed upon an exceeding high
mountain: there is a Castle, wherein are two fair Churches, in the one he
found a monument, which might well have been a mirror to himself, and
that was the Sepulchre of a notable Conjurer, which by his Magic had so
enchanted his Sepulchre, that whosoever set foot thereon, should be sure
never to die in their beds. From the Castle he came down, and went over
the Bridge. This Bridge hath twenty and four Arches. In the middle of this
Bridge stands a very fair monument, being a Cross builded of stone, and
most artificially carved. From thence, he came into the old Prage, the
which is separated from the new Prage, with an exceeding deep ditch, and
round about enclosed with a wall of Brick. Unto this is adjoining the Jews'
Town, wherein are thirteen thousand men, women, and children, all Jews.
There he viewed the College and the Garden, where all manner of savage
Beasts are kept; and from thence, he fetched a compass round about the
three Towns, whereat he wondered greatly, to see so mighty a City to
stand all within the walls. From Prage, he flew into the air and bethought
himself what he might do, or which way to take, so he looked round
about, and behold, he had espied a passing fair City which lay not far from
Prage, about some four and twenty miles, and that was Breslaw in Sclesia;
into which when he was entered, it seemed to him that he had been in
Paradise, so neat and clean was the streets, and so sumptuous was their
buildings. In this City he saw not many wonders, except the Brazen Virgin
that standeth on a Bridge over the water, and under the which standeth a
mill like a powder mill, which Virgin is made to do execution upon those
disobedient town-born children that be so wild, that their parents cannot
bridle them; which when any such are found with some heinous offence,
turning to the shame of their parents and kindred, they are brought to kiss
this Virgin, which openeth her arms, the person then to be executed, kis-

20 Perhaps "a bell."

seth her, then doth she close her arms together with such violence, that she crusheth out the breath of the person, breaketh his bulk, and so dieth: but being dead, she openeth her arms again, and letteth the party fall into the Mill, where he is stamped in small morsels, which the water carrieth away, so that not any part of him is found again. From Breslaw he went toward Cracovia, in the Kingdom of Polonia, where he beheld the Academy, the which pleased him wonderful well. In this City the King most commonly holdeth his Court at a Castle, in which Castle are many famous monuments. There is a most sumptuous Church in the same, in which standeth a silver altar gilded, and set with rich stones, and over it is a conveyance full of all manner silver ornaments belonging to the Mass. In the Church hangeth the jaw bones of an huge Dragon that kept the rock before the Castle was edified thereon. It is full of all manner munition, and hath always victual for three years to serve two thousand men. Through the Town runneth a river called the Vistula or Wissel, where over is a fair wooden bridge. This water divideth the Town and Casmere, in this Casmere dwelleth the Jews being a small walled Town by themselves, to the number of twenty-five thousand men, women, and children. Within one mile of the Town there is a salt mine, where they find stones of pure salt of a thousand pound, or nine hundred pound, or more in weight, and that in great quantity. This salt is as black as the Newcastle coals when it comes out of the mines, but being beaten to powder, it is as white as snow. The like they have four mile from thence, at a Town called Buchnia. From thence, Faustus went to Sandetz, the Captain thereof was called Don Spiket Iordan, in this Town are many monuments, as the tomb or sepulchre of Christ, in as ample manner as that is at Jerusalem, at the proper costs of a Gentleman that went thrice to Jerusalem from that place, and returned again. Not far from that Town is a new Town, wherein is a Nunnery of the order of Saint Dioclesian, into which order may none come, except they be Gentlewomen, and well formed and fair to look upon, the which pleased Faustus well: but having a desire to travel farther, and to see more wonders, mounting up towards the East over many lands and Provinces, as into Hungaria, Transilvania, Shede, Ingratz, Sardinia, and so into Constantinople, where the Turkish Emperor kept his Court. This City was surnamed by Constantine the founder thereof, being builded of very fair stone. In the same the great Turk hath three fair Palaces, the walls are strong, the pinnacles are very huge, and the streets large: but this liked not Faustus, that one man might have so many wives as he would. The Sea runneth hard by the City, the wall hath eleven Gates: Faustus abode there a certain time to see the manner of the Turkish Emperor's service at his table, where he saw his royal service to be such, that he thought if all the

Christian Princes should banquet together, and everyone adorn the feast
to the uttermost, they were not able to compare with the Turk for his
table, and the rest of his Country service, wherefore it so spited Faustus,
that he vowed to be revenged of him, for his pomp he thought was more
fit for himself: wherefore as the Turk sat and ate, Faustus shewed him a
little apish play: for round about the privy Chamber, he sent forth flashing
flames of fire, in so much, that the whole company forsook their meat
and fled, except only the great Turk himself, him Faustus had charmed in
such sort, that he could neither rise nor fall, neither could any man pull
him up. With this was the Hall so light, as if the Sun had shined in the
house, then came Faustus in form of a Pope to the great Turk, saying, all
hail, Emperor, now art thou honoured that I so worthily appear unto thee
as thy Mahumet was wont to do, hereupon he vanished, and forthwith it
so thundered, that the whole Palace shook: the Turk greatly marvelled
what this should be that so vexed him, and was persuaded by his chiefest
counsellors, that it was Mahumet his Prophet, the which had so appeared
unto them, whereupon the Turk commanded them to fall down on their
knees, and to give him thanks for doing them so great honour, as to shew
himself unto them; but the next day Faustus went into the Castle where
he kept his Wives and Concubines, in the which Castle might no man
upon pain of death come, except those that were appointed by the great
Turk to do them service, and they were all gelded. Which when Faustus
perceived, he said to his Spirit Mephostophiles, how likest thou this sport,
are not these fair Ladies greatly to be pitied, that thus consume their
youth at the pleasure of one only man? Why (quoth the Spirit) mayest not
thou instead of the Emperor, embrace his fairest Ladies, do what thy
heart desireth herein, and I will aid thee, and what thou wishest, thou
shalt have it performed: wherefore Faustus (being before this counsel apt
enough to put such matters in practice) caused a great fog to be round
about the Castle, both within and without, and he himself appeared
amongst the Ladies in all things as they use to paint their Mahumet, at
which sight, the Ladies fell on their knees, and worshipped him, then
Faustus took the fairest by the hand, and led her into a chamber, where
after his manner he fell to dalliance, and thus he continued a whole day
and night: and when he had delighted himself sufficiently with her, he put
her away, and made his Spirit bring him another, so likewise he kept with
her twenty-four hours' play, causing his Spirit to fetch him most dainty
fare, and so he passed away six days, having each day his pleasure of a sundry Lady, and that of the fairest, all which time, the fog was so thick, and
so stinking, that they within the house thought they had been in hell, for
the time, and they without wondered thereat, in such sort, that they went

to their prayers calling on their God Mahumet, and worshipping of his Image. Wherefore the sixth day Faustus exalted himself in the air, like to a Pope, in the sight of the great Turk and his people, and he had no sooner departed the Castle, but the fog vanished away, whence presently the Turk sent for his Wives and Concubines, demanding of them if they knew the cause why the Castle was beset with a mist so long? they said, that it was the God Mahumet himself that caused it, and how he was in the Castle personally full six days, and for more certainty, he hath lain with six of us these six nights one after another. Wherefore the Turk hearing this fell on his knees, and gave Mahumet thanks, desiring him to forgive him for being offended with his visiting his Castle and wives those six days: but the Turk commanded that those whom Mahumet had lain by, should be most carefully looked unto, persuading himself (and so did the whole people that knew of it) that out of their Mahumet should be raised a mighty generation, but first he demanded of the six Ladies of Mahumet had had actual copulation with them, according as earthly men have, yea my Lord, quoth one, as if you had been there yourself, you could not have mended it, for he lay with us stark naked, kissed and colled[21] us, and so delighted me, that for my part, I would he came two or three times a week to serve me in such sort again. From hence, Faustus went to Alkar, the which before time was called Chairam, or Memphis, in this City the Egyptian Soldan holdeth his Court. From hence the river Nilus hath his first head and spring, it is the greatest fresh-water river that is in the whole world, and always when the Sun is in Cancer, it overfloweth the whole land of Egypt: then he returned again towards the North-east, and to the Town of Ofen and Sabatz in Hungaria. This Ofen is the chiefest City in Hungaria, and standeth in a fertile soil, wherein groweth most excellent wine, and not far from the Town there is a well, called Zipzar, the water whereof changeth iron into Copper: here are mines of gold and silver, and all manner of metal, we Germans call this town Ofen[22], but in the Hungarian speech it is Start. In the town standeth a very fair Castle, and very well fortified. From hence he went to Austria, and through Slesia into Saxony, unto the Towns of Magdeburg and Liptzig, and Lubeck. Magdeburg is a Bishopric: in this City is one of the pitchers wherein Christ changed the water into wine at Cana in Galile. At Liptzig nothing pleased Faustus so well as the great vessel in the Castle made of wood, the which is bound

---

[21] Embraced.

[22] This is Buda. The statement that the Hungarians call the town "Start" springs from a misunderstanding of his source by the author of the *German Faust Book*.

about with twenty-four iron hoops, and every hoop weigheth two hundred pound weight, they must go upon a ladder of thirty steps high before they can look into it: he saw also the new church-yard, where it is walled, and standeth upon a fair plain, the yard is two hundred paces long, and round about in the inside of the wall, are goodly places separated one from each other to see sepulchres in, which in the middle of the yard standeth very sumptuous: therein standeth a pulpit of white work and gold. From hence he came to Lubeck and Hamburg, where he made no abode, but away again to Erfort in Duringen, where he visited the Freskold, and from Erfort he went home to Wittenberg, when he had seen and visited many a strange place, being from home one year and a half, in which time he wrought more wonders than are here declared.

Chapter XXIII

How Faustus had a sight of Paradise

AFTER this, Doctor Faustus set forth again, visited these countries of Spain, Portugal, France, England, Scotland, Denmark, Sweden, Poland, Muscovy, India, Cataia, Africa, Persia, and lastly into Barbaria amongst the Blackamoors, and in all his wandering he was desirous to visit the ancient monuments and mighty hills, amongst the rest beholding the high hill called the Treno Riefe, was desirous to rest upon it: from thence he went into the Isle of Brittany, wherein he was greatly delighted to see the fair water and warm Baths, the divers sorts of metal, with many precious stones, and divers other commodities the which Faustus brought thence with him, he was also at the Orchades behind Scotland, where he saw the tree that bringeth forth fruit, that when it is ripe, openeth and falleth into the water, whereof engendereth a certain kind of Fowl or Bird: these Islands are in number twenty-three but ten of them are not habitable, the other thirteen are inhabited: from hence, he went to the hill of Caucasus, which is the highest in all that Topic, it lieth near the borders of Scythia, hereon Faustus stood and beheld many lands and Kingdoms. Faustus being on such a high hill, thought to look over all the world and beyond, for he meant to see Paradise, but he durst not commune with his Spirit thereof: and being on the hill of Caucasus, he saw the whole land of India and Scythia, and towards the East as he looked he saw a mighty clear strike of fire coming from heaven upon the earth, even as it had been one of the beams of the Sun, he saw in the valley four mighty waters springing, one had his course towards India, the second towards Egypt, the third and fourth towards Armenia. When he saw these, he would need know of his Spirit what waters they were, and from whence they came. His Spirit gave him gently an answer, saying; it is Paradise that lieth so far in the East, the garden that God himself hath planted with all manner of pleasure, and the fiery stream that thou seest, is the walls or defence of the garden, but that clear light that thou seest so far off, is the Angel that hath the custody thereof, with a fiery sword: and although that thou thinkest thyself to be hard by, thou hast yet farther thither from hence, than thou hast ever been: the water that thou seest divided in four parts, is the water that issueth out of the Well in the middle of Paradise. The first is called Ganges or Phison, the second, Gihon or Nilus, the third Tigris, and the fourth Euphrates, also thou seest that he standeth under Libra and Aries right up towards the Zenith, and upon this fiery wall standeth the Angel Michael with his flaming sword to keep the tree of life the which he hath in charge; but the Spirit said unto Faustus, neither thou, nor I, nor any after us, yea all men whosoever are denied to visit it, or to come any nearer than we be.

Chapter XXIV

Of a certain Comet that appeared in Germanie, and how Doctor Faustus was desired by certain friends of his to know the meaning thereof

In Germanie over the Town of S. Eizleben was seen a mighty great Comet, whereat the people wondered; but Doctor Faustus being there, was asked of certain of his friends his judgment or opinion in the matter. Whereupon he answered, it falleth out often by the course and change of the Sun and Moon, that the Sun is under the earth, and the Moon above; but when the Moon draweth near the change, then is the Sun so strong that he taketh away all the light of the Moon, in such sort that he is as red as blood: and to the contrary, after they have been together, the Moon taketh her light again from him, and so increasing in light to the full, she will be as red as the Sun was before, and changeth herself into divers and sundry colours, of the which springeth a prodigious monster, or as you call it, a Comet, which is a figure or token appointed of God as a forewarning of his displeasure: as at one time he sendeth hunger, plague, sword, or such-like: being all tokens of his judgment: the which Comet cometh through the conjunction of the Sun and Moon begetting a monster, whose father is the Sun, and whose mother is the Moon, ☉ and ☽.

Chapter XXV

A question put forth to Doctor Faustus, concerning the Stars

THERE was a learned man of the Town of Halberstat, named N. V. W. invited Doctor Faustus to his table, but falling into communication before supper was ready, they looked out of the window, and seeing many stars in the firmament, this man being a Doctor of Physic and a good Astrologian, said: Doctor Faustus, I have invited you as my guest, hoping that you will take it in good part with me, and withal I request you to impart unto me some of your experience in the Stars and Planets. And seeing a Star fall, he said: I pray you, Faustus, what is the condition, quality, or greatness of the Stars in the firmament? Faustus answered him: My friend and Brother, you see that the Stars that fall from heaven when they come on the earth they be very small to our thinking as candles, but being fixed in the firmament there are many as great as this City, some as great as a Province or Dukedom, other as great as the whole earth, other some far greater than the earth: for the length and breadth of the heavens is greater than the earth twelve times, and from the height of the heavens there is scarce any earth to be seen, yea the Planets in the heavens are some so great as this land, some so great as the whole Empire of Rome, some as Turkie, yea one so great as the whole world.

Chapter XXVI

How Faust was asked a question concerning the Spirits that vex men

THAT is most true (saith he to Faustus) concerning the Stars and Planets: but I pray you in what kind or manner do the spirits use or vex men so little by day, and so greatly by night? Doctor Faustus answered: because the spirits are by God forbidden the light, their dwelling is in darkness, and the clearer the Sun shineth, the further the Spirits have their abiding from it, but in the night when it is dark, they have their familiarity and abiding near unto us men. For although in the night we see not the Sun, yet the brightness thereof so lighteneth the first moving of the firmament as it doth that on earth in the day, by which reason we are able to see the Stars and Planets in the night, even so the rays of the Sun piercing upwards into the firmament, the Spirits abandon the place, and so come near us on earth in the darkness, filling our heads with heavy dreams and fond fantasies, with screeching and crying in many deformed shapes: as sometimes when men go forth without light, there falleth to them a fear, that their hair standeth on end, so many start in their sleep thinking there is a Spirit by him, gropeth or feeleth for him, going round about the house in his sleep, and many such-like fantasies: and all this is for because that in the night the Spirits are more familiarly by us than we are desirous of their company, and so they carry us, blinding us and plaguing us more than we are able to perceive.

Chapter XXVII

How Doctor Faustus was asked a question concerning the Stars that fall from Heaven

DOCTOR FAUSTUS being demanded the cause why the Stars fell from heaven, he answered: that is but our opinion; for if one star fall, it is the great judgment of God upon us, as aforewarning of some great thing to come: for when we think that a Star falleth, it is but as a spark that issueth from a candle or a flame of fire, for if it were a substantial thing, we should not so soon lose the sight of them as we do. And likewise, if so be that we see as it were a stream of fire fall from the firmament, as oft it happeneth, yet are they no Stars, but as it were a flame of fire vanishing, but the Stars are substantial, therefore are they firm and not falling: if there fall any, it is a sign of some great matter to come, as a scourge to a people or country, and then such Star falling, the gates of heaven are opened, and the clouds send forth floods, or other plagues, to the damage of the whole land and people.

Chapter XXVIII

How Faustus was asked a question as concerning thunder

IN the month of August, there was over Wittenberg a mighty great lightning and thunder, and as Doctor Faustus was jesting merrily in the market place with certain of his friends and companions being Physicians, they desired him to tell them the cause of that weather. Faustus answered: it hath been commonly seen heretofore, that before a thunder-clap fell a shower of rain or a gale of wind, for commonly after a wind followeth a rain, and after a rain a thunder-clap: such things come to pass when the four winds meet together in the heavens, the airy clouds are by force beaten against the fixed crystalline firmament, but when the airy clouds meet with the firmament, they are congealed, and so strike and rush against the firmament, as great pieces of ice when they meet on the water, the echo thereof soundeth in our ears, and that we call thunder, which indeed is none other than you have heard.

The third and last part of Doctor Faustus his merry conceits, shewing after what sort he practised Necromancy in the Courts of great Princes, and lastly of his fearful and pitiful end

Chapter XXIX

How the Emperor Carolus Quintus requested of Faustus to see some of his cunning, whereunto he agreed.

THE Emperor Carolus the fifth of that name was personally with the rest of his Nobles and gentlemen at the Town of Innsbruck where he kept his Court, unto the which also Doctor Faustus resorted, and being there well known of divers Nobles and gentlemen, he was invited into the Court to meat, even in the presence of the Emperor: whom when the Emperor saw, he looked earnestly on him, thinking him by his looks to be some wonderful fellow, wherefore he asked one of his Nobles whom he should be: who answered that he was called Doctor Faustus. Whereupon the Emperor held his peace until he had taken his repast, after which he called unto him Faustus, into the privy chamber, whither being come, he said unto him: Faustus, I have heard much of thee, that thou art excellent in the black Art, and none like thee in mine Empire, for men say that thou hast a familiar Spirit with thee and that thou canst do what thou list: it is therefore (saith the Emperor) my request of thee that thou let me see a proof of thine experience, and I vow unto thee by the honour of mine Imperial Crown, none evil shall happen unto thee for so doing. Hereupon Doctor Faustus answered his Majesty, that upon those conditions he was ready in anything that he could, to do his Highness' commandment in what service he would appoint him. Well, then hear what I say (quoth the Emperor). Being once solitary in my house, I called to mind mine elders and ancestors, how it was possible for them to attain unto so great a degree of authority, yea so high, that we the successors of that line are never able to come near. As, for example, the great and mighty monarch of the world, Alexander Magnus, was such a lantern and spectacle to all his successors, as the Chronicles make mention of so great riches, conquering, and subduing so many Kingdoms, the which I and those that follow me (I fear) shall never be able to attain unto: wherefore, Faustus, my hearty desire is that thou wouldst vouchsafe to let me see that Alexander, and his Paramour, the which was praised to be so fair, and I pray thee shew me them in such sort that I may see their personages, shape, gesture, and apparel, as they used in their lifetime, and that here before my face; to the end that I may say I have my long desire fulfilled, and to praise thee to be a famous man in thine art and experience. Doctor Faustus answered: My most excellent Lord, I am ready to accomplish your request in all things, so far forth as I and my Spirit are able to perform: yet your Majesty shall know, that their dead bodies are not able substantially to be brought before you, but such Spirits as have seen Alexander and his Paramour alive, shall appear unto you in manner and form as they both lived in their most flourishing time: and herewith I hope to please your Imperial Majesty. Then Faustus went a little aside to speak to his Spirit, but he returned again presently, saying: now, if it please your Majesty, you shall see them, yet upon this condition that you demand no question of them, nor speak unto them, which the Emperor agreed unto. Wherewith Doctor Faustus opened the privy chamber door, where presently entered the great and mighty Emperor Alexander Magnus, in all things to look upon as if he had been alive, in proportion a strong thick-set man, of a middle stature, black hair, and that both thick and curled head and beard, red cheeks, and a broad face, with eyes like a Basilisk, he had on a complete harness burnished and graven exceeding rich to look upon; and so passing towards the Emperor Carolus, he made low and reverent curtsy: whereat the Emperor Carolus would have stood up to receive and greet him with the like reverence, but Faustus took hold of him and would not permit him to do it. Shortly after Alexander made humble reverence and went out again, and coming to the door his Paramour met him, she coming in, she made the Emperor likewise reverence, she was clothed in blue Velvet, wrought and embroidered with pearl and gold, she was also excellent fair like Milk and blood mixed, tall and slender, with a face round as an Apple, and thus she passed certain times up and down the house, which the Emperor marking, said to himself: now have I seen two persons, which my heart hath long wished for to behold, and sure it cannot otherwise be, said he to himself, but that the Spirits have changed themselves into these forms, and have not deceived me, calling to his mind the woman that raised the Prophet Samuel: and for that the Emperor would be the more satisfied in the matter, he thought, I have heard say, that behind her neck she had a great wart or wen, wherefore he took Faustus by the hand without any words, and went to see if it where also to be seen on her or not, but she perceiving that he came to her, bowed down her neck, where he saw a great wart, and hereupon she vanished, leaving the Emperor and the rest well contented.

Chapter XXX

How Doctor Faustus in the sight of the Emperor conjured a pair of Hart's horns upon a Knight's head that slept out of a casement

WHEN Doctor Faustus had accomplished the Emperor's desire in all things as he was requested, he went forth into a gallery, and leaning over a rail to look into the privy garden, he saw many of the Emperor's Courtiers walking and talking together, and casting his eyes now this way, now that way, he espied a Knight leaning out at a window of the great hall; who was fast asleep (for in those days it was hot) but the person shall be nameless that slept, for that he was a Knight, although it was done to a little disgrace of the Gentleman: it pleased Doctor Faustus, through the help of his Spirit Mephostophiles, to firm upon his head as he slept, a huge pair

of Hart's horns, and as the Knight awaked thinking to pull in his head, he hit his horns against the glass that the panes thereof flew about his ears. Think here how this good Gentleman was vexed, for he could neither get backward nor forward: which when the Emperor heard all the Courtiers laugh, and came forth to see what was happened, the Emperor also when he beheld the Knight with so fair a head, laughed heartily thereat, and was therewithal well pleased: at last Faustus made him quit of his horns again, but the Knight perceived how they came, *etc.*[23]

---

[23] There seems to be no explanation for the *etc.* here and at the end of the following two chapters. Cf. also end of Chapter IV.

Chapter XXXI

How the above-mentioned Knight went about to be revenged of Doctor Faustus

DOCTOR FAUSTUS took his leave of the Emperor and the rest of the Courtiers, at whose departure they were sorry, giving him many rewards and gifts: but being a league and a half from the City he came into a Wood, where he beheld the Knight that he had jested with at the Court with others in harness, mounted on fair palfreys, and running with full charge towards Faustus, but he seeing their intent, ran towards the bushes, and before he came amongst the bushes he returned again, running as it were to meet them that chased him, whereupon suddenly all the bushes were turned into horsemen, which also ran to encounter with the Knights and his company, and coming to them, they closed the Knight and the

rest, and told them that they must pay their ransom before they departed. Whereupon the Knight seeing himself in such distress, besought Faustus to be good to them, which he denied not, but let them loose, yet he so charmed them, that every one, Knight and others for the space of a whole month did wear a pair of Goat's horns on their brows, and every Palfrey a pair of Ox horns on their head: and this was their penance appointed by Faustus, *etc.*

Chapter XXXII

How three young Dukes being together at Wittenberg to behold the University,
requested Faustus to help them at a wish to the town of Menchen in Bavaria, there
to see the Duke of Bavaria his son's wedding

THREE worthy young Dukes, the which are not here to be named, but
being students altogether at the University of Wittenberg, met on a time
altogether, where they fell to reasoning concerning the pomp and
bravery that would be at the City of Menchen in Bavaria, at the wedding
of the Duke's Son, wishing themselves there but one half hour, to see the
manner of their jollity: to whom one replied, saying to the other two
Gentlemen, if it please you to give me the hearing, I will give you good
counsel that we may see the wedding, and be here again to night, and this
is my meaning; let us send to Doctor Faustus, make him a present of
some rare thing and so open our minds unto him, desiring him to assist
us in our enterprise, and assure ye he will not deny to fulfil our request.
Hereupon they all concluded, sent for Faustus, told him their mind, and
gave him a gift, and invited him to a sumptuous banquet, wherewith
Faustus was well contented, and promised to further their journey to the
uttermost. And when the time was come that the Duke his son should be
married, Doctor Faustus called unto him the three young Gentlemen
into his house, commanding them that they should put on their best apparel, and adorn themselves as richly as they could, he took off his own
great large cloak, went into a garden that was adjoining unto his house,
and set the three young Dukes on his cloak, and he himself sat in the
midst, but he gave them in charge that in any wise they should not once
open their mouths to speak, or make answer to any man so soon as they
were out, no not so much as if the Duke of Bavaria or his son should
speak to them, or offer them courtesy, they should give no word or
answer again, to the which they all agreed. These conditions being made,
Doctor Faustus began to conjure, and on a sudden arose a mighty wind,
heaving up the cloak, and so carried them away in the air, and in due time
they came unto Menchen to the Duke's Court, where being entered into
the outmost court, the Marshal had espied them, who presently went
to the Duke shewing his Grace that all the Lords and gentlemen were
already set at the table, notwithstanding, there were newly come three
goodly Gentlemen with one servant, the which stood without in the
court, wherefore the good old Duke came out unto them, welcoming
them, requiring what they were, and whence: but they made no answer
at all, whereat the Duke wondered, thinking they were all four dumb;
notwithstanding for his honour sake he took them into his court, and

feasted them. Faustus notwithstanding spake to them, if any thing happen otherwise then well, when I say, sit up, then fall you all on the cloak, and good enough: well, the water being brought, and that they must wash, one of the three had so much manners as to desire his friend to wash first, which when Faustus heard, he said, sit up, and all at once they got on the cloak, but he that spake fell off again, the other two with Doctor Faustus, were again presently at Wittenberg, but he that remained, was taken and laid in Prison: wherefore the other two Gentlemen were very sorrowful for their friend, but Faustus comforted them, promising that on the morrow he should also be at Wittenberg. Now all this while was this Duke taken in a great fear, and stricken into an exceeding dump, wondering with himself that his hap was so hard to be left behind, and not the rest, and now being locked and watched with so

many keepers, there was also certain of the guests that fell to reasoning with him to know what he was, and also what the others were that were vanished away, but the poor prisoner thought with himself, if I open what they are, then it will be evil also with me: wherefore all this while he gave no man any answer, so that he was there a whole day, and gave no man a word. Wherefore the old Duke gave in charge, that the next morning they should rack him until he had confessed: which when the young Duke heard, he began to sorrow and to say with himself, it may be that to-morrow, if Doctor Faustus come not to aid me, then shall I be racked and grievously tormented, in so much that I shall be constrained by force to tell more than willingly I would do: but he comforted himself with hope that his friends would entreat Doctor Faustus about his deliverance, as also it came to pass, for before it was day, Doctor Faustus was by him, and he conjured them that watched him into such a heavy sleep, that he with his charms made open all the locks in the prison, and therewithal brought the young Duke again in safety to the rest of his fellows and friends, where they presented Faustus with a sumptuous gift, and so they departed the one from the other, *etc.*

Chapter XXXIII

How Doctor Faustus borrowed money of a Jew, and laid his own leg to pawn for it

IT is a common proverb in Germanie, that although a Conjurer have all things at commandment, the day will come that he shall not be worth a penny: so is it like to fall out with Doctor Faustus, in promising the Devil so largely: and as the Devil is the author of lies, even so he led Faustus his mind, in practising of things to deceive the people and blinding them,

wherein he took his whole delight, thereby to bring himself to riches, yet notwithstanding in the end he was never the richer. And although that during four and twenty years of his time that the Devil set him, he wanted nothing; yet was he best pleased when he might deceive anybody: for out of the mightiest Potentates' Courts in all those Countries, he would send his Spirit to steal away their best cheer. And on a time being in his merriment where he was banqueting with other Students in a Inn, whereunto resorted many Jews, which when Doctor Faustus perceived, he was minded to play some merry jest to deceive a Jew, desiring one of them to lend him some money for a time, the Jew was content, and lent Faustus threescore dollars for a month, which time being expired, the Jew came for his money and interest, but Doctor Faustus was never minded to pay the Jew again: at length the Jew coming home to his house, and calling importunately for his money, Doctor Faustus made him this answer: Jew, I have no money, nor know I how to pay thee, but notwithstanding, to the end that thou mayest be contented, I will cut off a limb of my body, be it arm or leg, and the same shalt thou have in pawn for thy money, yet with this condition, that when I shall pay thee thy money again, then thou also give me my limb. The Jew that was never friend to a Christian, thought with himself, this is a fellow right for my purpose, that will lay his limbs to pawn for money, he was therewith very well content; wherefore Doctor Faustus took a saw, and therewith seemed to cut off his foot (being notwithstanding nothing so) well, he gave it to the Jew, yet upon this condition, that when he got money to pay, the Jew should deliver him his leg, to the end he might set it on again. The Jew was with this matter very well pleased, took his leg and departed: and having far home, he was somewhat weary, and by the way he thus bethought him, what helpeth me a knave's leg, if I should carry it home, it would stink, and so infect my house, besides it is too hard a piece of work to set it on again, wherefore what an ass was Faustus to lay so dear a pawn for so small a sum of money; and for my part, quoth the Jew to himself, this will never profit me anything, and with these words he cast the leg away from him into a ditch. All this Doctor Faustus knew right well, therefore within three days after he sent for the Jew to make him payment of his sixty Dollars, the Jew came, and Doctor Faustus demanded his pawn, there was his money ready for him: the Jew answered, the pawn was not profitable or necessary for anything and he had cast it away: but Faustus threateningly replied, I will have my leg again, or else one of thine for it. The Jew fell to entreating, promising him to give him what money he would ask, if he would not deal straightly with him, wherefore the Jew was constrained to give him sixty Dollars more to be rid of him, and yet Faustus had his leg on, for he had but blinded the Jew.

Chapter XXXIV

How Doctor Faustus deceived an Horse-courser

IN like manner he served an Horse-courser at a fair called Pfeiffring, for Doctor Faustus through his cunning had gotten an excellent fair Horse, whereupon he rid to the Fair, where he had many Chap-men that offered him money: lastly, he sold him for forty Dollars, willing him that bought him, that in any wise he should not ride him over any water, but the Horse-courser marvelled with himself that Faustus bade him ride him over no water (but quoth he), I will prove, and forthwith he rid him into the river, presently the horse vanished from under him, and he sat on a bundle of straw, in so much that the man was almost drowned. The

Horse-courser knew well where he lay that had sold him his horse, wherefore he went angrily to his Inn, where he found Doctor Faustus fast
asleep, and snorting on a bed, but the Horse-courser could no longer for-
bear him, took him by the leg and began to pull him off the bed, but he
pulled him so, that he pulled his leg from his body, in so much that the
Horse-courser fell down backwards in the place, then began Doctor Faustus to cry with an open throat, he hath murdered me. Hereat the Horse-
courser was afraid, and gave the flight,[24] thinking none other with himself, but that he had pulled his leg from his body; by this means Doctor
Faustus kept his money.

Chapter XXXV

How Doctor Faustus ate a load of Hay

DOCTOR FAUSTUS being in a Town of Germanie called Zwickaw, where
he was accompanied with many Doctors and Masters, and going forth to
walk after supper, they met with a Clown[25] that drove a load of Hay. Good
even good fellow said Faustus to the Clown, what shall I give thee to let
me eat my belly full of Hay? The Clown thought with himself, what a mad
man is this to eat Hay, thought he with himself, thou wilt not eat much,
they agreed for three farthings he should eat as much as he could: wherefore Doctor Faustus began to eat, and that so ravenously, that all the
rest of his company fell a-laughing, blinding so the poor Clown, that he
was sorry at his heart, for he seemed to have eaten more than the half of
his Hay, wherefore the Clown began to speak him fair, for fear he should

---

[24] i.e. took to flight.
[25] i.e. peasant.

have eaten the other half also. Faustus made as though he had had pity on the Clown, and went his way. When the Clown came in place where he would be, he had his Hay again as he had before, a full load.

Chapter XXXVI

How Doctor Faustus served the twelve Students

AT Wittenberg before Faustus his house, there was a quarrel between seven Students, and five that came to part the rest, one part being stronger than the other. Wherefore Faustus seeing them to be over-matched, conjured them all blind, in so much that the one could not see the other, and yet he so dealt with them, that they fought and smote at one another still, whereat all the beholders fell a-laughing: and thus they continued blind, beating one another, until the people parted them, and led each one to his own home: where being entered into their houses, they received their sight perfectly again.

Chapter XXXVII

How Faustus served the drunken Clowns

DOCTOR FAUSTUS went into an Inn, wherein were many tables full of Clowns, the which were tippling can after can of excellent wine, and to be short, they were all drunken, and as they sat, they so sang and hallowed, that one could not hear a man speak for them; this angered Doctor Faustus; wherefore he said to those that had called him in, mark my masters, I will shew you a merry jest, the Clowns continuing still hallowing and singing, he so conjured them, that their mouths stood as wide open as it was possible for them to hold them, and never a one of them was able to close his mouth again: by and by the noise was gone, the Clowns notwithstanding looked earnestly one upon another, and wist not what was happened; wherefore one by one they went out, and so soon as they came without, they were as well as ever they were: but none of them desired to go in any more.

Chapter XXXVIII

How Doctor Faustus sold five Swine for six Dollars apiece

DOCTOR FAUSTUS began another jest, he made him ready five fat Swine, the which he sold to one for six Dollars a piece, upon this condition, that the Swine-driver should not drive them into the water. Doctor Faustus went home again, and as the Swine had defiled themselves in the mud, the Swine-driver drove them into a water, where presently they were changed

into so many bundles of straw swimming upright in the water: the boor looked wishly about him, and was sorry in his heart, but he knew not where to find Faustus, so he was content to let all go, and to lose both money and Hogs.

Chapter XXXIX

How Doctor Faustus played a merry jest with the Duke of Anholt in his Court

DOCTOR FAUSTUS on a time came to the Duke of Anholt, the which welcomed him very courteously, this was in the month of January, where sitting at the table, he perceived the Duchess to be with child, and forbearing himself until the meat was taken from the table, and that they brought in the banqueting dishes, said Doctor Faustus to the Duchess, Gracious Lady, I have always heard, that the great-bellied women do always long for some dainties, I beseech therefore your Grace hide not your mind from me, but tell me what you desire to eat, she answered him, Doctor Faustus now truly I will not hide from you what my heart doth most desire, namely, that if it were now Harvest, I would eat my belly full of ripe Grapes, and other dainty fruit. Doctor Faustus answered hereupon,

Gracious Lady, this is a small thing for me to do, for I can do more than this, wherefore he took a plate, and made open one of the casements of the window, holding it forth, where incontinent he had his dish full of all manner of fruits, as red and white Grapes, Pears, and Apples, the which came from out of strange Countries, all these he presented the Duchess, saying: Madame, I pray you vouchsafe to taste of this dainty fruit, the which came from a far Country, for there the Summer is not yet ended. The Duchess thanked Faustus highly, and she fell to her fruit with full appetite. The Duke of Anholt notwithstanding could not withhold to ask Faustus with what reason there were such young fruit to be had at that time of the year? Doctor Faustus told him, may it please your Grace to understand, that the year is divided into two circles over the whole world, that when with us it is Winter, in the contrary circle it is notwithstanding Summer, for in India and Saba there falleth or setteth the Sun, so that it is so warm, that they have twice a year fruit: and gracious Lord, I have a swift Spirit, the which can in the twinkling of an eye fulfil my desire in any thing, wherefore I sent him into those Countries, who hath brought this fruit as you see: whereat the Duke was in great admiration.

Chapter XL

How Doctor Faustus through his Charms made a great Castle in presence of the Duke of Anholt

DOCTOR FAUSTUS desired the Duke of Anholt to walk a little forth of the Court with him, wherefore they went both together into the field, where Doctor Faustus through his skill had placed a mighty Castle: which when the Duke saw, he wondered thereat, so did the Duchess, and all the beholders, that on that hill, which was called the Rohumbuel, should on the sudden be so fair a Castle. At last Doctor Faustus desired the Duke and the Duchess to walk with him into the Castle, which they denied not. This Castle was so wonderful strong, having about it a great and deep trench of water, the which was full of Fish, and all manner of water-fowl, as Swans, Ducks, Geese, Bitterns, and suchlike. About the wall was five stone doors and two other doors: also within was a great open court, wherein were enchanted all manner of wild beasts, especially such as were not to be found in Germanie, as Apes, Bears, Buffs, Antelopes, and such like strange beasts. Furthermore, there were other manner of beasts, as Hart, Hind, and wild Swine, Roe, and all manner of land fowl that any man could think on, the which flew from one tree to another. After all this, he set his guests to the table, being the Duke and the Duchess with their train, for he had provided them a most sumptuous feast, both of meat and all manner of drinks, for he set nine messes of meat upon the board at once, and all this must his Wagner do, place all things on the board, the which was brought unto him by the Spirit invisibly of all things that their heart could desire, as wild fowl, and Venison, with all manner of dainty fish that could be thought on, of Wine also great plenty, and of divers sorts, as French wine, Cullin wine, Crabatsher wine, Rhenish wine, Spanish wine, Hungarian wine, Watzburg wine, Malmsey, and Sack: in the whole, there were an hundred cans standing round about the house. This sumptuous

banquet the Duke took thankfully, and afterwards he departed homewards, and to their thinking they had neither eaten nor drunk, so were they blinded with whilst that they were in the Castle: but as they were in their Palace they looked towards the Castle, and behold it was all in a flame of fire, and all those that beheld it wondered to hear so great a noise, as if it were great Ordinace should have been shot off: and thus the Castle burned and consumed away clean. Which done, Doctor Faustus returned to the Duke, who gave him great thanks for shewing them of so great courtesy, giving him an hundred Dollar, and liberty to depart or use his own discretion therein.

Chapter XLI

How Doctor Faustus with his company visited the Bishop of Saltzburg his Wine-cellar

DOCTOR FAUSTUS having taken his leave of the Duke, he went to Wittenberg, near about Shrovetide, and being in company with certain Students, Doctor Faustus was himself the God Bacchus, who having well feasted the Students before with dainty fare, after the manner of Germanie, where it is counted no feast except all the bidden guests be drunk, which Doctor Faustus intending, said: Gentlemen and my guests, will it please you to take a cup of wine with me in a place or cellar whereunto I will bring you, and they all said willingly we will: which when Doctor Faustus heard, he took them forth, set either of them upon an holly wand, and so were conjured into the Bishop of Saltzburg his Cellar, for there about grew excellent pleasant Wine: there fell Faustus and his company to drinking and swilling, not of the worst but of the best, and as they were merry in the Cellar, came down to draw drink the Bishop's butler: which when he perceived so many persons there he cried with a loud voice, thieves! thieves! This spited Doctor Faustus wonderfully, wherefore he made every one of his company to sit on their holly wand and so vanished away, and in parting Doctor Faustus took the Butler by the hair of the head and carried him away with them, until they came unto a mighty high-lopped tree, and on the top of that huge tree he set the Butler, where he remained in a most fearful perplexity, and Doctor Faustus departed to his house where they took their VALETE one of another, drinking the Wine the which they had stolen in great bottles of glass out of the Bishop's cellar. The Butler that had held himself by the hand upon the lopped tree all the night, was almost frozen with cold, espying the day, and seeing the tree of so huge great highness, thought with himself it is impossible to come off this tree without peril of death: at length he had espied certain Clowns which were passing by, he cried for the love of God help me down: the Clowns seeing him so high, wondered what mad man would climb to so huge a tree, wherefore as a thing most miraculous, they carried tidings unto the Bishop of Saltzburg, then was there great running on every side to see a man in a huge tree, and many devices they practised to get him down with ropes, and being demanded by the Bishop how he came there, he said, that he was brought thither by the hair of the head of certain thieves that were robbing of the Wine-cellar, but what they were he knew not, for (said he) they had faces like men, but they wrought like Devils.

Chapter XLII

How Doctor Faustus kept his Shrovetide

THERE were seven Students, and Masters that studied Divinity, Iuris Prudentia, and Medicina, all these having consented were agreed to visit Doctor Faustus and so to celebrate Shrovetide with him: who being come to his house he gave them their welcome, for they were his dear friends, desiring them to sit down, where he served them with a very good supper of Hens, fish, and other roast, yet were they but slightly cheered: wherefore Doctor Faustus comforted his guests, excusing himself that they stole upon him so suddenly, that he had not leisure to provide for them so well as they were worthy, but my good friends (quoth he) according to the use of our Country we must drink all this night, and so a draught of the best wine to bedward is commendable. For you know that in great Potentates' Courts they use as this night great feasting, the like will I do for you: for I have three great flagons of wine, the first is full of Hungarian wine, containing eight gallons, the second of Italian wine, containing seven gallons, the third containing six gallons of Spanish wine, all the which we will tipple out before it be day, besides, we have fifteen dishes of meat, the which my Spirit Mephostophiles hath fetched so far that is was cold before he brought it, and they are all full of the daintiest things that one's heart can devise, but (saith Faustus) I must make them hot again: and you may believe me, Gentlemen, that this is no blinding of you, whereas you think that it is no natural food, verily it is as good and as pleasant as ever you ate. And having ended his tale, he commanded his boy to lay the cloth, which done, he served them with fifteen messes of meat, having three dishes to a mess, the which were of all manner of Venison, and other dainty wild fowl, and for wine there was no lack, as Italian wine, Hungarian wine, and Spanish wine: and when they were all made drunk, and that they had almost eaten all their good cheer, they began to sing and to dance until it was day, and then they departed each one to his own habitation: at whose parting, Doctor Faustus desired them to be his guests again the next day following.

Chapter XLIII

How Doctor Faustus feasted his guests on the Ash-Wednesday

UPON Ash Wednesday came unto Doctor Faustus his bidden guests the Students, whom he feasted very royally, in so much that they were all full and lusty, singing and dancing as the night before: and when the high glasses and goblets were caroused one to another, Doctor Faustus began to play them some pretty jests, in so much that round about the hall was heard most pleasant music, and that in sundry places, in this corner a Lute, in another a Cornet, in another a Cittern, Gittern, Clarigolds, Harp, Horn pipe: in fine, all manner of music was heard there at that instant, whereat all the glasses and goblets, cups and pots, dishes, and all that stood on the board began to dance: then Doctor Faustus took ten stone pots, and set them down on the floor, where presently they began to dance and to smite one against the other that the shivers flew round about the whole house, whereat the whole company fell a-laughing. Then he began another jest, he set an Instrument on the table, and caused a monstrous great Ape to come in amongst them, which Ape began to dance and to skip, shewing them many merry conceits. In this and such-like pastime they passed away the whole day, where night being come, Doctor Faustus bade them all to supper, which they lightly agreed unto, for Students in these cases are easily entreated: wherefore he promised to feast them with a banquet of fowl, and afterwards they would all go about with a Mask, then Doctor Faustus put forth a long pole out of the window, whereupon presently there came innumerable of birds and wild fowl, and so many as came had not any power to fly away again, but he

took them and flung them to the Students: who lightly pulled off the necks of them, and being roasted they made their supper, which being ended they made themselves ready to the Mask. Doctor Faustus commanded every one to put on a clean shirt over his other clothes, which being done, they began to look one upon another, it seemed to each one of them they had no heads, and so they went forth unto certain of their neighbours, at which sight the people were wonderfully afraid. And as the use of Germanie is, that wheresoever a Mask entereth, the good man of the house must feast them: so when these maskers were set to their banquet, they seemed again in their former shape with heads in so much that they were all known what they were: and having sat and well eaten and drunk, Doctor Faustus made that every one had an Ass's head one, with great and long ears, so they fell to dancing and to drive away the time until it was midnight, and then every man departed home, and as soon as they were out of the house each one was in his natural shape again, and so they ended and went to sleep.

Chapter XLIV

*How Doctor Faustus the day following was feasted of the Students, and of his merry
  jests with them while he was in their company*

THE last Bacchanalia was held on Thursday, where ensued a great Snow,
and Doctor Faustus was invited unto the Students that were with him the
day before, where they had prepared an excellent banquet for him: which
banquet being ended, Doctor Faustus began to play his old pranks, and
forthwith were in the place thirteen Apes, that took hands and danced
round in a ring together, then they fell to tumble and to vaulting one
over another, that it was most pleasant to behold, then they leaped out of
the window and vanished away: then they set before Doctor Faustus
a roasted Calve's head: which one of the Students cut a piece off, and laid
it on Doctor Faustus his trencher, which piece being no sooner laid down,
but the Calve's head began to cry mainly out like a man, murther, murther,
but, alas, what doest thou to me! Whereat they were all amazed, but after
a while considering of Faustus his jesting tricks they began to laugh,
and then they pulled in sunder the Calve's head and ate it up. Whereupon
Doctor Faustus asked leave to depart, but they would in no wise agree to
let him go, except that he would promise to come again: presently then
Faustus, through his cunning, made a sledge, the which was drawn about
the house with four fiery dragons: this was fearful for the Students to behold, for they saw Faustus ride up and down as though he should have
fired and slain all them in the house. This sport continued until midnight
with such a noise that they could not hear one another, and the heads of
the Students were so light, that they thought themselves to be in the air all
that time.

Chapter XLV

*How Doctor Faustus shewed the fair Helena unto the Students upon the Sunday
  following*

THE Sunday following came these Students home to Doctor Faustus his
own house, and brought their meat and drink with them: these men were
right welcome guests unto Faustus, wherefore they all fell to drinking of
wine smoothly: and being merry, they began some of them to talk of the
beauty of women, and every one gave forth his verdict what he had seen
and what he had heard. So one among the rest said, I never was so desirous of anything in this world, as to have a sight (if it were possible) of fair
Helena of Greece, for whom the worthy town of Troie was destroyed and

razed down to the ground, therefore saith he, that in all men's judgment she was more than commonly fair, because that when she was stolen away from her husband, there was for her recovery so great bloodshed.

Doctor Faustus answered: For that you are all my friends and are so desirous to see that famous pearl of Greece, fair Helena, the wife of King Menelaus, and daughter of Tindalus and Læda, sister to Castor and Pollux, who was the fairest Lady in all Greece: I will therefore bring her into your presence personally, and in the same form of attire as she used to go when she was in her chiefest flowers and pleasantest prime of youth. The like have I done for the Emperor Carolus Quintus, at his desire I shewed him Alexander the great, and his Paramour: but (said Doctor Faustus) I charge you all that upon your perils you speak not a word, nor rise up

from the Table so long as she is in your presence. And so he went out of the Hall, returning presently again, after whom immediately followed the fair and beautiful Helena, whose beauty was such that the Students were all amazed to see her, esteeming her rather to be heavenly than an earthly creature. This Lady appeared before them in a most sumptuous gown of purple Velvet, richly embroidered, her hair hanged down loose as fair as the beaten Gold, and of such length that it reached down to her hams, with amorous coal-black eyes, a sweet and pleasant round face, her lips red as a Cherry, her cheeks of rose all colour, her mouth small, her neck as white as the Swan, tall and slender of personage, and in sum, there was not one imperfect part in her: she looked round about her with a rolling Hawk's eye, a smiling and wanton countenance, which near hand inflamed the hearts of the Students, but that they persuaded themselves she was a Spirit, wherefore such fantasies passed away lightly with them: and thus fair Helena and Doctor Faustus went out again one with another. But the Students at Doctor Faustus his entering again into the hall, re-

quested of him to let them see her again the next day, for that they would
bring with them a painter and so take her counterfeit: which he denied,
affirming that he could not always raise up her Spirit, but only at certain
times: yet (said he) I will give you her counterfeit, which shall be always
as good to you as if your selves should see the drawing thereof, which they
received according to his promise, but soon lost it again. The Students
departed from Faustus' home everyone to his house, but they were not
able to sleep the whole night for thinking on the beauty of fair Helena.
Wherefore a man may see that the Devil blindeth and enflameth the heart
with lust oftentimes, that men fall in love with Harlots, nay even with
Furies, which afterward cannot lightly be removed.

Chapter XLVI

How Doctor Faustus conjured away the four wheels from a clown's waggon

DOCTOR FAUSTUS was sent for to the Marshal of Brunswicke, who was
greatly troubled with the falling sickness. Now Faustus had this use, never
to ride but walk forth on foot, for he could ease himself when he list, and
as he came near unto the town of Brunswicke, there overtook him a
Clown with four horses and an empty waggon, to whom Doctor Faustus
jestingly to try him, said: I pray thee, good fellow, let me ride a little to ease
my weary legs; which the buzzardly ass denied, saying: that his horses were
also weary, and he would not let him get up. Doctor Faustus did this but
to prove the buzzard, if there were any courtesy to be found in him if
need were.

But such churlishness as is commonly found among clowns, was by
Doctor Faustus well requited, even with the like payment: for he said unto
him, Thou doltish Clown, void of all humanity, seeing thou art of so cur-
ish a disposition, I will pay thee as thou hast deserved, for the four wheels
of thy Waggon thou shalt have taken from thee, let me see then how canst
thou shift: hereupon his wheels were gone, his horses also fell down to
the ground, as though they had been dead: whereat the Clown was sore
affright, measuring it as a just scourge of God for his sins and churlishness: wherefore all troubled, and wailing, he humbly besought Doctor
Faustus to be good unto him, confessing he was worthy of it, notwithstanding if it pleased him to forgive him, he would hereafter do better.
Which humility made Faustus his heart to relent, answering him on this
manner, well, do so no more, but when a poor weary man desireth thee,
see that thou let him ride, but yet thou shalt not go altogether clear, for

although thou have again thy four wheels, yet shalt thou fetch them at the four Gates of the City, so he threw dust on the horses, and revived them again, and the Clown for his churlishness was fain to fetch his wheels, spending his time with weariness, whereas before he might have done a good deed, and gone about his business quietly.

Chapter XLVII

How four Jugglers cut one another's head off, and set them on again; and how Doctor Faustus deceived them

DOCTOR FAUSTUS came in the Lent unto Franckfort Fair, where his Spirit Mephostophiles gave him to understand that in an Inn were four Jugglers that cut one another's head off, and after their cutting off, sent them to the Barber to be trimmed, which many people saw. This angered Faustus (for he meant to have himself the only Cock in the Devil's basket), and he went to the place where they were, to behold them. And as these Jugglers were together, ready one to cut off the other's head, there stood also the Barbers ready to trim them, and by them upon the table stood likewise a glass full of distilled water, and he that was the chiefest among them stood by it. Thus they began, they smote off the head of the first, and presently there was a Lily in the glass of distilled water, where Faustus perceived this Lily as it were springing, and the chief Juggler named it the tree of life, thus dealt he with the first, making the Barber wash and comb his head, and then he set it on again, presently the Lily vanished away out of the water, hereat the man had his head whole and sound again; the like did they with the other two: and as the turn and lot came to the chief Juggler that he also should be beheaded, and that his Lily was most pleasant, fair, and flourishing green, they smote his head off, and when it came to be barbed, it troubled Faustus his conscience, in so much that he could not abide to see another do anything, for he thought himself to be the principal conjurer in the world, wherefore Doctor Faustus went to the table whereat the other Jugglers kept that Lily, and so he took a small knife and cut off the stalk of the Lily, saying to himself, none of them should blind Faustus: yet no man saw Faustus to cut the Lily, but when the rest of the Jugglers thought to have set on their master's head, they could not, wherefore they looked on the Lily, and found it a bleeding: by this means the Juggler was beguiled, and so died in his wickedness, yet not one thought that Doctor Faustus had done it.

Chapter XLVIII

How an old man, the neighbour of Faustus, sought to persuade him to amend his evil life, and to fall unto repentance

A GOOD Christian an honest and virtuous old man, a lover of the holy Scriptures, who was neighbour unto Doctor Faustus: when he perceived that many Students had their recourse in and out unto Doctor Faustus, he suspected his evil life, wherefore like a friend he invited Doctor Faustus to supper unto his house, unto the which he agreed; and having ended their banquet, the old man began with these words. My loving friend and neighbour Doctor Faustus, I have to desire of you a friendly and Christian request, beseeching you that you will vouchsafe not to be angry with me, but friendly resolve me in my doubt, and take my poor inviting in good part. To whom Doctor Faustus answered: My loving neighbour, I pray you say your mind. Then began the old Patron to say: My good neighbour, you know in the beginning how that you have defied God, and all the host of heaven, and given your soul to the Devil, wherewith you have incurred God's high displeasure, and are become from a Christian far worse than a heathen person: oh consider what you have done, it is not only the pleasure of the body, but the safety of the soul that you must have respect unto: of which if you be careless, then are you cast away, and shall remain in the anger of almighty God. But yet is it time enough Doctor Faustus, if you repent and call unto the Lord for mercy, as we have example in the Acts of the Apostles, the eighth Chap. of Simon in Samaria, who was led out of the way, affirming that he was Simon homo sanctus. This man was notwithstanding in the end converted, after that he had heard the Sermon of Philip, for he was baptized, and saw his sins, and repented. Likewise I beseech you good brother Doctor Faustus, let my rude Sermon be unto you a conversion; and forget the filthy life that you have led, repent, ask mercy, and live: for Christ saith, *Come unto me all ye that are weary and heavy laden, and I will refresh you.* And in Ezechiel: *I desire not the death of a sinner, but rather that he convert and live.* Let my words good brother Faustus, pierce into your adamant heart, and desire God for his Son Christ his sake, to forgive you. Wherefore have you so long lived in your Devilish practices, knowing that in the Old and New Testament you are forbidden, and that men should not suffer any such to live, neither have any conversation with them, for it is an abomination unto the Lord; and that such persons have no part in the Kingdom of God. All this while Doctor Faustus heard him very attentively, and replied: Father, your persuasions like me wondrous well, and I thank you with all my heart for your good will and counsel, promising you so far as I may to follow your discipline: whereupon he took his leave. And being come home, he laid him very pensive on his bed, bethinking himself of the words of the good old man, and in a manner began to repent that he had given his Soul to the Devil, intending to deny all that he had promised unto Lucifer. Continuing in these cogitations, suddenly his Spirit appeared unto him clapping him upon the head, and wrung it as though he would have pulled the head from the shoulders, saying unto him, Thou knowest Faustus, that thou hast given thyself body and soul unto my Lord Lucifer, and hast vowed thyself an enemy unto God and unto all men; and now thou beginnest to hearken to an old doting fool which persuadeth thee as it were unto God, when indeed it is too late, for that thou art the Devil's, and he hath good power presently to fetch thee: wherefore he hath sent me unto thee, to tell thee, that seeing thou hast sorrowed for that thou hast done, begin again and write another writing with thine own blood, if not, then will I tear thee all to pieces. Hereat Doctor Faustus was sore afraid, and said: My Mephostophiles, I will write again what thou wilt: wherefore he sat him down, and with his own blood he wrote as followeth: which writing was afterward sent to a dear friend of the said Doctor Faustus being his kinsman.

Chapter XLIX

How Doctor Faustus wrote the second time with his own blood and gave it to the Devil

I, DOCTOR JOHN FAUSTUS, acknowledge by this my deed and handwriting, that sith my first writing, which is seventeen years, that I have right willingly held, and have been an utter enemy unto God and all men, the which I once again confirm, and give fully and wholly myself unto the Devil both body and soul, even unto the great Lucifer: and that at the end of seven years ensuing after the date of this letter, he shall have to do with me according as it pleaseth him, either to lengthen or shorten my life as liketh him: and hereupon I renounce all persuaders that seek to withdraw me from my purpose by the Word of God, either ghostly or bodily. And further, I will never give ear unto any man, be he spiritual or temporal, that moveth any matter for the salvation of my soul. Of all this writing, and that therein contained, be witness, my own blood, the which with mine own hands I have begun, and ended.

Dated at Wittenberg, the 25th of July.

And presently upon the making of this Letter, he became so great an enemy unto the poor old man, that he sought his life by all means possible; but this godly man was strong in the Holy Ghost, that he could not be vanquished by any means: for about two days after that he had exhorted Faustus, as the poor man lay in his bed, suddenly there was a mighty rumbling in the Chamber, the which he was never wont to hear, and he heard as it had been the groaning of a Sow, which lasted long: whereupon the good old man began to jest, and mock, and said: oh what Barbarian cry is this, oh fair Bird, what foul music is this of a fair Angel, that could not tarry two days in his place? beginnest thou now to run into a poor man's house, where thou hast no power, and wert not able to keep thine own two days? With these and such-like words the Spirit departed. And when he came home Faustus asked him how he had sped with the old man: to whom the Spirit answered, the old man was harnessed, and that he could not once lay hold upon him: but he would not tell how the old man had mocked him, for the Devils can never abide to hear of their fall. Thus doth God defend the hearts of all honest Christians, that betake themselves under his tuition.

Chapter L

How Doctor Faustus made a marriage between two lovers

IN the City of Wittenberg was a Student, a gallant Gentleman, named N. N. This Gentleman was far in love with a Gentlewoman, fair and proper of personage. This Gentlewoman had a Knight that was a suitor unto her, and many other Gentlemen, the which desired her in marriage, but none could obtain her: So it was that this N. N. was very well acquainted with Faustus, and by that means became a suitor unto him to assist him in the matter, for he fell so far in despair with himself, that he pined away to the skin and bones. But when he had opened the matter unto Doctor Faustus, he asked counsel of his Spirit Mephostophiles, the which told him what to do. Hereupon Doctor Faustus went home to the Gentleman, and bade him be of good cheer, for he should have his desire, for he would help him to that he wished for, and that this Gentlewoman should love none other but him only: wherefore Doctor Faustus so changed the mind of the Damsel by a practice he wrought, that she would do no other thing but think on him, whom before she had hated, neither cared she for any man but him alone. The device was thus, Faustus commanded this Gentleman that he should clothe himself in all his best apparel that he had and that he should go unto this Gentlewoman, and there to shew himself, giving him also a Ring, commanding him in any wise that he should dance with her before he departed. Wherefore he followed Faustus his counsel, went to her, and when they began to dance they that were suitors began to take everyone his Lady in his hand, and this good Gentleman took her, who before had so disdained him, and in the dance he thrust the Ring into her hand that Doctor Faustus had given him, the which she no sooner touched, but she fell immediately in love with him, beginning in the dance to smile, and many times to give him winks, rolling her eyes, and in the end she asked him if he could love her and make her his wife; he gladly answered, he was content: and hereupon they concluded, and were married, by the means and help of Doctor Faustus, for which he received a good reward of the Gentleman.

Chapter LI

How Doctor Faustus led his friends into his Garden at Christmas, and shewed them many strange sights in his nineteenth year

In December, about Christmas in the City of Wittenberg, were many young Gentlewomen, the which were come out of the Country to make merry with their friends and Acquaintance; amongst whom there were certain that were well acquainted with Doctor Faustus, wherefore they were often invited as his guests unto him, and being with him on a certain time after dinner, he led them into his Garden, where he shewed them all manner of flowers, and fresh herbs, Trees bearing fruit and blossoms of all sorts, in so much that they wondered to see that in his Garden should be so pleasant a time as in the midst of summer: and without in the streets, and all over the Country, it lay full of Snow and Ice. Wherefore this was noted of them as a thing miraculous, each one gathering and carrying away all such things as they best liked, and so departed delighted with their sweet-smelling flowers.

Chapter LII

How Doctor Faustus gathered together a great army of men in his extremity against a Knight that would have injured him on his journey

Doctor Faustus travelled towards Eyszleben, and when he was nigh half the way, he espied seven horsemen, and the chief of them he knew to be the Knight to whom he had played a jest in the Emperor's Court, for he had set a huge pair of Hart's horns upon his head: and when the Knight now saw that he had fit opportunity to be revenged of Faustus he ran upon him himself, and those that were with him, to mischief him, intending privily to shoot at him: which when Doctor Faustus espied, he

vanished away into the wood which was hard by them. But when the
Knight perceived that he was vanished away, he caused his men to stand
still, where as they remained they heard all manner of war-like instruments of music, as Drums, Flutes, Trumpets, and such-like, and a certain
troop of horsemen running towards them. Then they turned another way,
and there also were assaulted on the same side: then another way, and yet
they were freshly assaulted, so that which way soever they turned themselves, he was encountered: in so much that when the Knight perceived
that he could escape no way, but that they his enemies laid on him which
way soever he offered to fly, he took a good heart and ran amongst the
thickest, and thought with himself better to die than to live with so great
an infamy. Therefore being at handy-blows with them, he demanded the
cause why they should so use them: but none of them would give him
answer, until Doctor Faustus shewed himself unto the Knight, where
withal they enclosed him around, and Doctor Faustus said unto him, Sir,
yield your weapon, and yourself, otherwise it will go hardly with you. The
Knight that knew none other but that he was environed with an host of
men (where indeed they were none other than Devils) yielded: then Faustus took away his sword, his piece, and horse, with all the rest of his companions. And further he said unto him; Sir, the chief General of our army
hath commanded to deal with you according to the law of Arms, you shall
depart in peace whither you please: and then he gave the Knight an horse
after the manner, and set him thereon, so he rode, the rest went on foot
until they came to their Inn, where being alighted, his Page rode on his
horse to the water, and presently the horse vanished away, the Page being
almost sunk and drowned, but he escaped: and coming home, the Knight
perceived his Page so bemired and on foot, asked where his horse was become? Who answered that he was vanished away: which when the Knight
heard, he said, of a truth this is Faustus his doing, for he serveth me now
as he did before at the Court, only to make me a scorn and a laughing
stock.

Chapter LIII

*How Doctor Faustus caused Mephostophiles to bring him seven of the fairest women
that he could find in all those countries he had travelled in, in the twentieth year*

WHEN Doctor Faustus called to mind, that his time from day to day
drew nigh, he began to live a swinish and Epicurish Life, wherefore he
commanded his Spirit Mephostophiles, to bring him seven of the fairest
women that he had seen in all the time of his travel: which being brought,

first one, and then another, he lay with them all, in so much that he liked them so well, that he continued with them in all manner of love, and made them to travel with him in all his journeys. These women were two Netherlanders, one Hungarian, one English, two Wallons, one Franck-lander: and with these sweet personages he continued long, yea even to his last end.

Chapter LIV

How Doctor Faustus found a mass of money when he had consumed twenty-two of his years

To the end that the Devil would make Faustus his only heir, he shewed unto him where he should go and find a mighty huge mass of money, and that he should have it in an old Chapel that was fallen down, half a mile distant from Wittenberg, there he bade him to dig and he should find it, the which he did, and having digged reasonable deep, he saw a mighty huge serpent, the which lay on the treasure itself, the treasure itself lay like a huge light burning: but D. Faustus charmed the serpent that he crept into a hole, and when he digged deeper to get up the treasure, he found nothing but coals of fire: there also he heard and saw many that were tormented, yet notwithstanding he brought away the coals, and when he was come home, it was all turned into silver and gold, as after his death was found by his servant, the which was almost about estimation, a thousand gilders.

Chapter LV

How Doctor Faustus made the Spirit of fair Helena of Greece his own Paramour and bedfellow in his twenty-third year

To the end that this miserable Faustus might fill the lust of his flesh, and live in all manner of voluptuous pleasures, it came in his mind after he had slept his first sleep,[26] and in the twenty-third year past of his time, that he had a great desire to lie with fair Helena of Greece, especially her whom he had seen and shewed unto the Students of Wittenberg, wherefore he called unto him his Spirit Mephostophiles, commanding him to bring him the fair Helena, which he also did. Whereupon he fell in love with her, and made her his common Concubine and bedfellow, for she was so beautiful

---

[26] The German text has "at midnight, when he awoke."

and delightful a piece, that he could not be one hour from her, if he should therefore have suffered death, she had so stolen away his heart: and to his seeming, in time she was with child, and in the end brought him a man child, whom Faustus named Justus Faustus: this child told Doctor Faustus many things that were to come, and what strange matters were done in foreign countries: but in the end when Faustus lost his life, the mother and the child vanished away both together.

Chapter LVI

How Doctor Faustus made his Will, in the which he named his servant Wagner to be his heir

DOCTOR FAUSTUS was now in his twenty-fourth and last year, and he had a pretty stripling to his servant, the which had studied also at the University of Wittenberg: this youth was very well acquainted with his knaveries and sorceries, so that he was hated as well for his own knaveries, as also for his Master's: for no man would give him entertainment into his service, because of his unhappiness, but Faustus: this Wagner was so well beloved with Faustus, that he used him as his son: for do what he would his master was always therewith well content. And when the time drew nigh that Faustus should end, he called unto him a Notary and certain masters the which were his friends and often conversant with him, in whose presence he gave this Wagner his house and Garden. Item, he gave him in ready money one thousand six hundred gilders. Item, a Farm. Item, a gold chain, much plate, and other household stuff. This gave he all to his servant, and the rest of his time he meant to spend in Inns and Students' company, drinking and eating, with other jollity: and thus he finished his Will for that time.

Chapter LVII

How Doctor Faustus fell in talk with his servant touching his Testament, and the covenants thereof

NOW when this Will was made, Doctor Faustus called unto him his servant, saying: I have thought upon thee in my Testament, for that thou hast been a trusty servant unto me and a faithful, and hast not opened my secrets: and yet further (said he) ask of me before I die what thou wilt, and I will give it unto thee. His servant rashly answered, I pray you let me have your cunning. To which Doctor Faustus answered, I have given thee all my books, upon this condition, that thou wouldst not let them be common, but use them for thine own pleasure, and study carefully in them. And dost thou also desire my cunning? That mayest thou peradventure have, if thou love and peruse my books well. Further (said Doctor Faustus) seeing that thou desirest of me this request, I will resolve thee: my Spirit Mephostophiles his time is out with me, and I have nought to command him as touching thee, yet will I help thee to another, if thou like well thereof. And within three days after he called his servant unto him, saying: art thou resolved? wouldst thou verily have a Spirit? Then tell me in what manner or form thou wouldst have him? To whom his servant answered, that he would have him in the form of an Ape: whereupon presently appeared a Spirit unto him in manner and form of an Ape, the which leaped about the house. Then said Faustus, see, there hast thou thy request, but yet he will not obey thee until I be dead, for when my Spirit Mephostophiles shall fetch me away, then shall thy Spirit be bound unto thee, if thou agree: and thy Spirit shalt thou name Akercocke, for so is he called: but all this is upon condition that thou publish my cunning, and my merry conceits, with all that I have done (when I am dead) in an history: and if thou canst not remember all, thy Spirit Akercocke will help thee: so shall the great acts that I have done be manifested unto the world.

Chapter LVIII

How Doctor Faustus having but one month of his appointed time to come, fell to mourning and sorrow with himself for his devilish exercise

TIME ran away with Faustus, as the hour-glass, for he had but one month to come of his twenty-four years, at the end whereof he had given himself to the Devil body and soul, as is before specified. Here was the first token, for he was like a taken murderer or a thief, the which findeth himself guilty in conscience before the Judge have given sentence, fearing every hour to die: for he was grieved, and wailing spent the time, went talking to himself, wringing of his hands, sobbing and sighing, he fell away from flesh, and was very lean, and kept himself close: neither could he abide to see or hear of his Mephostophiles any more.

Chapter LIX

How Doctor Faustus complained that he should in his lusty time and youthful years die so miserably

THIS sorrowful time drawing near so troubled Doctor Faustus, that he began to write his mind, to the end he might peruse it often and not forget it, and is in manner as followeth.

Ah Faustus, thou sorrowful and woeful man, now must thou go to the damned company in unquenchable fire, whereas thou mightest have had the joyful immortality of the soul, the which thou now hast lost. Ah gross understanding and wilful will, what seizeth on my limbs other than a robbing of my life? Bewail with me my sound and healthful body, wit and soul, bewail with me my senses, for you have had your part and pleasure as well as I. Oh envy and disdain, how have you crept both at once into me, and now for your sakes I must suffer all these torments? Ah whither is pity and mercy fled? Upon what occasion hath heaven repaid me with this reward by sufferance to suffer me to perish? Wherefore was I created a man? The punishment that I see prepared for me of myself now must I suffer. Ah miserable wretch, there is nothing in this world to shew me comfort: then woe is me, what helpeth my wailing.

Chapter LX

Another complaint of Doctor Faustus

OH poor, woeful and weary wretch: oh sorrowful soul of Faustus, now art thou in the number of the damned, for now must I wait for unmeasurable pains of death, yea far more lamentable than ever yet any creature hath suffered. Ah senseless, wilful and desperate forgetfulness! O cursed and unstable life! O blind and careless wretch, that so hast abused thy body, sense, and soul! O foolish pleasure, into what a weary labyrinth hast thou brought me, blinding mine eyes in the clearest day? Ah weak heart! O troubled soul, where is become thy knowledge to comfort thee? O pitiful weariness! Oh desperate hope, now shall I never more be thought upon! Oh, care upon carefulness, and sorrows on heaps: Ah grievous pains that pierce my panting heart, whom is there now that can deliver me? Would God that I knew where to hide me, or into what place to creep or fly. Ah, woe, woe is me, be where I will, yet am I taken. Herewith poor Faustus was so sorrowfully troubled, that he could not speak or utter his mind any further.

Chapter LXI

How Doctor Faustus bewailed to think on Hell, and of the miserable pains therein provided for him

Now thou Faustus, damned wretch, how happy wert thou if as an unreasonable beast thou mightest die without soul, so shouldst thou not feel any more doubts? But now the Devil will take thee away both body and soul, and set thee in an unspeakable place of darkness: for although others' souls have rest and peace, yet I poor damned wretch must suffer all manner of filthy stench, pains, cold, hunger, thirst, heat, freezing, burning, hissing, gnashing, and all the wrath and curse of God, yea all the creatures that God hath created are enemies to me. And now too late I remember that my Spirit Mephostophiles did once tell me, there was a great difference amongst the damned; for the greater the sin, the greater the torment: for as the twigs of the tree make greater flame than the trunk thereof, and yet the trunk continueth longer in burning: even so the more that a man is rooted in sin, the greater is his punishment. Ah thou perpetual damned wretch, now art thou thrown into the everlasting fiery lake that never shall be quenched, there must I dwell in all manner of wailing, sorrow, misery, pain, torment, grief, howling, sighing, sobbing, blubbering, running of eyes, stinking at nose, gnashing of teeth, fear to the ears, horror to the conscience, and shaking both of hand and foot. Ah that I could carry the heavens on my shoulders, so that there were time at last to quit me of this everlasting damnation! Oh who can deliver me out of these fearful tormenting flames, the which I see prepared for me? Oh there is no help, nor any man that can deliver me, nor any wailing of sins can help me, neither is there rest to be found for me day nor night. Ah woe is me, for there is no help for me, no shield, no defence, no comfort. Where is my hold? knowledge dare I not trust: and for a soul to Godwards that have I not, for I shame to speak unto him: if I do, no answer shall be made me, but he will hide his face from me, to the end that I should not behold the joys of the chosen. What mean I then to complain where no help is? No, I know no hope resteth in my groanings: I have desired that it should be so, and God hath said Amen to my misdoings: for now I must have shame to comfort me in my calamities.

Chapter LXII

Here followeth the miserable and lamentable end of Doctor Faustus, by the which all Christians may take an example and warning

IN the twenty-fourth year Doctor Faustus his time being come, his Spirit appeared unto him, giving him his writing again, and commanding him to make preparation, for that the Devil would fetch him against a certain time appointed. D. Faustus mourned and sighed wonderfully, and never went to bed, nor slept wink for sorrow. Wherefore his Spirit appeared again, comforting him, and saying: My Faustus, be not thou so cowardly minded; for although that thou losest thy body, it is not long unto the day of Judgment, and thou must die at the last, although thou live many thousand years. The Turks, the Jews, and many an unchristian Emperor, are in the same condemnation: therefore (my Faustus) be of good courage, and be not discomforted, for the Devil hath promised that thou shalt not be in pains as the rest of the damned are. This and such-like comfort he gave him, but he told him false, and against the saying of the Holy Scriptures. Yet Doctor Faustus that had none other expectation but to pay his debts with his own skin, went on the same day that his Spirit said the Devil would fetch him, unto his trusty and dearest beloved brethren and companions, as Masters, and Bachelors of Arts, and other Students more the which had often visited him at his house in merriment: these he entreated that they would walk into the Village called Rimlich, half a mile from Wittenberg, and that they would there take with him for their repast part of a small banquet, the which they all agreed unto: so they went together, and there held their dinner in a most sumptuous manner. Doctor Faustus with them (dissemblingly) was merry, but not from the heart: wherefore he requested them that they would also take part of his rude supper: the which they agreed unto: for (quoth he) I must tell you what is the Victualler's due: and when they slept (for drink was in their heads) then Doctor Faustus paid and discharged the shot, and bound the Students and the Masters to go with him into another room, for he had many wonderful matters to tell them: and when they were entered the room as he requested, Doctor Faustus said unto them, as hereafter followeth.

Chapter LXIII

An Oration of Faustus to the Students

MY trusty and well-beloved friends, the cause why I have invited you into this place is this: Forasmuch as you have known me this many years, in what manner of life I have lived, practising all manner of conjurations and wicked exercises, the which I have obtained through the help of the Devil, into whose Devilish fellowship they have brought me, the which use the like Art and practice, urged by the detestable provocation of my flesh, my stiff-necked and rebellious will, with my filthy infernal thoughts, the which were ever before me, pricking me forward so earnestly, that I must perforce have the consent of the Devil to aid me in my devices. And to the end I might the better bring my purpose to pass, to have the Devil's aid and furtherance, which I never have wanted in mine actions, I have promised unto him at the end and accomplishing of twenty-four years, both body and soul, to do therewith at his pleasure: and this day, this dismal day, those twenty-four years are fully expired, for night beginning my hour-glass is at an end, the direful finishing whereof I carefully expect. for out of all doubt this night he will fetch me, to whom I have given myself in recompense of his service both body and soul, and twice confirmed writings with my proper blood. Now have I called you my well-beloved Lords, friends, brethren, and fellows, before that fatal hour to take my friendly farewell, to the end that my departing may not hereafter be hidden from you, beseeching you herewith courteous, and loving Lords and brethren, not to take in evil part anything done by me, but with friendly commendations to salute all my friends and companions wheresoever: desiring both you and them, if ever I have trespassed against your minds in anything, that you would all heartily forgive me: and as for those lewd practices the which this full twenty-four years I have followed, you shall hereafter find them in writing: and I beseech you let this my lamentable end to the residue of your lives be a sufficient warning, that you have God always before your eyes, praying unto him that he would ever defend you from the temptation of the Devil, and all his false deceits, not falling altogether from God, as I wretched and ungodly damned creature have done, having denied and defied Baptism, the Sacraments of Christ's body, God himself, all heavenly powers, and earthly men, yea, I have denied such a God, that desireth not to have one lost. Neither let the evil fellowship of wicked companions mislead you as it hath done me: visit earnestly and oft the Church, war and strive continually against the Devil with a good and steadfast belief on God, and Jesus Christ, and use your vocation in holiness. Lastly, to knit up my troubled Oration, this is my friendly request, that you would to rest, and let nothing trouble you: also if you chance to hear any noise, or rumbling about the house, be not therewith afraid, for there shall no evil happen unto you: also I pray you arise not out of your beds. But above all things I entreat you, if you hereafter find my dead carcass, convey it unto the earth, for I die both a good and bad Christian;

a good Christian, for that I am heartily sorry, and in my heart always pray for mercy, that my soul may be delivered: a bad Christian, for that I know the Devil will have my body, and that would I willingly give him so that he would leave my soul in quiet: wherefore I pray you that you would depart to bed, and so I wish you a quiet night, which unto me notwithstanding will be horrible and fearful.

This oration or declaration was made by Doctor Faustus, and that with a hearty and resolute mind, to the end he might not discomfort them: but the Students wondered greatly thereat, that he was so blinded, for knavery, conjuration, and such-like foolish things, to give his body and soul unto the Devil: for they loved him entirely, and never suspected any such thing before he had opened his mind to them: wherefore one of them said unto him; ah, friend Faustus, what have you done to conceal this matter so long from us, we would by the help of good Divines, and the grace of God, have brought you out of this net, and have torn you out of the bondage and chains of Satan, whereas now we fear it is too late, to the utter ruin of your body and soul? Doctor Faustus answered, I durst never do it, although I often minded, to settle myself unto godly people, to desire counsel and help, as once mine old neighbour counselled me, that I should follow his learning, and leave all my conjurations, yet when I was minded to amend, and to follow that good man's counsel, then came the Devil and would have had me away, as this night he is like to do, and said so soon as I turned again to God, he would dispatch me altogether. Thus, even thus (good Gentlemen, and my dear friends) was I enthralled in that Satanical band, all good desires drowned, all piety banished, all purpose of amendment utterly exiled, by the tyrannous threatenings of my deadly enemy. But when the Students heard his words, they gave him counsel to do naught else but call upon God, desiring him for the love of his sweet Son Jesus Christ's sake, to have mercy upon him, teaching him this form of prayer. O, God, be merciful unto me, poor and miserable sinner, and enter not into judgment with me, for no flesh is able to stand before thee. Although, O Lord, I must leave my sinful body unto the Devil, being by him deluded, yet thou in mercy mayest preserve my soul.

This they repeated unto him, yet it could take no hold, but even as Cain he also said his sins were greater than God was able to forgive; for all his thought was on his writing, he meant he had made it too filthy in writing it with his own blood. The Students and the others that were there, when they had prayed for him, they wept, and so went forth, but Faustus tarried in the hall: and when the Gentlemen were laid in bed, none of them could sleep, for that they attended to hear if they might be privy of his end.

It happened between twelve and one o'clock at midnight, there blew a mighty storm of wind against the house, as though it would have blown the foundation thereof out of his place. Hereupon the Students began to fear, and got out of their beds, comforting one another, but they would not stir out of the chamber: and the Host of the house ran out of doors, thinking the house would fall. The Students lay near unto that hall wherein Doctor Faustus lay, and they heard a mighty noise and hissing, as if the hall had been full of Snakes and Adders: with that the hall door flew open wherein Doctor Faustus was, then he began to cry for help, saying: murther, murther, but it came forth with half a voice hollowly: shortly after they heard him no more. But when it was day, the Students that had taken no rest that night, arose and went into the hall in the which they left Doctor Faustus, where notwithstanding they found no Faustus, but all the hall lay besprinkled with blood, his brains cleaving to the wall: for the Devil had beaten him from one wall against another, in one corner lay his eyes, in another his teeth, a pitiful and fearful sight to behold. Then began the Students to bewail and weep for him, and sought for his body in many places: lastly they came into the yard where they found his body lying on the horse dung, most monstrously torn, and fearful to behold, for his head and all his joints were dashed in pieces.

The forenamed Students and Masters that were at his death, have obtained so much, that they buried him in the Village where he was so grievously tormented. After the which, they returned to Wittenberg, and coming into the house of Faustus, they found the servant of Faustus very sad, unto whom they opened all the matter, who took it exceeding heavily. There found they also this history of Doctor Faustus noted, and of him written as is before declared, all save only his end, the which was after by the Students thereto annexed: further, what his servant had noted thereof, was made in another book. And you have heard that he held by him in his life the Spirit of fair Helena, the which had by him one son, the which he named Justus Faustus, even the same day of his death they vanished away, both mother and son. The house before was so dark, that scarce anybody could abide therein. The same night Doctor Faustus appeared unto his servant lively, and shewed unto him many secret things the which he had done and hidden in his lifetime. Likewise there were certain which saw Doctor Faustus look out of the window by night as they passed by the house.

And thus ended the whole story of Doctor Faustus his conjuration, and other acts that he did in his life; out of the which example every Christian may learn, but chiefly the stiff-necked and high minded may thereby learn to fear God, and to be careful of their vocation, and to be at defiance with all Devilish works, as God hath most precisely forbidden, to the end we should not invite the Devil as a guest, nor give him place as that wicked Faustus hath done: for here we have a fearful example of his writing, promise, and end, that we may remember him: that we go not astray, but take God always before our eyes, to call alone upon him, and to honour him all the days of our life, with heart and hearty prayer, and with all our strength and soul to glorify his holy name, defying the Devil and all his works, to the end we may remain with Christ in all endless joy: Amen, Amen, that wish I unto every Christian heart, and God's name to be glorified. Amen.

FINIS

Appendix

LIST OF LOCALITIES
(*Where they vary from the modern usage*)

ACH: Aachen (Aix-la-Chapelle).
ANHOLT: Anhalt.
AUSPURG: Augsburg.
AUSTRICH: Austria.
BASILE ⎱ Basle
BASYL ⎰
BATOBURG: Battenburg.
BETHELEM: Bethlehem.
BEYERLANDT: Bavaria.
BREAME: Bremen (?).
CAMPA DE FRIORE: Campo de' Fiori.
CAMPANY: Campania.
CATHAI: China.
COSTUITZ (COSTNITZ): Constance.
CRACOVIA: Cracow.
CULLIN: Cologne.
DURING: Thuringia.
ELVE: Elbe.
ERFORT: Erfurt.
GEUF (GENF): Geneva.
GIBLATERRA: Gibraltar.
GINNIE: Guinea.
GOSLARYENS: Citizens of Goslar.
GRACOVIA: Cracow.
KUNDLING: Knittlingen.
LIEFLAND: Livonia.
LIPTZIG: Leipzig.
LITAW: Lithuania.
LUSITANY: Lusitania, Portugal.
MAYNE: Main.
MEDERI: Madeira (?).
MENCHEN: Munich.
MENTZ: Mainz.
MILLAIN: Milan.
MISSENE: Meissen.
MOSA: Maas.

NORENBERG: Nuremberg.
NOVA HISPANIOLA: Mexico.
PADOA: Padua.
POLONIAN: Polish.
PRAGE: Prague.
RAVENSPURG: Regensburg.
RHODE: Roda.
SANDETZ: Sandec, in Galicia.
SCLESIA ⎫ Silesia.
SLESIA ⎭
SENA: Siena.
SHAWBLANDT: Schwabenland, Swabia.
SWEITZ: Switzerland.
S. MICHAEL'S ⎫ Two of the Azores.
TERZERA   ⎭
TERGESTE: Triste.
TERRA INCOGNITA: America.
TENORRIFOCIE ⎫ Teneriffe (?).
TRENO RIEFE ⎭
TREIR: Trier (Trèves).
ULME ⎫ Ulm.
ULMA ⎭
WARTZBURG ⎫ Würzburg.
WATZBURG ⎭
WEIM: Vienna.
WEIMER: Weimar.

III Early Faust Plays and Music

Marlowe's *Doctor Faustus* and the *English Faust Book*

David Wootton

The story of *Doctor Faustus* begins with the *Historia von Johann Fausten*, published in Frankfurt in 1587. Fourteen editions were published in the next six years, and six more by the end of the century. Translations appeared in Danish (1588), Dutch (1592), French (1598), and Czech (1611). In late 1588 (or perhaps very early in 1589), a translation appeared in England, *The History of the Damnable Life and Deserved Death of Doctor Faustus*, known for short as the *English Faust Book*.[1] The translator was "P. F.," who described himself as a gentleman. John Henry Jones has identified him as Paul Fairfax, who was in London from June 1588, apparently arriving there from Frankfurt, and who quickly got into trouble with the authorities for practicing medicine without a license. His *History* was reprinted at least eight times in the next sixty years.

Doctor Faustus is the last play on the Elizabethan stage to deal directly with religion. Religious issues were inherently contested and controversial, but there were many who claimed that the stage was a peculiarly irreligious space, one in which it was entirely inappropriate to refer to religious matters. In 1606 an Act of Parliament forbade the use onstage of "the holy name of God or of Christ Jesus, or of the Holy Ghost, or of the Trinity," but already in the 1602 revisions to *Doctor Faustus* some of these references were being deleted: Mephistopheles' advice to "abjure the Trinity," for example, becomes "adjure all godliness." Marlowe dared stage the story of Faustus because his source was officially approved, and because the story dealt with the relations between human beings and devils. This was perhaps the subject on which there was most general agreement among Christians of all persuasions, whether Catholics, Lutherans, Calvinists, or members of the Church of England (a church that had deliberately blurred key doctrinal distinctions, so that among its members were people who would have preferred to be Catholics, Lutherans, or Calvinists); for Christianity in all its different official forms was united in believing that humans could enter into pacts with the devil

---

[1] The key authority is *The English Faust Book*, ed. J. H. Jones (Cambridge: Cambridge University Press, 1994).

and that witches must be executed. In avoiding theological controversy, Marlowe was following the example of the *English Faust Book* (which, in this respect, faithfully copies the German original), for although Protestants such as Luther and Melanchthon had led the attack on the historical Faustus, and although the *English Faust Book* was written and published by Protestants, there is little that is distinctively Protestant about it (with the exception, of course, of the hostility to the Catholic clergy that appears in the account of Faustus' visit to Rome in Chapter 22). The story of Faustus is presented as one from which "every Christian" may learn; it is not addressed to Christians of any particular confession or variety of belief.

Nevertheless, Marlowe introduces crucial modifications into the story as told by the *English Faust Book*. In the *English Faust Book*, the Old Man comes to Faustus (Chapter 48) and urges him to repent and ask God's forgiveness. Faustus is on the point of doing so ("He laid him very pensive on his bed, bethinking himself of the words of the good old man, and in a manner he began to repent that he had given his soul to the devil, intending to deny all that he had promised unto Lucifer") when Mephistopheles appears, terrifies Faustus, and forces him to sign a second contract, promising "I will never give ear unto any man, be he spiritual or temporal, that moveth any matter for the salvation of my soul." Any doubt that there might be about Faustus' fate (and there is precious little uncertainty in the *English Faust Book*) disappears at this point. The "Five complaints of Doctor Faustus before his end" all assume there is no doubt that he will go to hell. His students, on the day of his death, say that if they had known in time they could have rescued him, "whereas now we fear it is too late." Faustus agrees, telling again the story of his meeting with the Old Man, and his second contract. Still the students summon up hope: perhaps, if Faustus prays, he may yet be saved – even if the devil must have his body, perhaps his soul may be preserved. "This they repeated unto him, yet it could take no hold, but even as Cain he also said that his sins were greater than God was able to forgive; for all his thought was on his own writing: he meant that he had made it too filthy in writing it with his own blood." And this is the last we hear of Faustus' thoughts on the possibility of his own salvation. Clearly, whatever theoretical possibility there might be of his saving himself, there is no real prospect of his doing so.

Marlowe's story is quite different. In *Doctor Faustus*, as in the *English Faust Book*, the Old Man offers Faustus a real hope of salvation. The Old Man, whose faith can triumph over hell, knows that Faustus' guilt can be washed away by Christ's blood, if Faustus will only repent. He sees an angel hovering over Faustus, ready to save him through Christ's grace.

Faustus nearly repents; but Mephistopheles intervenes, the second contract is signed, and Faustus is seduced by Helen.

Yet still, that is not the end of the story. The students assure Faustus that "God's mercies are infinite," and Faustus responds by longing to weep and lift up his hands to heaven. Even when the students leave him, he has some faint hope of living until morning. As the clock strikes eleven, he sees Christ's blood streaming in the firmament and knows one drop could save him. The wish the students had voiced in the *English Faust Book*, that Faustus' soul might be saved even at the expense of his body, becomes here his wish. To the very end, Faustus hopes for an escape.

The B-text, the version including the additions of 1602, first published in 1616, is very different. Here, too, the Old Man offers Faustus hope of salvation, though now his theology has been revised ("Yet, yet thou hast an amiable soul, / If sin by custom grow not into nature" – here the Old Man seems to deny the dreadful consequences of the Fall, so central to Protestant theology). But once Mephistopheles has extracted the second contract from Faustus and Faustus has been seduced by Helen, then Lucifer and Beelzebub come on stage "to view the subjects of our monarchy ... bringing with us lasting damnation." Any thoughts Faustus might have of escape are dismissed by Mephistopheles as "idle fantasies." The scholars seek to offer Faustus hope, but as soon as they leave, Mephistopheles says, "Aye, Faustus, now thou hast no hope of heaven, / Therefore despair"; and the Good Angel appears in order to announce, "The jaws of hell are open to receive thee," and then formally abandons Faustus to his fate. Faustus, during his last hour, still dreams of escape, but Christ's blood no longer streams in the firmament, and we know that Faustus is merely indulging in "idle fantasies." At the end, pieces of his body are discovered on the stage.

I have gone through the three versions of Faustus' end in some detail because three central issues in the interpretation of the play arise from them. First, is the theology of the play Protestant, or more particularly Calvinist? Some scholars read *Doctor Faustus* as representing a peculiarly Calvinist anxiety in which fear that one is predestined to damnation leads to despair.[2] Others read the play as an expression of "orthodox" Chris-

---

[2] Arieh Sachs, "The Religious Despair of Doctor Faustus," *Journal of English and German Philology* 63 (1964), 625–47. Richard Waswo offers a Protestant reading: "Damnation, Protestant Style: *Macbeth, Faustus*, and Christian Tragedy," *Journal of Medieval and Renaissance Studies* 4 (1974), 63–99; for a Lutheran reading, see Clifford Davidson, "Doctor Faustus of Wittenberg," *Studies in Philology* 59 (1962), 514–23. Pauline Honderich sees a conflict between Calvinism and Ang-

tianity (by which they sometimes mean Christianity as it was taught before the Reformation), comparing it with the teachings of Aquinas and medieval morality plays.[3] These scholars see nothing distinctively Protestant in Marlowe's version of Faustus' story. A good deal depends here on whether you read the A-text, the B-text, or (as scholars often did between 1950 and 1990) an edition that presents a conflation of the two. Scholars who compare the A-text with the B-text are generally agreed that the A-text is Calvinist and the B-text is not.[4]

Moreover, the A-text's insistence on redemption through faith in Christ's sacrifice of himself on the cross is Marlowe's own contribution, perhaps under the influence of accounts of the death of an Italian Protestant, Francisco Spira, who had died convinced of his own damnation; or of the play based on the Spira story, Nathaniel Woodes' *The Conflict of Conscience* (1581).[5] The Protestantism of the Old Man in the A-text invites us to think back to Faustus' own reading of the Bible (lines 68–77): there Faustus had found that the reward of sin is death and that if we say that we have no sin, we deceive ourselves. He had also found the Calvinist doctrine of predestination: *che sera sera*. What he did not find was the comforting words, promising salvation, that accompany the texts on which his eyes settled; but then, Calvinists held that those words of comfort were applicable only to a few, the elect. For the majority, Faustus' interpretation of the text is sound theology. For them, religion has nothing to offer.

The Old Man of the B-text (and the Old Man seems to be presented as our best guide to true religion) is, by contrast, no Calvinist. Where the

licanism at the heart of the play: "John Calvin and Doctor Faustus," *Modern Language Review* 68 (1973), 1–13.

3 *Faustus*, ed. Bevington and Rasmussen, 15–22; Joseph Westlund, "The Orthodox Christian Framework of Marlowe's *Faustus*," *Studies in English Literature* 3 (1963), 191–205. According to Gerard H. Cox ("Marlowe's *Doctor Faustus* and 'Sin Against the Holy Ghost,'" *Huntington Library Quarterly* 36 [1973], 119–37), "Faustus's tragedy is one of free will gone wrong" (136). Margaret Ann O'Brien ("Christian Belief in *Doctor Faustus*," *English Literary History* 37 [1970], 1–11) and Ceri Sullivan ("Faustus and the Apple," *Review of English Studies* 47 [1996], 47–50) offer a Catholic reading.

4 The key article here is Michael J. Warren, "*Doctor Faustus*: The Old Man and the Text," *English Literary Renaissance* 11 (1981), 111–4. See also Sachs, "Religious Despair," 641; and Leah S. Marcus, "Textual Instability and Ideological Difference," in her *Unediting the Renaissance* (London: Routledge, 1996), 38–67.

5 Lily B. Campbell, "*Doctor Faustus*: A Case of Conscience," *PMLA* 67 (1952), 219–39. On Spira: Michael MacDonald, "The Fearful Estate of Francis Spira," *Journal of British Studies* 31 (1992), 32–61.

A-text offers the prospect of salvation by faith alone, the B-text seems to offer salvation if Faustus amends his life: it comes very close to offering salvation by works, and thus might be taken to verge on Arminianism (by the early 17th century, Arminians in the Church of England were stressing the possibility of free will and the importance of the sacraments), or even Catholicism.

The second central issue in the interpretation of the play results from Marlowe's placing Faustus' seduction by Helen immediately after he signs the second demonic pact, when in the *English Faust Book* there is no connection between the two. In both the A-text and the B-text, Faustus' kiss with Helen seems to be his final and ultimate act of wickedness. In the B-text it apparently seals his fate; in the A-text, the consequences are not quite so drastic, yet the Old Man watches the scene and sees in it every indication of Faustus' rejection of salvation.

In a famous essay, "The Damnation of Faustus" (1946), Walter Greg argued that the Helen who appears on stage is a demon in human shape (she is what is technically known as a *succubus*, a devil in female form, while a devil in male human form who has sex with a woman is an *incubus*), that by having sex with her (for this is what the kiss represents), Faustus commits the sin of "demoniality" (a word modeled on "bestiality," which means having sex with beasts), and that this is what seals his fate.[6] A number of scholars have effectively refuted Greg's implication that "demoniality" was an unforgivable sin (the very word "demoniality" was not coined until the 17th century); even if Faustus had had sex with a devil, orthodox theology, both Protestant and Catholic, would have maintained that he could still repent and be saved. Nor does Marlowe seek to lay emphasis on the fact that Helen is in fact a devil (although there can be no doubt that this is what she must be): here he follows the *English Faust Book*, which consistently eliminates the references to *succubi* in the German original.

Yet there can be no doubt that Marlowe deliberately makes the kiss the supreme moment of Faustus' life on earth, and he makes Faustus worship Helen (in the process, she turns, astonishingly, from a woman into a man – into Jupiter, who seduces Semele and Arethusa). One can certainly say

---

[6] W. W. Greg, "The Damnation of Faustus," *Modern Language Review* 41 (1946), 97–107 (reprinted in *Marlowe: Doctor Faustus*, ed. J. Jump [London: MacMillan, 1969]); T. W. Craik, "Faustus' Damnation Reconsidered," *Renaissance Drama* new series 2 (1969), 189–96; Nicholas Kiessling, "Doctor Faustus and the Sin of Demoniality," *Studies in English Literature* 15 (1975), 205–11; Warren, "The Old Man and the Text," 131–39. See also Walter Stephens, *Demon Lovers: Witchcraft, Sex, and the Crisis of Belief* (Chicago: University of Chicago Press, 2002).

that sexual passion has blinded Faustus to the fate of his soul; one can also say that Faustus is guilty of idolatry. But perhaps one should also note that on stage, Helen (like all women on the Elizabethan and Jacobean stage) would have been played by a boy. Faustus, we may say, is having three kinds of sex at once: with a woman, a man, and a demon. In appearance, Helen is a woman; Mephistopheles is there to remind us she is a demon; it is Faustus himself who changes her gender as he speaks, turning himself from Paris into Semele or Arethusa, and her into Jupiter. (As David Riggs neatly puts it, "The devil is in the gender reversals.")[7] It is Marlowe's choice to have sex mark the dramatic crisis of the play, and Marlowe's choice to leave us profoundly unclear as to how we are to understand the sex between Faustus and Helen. All we seem to be able to conclude is that there is something enormously powerful, demonic, deadly, and divine about sex itself. Christian faith, if it involves forswearing sexual passion, would seem to involve a terrible sacrifice.

The third central issue in the interpretation of the play derives from the fact that there is far greater possibility in the A-text than in the B-text that Faustus can yet, up until the end, save himself through repentance. For any orthodox Protestant (whether Lutheran or Calvinist), who is to be saved and who is to be damned has been predestined from the beginning of time, and human beings have no free will with which to affect the outcome. But an orthodox Protestant can also insist (as the Old Man does in the *English Faust Book*) a notorious sinner can be saved at the end of a wicked life through God's granting him or her faith. This means that orthodox Protestants hold that God knew from the beginning of time who would be saved; but that it is irreligious for any individual to despair and declare they are doomed to damnation (as Spira had done). With hindsight one could say for sure that both Spira and Faustus were damned from the beginning; but so long as they lived, one could never preclude the possibility of salvation. The A-text stresses this possibility to the end and perhaps, in doing so, shows its awareness of discussions of the fate of Spira; the B-text reverts to a far less subtle position, wherein Faustus is condemned beyond hope, either by his second contract with the devil or by his union with Helen. Once Faustus has finally made his choice, then there is no going back.

But behind this lies a further difference between *Doctor Faustus* and the *English Faust Book*, a difference so fundamental that it cannot be overemphasized. In order to understand it, we need to turn to a book that Marlowe had probably read, Reginald Scot's *The Discovery of Witchcraft*

---

[7] David Riggs, *The World of Christopher Marlowe* (London: Faber, 2004), 244.

(1584).[8] Marlowe borrows from Scot (or from one of the books influenced by Scot) the use of "familiar" as a noun to substitute for the phrase "familiar spirit," meaning the devil, in animal or human form, accompanying a witch or wizard.[9] Scot's *Discovery* is nowadays regarded as a key text because Scot is the first person in modern European history to write a book denying the existence of witches. In Scot's view, all those convicted of witchcraft are charged with an impossible crime (human beings simply cannot make a pact with the devil, as the devil is an immaterial being, with whom there can be no direct communication), and every witch executed is innocent of the crime with which she (for it is usually a she) is charged.

Scot mocked the idea of familiars, and Marlowe follows his example by imagining that all the lice on one's body might be familiars (lines 386–87): an idea that is subversive of the very idea of a familiar, since a familiar needs a stable identity (he is usually a cat, or a dog, or a toad) so that the witch can look after him. Demonologists were being perfectly consistent when they argued that the devil "can make no creature under the quantity [i.e., size] of barleycorn, and lice being so little cannot therefore be created by them."[10] What all familiars do is suckle on their hosts (witches were supposed to grow extra teats so that their familiars could suck), so that, apart from the fact that lice are short lived and indistinguishable from each other, there is something perfectly appropriate in the idea of a louse as a familiar. Marlowe is subverting the idea of devils by miniaturizing them: the same tactic is followed exactly by Marlowe's friend Nashe in *The Terrors of the Night* (1594), a work in which Scot is cited.

Most Elizabethans believed in the possibility of pacts with the devil, and believed that witches (and, in their view, Faustus would unquestionably have been a witch) were capable of apparently magical feats: of traveling through the air from one country to another, of making themselves invisible, of turning a bundle of hay into a horse. On stage, Faustus exercises the powers of a witch. Scot, who denied that there were any witches, had to explain why there were accounts of people, like Faustus,

---

[8] On Scot, see entry in *Dictionary of National Biography* (Oxford: Oxford University Press, 2004), and D. Wootton, "Reginald Scot / Abraham Fleming / The Family of Love," in *Languages of Witchcraft*, ed. S. Clark (MacMillan, 2000), 119–39.

[9] See *Oxford English Dictionary* s.v. "familiar." The *English Faust Book* has only "familiar spirit."

[10] Reginald Scot, *The Discoverie of Witchcraft*, ed. B. Nicholson (Totowa, NJ: Rowman and Littlefield, 1973), 314 (pagination of the 1584 edition).

doing apparently astonishing things. His answer was that such things were accomplished by *legerdemain*[11] or slight of hand. He devoted one book of the *Discovery* to explaining how one could fool people into thinking that impossible events have actually happened. He explained in detail how to perform a whole series of "magic" tricks. This book was frequently republished on its own later as the first practical guide to how to perform what we might call "staged" magic, of the pulling-rabbits-out-of-hats variety.

The *Discovery* provides an important clue as to why Marlowe was interested in dramatizing the *English Faust Book*. Of course, the story is one in which devils and hell are real, and there is no salvation aside from that of the Christian religion. There is one sense in which the Faustus story is Christian propaganda. But at the same time, to stage the Faustus story is to perform magic; and to perform magic is to show the power of illusion, and thus to demonstrate that all miracles may be false. We see a simple example of this when Robin and Rafe hide the silver goblet from the Vintner: they render it invisible simply by passing it back and forth from one to the other, so that it is never where the Vintner looks for it. This is classic *legerdemain*. We see a more complicated example when the horse-courser is tricked into thinking that he has pulled off Faustus' leg. Clearly he has been tricked into mistaking a prosthesis for the real thing. Thus Marlowe demonstrates the truth of Scot's claim that it is impossible to distinguish reality from illusion when it comes to magic (and miracles). Indeed, by bringing Mephistopheles and Lucifer onto the stage (and frightening the audience with their firecrackers), Marlowe shows that even the devil may be an illusion. Part of Richard Baines' testimony against Marlowe was that "He affirmeth that Moses was but a juggler, and that one Heriotes [i.e., the scientist, Thomas Hariot], being Sir W. Raleigh's man, can do more than he"; in other words, that the miracles attributed to Moses in the book of Exodus were mere tricks that those skilled in *legerdemain* could equal. And part of Thomas Kyd's testimony was that Marlowe had said, "That things esteemed to be done by divine power might have as well been done by observation [i.e., expertise or skill] of men." This is Scot's argument, and it relates directly to the tricks performed on stage in *Doctor Faustus*.

---

[11] Rob Iliffe, "Lying Wonders and Juggling Tricks: Religion, Nature, and Imposture in Early Modern England," in *Everything Connects*, ed. J. E. Force and D. S. Katz (Leiden: Brill, 1999), 185–209.

Scott also printed, from a manuscript in his possession, a complete set of instructions for summoning up a devil, including illustrations of the signs and characters to be drawn on the ground. Scot's approach was resolutely empirical (he sent old women out into neighboring villages to see if they could find anyone to teach them witchcraft), and his intent was presumably that his readers would try summoning the devil and discover that he would not come. He wrote, "I for my part have read a number of their conjurations [that is to say, he had recited the spells claimed by witches and conjurors to be effective in conjuring up demons], but never could see any devils of theirs, except it were in a play."[12] This was certainly the lesson learnt from Marlowe himself by a young man from Canterbury, Thomas Fineaux, who was a student at Cambridge from 1587 to 1590, when Marlowe was writing *Doctor Faustus*. Fineaux, who had "learned all Marlowe by heart, ... would go out at midnight into a wood and fall down upon his knees and pray heartily that the devil would come and he would see him; for he did not believe there was a devil. ... Marlowe made him an atheist."[13]

It should be apparent already that Scot's argument is highly subversive of orthodox religion (at least as it was understood in the 16th century), for it renders the devil invisible and casts doubt on the reality of miracles. In a final book of the *Discovery*, on spirits and devils (this book is unfortunately omitted from most modern reprints of Scot), Scot argued that spirits and devils are essentially promptings to good and evil with the minds of human beings. This led James VI of Scotland (later James I of England) to conclude in his *Demonology* that Scot had denied the existence of spirits, but it would be more accurate to say that Scot argues that spirits exist only within the mind, and that within each of us there is a constant tension between good and evil that can be described as a constant conflict between a good spirit and an evil spirit.[14]

In order to put the *English Faust Book* on the stage, Marlowe and his collaborator introduce some new characters (Valdes and Cornelius, Rafe and Robin) without altering the fundamental nature of the story. But Marlowe also introduces the Good and Evil Angels, who appear four times in the A-text (and five times in the B-text). Scholars normally link these angels to the appearance of good and evil angels in an early–15th-century moral-

---

[12] Scot, *Discoverie*, 443.

[13] Quoted in Riggs (*Marlowe*, 235).

[14] Scot, *Discoverie*, 547. I therefore sympathize with the views of Wilbur Sanders, as described by Robert H. West in "The Impatient Magic of *Dr. Faustus*" (*English Literary Renaissance* 4 [1974], 218–46).

ity play, *The Castle of Perseverance*; although, as David Bevington and Eric Rasmussen point out, there is no reason to think that Marlowe was familiar with this play.[15] It is much more likely, I think, that what Marlowe was doing was embodying the internal conflict between good and evil spirits as described by Scot. And of course, in Faustus' final soliloquy, where invisible demons hold him down as he tries to leap toward God, Faustus himself describes this conflict – it is no longer materialized outside himself, in the figures of the angels, but is internalized – as a purely psychic crisis.

In order to describe this internal conflict and the way in which the Good and Evil Angels embody it, scholars often write about *Doctor Faustus* as a *psychomachia*, a dramatization of an internal struggle. In doing so, they are referring back to medieval texts that sought to portray the conflict between good and evil within the soul. It is therefore striking that Abraham Fleming, a close associate of Scot's, had in 1582 published an adaptation of the key text in this medieval tradition under the title *Monomachie of Motives in the Mind of Man*. What distinguishes Fleming's adaptation from its medieval predecessors is that, where the latter always give longer and better arguments to virtue than they give to vice, Fleming, like Marlowe, places the two on an exactly equal footing.

"Hell strives with grace for conquest in my breast," says Faustus (line 1331). The title page of the 1604 edition shows somebody whose left hand is weighted down by a boulder, while his right arm is winged and lifts him toward heaven. The illustration was probably not produced especially for the volume – it is a conventional image that could be recycled for the occasion. In Whitney's *A Choice of Emblemes* of 1586, a similar image is labeled: "One hand with wings, would fly unto the stars, / And raise me up to win immortal fame ... th'other still is bound, / With heavy stone, which holds it to the ground."[16] But the illustration exactly represents this internal conflict that is one of Marlowe's crucial innovations in the Faust story.

It is notable that a number of elements (in addition to the belief that "every man hath assigned him, at the time of his nativity, a good angel and a bad" [506]) that are missing from the *English Faust Book*, but present in *Doctor Faustus*, are also to be found in the *Discovery of Witchcraft's* "Discourse upon Devils and Spirits" – such as the magician who burns his books (A1508; Scot 497), and the alliance between the devil and the

---

[15] *Faustus*, ed. Bevington and Rasmussen, 9.
[16] *Faustus*, ed. Ormerod and Wortham, note to line 1483.

seven deadly sins (A731–95; Scot 508). According to the *Oxford English Dictionary*, Marlowe was the first to use the phrase "old wives' tales" (A582); but the phrase had already been used by Scot (449; see also 508–509, 533).

In tracing these connections between Scot's *Discovery* and Marlowe's *Doctor Faustus*, we are, I think, on safe ground. I want to end with a suggestion that is more adventurous. Faustus' ambition is to become a spirit, even to become "a mighty god" and "gain a deity." (This is to take a step beyond the *English Faust Book*, where Faustus wants to become a spirit, but not a god.) Presumably he wants to become a spirit partly because he doubts that he has an immortal soul. To become a spirit is to gain immortality – earlier he had become disillusioned with medicine because it could not teach him how to raise the dead or make men live eternally (lines 54–55). In addition, he wants superhuman powers. The idea of becoming a god would have been less incomprehensible to an Elizabethan than to us. They knew that the great men of the Greek and Roman past had been worshiped as gods, sometimes during their own lifetimes. They knew that Lucifer had sought to be a god, which is what had brought him into conflict with God himself.

In *Doctor Faustus*, Marlowe set out to dramatize a recent, popular narrative that most of his contemporaries would have accepted as literally true, the story of Doctor John Faustus. But he added to that story a number of themes that were his own contribution: the idea of sex as divine, which was surely based on Marlowe's own experience; the idea, perhaps derived from the Spira story, that Calvinism can lead to despair, and that this despair can find itself in tension with an ineradicable, inexhaustible, constantly reborn hope; the idea of an internal, psychological conflict between good and evil, probably derived from Scot; the idea that Faustus aspired not only to be a spirit, but to be a God, perhaps derived from the Family of Love.[17] These were small and subtle changes in a script, which for the most part, remained remarkably faithful to its source. But they turned an entirely predictable (if remarkably well-written) story into a tense and thrilling drama, a drama in which orthodox Christian teaching triumphs, but in which Faustus has all the best lines.

---

[17] On the Family of Love: Christopher Marsh, *The Family of Love in English Society, 1550–1630* (Cambridge: Cambridge University Press, 1994); and Peter Lake, *The Boxmaker's Revenge* (Manchester: Manchester University Press, 2000).

Early Faust Music

Osman Durrani

The earliest music associated with Faust was composed almost before the ink had dried on the Faust Book of 1587. Fritz Beer's 'Faustus conjures twelve students' and 'Faustus silences the howling peasants' were set to music in 1588 (Bolte, Mertens). The former tells of students who were brawling in two groups of 7 and 5. Faustus considers the larger group to have an unfair advantage and makes them blind, so that they cannot recognise who is fighting against whom. The noisy peasants are given a similar lesson in civic virtue: they have their jaws fixed wide open as a punishment for their unruly behaviour. The tunes to these two moral ditties were by two prominent Mastersingers, Heinrich Frauenlob and Heinrich Mügling (Aign, 15).

An English ballad was granted permission by Bishop Aymler in the same year. Walter Aign assumes it was identical with 'The Just Judgment of God shew'd upon Dr John Faustus', a ballad printed on a broadsheet around 1670 and believed to be based on a much earlier source.

This, too, was not an original composition, but sung to the tune of 'Fortune my Foe'. A number of similar items have been preserved from later years. The ballads normally purport to illustrate a single episode from the magician's life; they were sometimes accompanied by a woodcut image and usually sold as broadsheets.

Works Cited

Walter Aign, *Faust im Lied*, Stuttgart: K. Theens, 1975.

Johannes Bolte, 'Ein Meisterlied von Doktor Faust', *Euphorion* 1 (1894), 787 f.

Volker Mertens, 'Doktor Faust im Meisterlied', in Franz V. Spechtler (ed.), *Lyrik des ausgehenden 14. und 15. Jahrhunderts*. Amsterdam: Rodopi, 1984, 97–114.

The Juſt Judgment of GOD ſhew'd upon Dr. *John Fauſtus.*

To the Tune of, *Fortune my Foe,* &c.

ALL Chriſtian Men give Ear a while to me,
How I am plung'd in Pain, but cannot ſee:
I liv'd a Life, the like did none before,
Forſaking Chriſt, and I am damn'd therefore.

At *Wertemburgh,* a Town in *Germany,*
There was I born and bred of good Degree,
Of honeſt Stock, which afterwards I ſham'd,
Accurſt therefore, for *Fauſtus* was I nam'd.

In learning high my Uncle brought up me,
And made me Doctor of Divinity:
And when he dy'd he left me all his Wealth,
Which curſed Gold did hinder my Soul's Health.

Then did I ſhun the Holy Bible Book,
Nor on God's Word would never after look;
But ſtudied the accurſed Conjuration,
Which was the Cauſe of my utter Damnation.

The Devil in Fryers Weeds appeared to me,
And ſtraight to my Requeſt he did agree,
That I might have all Things at my Deſire,
I gave him Soul and Body for his Hire.

Twice did I make my tender Flefh to bleed,
Twice with my Blood I wrote the Devil's Deed,
Twice wretchedly I Soul and Body fold,
To live in Pleafure, and do what Things I would.

For four and twenty Years this Bond was made,
And then at length my Soul for it was paid;
Time ran away, and yet I never thought,
How dear my Soul our Saviour Chrift had bought.

Would I at firft been made a Beaft by Kind,
Then had not I fo vainly fet my Mind;
Or would not when Reafon began to bloom,
Some darkfome Den had been my deadly Tomb.

Wo to the Day of my Nativity!
Wo to the Time that once did fofter me!
And wo unto the Hand that fealed the Bill!
Wo to myfelf the Caufe of all my Ill!

The Time I pafs'd away with much Delight,
'Mongft Princes, Peers, and many a worthy Knight,
I wrought fuch Wonders by my Magick Skill,
That all the World may talk of *Fauftus* ftill.

The Devil carried me up in the Skie,
Where I did fee how all the World did lie:
I went about the World in eight Days Space,
And then return'd into my native Place.

What Pleafure I did wifh to pleafe my Mind,
He did perform, as Bond and Seal did bind:
The Secrets of the Stars and Planets told,
Of Earth and Sea, with Wonders manifold.

When four and twenty Years was almoft run,
I thought on Things that then was paft and done;
How that the Devil will foon claim his Right,
And carry me to everlafting Night.

Then all too late I curft my wicked Deed,
The Dread thereof does make my Heart to bleed:
All Days and Hours I mourned wond'rous fore,
Repenting then of all Things done before.

I then did wifh both Sun and Moon to ftay,
All Times and Seafons never to decay:
Then had my Time ne'er come to dated End,
Nor Soul and Body down to Hell defcend.

At laft when I had but one Hour to come,
I turn'd the Glafs for my laft Hour to run:
And call'd in learned Men to comfort me,
But Faith was gone, and none could fuccour me.

By Twelve o'Clock was almoft out,
My grieved Confcience then began to doubt:
I pray'd the Studious to ftay in Chamber by,
But as they ftaid they heard a doleful cry.

Then prefently they came into the Hall,
Whereas my Brains were caft againft the Wall;
Both Arms and Legs in Pieces they did fee,
My Bowels gone, there was an End of me.

You Conjurors and damned Witches all,
Example take by my unhappy Fall:
Give not your Souls and Bodies unto Hell,
See that the fmalleft Hair you do not fell.

But hope in Chrift his Kingdom you may gain,
Where you fhall never fear fuch mortal Pain;
Forfake the Devil and all his crafty Ways,
Embrace true Faith that never more decays.

FINIS.

Transformations of the Faust Theme

Klaus L. Berghahn

English theater troupes brought [Marlowe's famous play *Tragical History of D. Faustus*] to the continent where it became tattered, ending up as a puppet play in the 18th century. The same happened to the original chapbook, which underwent numerous editions and revisions until it reached the 18th century in two different versions: one by Pfitzer, which is still fairly close to the original; the other by the "Christlich Meinender" which is basically a plot summary. It was in these distorted or trivialized forms that the serious writers of the 18th century rediscovered the poetic and philosophical qualities of the Faust myth. Faust seemed to be the ideal character for the Age of Enlightenment, during which the attitudes toward faith and knowledge changed radically, and intellectual curiosity became the noblest of human characteristics. "A desire for knowledge is the natural feeling of mankind," states Dr. Johnson, "and every human being, whose mind is not debauched, will be willing to give all he has, to get knowledge."[18] This, from now on, is Faust's case. For a secularized age that measures everything against the yardstick of reason, even the Devil loses his sting: he becomes "part of that force which would do ever evil, and does ever good," as Goethe later put it.[19]

By the time Lessing became aware of the Faust theme and began working on it, many writers seemed to be busy with it, which made Gottsched, the archenemy of popular literature, rather nervous.[20] Lessing wanted to wait to publish his *Faust* until all the other versions including Goethe's had appeared – this in order to make their authors waste paper. He waited too long – although it may be true that a finished manuscript was lost in the mail between Dresden and Wolfenbüttel in 1775, as an often-repeated story has it. What came down to us are only fragments of Lessing's work: one scene which he published in his famous 17th *Literaturbrief* in 1759, and the so-called "Berlin Scenario," a summary of an opening sequence consisting of a Prologue and four scenes published posthumously by his brother Karl in 1786. In addition to these five pages and many letters that mention Lessing's work on Faust over a period of twenty years, we have two reliable accounts (by Lessing's friends C. F. von Blanckenburg and

---

[18] Quoted from J. W. Smeed, *Faust in Literature* (Oxford, 1975), 18.
[19] Erich Trunz, ed., *Goethes Faust*, 5th ed. (Hamburg, 1959), v. 1336.
[20] Robert Petsch, *Lessings Faustdichtung* (Heidelberg, 1911), 51 ff.

J. J. Engel) of the tragedy's outline and its ending, Faust's redemption.[21] There is not much to work with, and interpretation here seems to become an art of overcoming absence. Nothing loftier than to speculate about a text that hardly exists, one might say. Not quite! For Lessing's labor with the Faust myth is clearly reconstructible.

It is quite obvious why Lessing is fascinated by Faust, who represents the modern myth of the human quest for knowledge and truth – a symbol with which he himself could easily identify. That Lessing's conception of his *Faust* tragedy is closely, if not exclusively, connected with the modern drive for knowledge becomes clear when we look at the "Berlin Scenario." Its prologue shows an assembly of devils in an old cathedral where various demons report on their day's work to Beelzebub. At the end, they also talk about Faust, who seems to be indifferent to any temptation, whereupon one devil promises to make him the prey of hell within twenty-four hours.

Faust's desire for knowledge, which is his only flaw, will bring him down. It seems that Lessing wanted to develop Faust's tragic fate entirely out of this passion for truth. Faust achieves his goal with the help of the Devil which at the same time guarantees his downfall. In contrast to the traditional myth where Faust seeks every pleasure of the world – lust, power, and wealth – and pays for it after twenty-four years, Lessing's Faust is only consumed by one pure desire which is not a vice. In accordance with Aristotle's and his own concepts of tragedy, ἁμαρτία should lead to the tragic ending. But this Lessing could not do. He could not sacrifice Faust for the noblest of all human qualities. Faust must be saved at any price. In the best of all worlds, which is ruled by reason, the passion for knowledge had to be vindicated. Here, exposition and ending clearly conflict with each other; the result of Faust's sole flaw, which, of necessity, must lead to his tragic downfall, can be eliminated only by a trick: Faust merely dreamt his excesses (of the missing middle part) and the Devil is cheated out of his work. What the devils carry away is just a "phantom" of Faust.[22]

This is a clear break with the damnation of Faust. The modern playwright working with the old myth could not follow through on the premise that Faust's thirst for knowledge should end in hell. Faust must be saved even if only a *deus ex machina* can save him, and even if the concept of tragedy suffers. Here, Lessing's philosophy triumphs over his dramatic

---

[21] Ibid., 32–39 ("Texte"), 40–50 ("Die wichtigsten Zeugnisse").
[22] Ibid., 47.

art. He must have felt this contradiction but did not know how to solve
the problem. The Faust myth was no longer suitable for a modern tragedy, or else it had to be altered drastically, in order to be altered drastically, in order to fit the anthropology of Enlightenment. Faust's damnation had to be revoked even if the tragedy came dangerously close to
becoming a morality play. This is precisely the solution which Engel's outline offers us. Faust has received and understood the "warning." A very
heavy-handed and didactic ending, unlike Lessing's dramatic art; and we
wonder whether Faust has renounced even his desire for knowledge and
become a pious philistine. Lessing's break with the tradition is clearly visible, but the fragments and endings as reported by his friends leave too
many questions unanswered.

There is one more observation which could explain why Lessing was
unable to finish his *Faust*. Granted, he felt congenial and sympathetic to
Faust's desire for truth. But, unlike Faust who wanted the whole truth at
once – or, at least, in twenty-four hours – Lessing followed the principle
of gradualism, as we know from his famous *Duplik* of 1778.

In Lessing's fragment published in his 17th *Literaturbrief*, [Faust]
chooses from among the seven devils the fastest one, who is as fast as the
change from good to evil. Faust has not only "too much desire for knowledge," he also wants to have it in the shortest time. For Lessing, in
contrast, the process of *Bildung* is slow and includes detours. Faust is impatient; he wants to accelerate time and cannot reach the future fast
enough. He is unlike Lessing who knows that the "education of mankind" is a gradual process which cannot be finished in one generation,
and certainly not by one man – even if his name is Faust. It seems, in the
end, that Faust could not be the ideal character or myth for Lessing,
whose understanding of time was not limited to one life.

Maybe it is a blessing for German literature that Lessing finished his
Nathan der Weise instead of his *Faust*, and that he left the Faust myth for
Goethe to work with. To do justice to Goethe's *Faust*, on which he la-
bored – off and on – for almost sixty years, a complete interpretation has
to include two perspectives. First, all major and minor changes of the old
myth must be taken into consideration, and, second, they must be interpreted in view of the changing circumstances of Goethe's life. His work
on and with this myth is a constant searching for, and selecting of, images
to understand and create his own world, to find answers to the changing
times and to social or political developments; it is an instrument of world
orientation. To analyze Goethe's reinterpretation of the Faust myth
would mean nothing less than a reconstruction of his literary life between
1772 and 1832, as it unfolds within the interrelation of myth and history.

Goethe worked so freely with the old myth, and integrated it so completely into his world view, that his *Faust* replaced the old myth. Even passages which are largely taken from, or inspired by, the chapbook were transformed into a new symbolic meaning. A case in point, which I can mention only in passing, is the Helena subplot.

Goethe was well aware of his indebtedness to the old legend, as he called it. He considered the Helena episodes "a significant motif," which he used for *Faust II*. The material similarities between Spies's chapbook and Goethe's *Faust* are striking indeed. In both texts, Helena appears twice: first, she is brought back to life in order to satisfy the curiosity of Faust's students, or to entertain the guests at the emperor's palace; then she appears a second time, in order to stay with Faust, become his mistress, and have a son by him. What for Spies are but examples of Faust's trickery and lust becomes in Goethe's adaptation the "Classical Walpurgis Night." For Goethe, Helena symbolizes the reincarnation of classical antiquity: first, as a shadow, a memory of the past; then, in her real appearance, as an appropriation of the past for the present. She is, in short, the embodiment of Goethe's poetic philosophy of history. For Faust, the whole Helena episode is just one important moment in his development: he experiences beauty in its highest and most sensuous form, and at the same time recognizes that he cannot possess and hold her, that beauty is merely an illusion. In the end, he holds only Helena's veil in his hands.

To come back to our original question: How does Goethe use the Faust myth and what does its transformation mean? Of the numerous changes he made, I have to limit myself to the three most important ones: the beginning, the Gretchen tragedy, and the ending.

We enter Goethe's *Faust* through three prologues. These are: the "Dedication" (a personal reflection on his work when Goethe returned to it in 1797), the "Prelude in the Theater" (an improvisational scene between a theater director, a poet, and a "merry person," or harlequin figure, which puts the play into the social context of the literary life of the time), and the "Prologue in Heaven." Of these three, the "Prologue in Heaven" is, from our perspective, the most important one since it provides a transcendental frame for the *Faust* tragedy. It is that of the theater as the whole world, *theatrum mundi*, where man stands between God and the Devil and where the sequence of acts will show what choices he has and how he chooses; it is history presented as salvation history, and man's passage through the world embedded in a morality play. From God's perspective, the world is a stage and Faust is merely a player. This rather traditional theatrical device, with all its metaphysical implications, already prepares the audience for the solution: Faust shall not fall prey to the Devil.

There is no question that God is the superior character who knows Faust and is confident that he will win his wager with Mephistopheles – if it is a bet at all. The stage is set; enter Faust.

Faust's famous opening monologue is a desperate negation of human intelligence and science, which leads him to skepticism and even cynicism. Wherever he restlessly searches he faces nothing but limitations. Or as Goethe himself characterized the situation of his hero in 1826:

> The character of Faust, at the exalted level to which our new version has raised him out of the rough old folktale, represents a man who [feels] impatient and uncomfortable within the general limits of earthly life, ... a mind which, turning in every direction, always returns in a more unhappy state. Such a disposition is similar to the modern one.[23]

Goethe's characterization is, as his usually are, rather general, but it bridges the gap between Renaissance and Enlightenment. Faust becomes a symbol of modern man. His thirst for knowledge is not only frustrated by the limits of scholastic sciences but also by the narrow confines of his life. His "narrow Gothic chamber" is the most powerful image of Faust's limitations. If we look at this scene from the perspective of its origin, it bespeaks the spirit of Goethe's *Prometheus* fragment of 1772, the protest of the self that wants to be God. From a modern perspective, and in the context of the drama as a whole, it seems that Faust suffers from lack of knowledge and of self-fulfillment. Therefore, *Faust* is not just the tragedy of a modern scientist but that of modern man at large, who suffers from want of wholeness, of totality. If this inner conflict is not to end in despair or suicide, Faust needs some help. That's where Mephisto comes in.

He offers Faust his services, yet not in the form of the well-known pact, but as a wager – the second one in the play, which, like the first, underscores its central motif: Faust's striving for total understanding and his longing for self-perfection. It is, however, Faust who proposes the wager.

[The] central point of Faust's wager [is] the fulfilled moment. It keeps his relation to Mephisto a mystery, making his life an experiment. Already here, the misunderstanding between them begins, for Faust seeks knowledge, understanding of the world, development of all his potentials, and aims for a utopian moment of self-perfection, whereas Mephisto wants only to satisfy Faust's lust for life and to drag him "through shallow insignificance." What Faust desires, Mephisto cannot understand or satisfy.

---

[23] Zweiter Entwurf zu einer Ankündigung der "Helena," Dezember 1826; in Trunz, *Goethes Faust*, 438.

Goethe's important changes of the old myth, the "Prologue in Heaven" with its wager and Faust's bet with Mephisto, anticipate the ending: Faust, the modern man, will be saved, and the Devil will be betrayed twice. Goethe knew what he was doing when he changed the beginning.

The second and most radical change of the Faust myth is more difficult to deal with. How is one to explain that the tragedy of an infanticide constitutes part of the Faust drama? Strictly speaking, the Faust myth and the Gretchen tragedy do not fit together. And yet, when we speak of Faust, common knowledge has it that Gretchen's tragedy comes to mind as well. Goethe made it possible. The old chapbook, of course, mentions nothing of this sort. When Faust, once his dusty academic career and his monastic life-style are behind him, becomes aware of his sexual desires, he wants to marry. The Devil has a hard time convincing Faust that this isn't necessary. He will provide him each night with a new mistress. Faust accepts, and the episode ends with Faust trembling in anticipation. There is only one hint in Pfitzer's *Faust* book of 1674 of Faust falling in love with a beautiful yet poor maiden. But nothing more – no seduction, no infanticide, and, least of all, no tragedy that leads to heaven. No, the old myth did not inspire Goethe's Gretchen tragedy. It has other roots, roots which are closer to his own literary and existential experiences.[24]

The Gretchen tragedy is the central part of the oldest formation of *Faust*, the so-called *Urfaust* which Goethe brought to Weimar in 1775, read to small circles, but never published. It is a bourgeois tragedy in typical Storm-and-Stress fashion. As we know from Goethe's *Dichtung und Wahrheit*, Lessing's tragedy *Emilia Galotti* (1772) had a tremendous impact on the younger generation of writers. The Storm-and-Stress playwrights radicalized the new genre by making the plot contemporary and by presenting the tragic conflict as a class conflict: a young maiden of the middle, or lower-middle, class is seduced by a nobleman; when she is pregnant he deserts her; in despair, and under social pressure, she kills the newborn, and as the law dictates, she is condemned and executed. That is Gretchen's case even though Faust only appears to her as an aristocrat – but he certainly acts like one. Biographical evidence from the years 1771 to 1772 allows us to speculate about Goethe's model in real life: Susanna Margaretha Brandt, who was tried for the murder of her newborn and executed in Frankfurt. She claimed that her seduction was the work of the Devil, who even spoke to her. All of this, and more, explains Goethe's interest in the Gretchen tragedy; it fails, however, to explain why he con-

---

[24] Valters Nollendorfs, *Der Streit um den Urfaust* (The Hague, 1967).

nected this tragedy, which could easily stand on its own, with the Faust complex. Goethe felt the discrepancy, and for a long time was unable to finish the first part. In 1790, as part of the first edition of his collected works, he published *Faust* as a fragment. Only in 1806 did he finish *Faust I*, which gives us an idea of how he integrated the tragedy of Gretchen.

Structurally, the two segments are connected by the actions of the protagonist, who experiences the "enjoyment of life" in the "small world" of Gretchen before taking off into the higher regions of the "great world."[25] In the finished version of *Faust I*, the new scene "Witch's Kitchen" bridges the gap between the Faust and the Gretchen episodes. Faust, rejuvenated by the witch's potion – let's say, made younger by thirty years – will soon "see Helena in every woman" (2604), as Mephisto remarks. And the first woman who crosses Faust's path in the following "Street" scene is precisely Gretchen. Mephisto cannot foresee that Faust will fall in love with Gretchen. What on Mephisto's part was meant to be a stepping-stone to the "enjoyment of life" becomes for Faust personal love, and thus complicates their relationship. To make this unmistakably clear, Goethe injected another new scene, "Forest and Cave," where Faust contemplates his ecstasy of love and its contradictions, while at the same time, in a parallel scene, Gretchen at the spinning wheel sings of her love, which transforms during her song into desire. But Faust's restlessness and Mephisto's cynical commentaries on Faust's love already anticipate Gretchen's tragedy. When she is finally ruined, Mephisto wants to distract the guilt-ridden Faust with the spectacle of the Walpurgis Night. This third new scene ends with Faust's vision of Gretchen, a moment of ἀναγνώρισις, which brings back both his love and the recognition of her fate. In a rage, Faust tries to rescue Gretchen from the dungeon, but she, in the twilight of despair and madness, refuses to follow him and Mephisto, whom she senses to be the Devil. Gretchen surrenders herself to the judgment of God while Mephisto drags Faust off to what seems to be his damnation. Here, the last important change occurs. When Mephisto proclaims: "She is condemned," a voice from above answers: "She is redeemed" (4611). Gretchen's salvation anticipates Faust's, who follows Mephisto on a journey through the "great world." Thus, the Gretchen episode is now fully integrated into the *Faust* drama. What Mephisto intended as sexual enjoyment of life and the first step down to hell has been transformed into personal love and the first step toward heaven. Faust's love for Gretchen, which is inscribed on his body and mind, becomes

---

[25] Schema zu "Faust" (1797–1799?), in *Goethes Faust*, 427.

part of his life experience and of his self-development. The Gretchen tragedy foreshadows, as do the other changes of the original myth, Faust's redemption.

What a miraculous ending for him who had moved from one extreme to another, this man of action responsible for outrageous acts! And the list in long: Faust is responsible for the deaths of Gretchen's mother, of her brother, of Gretchen herself; for a paper money fraud, the annihilation of an army, piracy, exploitation, slave labor; and, finally, for the murder of Philemon and Baucis – this Faust is to be redeemed? He is not the Faust whom Lessing would have saved. Goethe's Faust would rightly deserve the verdict: *In aeternum damnatus est!* Instead, Maria in person appears as *dea ex machina*, and Faust's sinful acts are covered with the veil of love and grace. There is much room for metaphysical speculation and cheerful misunderstanding. And yet, there seems to be more than meets the skeptic's eye; otherwise, the quarrel about the conclusion of *Faust* would not have attracted the attention of so many illustrious spirits. And let us not forget that the finale of *Faust* is Goethe's poetic testament. These are his sacred last words – piety seems to be in order.

Since my interpretation of Goethe's *Faust* rests on the premise that the two wagers in the beginning and the Gretchen tragedy prefigure the ending, I have to make my final interpretative move. Clearly, Faust's end is a radical break with the myth. As Goethe already knew from Lessing's fragments, Faust could no longer be condemned in a secular age like that of Enlightenment, when hell had lost its chill and the Devil his sting. In a letter to K. E. Schubarth of 1820, Goethe states his intention: "You felt correctly about the ending of the play. Mephistopheles is only permitted to win half of the wager, and when the other half of the guilt rests with Faust, then the Old Man can use his right of grace to the merriest of endings."[26] Judging from Goethe's intention, the wager in heaven – half won, half lost – decides Faust's fate: mercy comes before justice. The natural order of things vanishes and is replaced by a new order we do not yet know. These are the metaphysics of *Faust* as Adorno sees them.[27]

The outcome of the second wager, the one between Faust and Mephisto, is more hotly debated. The theme of this wager is the moment of fulfillment, which Faust seems to have reached (11581 ff.). Mephisto triumphs. But is this really the moment he has been waiting for? Mephisto

---

[26] Goethe to Karl Ernst Schubarth, 3 November 1820, in Trunz, *Goethes Faust*, 433.

[27] Theodor W. Adorno, "Zur Schlußszene des Faust," in his *Noten zur Literatur II* (Frankfurt, 1961), 7–18.

takes for real what Faust is only anticipating. Goethe's language is quite precise here: Faust speaks of "foretasting," and he uses the optative. Faust's moment of fulfillment is merely a vision; what he foresees has not yet been experienced.

Faust's absolute striving, which could not be satisfied even by the presence of Helena, comes to rest when he envisions his utopia: a free people on free land. As with any vision of a promised land, the content, or even the contours, of Faust's utopia are undetermined; and yet, freedom is the magic word that gives imagination latitude. That Goethe had a socialist utopia in mind is rather doubtful.[28] Bloch, who is the legitimate father of this interpretation, concentrates on the utopian moment when the "not-yet" becomes visible on the horizon, while he calls the content of Faust's vision "capitalistic."[29] One should not overburden Goethe's famous line, and certainly not try to reconstruct a blueprint for Goethe's utopia from it. One should, however, not overlook Goethe's irony, either: the old Faust is already blind, and his blindness does not make him a prophet – on the contrary. When he gives his final speech, he imagines that his workers are tilling the land, while actually they are digging his grave. Faust's illusion of his highest moment is also his last illusion. And one should certainly not forget that this is not yet the ending of *Faust*. The drama does not end with Faust's utopian moment, nor with his death, but with his ascension to heaven.

Therefore, Heinz Schlaffer seems to be right when he stresses once more the importance of Gretchen or, better still, of love, in the final scenes.[30] In this metaphysical "liturgy of love" (Schlaffer), it is Gretchen, as a penitent, who leads Faust to higher spheres, and it is she who educates him now (12090), Gretchen completes Faust's educational journey in heaven. So much for Goethe's apotheosis of woman eternal.

Or is it not even that? Is there underneath all the metaphysical symbolism yet another message, a final myth? Let us once more recall what Faust stands for. He is a man who defies natural limits and restlessly strives for the absolute. He wants to experience the cumulative experience of mankind, in order to enrich and expand his own self. For a restless character like this, who longs for self-fulfillment, one life is far too short. Even Mephisto, viewing Faust's corpse, seems to feel that (11595f.). Since only

---

28 Thomas Metscher, "Faust und die Ökonomie," in *Vom Faustus bis Karl Valentin* (Berlin, 1976 [*Das Argument*, AS 3]), 28–155.

29 Ernst Bloch, "Faust, Makrokosmos, Verweile doch, du bist so schön," in his *Das Prinzip Hoffnung* (Frankfurt, 1973), 1188–1194.

30 Heinz Schlaffer, "Fausts Ende," *Das Argument* 99 (1976): 772–779.

Faust's earthly path ends there, does his continued existence in heaven not suggest more than just redemption, does it not also imply immortality as a means of self-perfection? Lessing's eternal optimism, in the last sentence of his *Education of Mankind*, comes to mind again. Perhaps Faust's end is just another variation on the same theme contemplated by Kant, Schopenhauer, and many other contemporaries, too. Goethe, confronted with his own demise, gives Faust this chance. Faust's immortality is Goethe's final myth.

The Faust myth reached its most artistic and symbolic form in Goethe's *opus magnum*. Goethe's work on this myth is comparable only to what Hesiod and Homer did for Greek mythology. His classical form of the Faust myth has inspired many creative minds in literature, art, and music to work with it and transform it again. However, this new work on the Faust myth does not, and cannot, continue *ad infinitum*. As we know from Jolles and Blumenberg, a myth can also be brought to an end. For the Faust myth, that has certainly happened in this century. I think of Paul Valéry's *Mon Faust* and Thomas Mann's *Doktor Faustus*, of Hanns Eisler's *Faust* libretto and Volker Braun's *Hinze und Kunze*. When Günther Anders states categorically that Faust is dead, he implies that the Faust myth, certainly as a German myth, has outlived its usefulness as a symbol for Germany's highest and darkest period. And yet – what if there were still something to say?

Documents

I. Description of a Faust Performance in Danzig in 1668.
Found in the Diary of Georg Schröder, Councilman of Danzig.[1]

First Pluto comes out of hell and summons one devil after the other –
the tobacco devil, the bawdy devil, and among others the cunning devil –
and gives them orders to deceive people to the best of their ability. Following this it develops that Dr. Faust, discontented with ordinary wisdom,
acquires books on magic and conjures the devils into his service. In doing
so he investigates their speed and wishes to choose the speediest. It is not
enough for him that they be as quick as stags, or clouds, or the wind; he
wishes one who is as quick as the thoughts of man. And after the canny
devil has represented himself as meeting this requirement, Faust demands
that he serve him for twenty-four years, in return for which Faust would
surrender himself to the devil. This the canny devil will by no means do,
but he refers the proposal to Pluto, and when the latter is agreed, the canny
devil enters into a compact with Faust, who signs a contract in blood.

Later a hermit tries to warn Faust, but in vain. All Faust's conjurings
turn out well. He causes Charlemagne to appear to him, and likewise the
beautiful Helen, with whom he has his pleasure. Finally his conscience
awakes and he counts the hours until the clock strikes twelve. Then he ad-
dresses his servant and warns him to abstain from magic. Soon Pluto
comes and sends his devils to fetch Dr. Faust. This is done and they throw
him into the air and tear him to pieces. It is also presented how he is tormented in hell, where he is drawn up and down and these words of fire are
seen: Accusatus est, judicatus est, condemnatus est (he has been accused,
judged, and condemned).

II. Announcement of a Performance of Faust in Bremen.[2]

"The Life and Death of the great archconjurer Dr. John Faust, excellently
presented, with Pickelhäring comedy, from beginning to end." The fol-

---

[1] See W. Creizenach, *Versuch einer Geschichte des Volksschauspiels vom Doctor Faust.*
Halle, 1878, p. 5.

[2] Cf. Creizenach, op. cit., p. 6 f. The performance was by a company of "Saxon
high German comedians," probably in the ninth decade of the seventeenth
century. The spectacular features advertised point towards the beginning of the
Italian influence.

lowing scenes are offered for the admiration of the public: Pluto rides in
the air on a dragon. Then Faust appears and conjures the spirits. Pickelhäring wants to gather money but is tormented by all sorts of magic birds
in the air. Following this, Dr. Faust gives a banquet at which the center-
piece (épergne) is tranformed into all kinds of wonderful figures, so that
human beings, dogs, cats, and other animals come out of a pastry and fly
through the air. Then a fire breathing raven, in flight, announces to Faust
his approaching death and Faust is carried away by the spirits. Hell is pic-
tured, adorned with beautiful fireworks. Finally, the whole action is once
more presented in shadow pictures, in connection with which there is a
masquerade of six persons, a Spaniard, two jugglers, a schoolmaster, a
farmer and a farmer's wife, who put on an especially humorous dance ...

III. Announcement of a Performance in Hamburg.[3]

The court players of His Royal Highness, the King of Poland and Elector
of Saxony, and the Prince of Brunswick, Lüneburg and Wolfenbüttel, and
of the Prince of Schleswig-Holstein will present today, by permission of
the authorities, a German play, entitled: The impious life and terrible end
of the world renowned archconjurer Dr. John Faust. The following features will form part of the production:

A great courtyard in the palace of Pluto on the rivers Lethe and Acheron in Hades. Charon comes sailing in his boat on the river and with him
on a fiery dragon appears Pluto, accompanied by his whole hellish retinue
and spirits.

Dr. Faust's study and library. An attractive celestial spirit sings the following affecting aria to the accompaniment of soft music:

Faust! what hast thou undertaken?
Oh, alas! what hast thou done?
Hast thou all good sense forsaken?
Thinkest thou no more upon
The eternal grief and pain,
And the bliss ne'er known again?

---

[3] July 7, 1738, by Johann Neuber, husband of the actress Karolina Neuber, and,
with her, director of the famous Neuber troupe. To please Gottsched, Frau
Neuber had burned Harlekin or Hans Wurst publicly on the Leipzig stage in
1737 as a sign that henceforth Hans Wurst and all he stood for was banished
from the stage!!! The program is printed in Geissler, *Gestaltungen des Faust*,
Munchen, 1927. Vol. 1, pages 222–223.

Does the prick of sinful longing
Far outweigh your soul's delight?
Wouldst thou be to hell belonging
When thou shouldst in heaven abide?
Holdest thou the sinner's groan
Dearer than the heavenly throne?

Is there naught your mind can alter?
Oh, so gaze on heaven above
If perchance its bounteous water
May arouse in you God's love.
Let it work upon your heart
And in heaven seek your part.

A raven comes out of the air and fetches Dr. Faust's signature.

Hans Wurst comes by chance upon his master, Dr. Faust, as he is engaged in conjuring. He has to stand still and cannot move from the spot until he has taken off his shoes. The shoes dance together merrily.

An impertinent courtier, who makes fun of Dr. Faust, gets horns on his forehead in sight of all.

A peasant buys a horse from Dr. Faust and as soon as he rides it, the horse changes into a bundle of hay. The peasant wants to call Dr. Faust to account for this, Faust pretends to be asleep, the peasant pulls at him and tears out his leg.

Hans Wurst wants to have a lot of money and, to please him, Mephistophiles permits him to cause a shower of gold.

Beautiful Helen, to the accompaniment of pleasant music, sings to Dr. Faust an aria which he does not like, because in it she prophesies his destruction.

Dr. Faust takes leave of his servant Christopher Wagner. Hans Wurst also clears out and the spirits carry away Dr. Faust during a display of fireworks.

The palace of Pluto in Hades is again seen. The furies have Dr. Faust and hold a ballet around him because they have succeeded in bringing him to their realm.

The rest will be pleasanter to see than to read about.

IV. Announcement of a Performance of Faust in Frankfurt a.M.[4]

With the gracious permission of the very noble and wise Council, the High German Comedians located here will again open their theater today and present the familiar but none the less favorite tragedy entitled Ex doctrina Interitus, or Unfortunate Learning, presented in the life and wretched death of Dr. John Faust. With Hans Wurst, a servant tormented by many kinds of spirits. – Noteworthy scenes which are presented: (1) Pluto appears, traveling through the air on a dragon. (2) Hans Wurst comes into Faust's magic circle and is tormented by the spirits. (3) Mephistophiles comes flying through the air into Faust's room. (4) Faust shows the following to the Duke of Parma: the torments of Tantalus; the vulture of Tityos; the stone of Sisyphus; the death of Pompey. (5) A woman is publicly changed into a fury. (6) To the accompaniment of a ballet of spirits, Faust is torn to piece by the furies. In conclusion there is a ballet and a merry comedy.

V. Announcement of a Performance in Frankfurt a.M.[5]

With the gracious permission of the very noble and wise Council of the imperial, electoral, and commercial free city of Frankfurt, the newly built stage will be opened today under the direction of Mr. Joseph von Kurz. There will be presented a grand mechanical comedy, old, world famous, often staged and presented in various ways. But it is to be presented by us today in such fashion that the like will hardly have been seen put on by other companies. Entitled: In doctrina interitus or The infamous life and terrible end of the world famed and universally known archconjurer Dr. John Faust, professor of theology at Wittenberg. According to the epigram:

Multi de stygia sine fronte palude jocantur
Sed vereor fiat, ne jocus iste focus.

That is:

Many but jest at hell and scoff at fears,
Until their brazen laughter's turned to tears.

---

[4] Cf. Creizenach, op. cit., p. 10. The performance was given in 1742 by a company of German actors, directed by Walleroti.

[5] Cf. Creizenach, op. cit., p. 11. The performance was given in October, 1767, under the directorship of Joseph Felix von Kurz.

Together with Crispin, a dismissed students'fag, a traveller evilly beset by spirits, the tormented comrade of Mephistopheles, an unfortunate aerial traveller, a laughable settler of his debts, a natural wizard and a foolish night watchman. Here follow the individual attractions, mechanical contrivances, transformations and scenes. (1) Faust's learned discussion in his study as to whether the study of theology or of nigromancy is preferable. (2) Faust's remarkable conjuration in a dark wood at night, at which appear amid thunder and lightning various hellish monsters, spirits, and furies, among whom is Mephistopheles. (3) Crispin, the magic circle, performs laughable tricks with the spirits. (4) Faust's personal contract with hell, which is fetched through the air by a raven. (5) Crispin impudently opens a book in Dr. Faust's library and little devils come out of it. (6) Faust's journey through the air with Mephistopheles. (7) Crispin receives from Mephistopheles a fiery rain of gold. (8) Faust, at the court of the Duke of Parma, presents various noteworthy scenes from biblical and profane history, viz., (1) How Judith cuts off the head of Holofernes on a bed in his tent. (2) How Delilah robs the mighty Samson of his hair and the Philistines overcome Samson. (3) The martyrdom of Titius, whose entrails the ravens devour out of his body. (4) The camp of Goliath who is slain by little David with a stone from a sling. (5) The destruction of Jerusalem, surely a fine spectacle. (9) Faust will make merry with the councillors of the Prince of Parma and conjure horns on the head of one of them. (10) Shows a cemetery or graveyard with many epitaphs and inscriptions. Faust wants to excavate the bones of his dead father and misuse them in his magic, but he is urged to penitence by his father's spirit. (11) Faust is converted, but is again seduced by Mephistopheles through various illusions, in which the mournful cemetery is changed into a pleasure garden. (12) Faust recognized the deception when it is too late. The pleasant park is turned into an open hell and the despairing Faust, after a plaint in verse, is carried to hell by the furies amid thunder and lightning. (13) A ballet of furies. (14) Mephistopheles, to the accompaniment of firewords, draws Faust into the jaws of hell. (15) A great finale of fireworks.

The Puppet-Play
of
Doctor Faust

AN HEROI-COMIC DRAMA IN FOUR ACTS

From the manuscript of the puppet-showman Guido Bonneschky. Published for the first time faithfully in its original form by Wilhelm Hamm, 1850.

DRAMATIS PERSONÆ

FERDINAND, *Duke of Parma*
BIANCA, *his wife*
ORESTES, *his counsellor*
JOHANNES FAUST, *doctor in Wittenberg*
WAGNER, *his famulus*
KASPERLE, *a travelling genius*
MEPHISTOPHELES ⎫
AUERHAHN ⎪
MEXICO ⎪
ALEXO ⎬ *supernatural spirits*
VITZLIPUTZLI ⎪
A GOOD GENIUS ⎭
GOLIATH AND DAVID ⎫
THE CHASTE LUCRETIA ⎪
SAMSON AND DELILAH ⎬ *apparitions*
JUDITH, *with the head of Holofernes* ⎪
HELENA, *the Trojan beauty* ⎭

Act I

FAUST'S *study. To the left is a table on which are lying various books and astronomical instruments. In front of the table stands a magic globe.*

Scene I

FAUST [*sitting alone and reading*]. Varietas delecta ... "Variety in all things shall create joy and pleasure for man." This is truly a beautiful sentence; I have read it often and often, yet it does not reach far enough for the satisfaction of my desire. One man likes this, another likes that, but we have all the impulse in our hearts to grasp at something higher

than we possess. It is true that I might think myself more fortunate
than many of my fellows; lacking wealth, lacking support, I have attained by my own efforts to the rank of doctor, and I have carried on this
profession honourably for eighteen years. But what is all this to me?
Doctor I am, doctor I remain, and beyond that I cannot go in the field
of theology. Ha! That is too little for my spirit, which aims at being re-
vered by posterity. I have resolved to apply myself to necromancy, and
through that to reach my heart's desire – to make my name immortal.

A VOICE TO THE RIGHT [*invisible*]. Faust! Faust! Leave off this project! Pur-
sue the study of theology and you will be the happiest of men!

A VOICE TO THE LEFT. Faust! Leave off the study of theology! Take up
the study of necromancy and you will be the happiest of men!

FAUST. Heaven! What is that? To my intense amazement I hear two invisible voices! One on the right warns me to keep to the study of theology, and says that if I do so I shall be the happiest of men; that on the
left advises me to take up the study of necromancy, and says that if I do
so I shall be the happiest of men. Well, then, I shall follow you, you
voice to the left!

THE VOICE TO THE RIGHT. Woe, O Faustus, to your miserable soul! Ha!
Then you are lost!

THE VOICE TO THE LEFT [*laughs*]. Ha! ha! ha! What a jest!

FAUST. Again do I hear these two voices, one on the right bewailing
and one on the left laughing at me? Yet must I not alter my purpose,
since I feel that only through the study of necromancy can I bring my
desires to satisfaction! Yet again, I shall follow you, you voice to the
left!

Scene II
FAUST *and* WAGNER.

WAGNER. I come to inform your Magnificence that two students gave
me, to be handed to your Magnificence, a book which you have long
wished to possess, since it deals with the study of necromancy.

FAUST. Since yesterday I have been hoping you would bring it me, and
I have been eagerly awaiting it. Where is the book?

WAGNER. I have laid it in your lecture-room.

FAUST. Good! Leave me!

WAGNER. In all humility, your Magnificence, I should like respectfully to
ask about something that worries me.

FAUST. Speak on, my dear Wagner! You know that I have never refused
you anything that lay in my power to give.

WAGNER. Your Magnificence, I would humbly beg you to let me engage a young lad to be taken into your service, for it will be too difficult for me to manage the household and at the same time carry on my studies.

FAUST. Do so, my dear Wagner! It has long been my wish to see you less burdened by the management of the house so that you can apply yourself more freely to your study. You can therefore look round for a young lad, and when you have found a fit person, who can show you good testimonials, you may bring him to me, and I shall make further arrangements with hin.

WAGNER. Very good, your Magnificence! I shall do all in my power to fulfil your commands.

FAUST. Then the book that the students handed over to you is in the lecture-room?

WAGNER. Yes, your Magnificence!

FAUST. Then I will go and see whether it is the same that I have vainly sought to get for so long.   [*Goes out.*

SCENE III

WAGNER. What a noble-minded master is this! What would have become of me without his help? He has taken me, a lonely orphan, into his house, and has always taken such pains over my education and my progress. Can I ever repay him for all his kindness? I think not. But I will work honestly, do all I can to anticipate his wishes, and at least show him that he did not expend his kindnesses in vain, that a thankful heart beats in my bosom for him. I shall therefore go to a good friend of mine and inquire whether perhaps he knows of a suitable young man to enter his service. Accomplishment of a duty is the greatest proof for a man who wishes to show his gratefulness.   [*Goes out.*

SCENE IV

FAUST [*who enters a little earlier with a book in his hand*]. Good man! Just remain as I have found you hitherto and I will truly strive to recompense you for your trust, and to further your fortunes so far as I can. Now, however, I desire also to carry out my resolution to devote myself solely to the study of necromancy by means of this book, and I desire immediately to test this art by a conjuration. "I charge you, you furies of hell, by hell's gates, by Styx and Acheron, to appear immediately before me! Break out, you howling storm, that Ixion's wheel may stop and Prometheus' vulture forget to torment him, and carry out my will! Despair, Fury, and rage – hurl you at my feet!"

Scene V
FAUST, ALEKSO, VITZLIPUTZLI, AUERHAHN, MEXICO
[*hurled in with wild thunder and lightning*]. LATER MEPHISTOPHELES.

FAUST. A pretty crew! Yet you are very negligent! Don't do that again to me! Tell me, you first fury of hell, what's your name?
MEXICO. Mexico.
FAUST. And how quick are you?
MEXICO. As quick as a bullet fired from a gun.
FAUST. You have a great speed, but not enough for me. Vanish!
                                      [MEXICO *disappears through the sky.*
FAUST. And what name have you, hellish fury, and how quick are you?
AUERHAHN. Auerhahn, and I am as quick as the wind.
FAUST. That's very quick, but not enough for me. Vanish!
                        [AUERHAHN *disappears in the same way as* MEXICO *did.*
FAUST. What's your name, hellish spirit?
VITZLIPUTZLI. Vitzliputzli.
FAUST. And how quick are you?
VITZLIPUTZLI. As quick as a ship sailing on the sea.
FAUST. As a ship sailing on the sea? That is a fair speed, but with unfavourable winds it doesn't always reach its goal. Vanish!
                                      [VITZLIPUTZLI *goes off.*
FAUST. Say on, hellish fury – what's your name?
ALEKSO. Alekso.
FAUST. Alekso? And what's your speed?
ALEKSO. I am as quick as a snail.
FAUST. As a snail? So you are truly the slowest of all the hellish spirits? I can't make any use of you at all. Vanish!   [ALEKSO *goes slowly off.*
FAUST. Tolerably slow!   [MEPHISTOPHELES *comes in dressed like a hunter.*
FAUST. Ha! What do I see? A hellish fury in the likeness of a man?
MEPHISTOPHELES. You must know, Faust, that I am a prince of hell, and have the power to assume, and to appear in, whatsoever shape I please.
FAUST. You a prince of hell? What's your name?
MEPHISTOPHELES. Mephistopheles.
FAUST. Mephistopheles? That's a good-sounding name. And how quick are you?
MEPHISTOPHELES. As quick as man's thoughts.

FAUST. As man's thoughts? Ha! That is an extraordinary speed; for I can be with my thoughts one moment in Africa, another in America. Say, hellish fury, if you wish to serve me. I shall promise you to be yours, body and soul, at the end of the time I shall settle on.

MEPHISTOPHELES. Tell me the conditions, Faust, to which I must submit.

FAUST. The first condition is this, that you get me as much money as I ask from you. The second is that you make me a person of consequence among all great men and at all great courts, that you carry me wherever my desire takes me, that you warn me of all dangers. And the third condition is that you tell me before our contract comes to an end and that you obey me for four and twenty years. Are you willing?

MEPHISTOPHELES. Why four and twenty years, Faust? Half of that is enough.

FAUST. Four and twenty years – no less.

MEPHISTOPHELES. Well, I am satisfied. [*Aside*] I'll cheat him all right; he doesn't count on my skill. [*Aloud*] But, Faust, I must leave you just now to tell my prince Pluto of our agreement and ask him whether I may conclude this contract with you.

FAUST. Leave me then! But when will you return to me?

MEPHISTOPHELES. As soon as you think of me, Faust.   [*Goes off.*

FAUST [*alone*]. As soon as I think of you? I ought not certainly to enter into an agreement with a hellish spirit, but it is the only way to accomplish my desires quickly. And have I not sufficient power through my knowledge to get out of his clutches when half the time of the contract is over? Yes, so be it! Yet I feel so weary, so exhausted; this is certainly the result of the exertion of my spirit. I will go into my cabinet to rest for an hour or so, and then I shall carry on my plan with renewed energy.   [*Goes out.*

Scene VI

CASPER [*comes in with a bundle on his back*]. Pox on't! There's travelling for you! I have walked fourteen miles in thirteen days, and only every half-hour I've struck an inn! I've come to-day from – here. Here in my knapsack I have my whole equipage: I have the lining for a new over-coat – the cloth for it, however, is still with the shopkeeper. And here a half-dozen good stockings without heels, and a whole dozen of shirts. The only trouble is that the best of them has got no sleeve, and the eleventh is patched with the twelfth. I bought myself this fine beaver in Leipzig. It cost me twenty-one groschen, and a pair of new turned-up shoes of the latest style, the heels tipped with nails, cost me likewise seventeen groschen six pfennigs. Yes, yes, travelling costs money; I note that my purse has fallen into a galloping consumption. I've been journeying in Holland, Scotland, Brabant, England – but I've got to get there first. But in Danzig, Breslau, Vienna, Regensburg, Friessland, Nürnberg, Dresden – I've never been there at all. I was even three hundred miles behind the New World, but all at once I came on a wall and couldn't go on any farther; then I turned back, and now fortunately I find myself in Wittenberg and shall see whether I can get a situation, for I'm fed up with wandering about. When my father took leave of me said he: "Casper, try only to set your affairs a-swinging." That I've done, for my bundle is so light I could chuck it over the biggest house. But zounds! What sort of an inn is this, where neither landlord nor waiter is to be seen! Hullo, there! Wake up, household! There's a new customer here who wants to get a two-groschen bottle of wine! Mr Landlord! Waiter! What the devil's become of you! Aha! Now I hear some one coming. I'll give him a good fright! [*He creeps under the table.*

SCENE VII
CASPER *and* WAGNER.

WAGNER. I'd like to know how it is that I can't find anybody who wants to go into service. The friends I was with are quite unable to recommend a suitable person to me. [CASPER *comes out and frightens him.*
WAGNER. Oh, heavens! What is it? A strange man in my master's room?
CASPER. You're trembling like an anvil.
WAGNER. Who are you, my friend? How dare you come into this room without getting yourself announced? How did you get in?
CASPER. What a comic question! I came in on my feet, of course! But tell me – is it the habit and practice in Wittenberg for a customer to get himself announced when he wants to buy a bottle of wine?
WAGNER. My friend, you're not in an inn.
CASPER. No?
WAGNER. No, on the contrary, you are standing in the study of his Magnificence Doctor Faust.
CASPER. Well, well! What mistakes one can make! I thought, seeing so many young men go into this house here, that It must be an inn, for there also many folks are constantly going in and out.
WAGNER. That doesn't follow, as you shall hear, for all the young men you saw are students who come daily to the lectures which are delivered in this house.

CASPER. Students? And I thought they were customers! Then I made a pretty mistake! Well, I'll set myself on my feet to find an inn.

[*Makes as if to go off.*

WAGNER. Wait a minute, my friend! To judge by your clothes you are a servant?

CASPER. Yes, I've got my master on my back.

WAGNER. And were have you come from now?

CASPER. From Italy.

WAGNER. Yes, my friend, but Italy is big. What I wanted to know was the precise place of your birth.

CASPER. Oh! You wanted to know the place of my birth?

WAGNER. Yes.

CASPER. I was born in Calabria.

WAGNER. What? In Calabria?

CASPER. Yes, in Calabria.

WAGNER. And what made you leave it?

CASPER. There I was engaged as companion in the house of a study-maker.

WAGNER. In the house of a student I suppose you mean?

CASPER. No, in the house of a study-maker! Surely I know best in whose house I was?

WAGNER. So you were given a situation in the house of a student?

CASPER [*aside*]. Oh, jeminy! Isn't that a stupid fool! But I'll let him be, [*Aloud*] Yes, in the house of a student.

WAGNER. And what made you give up this situation?

CASPER. Well, do you see, that was a curious story. Every morning in Calabria I had to bring into the college for my former master his copy of donatus, a very big book, and every day had to go over a certain plank. Now, one morning in the middle of this plank I met a pretty girl; I made her a couple of compliments, missed my footing, and let the book fall into the water. When my master heard of this he chucked me out of the job.

WAGNER. And then you started to travel?

CASPER. Yes, *per petes apostolorum.*

WAGNER. You've got some kind of a testimonial?

CASPER. Oh, yes! My master wrote a testimonial for me in black letter, chancery hand, and current script so naturally on my back with a gnarled stick that the letters will be legible till domesday.

WAGNER. Do you want to take up service again?

CASPER. Oh, yes! Do you want a servant?

WAGNER. Yes, if only you had good testimonials to show.

CASPER. Well, I've got them on my back.

WAGNER. Yes, sir, but he whose famulus I am will not be satisfied with that.

CASPER. Who are you?

WAGNER. Famulus to Doctor Faust.

CASPER. You are his famulus and want to engage me? Then I'd be a servant's servant?

WAGNER. No, you don't understand me; I will explain. My master has asked me to find a young fellow who wishes to go into service.

CASPER. Oh, that is a different story.

WAGNER. If you desire to enter his service you need only say so.

CASPER. Of course! But listen – there isn't too much work to be done here, is there? Because, do you see, I'm no great friend of work. I have so long a finger on each hand that I'm always knocking myself.

WAGNER. Oh, you'll get a very good place, with good food and wages, for my master is not married. Only one thing I must advise you about – keep secrets!

CASPER. Don't you worry about that! Just you wrap up the secrets I must keep in a piece of roast beef and a bottle of wine, for as long as my mouth has something to chew and my throat to swallow I'm as dumb as a fish.

WAGNER. Well, that will be all right. I can also tell you at once what duties you have. In the morning you must remove the dust from the *repositorium* and the books.

CASPER. Remove the books from the *repositorium* and the dust? Oh, that I can do; I've often done that in the house of my former master.

WAGNER. Then chop wood and draw water; that's all you have to do.

CASPER. Chop wood and draw water? Oh, the devil!

WAGNER. Don't worry about that! You'll certainly like working at my master's. And moreover, if only you are trustworthy and industrious, and when we're better known to one another, then I'll do still more for you, for I have the key of the wine-cellar in my keeping.

CASPER. See here, Mr Famulus, how would it be if we exchanged places? You would give me the key of the wine-cellar and you could see to the wood-chopping and the water-drawing.

WAGNER [*laughs*]. Ha! ha! ha! That wouldn't be bad, but, as I said just now, all that will come in time.

CASPER. Yes, yes, all that will come. But couldn't you give me something to eat and drink just now – a leg of mutton, say, or a pheasant and a bottle of wine – for I've come from a journey and have such a desperate hunger that my stomach is as shrunk up as an empty tobacco-pouch?

WAGNER. Follow me!   I'll fulfil your wish directly.   [*Goes.*

CASPER [*calls to him*]. Mr. Famulus! Mr Famulus!

WAGNER [*comes back*]. Well, what do you want?

CASPER. Just show me a spot where I may put away my wardrobe, so that once and for all I may take the hump out of my bundle.

WAGNER. Just come with me into another room. There you can put away your clothes and can apply yourself to eating and drinking. [*Goes out.*

CASPER. Rejoice, belly; now a treat's in store for you! He! he! Mr Famulus, just take me with you! I don't know my way about this house.

[*Goes out.*

SCENE VIII

CASPER [*runs in*]. Zounds once more! I've been in the kirchen and have inspected what there is to eat – bacon frizzling loud and wine from a pump! The boot-polish is good for nothing. Well, I'm glad that I have got a new situation and that a good one. I have taken off my knapsack and wish to look round. Zounds once more! Where has the plum jam been put? This is a queer house, with all the rats' tails and the piles of books, which are as big as my grandmother's bread-board. Zounds! What is there? Is that truly a tailor's measure? Am I then to serve a tailor? [*He steps on to the magic circle which is traced on the ground and turns over the pages of the books that lie on the table.*] Zounds once more! A tailor hasn't so many books. I can read them too. What's this? *Brrrr!* What's this? *Brrr!* [*Shakes his head vigorously.*] That is a K-Katz-D, B, U, B-Pudel-Katzpudel; K-E-K–Karek Barek, B-E-R–Berlicke! [*Three infernal spirits appear.*] Berlicke! Berlicke! [*He looks round.*] Oh! Lord Jesus! Lord Jesus! Help! Help! What do you black fellows want? There's no chimney to clean here. What do you want, you charcoal-burner with the red nose? Oh, dear god! Dear god! Zounds once more!

THE SPIRITS. Just come out of that circle, and we shall tell you. We await your commands.

CASPER. No! no! I won't come out of this because you ask me to! Zounds once more!

THE SPIRITS. But you must step out and give us your hand, or we do not go away.

CASPER. Come out? Ne – give you my hand? Ne – then you'll go, you dirty chimney-sweeps? No, I'm not coming out! I'm not coming out! Stay as long as you will! Who asked you to come here?

THE SPIRITS. You yourself summoned us through saying Berlicke.

CASPER. Then I'll just summon you off again. How am I to do it? Zounds once more!

THE SPIRITS. That you must do through saying Berlocke.

CASPER. Aha! Spiritus, do you mark that? You wait, you rats' tails! I will hunt you down now! So, now watch! Berlocke! [*They vanish.*] Berlicke! [*They come again.*] Berlocke! Berlicke! Berlocke! Berlicke! Berlocke! Berlicke! Berlocke! Berlicke!

[*He calls out ever quicker and quicker, the infernal spirits come and vanish ever more swiftly, until at last they fling Casper over the houses with woeful shrieks.*]

Act II
The same room as in Act I. The chair stands on the left.

SCENE I

FAUST [*enters*]. Oh, heavens! What a strange dream has disturbed me to-night and thrown my soul into torment! I thought I saw an angel who warned me to abandon my project of entering into an agreement with the hellish spirits, else now and hereafter I should be utterly lost. But I cannot bring myself to change my plan, for I feel that I am cunning enough to cheat Satan, with all his craft and his tricks, and to cancel the bond itself whenever my wishes are fulfilled. That vision was probably but a figment of my troubled imagination, a phantom of the mind, designed to frighten me as I stretched out my hand for this treasure. But the ancients say, if one grasps it fearlessly it will vanish completely. So I will if Mephistopheles ...

SCENE II
MEPHISTOPHELES *enters.*

MEPHISTOPHELES. Well, Faust, have I kept my word?

FAUST. To my greatest astonishment. Have you got permission from your Pluto to serve me?

MEPHISTOPHELES. Yes, Faust. But he requires a deed made out in your writing, saying that you will be his property, body and soul, at the expiration of the time fixed by you.

FAUST [*goes to the table*]. I will fulfil his desires immediately.

MEPHISTOPHELES. What are you going to do, Faust?

FAUST. Sign my name.

MEPHISTOPHELES. Among us of the Plutonic realm no signature with ink is valid. Among us it must be written in blood.

FAUST. But how can I get blood without cutting one of my limbs and so giving pain to myself?

MEPHISTOPHELES. Put your hand to my mouth and I will provide you with some blood painlessly.

FAUST [*gives him his hand*]. Here!   [MEPHISTOPHELES *blows on it.*

FAUST. In truth, my blood flows without my feeling anything at all, and to my amazement it comes forth in two letters – an H and an F. What do these two letters mean, Mephistopheles?

MEPHISTOPHELES. What, Faust? Can't you, who are so great a scholar, interpret these letters? Well, then, these signify *Homo, fuga*, or "Man, flee."

FAUST. Ha! From whom should I fly, infernal spirit?

MEPHISTOPHELES. You must not interpret it as a bad omen – it means fly into the arms of your true servant Mephistopheles.

FAUST. If that is so I shall, without other thought, sign the document with it. [*He writes.*] "Johannes Faust"! So, now you can carry this contract to your prince Pluto.

MEPHISTOPHELES. No, Faust; henceforth I do not move a step from you. Tell me, who should carry off this document – a wolf, a bear, or a tiger?

FAUST. What should such fierce beasts be doing in my room? Let a crow take it.

MEPHISTOPHELES [*nods*]. Watch, Faust!

[*Thunder and lightning. A crow appears, takes the bond in its mouth, and flies off.*

FAUST. But will the crow deliver the bond correctly?

MEPHISTOPHELES. You can rest assured of that. Have you now any commands for me, so that I can show you how quickly I can fulfil them?

FAUST. No. Withdraw now until I call you.

MEPHISTOPHELES. Very well, my Faust, only mention my name and in the twinkling of an eye I shall be with you.   [*Goes off.*

FAUST [*alone*]. Now I should only like to know where my famulus remains so long. He could have done my bidding and been back ages ago. I hope no misfortune has befallen him; his long absence makes me very anxious. Ah! There he comes at last!

SCENE III

WAGNER *enters.*

WAGNER. I inform your Magnificence that I have done everything you command me.

FAUST. Good, my dear Wagner. But how comes it then that you have not brought back a young lad as I gave you leave and as you yourself wished? Perhaps you have not been able to find anybody suitable?

WAGNER. Oh, yes, your Magnificence, when you bid me I'll bring him to you at once.

FAUST. Good! Bring him in! Where is he?

WAGNER. In my room. He has just come from a journey and has asked me to give him something to eat and drink. I will call him at once. [*Goes to the side.*] My friend!

CASPER [*from without*]. What is it?

WAGNER. Come here! His Magnificence wants to speak to you.

CASPER. In a minute! Let me just eat up my leg of mutton!

WAGNER. His Magnificence can't wait for you. Come at once!

CASPER. Just let me drink down this little glass of wine!

WAGNER. Don't be so rude! Come at once!

CASPER. What are you shouting about? I'm ready and waiting all the time.

SCENE IV

CASPER *enters.*

CASPER. Well, what's the matter that you make such a fuss that one can't eat in quiet?

WAGNER. Here! His Magnificence wants to speak to you.

CASPER. Ah! That's quite a different matter – I'll make my compliments to him at once. Your Insolence, it gives me uncommon pleasure that you have the honour of making my acquaintance.

FAUST. Have you been in service before?

CASPER. Yes, your Insolence, in Calabria, where I was in the service of a study-maker.

FAUST. Are your parents still alive, my friend?

CASPER. I'm not quite sure. I always think that the drum-pigeons hatched me.

FAUST. You have good testimonials to show, I suppose?

CASPER. Rest assured; I have a most magnificent testimonial – [*aside*] on my back.

WAGNER. Yes, your Magnificence, he has assured me of it [*speaking confidentially to* FAUST].

CASPER [*sits on the chair*]. Ah! Here's a chair; I can make myself comfortable. [*Sits down.*] Zounds! What a charming seat! This chair must be upholstered with fat steel springs! *Prr! Prr!* Here one can give oneself an air of authority.

WAGNER. My friend!

CASPER. Well, what is it?

WAGNER. Get up at once!

CASPER. Why?

WAGNER. It isn't proper to sit down in the presence of his Magnificence.

CASPER. Oh, that doesn't apply to me! I've come from a journey, and he who comes from a journey is tired and desires to be comfortable.

WAGNER. But this chair is his Magnificence's own!

CASPER. Just now it is Casper's own! I don't know at all why Mr Famulus finds fault with it. Your Insolence hasn't said a single word, but every moment you, Mr Famulus, find something that doesn't seem right. I say this to you: if this goes on and once I get up my temper, then ... [*At this moment the chair on which he sits is enveloped in flame.*] Oh! Oh! Help! Help! [*Goes out.*

SCENE V

MEPHISTOPHELES, CASPER *singing.*

CASPER [*joining* MEPHISTOPHELES]. Well, who are you, *mon cher ami*? Is it good manners to come into his Insolence's room with your hat on your head?

MEPHISTOPHELES. Do you not recognize me then? I am the master's huntsman.

CASPER. The master's huntsman? And what does master want a huntsman for? He's a theologian.

MEPHISTOPHELES. But a very great lover of the hunt. I stand very high in his favour, for I catch foxes and hares with my hands.

CASPER. Zounds! Then you're a clever fellow! You know how to spare powder! What's your name?

MEPHISTOPHELES. Mephistopheles.

CASPER. What? Stoffelfuss, did you say?

MEPHISTOPHELES. Mephistopheles! Don't mutilate my name, or —

CASPER. Well, well, don't shout in that way and take on so! I didn't get it right.

MEPHISTOPHELES. Have you heard that our master is going to travel?

CASPER. Travel? Where to?

MEPHISTOPHELES. Just travel.

CASPER. Just so, travel. Where to?

MEPHISTOPHELES. To Parma.

CASPER. Oh, you can't make a fool of me! What would he want to get into a *Barme*[1] for, when he's so fat?

MEPHISTOPHELES. No! no! Parma is a principality where a great nuptial ceremony is to take place.

---

[1] Manger.

CASPER. Oh! That's quite another matter. But what's a nuptial ceremony?

MEPHISTOPHELES. A nuptial ceremony is a marriage.

CASPER. Do they give you much to eat and drink there?

MEPHISTOPHELES. Oh, yes: lots.

CASPER. Rejoice, my belly: there's going to be another downpour! Is master to take me with him or not?

MEPHISTOPHELES. No, he has ordered that you should remain behind. He is to journey quite alone to Parma on his robe.

CASPER. On his robe? That will be a pretty wear and tear.

MEPHISTOPHELES. Yet I will take it on my own responsibility to take you along with us, without his being aware of it.

CASPER. Oh, yes, do that, good Stoffelfuss, for I simply adore eating and drinking!

MEPHISTOPHELES. Would you prefer to ride or go in a carriage?

CASPER. You know best. Get something sent here for me to ride.

MEPHISTOPHELES. Very well, I'll see to it at once. But I expressly forbid you to tell anyone in Parma who our master is or what his name is – otherwise I'll break your neck. Do you understand me?   [Goes out.

CASPER [alone]. Oh, yes, I've understood all right. One would need cotton-wool in one's ears not to have understood. Well, I must go and get my equipage packed up. And he will get me something to ride on; if only he brought me here a nice little Polish or Hungarian pony, for I like riding, and – [A dragon enters and gives him a knock on the shoulders; he falls down.] What kind of behaviour is that? [Gets up.] He! he! Help! help! Stoffelfuss! Stoffelfuss! Is that the horse you promised me?

MEPHISTOPHELES [coming in]. Just get up on it. It won't harm you.

CASPER. Oh, yes, just get up on it! That's a new-fangled horse. I must think it over a bit. Zounds! It's got a walking-stick behind! If the animal hits me a knock on the nose it'll upset the applecart. It's even got wings! Won't I suffer if it flies off? Courage! I'll get up. [He mounts.] That's not a bad seat! Hi! hi! Little fox! Hi! [The dragon gives him a knock at the back of his head with its tail.] Well! And who's the lout who's given me a blow as if he wanted to knock out my four senses? I'll put a stop to that! Well, little fox, gee up, gee up! Hi! hi! [The dragon gives him another blow.] Thunder and lightning! Some one has struck me again! [He turns round.] I believe it was you with your walking-stick! Just you wait! I'll takes another seat so as to get out of the line of fire. [He sits farther forward.] This beast's contrived not badly for a learner in riding, for if one were to fall off one couldn't fall far. [Makes movements as if he were walking.] But I hope there won't be bad weather to-day; I fear this journey will cost me more in shoe leather than I get in salary. Now, little fox. Hi! hi! [The dragon rises *suddenly, and flies upward amid thunder and lightning. He cries out.*] He! he! Help! help! Stoffelfuss! Stoffelfuss! The animal's going up into the sky! He! he! he! [*He vanishes.*

Act III
SCENE I: *A garden.*
DUKE, BIANCA, ORESTES.

DUKE. Well, dearest spouse, how do you like my Court? Can you find in me and my subjects sufficient recompense for the sacrifice you have made in leaving your parents and your native country?

BIANCA. Oh, my husband, how deeply you shame me in asking that question! Have I not received proofs sufficient of your love and of the esteem of your subjects to make me happy in the thought of spending my life at your side?

DUKE. And yet it seems to me as if a secret grief sometimes clouded your face. Have you perhaps a secret in your breast in which you do not feel perhaps that I am worthy to participate?

BIANCA. No, I am only troubled by sorrow for my father, who was seriously ill when I accompanied the ambassadors here to you. Feeble and exhausted, he raised himself in his bed when I took leave of him and said: "Be as good a wife as you have been a daughter and my blessing will follow you always." Oh, my husband, from that time I have been unable to repress the anxiety which grief for my father's health occasions me. Will you grant me a request?

DUKE. Speak, dear Bianca – it shall be granted.

BIANCA. Allow me to leave you now, so that I can give the ambassadors some consoling words to carry to my father, telling him of the love and kindness which I have met with here.

DUKE. With pleasure I accede to your wish. Only I beg you not to withdraw your gracious presence overlong.

BIANCA. I will hasten as quickly as I can and come to you again.

[*Goes off.*

Scene II
DUKE *and* ORESTES.

DUKE. Well, dear Orestes, what do you say to my choice of a wife?

ORESTES. That you must consider yourself and the whole country lucky to have gained so virtuous a consort and duchess, and may Heaven grant the happiness to us all to be ruled right long by such an excellent pair of princes!

DUKE. I thank you for your wish, and hope that you will aid me even further with your wise counsel to make my subjects happy.

ORESTES. Truly, your Highness, I will try to show myself worthy of the great favour you display towards me.

DUKE. Have you prepared, as well as possible, everything that will be needed for these nuptials?

ORESTES. Yes, your Highness. I have not failed to carry out your orders to the best of my ability. I have also got it announced by means of a proclamation that all artists and scholars should come here to embellish this marriage by their presence. [CASPER *is hurled down from the sky on to the stage.*

DUKE. Good heavens! What's that?

ORESTES. Your Highness, I am amazed. This man —

DUKE. Ask him, dear Orestes, how it can possibly be that he could come down here out of the sky?

CASPER. Him! ham! hum!

ORESTES. My friend, who are you?

CASPER. Him! ham! hum!

ORESTES. How can it be that you have fallen down here out of the sky without injuring yourself?

CASPER. Him! ham! hum! Him! ham! hum!

DUKE. He seems to be dumb, if he's not dissembling. Promise him twenty ducats if he reveals this secret to us; if not, he'll get twenty good lashes.

CASPER. Him! ham! hum! Bum! bum!

ORESTES. My friend, you have heard what his Highness has promised you. If you can speak, don't delay any longer in fulfilling his Highness's desire.

CASPER. Him! ham! hum! Him! ham! hum!

DUKE. I truly believe that this man is merely laughing at us. Orestes, call the watch at once!

ORESTES. In a moment, your Highness.   [*Prepares to go off.*

CASPER [*holds him back*]. No! no! Just wait, old sir!

DUKE. What? You can speak? You're not dumb? —

CASPER. That's just the trick.

DUKE. You seem to me to be a very obstinate fellow.

CASPER. Oh, no. I'm a very good man, but I have a very bad companion, and he has forbidden me to speak.

DUKE. What's your name?

CASPER. Ah! That's what I must not tell.

DUKE. Then you must have been guilty of some terrible crime if you dare not reveal your name.

CASPER. You don't think, do you, that I've stolen anything? God forbid! Casper can go wherever you will, but no one can say that about Casper.

DUKE. So Casper's your name?

CASPER. Who told you that I was called Casper?

DUKE. You yourself.

CASPER. I? [*To himself*] Oh, you damned blubberer!

DUKE. To judge by your dress you are a servant?

CASPER. You've guessed it.

DUKE. What's your master's name?

CASPER. Ah, there's the rub! I must not reveal it, else my neck'll be broken.

DUKE. You can always tell it to me. No harm shall come to you.

CASPER. Who, then, are you?

DUKE. I am the Duke of Parma.

CASPER. What? The Duke of Parma? Pray pardon me for not having yet made you my compliments. I am very glad that you have the honour of my acquaintance. Go on!

DUKE. Very good, my friend. Well, I should gladly know the name of your master.

CASPER. I must not tell it; but I'll show it you pantomimically.

DUKE. Well, I am content.

CASPER [*raises his arm*]. See here! What is that?

DUKE. That's an arm.

CASPER. Well, what is this just in front? Just in front?

DUKE. A hand, and if you close it it's a *Faust*.[2]

CASPER. Right – I serve him. But I didn't tell you.

DUKE. What? The great scholar? You're in Doctor Faust's service?

CASPER. Yes, I am. It's great to be able to speak to people and yet not give away secrets. That's the point – I am a true genius; I've always got a bunch of tricks in my head.

DUKE. Since you live with this famous man, have you not learned some of his art?

CASPER. My master learned everything from me.

DUKE. From you?

CASPER. Oh, yes! I am Faust's teacher. Haven't you heard, then, of my skill? My name has been blazoned abroad to all four corners of the earth.

---

2 Fist.

DUKE. No, I haven't heard anything about it.

CASPER. Aha! Now I call to mind, we had so hard a winter then that all the sounds were frozen; but just let it thaw, and my fame will make a devil of a row.

DUKE. I should be glad to see some of your art.

CASPER. So you want to see some of my art?

DUKE. Yes!

CASPER. You shall have it directly. [*Aside*] See, Casper, if you had learned anything now, how you could have profited. [*Aloud*] Do you wish to see something big, something grand?

DUKE. Yes, something extraordinary.

CASPER. Would you like to see a great big wave come rolling in to drown all three of us?

DUKE. No, I shouldn't like to see that.

CASPER. That's a very big piece.

DUKE. I'd rather you showed me something else.

CASPER. Something else? Perhaps you'd like to see a great millstone crashing down from the sky to beat us down ten fathoms deep in the bosom of the earth? That's a very impressive piece.

DUKE. No, I shouldn't like to see that; my life would be endangered in this as in your first piece. Something fine, something pleasant – that's what I want.

CASPER. Oh! Something fine? Perhaps you'd like to see an Egyptian darkness wrapped up in cotton-wool? That's a very fine piece. But I need four weeks' time to pack it in its box.

DUKE. Don't go on talking such utter nonsense!

CASPER. Utter nonsense? Can you do it then?

DUKE. No – but —

CASPER. Well, you mustn't say that it is utter nonsense, for I can become offended so quickly as to make my body all run into gall when a person steps up and says it is utter nonsense, and yet can't do it himself.

DUKE. Don't be so indignant about it! Show me something else.

CASPER. Perhaps you'd like to see a devilry?

DUKE. Yes, I should like to see a *Salto mortale*.

CASPER. But what's my reward if I do show a devilry?

DUKE. I have laid aside twenty ducats for you, and these you shall get.

CASPER. I should be right glad if you gave me the money in advance.

DUKE. Why? You don't doubt my promise, do you?

CASPER. Oh! God forbid! But, do you see, when I make a devilry, usually I stay three or four months in the sky, so it would be an advantage if

I had the money in advance wherewith, among other things, to pay for my lodgings.

DUKE. So soon as I am convinced of your skill you shall have the ducats – but not before.

CASPER. So I get no money in advance?

DUKE. No.

CASPER. Well, for my part, if an accident happens to me I'll have no gold with me, and you shall have it on your conscience.

DUKE. Yes! yes! Just give me a proof of your skill.

CASPER. At once! At once! Just stand a little to the side, and I will start my invocation. [*He turns always on one foot.*] *Br! br! br!*

DUKE. What does that mean?

CASPER. That's the invocation. You mustn't put me out. *Br! br! br!* Well, sirs, shut your eyes, in case things spring into your face.

DUKE. What kind of things?

CASPER. Sugar and coffee! *Br! br! br!* What do you really want to see, sirs?

DUKE. Well, a caper!

CASPER. Make it yourself! I can't do it!   [*Goes off.*

DUKE. Wait, you damned rascal! Orestes, go and get the watch to arrest him and let him suffer for his villainy.

ORESTES. At once, your Highess.   [*Goes off.*

SCENE III

Duke alone.   Then FAUST.   *Later little by little the apparitions.*

DUKE. I will not let him be punished too severely for his audacity in having ridiculed me, for he has given me real pleasure with his droll conceits. If I'm not mistaken, a man whom I don't know is coming down the alley towards me.

FAUST [*enters*]. Most serene Duke, with deepest humility I beg you to pardon me for making so free a visit. But as it has been proclaimed that all artists and scholars are invited to come to your princely marriage, I have hastened to fulfil your Highness's commands, and humbly beg that you will permit me to present here my art and my skill.

DUKE. What is your name?

FAUST. Johannes Faust.

DUKE. What? You are the world-famous Doctor Faust, whom all men admire, you who are able in one minute to summon summer and winter, like nature itself? You are very welcome to my Court: for long I have desired to make your personal acquaintance.

FAUST. Your Highness overwhelms me with your praise, which up to now
I have not done anything to deserve. Perhaps your Highness would desire to see some proofs of my art?

DUKE. If it gives you no trouble, I should accept your offer with pleasure.

FAUST. At all time and in every place, your Highness, I am ready to fulfil
your commands.

DUKE. Well, then, I should like to see here the big giant Goliath and the
little David.

FAUST. Your Highness shall immediately be satisfied! Mephistopheles!
Do you hear? Cause the giant Goliath and the little David to appear immediately!

[*An adagio sounds, and* GOLIATH *and* DAVID *appear. The latter has his sling
in his hand. After some minutes, during which the* DUKE *speaks to* FAUST, *the*
DUKE *indicates that he has seen enough.* FAUST *bows and nods; the apparitions
vanish; and the music ceases.*

DUKE. Indeed, you have shown me these two persons beyond my expectation. I have long wondered how it was possible that this giant
could be killed by a sling wielded by so small a man.

FAUST. It is a proof that the strong must not always trust to their strength.
What would your Highness like to see further?

DUKE. The chaste Lucrece, as she stabs herself in the breast on the Capitol at Rome, since her virginity was in danger of being violated by force.

FAUST. Very well, your Highness! Do you hear, Mephistopheles? Cause
the chaste Lucrece to appear!

[*He nods. Adagio.* LUCRECE *appears with the dagger at her breast. Then the same
dumb show as before.*

DUKE. Upon my honour! Most excellently do you gratify my wishes. This
woman through her chastity redeemed Rome's tottering imperial
throne. She will shine in history as the greatest example of womanly
virtue.

FAUST. Your Highness is right! What would your Highness desire to see
now?

DUKE. Samson and Delilah, as she was cutting off his hair.

FAUST. In a moment, your Highness! Mephistopheles, cause Samson and
Delilah to appear!

[*He nods. Adagio. The curtain at the back opens and reveals* DELILAH *sitting in a
chair with scissors in her hand; before her sits* SAMSON, *sleeping with his head laid
on her bosom; she is about to cut off his hair. Then dumb show as above.*

DUKE. You are giving me more and more proof that you are one of the
greatest magicians of our time. But I should like to ask for one thing
more.

FAUST. Make your command, your Highness!

DUKE. I should like to see the heroic Judith with the head of Holofernes.

FAUST. Very well, your Highness! Mephistopheles! Do you hear? Cause her to appear at once – Judith with the head of Holofernes!

[*He nods:* JUDITH *appears to the music of an adagio. In her right hand is a sword, in her left the head of Holofernes. Dumb show as above.*

DUKE. I thank you for the pleasure you have given me. You are my guest from to-day; and for as long as you stay in my Court you are my close companion. Follow me, for I wish to introduce you to my wife as the most renowned magician.

FAUST. I obey, your Highness.   [*They go out.*

SCENE IV

CASPER *and* MEPHISTOPHELES *enter.*

MEPHISTOPHELES [*dragging in Casper by the neck*]. Just you come here, you scoundrel! Why have you betrayed our master?

CASPER. Oh! oh! I haven't betrayed him. Let me alone, Stoffelfuss, golden Stoffelfuss – won't you let me go?

MEPHISTOPHELES. Why did you tell your master's name to the Duke?

CASPER. I didn't tell him a word; I just showed it to him pantomimically, and he understood at once who our master was and what was his name. But, dear Stoffelfuss, just let me go this time! Don't break my neck; I won't do it again as long as I live.

MEPHISTOPHELES. Well, it shall be allowed to pass this time. But as a punishment you will remain here in Parma alone. Master has dismissed you from his service. You'll see now how you'll perish!   [*Goes out.*

CASPER [*alone*]. Stoffelfuss! He! Stoffelfuss! Golden Stoffel! Don't leave me alone! Stoffelchen! He's gone, by my soul, and left me here! First give me at least my wages! You owe me two months' wages. It's all in vain! The devil has taken it! Ah! You poor Casper, how will you get on now, without a place, without a master? And the Duke is sending round four men with big sticks to arrest me for my magic. [*Weeps.*] Hu! hu! ha! ha! If my grandmother knew what's happening to me I think the good woman would weep her eyes out of her head! Hu! hu! ha! ha!

SCENE V
AUERHAHN *enters.*

AUERHAHN [*descending from the sky*]. Casper!

CASPER. I thought some one called me by name?

AUERHAHN. Casper, why are you in such grief?

CASPER. And shouldn't I be grieved? My master has chucked me out of my place. Here I am in a foreign land where I don't know one street from another.

AUERHAHN. You are truly in a difficult position, for here there are many bandits, who knock men dead for two halfpennies.

CASPER. Two halfpennies? And I have just threepence in my pocket. Will they knock me dead thrice?

AUERHAHN. Yes, they will knock you dead thrice!

CASPER. Oh! oh! Poor Casper, all's over with you. Hu! hu! hu!

AUERHAHN. Listen, Casper! I really pity you!

CASPER. Well, here is one, at any rate, in the world who is affected by my position!

AUERHAHN. Do you know? In Wittenberg the night-watchman has died, and if you promise me your soul, guaranteeing that I can carry it off after twelve years, I shall bring you to Wittenberg and put you in the night-watchman's place there.

CASPER. No, nothing can come of this contract.

AUERHAHN. Why not?

CASPER. I haven't got a soul. My maker forgot to put one into me!

AUERHAHN. Don't be so silly! Don't you consider yourself a man? Consequently you must have a soul.

CASPER. Do you really believe I have a soul?

AUERHAHN. Of course!

CASPER [*aside*]. I can cheat the silly devil in this! [*Aloud*] All right! I remember now – I have got a soul! I don't know how I could have forgotten. But what's your name?

AUERHAHN. Auerhahn!

CASPER. Kickelhahn? Well, my dear Kickelhahn, I promise you my soul after twelve years – and you'll get me the night-watchman's place?

AUERHAHN. Yes, I'll get it for you.

CASPER. And bring me at once to Wittenberg?

AUERHAHN. Yes, we shall be at Wittenberg in a twinkling. Just hold on to me.

CASPER [*grips him*]. I'm holding on! [*Springs back and blows on his hands.*]

Thunder and lightning! I have burned myself; my hands must be full of blisters.

AUERHAHN. Yes, I've got an ardent disposition!

CASPER. I've noticed that. Just cool it off a little!

AUERHAHN. Well, then, hold on to me once more!

CASPER. Well, once more I'm holding on.

AUERHAHN. Say, now: Capo cnallo!

CASPER. Capers and quails.

AUERHAHN. Capo cnallo!

CASPER. Capo cnallo!   [*Flies off with him.*

Act IV

SCENE I

FAUST's *room as in Act I.   The chair stands at the table.*

FAUST [*entering*]. Greetings, home of my earliest joy! Remove from me my depression, my ill-will! Oh, why have I renounced my hope of salvation for such an ordinary existence? Here is the wound whereby I subscribed my heart's blood to him, sure mortgage to hell. Of course, I may be of good hope, for I can laugh at Satan, since four and twenty years must pass after our contract before I become his bondslave, and now only half of that time has gone by. Yes, I shall make use of his help only for a few years more, to make myself famous, and then I shall endeavour to get out of his clutches, and seek to gain back the salvation I cast away so lightly on my abandoned path. [*He sets himself.*] But I do not know why such an overpowering desire for sleep has suddenly come on me and forces me here to take a rest. Ah! Rest – rest that since my bond has left me quite, so that up to now I have only known it as a name!

[*He falls asleep.*

SCENE II

The GENIUS *enters.*

GENIUS. Faust! Faust! Wake from your sinful sleep! What have you undertaken? Consider that the joys which you gain from this infernal bond are transitory, that you have destroyed thereby your hope of salvation and go to eternal damnation! Were you not born a man, and do you sacrifice yourself so wantonly to this hellish spirit? Oh, abandon the road which you have been travelling up to now! Return to virtue! You have no time to lose if you desire still to save your soul. You can break the bond, but only if you do it to-day. Oh, Faust! Follow the warning of your guardian genius, so that I may flutter round protecting you as of yore!   [*Goes out.*

FAUST [*awaking*]. Ha! What was that? This is the second time I thought I saw my genius warning me to break my bond with Satan as soon as possible. Yes, yes, I will go back to the path of virtue, and consecrate myself to it, and through it seek to make myself worthy of the joys of heaven. Mephistopheles!

SCENE III
MEPHISTOPHELES *enters.*

MEPHISTOPHELES. What you want, Faust?

FAUST. You know that you are forced by our contract to answer all my questions. Tell me then: what would you do if you could obtain salvation?

MEPHISTOPHELES. I am not compelled to give you an answer to such a question. Yet hear and despair! If I could gain eternal salvation I should climb a ladder all the way to heaven, even if every rung were a sharp knife. And do you, a man, throw your being so wantonly away in order to enjoy the transitory pleasures of earth?

FAUST. Ha! I am not yet in your power! Get away from me for ever!

MEPHISTOPHELES [*aside*]. Well, I will go away, and seek to bind him to me again by some means or other.   [*Goes out.*

FAUST [*alone*]. Miserable wretch! How deep am I sunk! Yet there is still time to repent and to regain salvation. Yes, I will follow the words of my guardian spirit and at once relieve my heart by an ardent prayer to God. [*Kneels down.*] All-compassionate, look down from Your throne upon me, a sinning man. Listen to my sighs; let my prayer ascend through the clouds; forgive me my past sins; take me again into Your grace, and lead me ...

SCENE IV
MEPHISTOPHELES *enter with* HELEN.

MEPHISTOPHELES. Faust! Faust! Leave off praying! Here, I'm bringing you the lovely Helen, for whom the whole of Troy was destroyed!

FAUST. Get away, you infernal spirit! I am in your power no more!

MEPHISTOPHELES. Just look here, Faust! She shall be your own, Faust, if only you stop praying!

FAUST [*looks round*]. Ha! What a charming shape do I see!

HELEN. Gracious sir, your huntsman told me you had some commands
for me.

FAUST [*aside*]. Am I no longer myself? Ha! Are these my eyes which are
devouring her eagerly and ardently as the sunbeams do the earth? Oh!
The flame of life has blazed up in me anew; I shall try no more to gain
heaven, for the earth blooms for me in amorous luxury.

MEPHISTOPHELES. Look, Faust, what trouble I've taken to dissipate your
ill-humour! Amuse yourself with her as you please; only banish all sad
thoughts.

FAUST. I thank you, Mephistopheles, for your lovely present. Now, charming Helen, are you desirous of living with me?

HELEN. You are lord of my person, and I will not fail to carry out your
commands.

FAUST. Accompany me, dear Helen; I shall show you my jewels to con-
vince you how happy your life with me will be.

HELEN. I follow you gladly!   [*Goes out with* FAUST.

MEPHISTOPHELES [*alone*]. Ha! ha! ha! He's ours now; he's got no power
now to escape us! He had almost overreached me and escaped from my
clutches, but a woman was the thing to put him again into our hands.

SCENE V

FAUST RUNS *in*.

FAUST. Oh, vanity! Ha! Damned false being! When I sought to embrace
this charming form I found myself embracing a hellish fury! Oh, Faust!
What have you done? Now I have provoked Heaven anew! Once more
I have allowed myself to be beguiled by Satan! Ha! Cursed spirit, are
you still here? Get away from my side for ever, for I shall never see you
again!

MEPHISTOPHELES. Ha! ha! ha! Rage on – it hurts me not! For know that
our contract is nearly at an end; without any other chance of escape you
will be my property.

FAUST. The contract at an end! I your property! Yet hardly half the four
and twenty years have passed since I sold my soul to you!

MEPHISTOPHELES. No, Faust, you have made a bad mistake; just count in
the nights and you will see that our contract is at an end.

FAUST. Ha! Lying spirit, you have betrayed me! But rejoice not so soon!
I yet feel I have the power to defy you!

MEPHISTOPHELES. I laugh at your threats; your blood is mine; the bond is
ended, and soon we shall come to take you in triumph to our prince
Pluto.   [*Goes out.*

Scene VI

FAUST [*alone*]. Ha! Will my life's course then be ended in a few hours?
[*Kneels down.*] Oh, may my prayer ascend yet once more to the all-good
God! There where the rosy flames of evening soar, there is – ha!
Curses! The fiery gate of hell! Listen! Never – there must I go – *Ave* –
the music of the celestial choir is broken! Oh, demon, why do you twist
my words so that my prayer is turned into curses? No, no, I cannot
pray! The fountain of eternal mercy is sealed from me. Even if the
angels were to weep tears on my account it would never be opened for
me again! I can hope for mercy no more.
MEPHISTOPHELES [*within*]. Fauste, prepara te!
FAUST. Ha! Now must I prepare for the last hour of my life: now must
I receive punishment for my sinful life – there in the pit of hell! My
heart will be fettered by Pluto's heavy chains, and the furies wait eagerly
for my body in order to tear it to pieces.   [*It strikes ten.*

Scene VII

CASPER *enters as a night-watchman with his lantern.*

CASPER [*still without*]. Grethel! Light the lantern for me. I must start my
duties as night-watchman to-day. The citizens have just given me
the job, but the town council hasn't yet confirmed it; it desires first a
plain proof of my worth. Well, I'll do it as well as I can. [*Enters singing.*]

> Masters all, now list to me:
> If your wives they plaguy be
> Into bed them straightway cast;
> All the quarrel will be past.
> Ten has struck.
> Dra, la, la, la, la, la!   [*Dances.*
> Ladies all, now list to me,
> You must bear much – that I see.
> Yet this is no new device –
> Sometime you've got to break the ice!
> It's been broken quite a lot.
> Dra, la, la, la, la, la!   [*Dances.*

FAUST. How dare you enter my room when I have forbidden you ever to
come to my house again?
CASPER. Your Insolence, pray pardon me; I desired only to give a proof of
my skill as a night-watchman.

FAUST. Very good. But stay no longer in my presence.

CASPER. And then I wish also to talk to your Insolence about the wages owing to me; for I'm pressed for money. I must buy some trade equipment in order to carry on my new duties.

FAUST. Go to my famulus and get him to pay you the money – and now begone to the street where you belong.

CASPER. Well, if you are not glad to see me, I'll go. I thought to make my affairs right if I brought my first serenade to your Insolence's house, but since it doesn't appeal to you I'll make off again immediately.

[Goes out humming.

FAUST [*alone*]. Now at this moment I am being accused and tried by the Almighty Judge! Oh, terrible thought!

MEPHISTOPHELES [*without*]. Fauste, judicatus es!

FAUST [*springs up*]. Ha! It is done! I am judged – my sentence is passed; the Almighty has broken his staff over me! I am in Satan's power! Oh, cursed be the day when I was born!   [*Seats himself. It strikes eleven.*

SCENE VIII

FAUST, CASPER, *and later all the Furies.*

CASPER [*within*]. Grethel, give me the lantern. It's struck again; the clock can't be quite right in its head. But pour me out first a little oil on the wick so that I can see a bit better. So!   [*Enters singing.*

All ye widowers, list to me:
If a new wife you wish to see,
Do not praise the first too much,
Else you'll not get another such.
Eleven has struck!
Dra, la, la, la, la, la!
All ye widows, list to me:
Truly you live in misery,
For, alas! you have not got
From experience you know what.
Eleven twenty!
Dra, la, la, la, la!

Zounds! How have I got into this room again! Pray pardon, your Insolence, that I have come into your house once more; I truly don't know how I manage to lose my path always! In a way, however, I'm glad that I have the honour of meeting your Insolence again, for I have a right big request to make to you.

FAUST. Well, what does your request concern?

CASPER. I have heard that your Insolence is to make a journey into the Plutonic realm, and I would wish to beg you to bear many compliments from me to my grandmother. She sits on the left hand as you enter hell, number one, and mends slippers.

FAUST. Get out this very minute, or I will drive your impertinence off by force!

CASPER. Well, well, don't take it so ill! I can easily go by myself. [*Goes out humming.*

MEPHISTOPHELES [*within*]. Fauste, in eternum damnatus es!

FAUST [*springs up*]. Ha! Now the moment has come when I am expected in the pit of hell, where resin and brimstone burns for me, where Pluto's monsters wait for me. Soon I shall feel hell's torments in my body! The thunder rolls – the earth vomits fire! Oh, help! Oh, save me, might of Heaven! In vain! In vain is my cry for help – I must hence to a place where I have to suffer punishment for my sins. Ha! Come then, you hellish furies, rend, tear my body, and bring me to the place of my fate! [*At the beginning of this speech thunder and lightning start. These grow fiercer. At the end the* FURIES *arrive and go off carrying* FAUST *into the sky. Slowly it grows quieter, then twelve strikes.*

SCENE IX
CASPER. *Later* AUERHAHN.

CASPER [*without*]. Devil take it! That clock strikes as if Satan were pulling at the rope! I must go my rounds again. Grethel, make a couple of pans of coffee, but don't put too many grounds in it. Now give me the lantern. So! I will be back soon. See and be quick about it! [*Enters singing.*]

All my lads, now list to me!
If a maiden you go to see,
Do it nicely, do't with poise,
See the house door makes no noise:
Twelve has struck!
Dra, la, la, la, la!
All my virgins, list to me!
Should one ask you a question free –
"Are you, my dear, a virgin yet?" –
Just you answer: "Yes, I regret."
Null null has struck!
Dra, la, la, la, la!

[*He dances and bumps with the lantern into* AUERHAHN, *who has descended from the sky.*

CASPER [*shrieks*]. Kibi! Who's that?

AUERHAHN. Do you know me, Casper?

CASPER. No, I don't! Who are you, *mon cher ami?*

AUERHAHN. I am Auerhahn.

CASPER. Oh! Let me just throw a little light on your face! [*Holds up the lantern.*] Yes, you're right. You are Kickelhahn. What do you want?

AUERHAHN. Casper, your time is up. You must go with me to hell!

CASPER. To hell? I thought the chimney was your place. I do believe you're not right in the head! Have the twelve years passed then?

AUERHAHN. Yes.

CASPER. But I made my first round as night-watchman only to-day.

AUERHAHN. That's nothing. The twelve years have passed, and you are now mine.

CASPER. What do you say? As I can see, you've cheated me!

AUERHAHN. Of course!

CASPER. Well, you're cheated too, for I haven't got a soul! Ha! ha! ha!

AUERHAHN. And even if you haven't got a soul you must come with me.

CASPER. Listen, Kickelhahn, don't make me wild! Go your way or my lantern will make companionship with your head!

AUERHAHN. Well, you know that since you are a night-watchman I can't get you. [*Ascends through the sky.*

CASPER [*alone*]. That's charming – even the devil will have nothing to do with night-watchmen! Well, I'll go back to my comrades, and we'll make right merry with a can of schnaps and laugh at the silly devils.

[*Goes out dancing.*

The curtain falls

IV The Faust Theme in Romantic Music

Henry Bacon

In his *Tragedy of Faust* Johann Wolfgang von Goethe gave an old folk tale a remarkable, unique form. He also infused the story with a philosophy which captured some of the most painful dilemmas that have haunted the Western mind throughout the modern era. Most Romantic composers who treated the Faust theme claimed to have been inspired by this extraordinary work. However, they all used only certain fragments of Goethe's tragedy and most of them drastically revised the story line. The results were splendid, even awe-inspiring, but often the revisions carried them quite far away from the poet's philosophy. Already in connection with Hector Berlioz's *The Damnation of Faust* controversy raged over whether it was even possible to adapt Goethe's sublime work into music without compromising its very essence, the ideas expressed in his sublime poetry. Gradually there emerged the opposing view, the idea of music as the highest expression of the spirit. Frantz Liszt argued that programmatic symphonic music had the unique power to express the sensibility of the era, just as in their poetry Goethe and Byron had expressed the sensibility of their times. Liszt's notion and similar ideas expressed by other composers led to the creation of wholly new musical and music dramatic forms. This is very much evident in adaptations of *Faust*, each of which exemplifies a highly individual solution to the problem of interrelating music, words, and drama. Consequently, the works express different ideas and attitudes as well as philosophical outlooks.

The most important adaptations of Goethe's *Faust* into music are Berlioz's *The Damnation of Faust* (1846), Schumann's *Scenes from Goethe's Faust* (1862), Liszt's *A Faust Symphony* (1857), Gounod's *Faust* (1859), Boito's *Mefistofele* (1868), and Mahler's *Symphony No. 8* (1910). Berlioz and Gounod restricted themselves to the romantic love story of the first part of the tragedy. Schumann chose a selection of scenes from almost the entire length of the tragedy without attempting to present a continuous narrative, while Boito quite dexterously succeeds in fusing selected scenes from both parts into a single narrative. Mahler set to music only the concluding scene of the second part. Liszt is the only major composer to have opted for expressing the ideas of the drama purely in music.

Berlioz: *The Damnation of Faust*

Goethe's *Faust* made a tremendous impression on the French Romantics. Hector Berlioz first read it in 1827 and next year composed *Eight Scenes from*

Faust. The young composer was exceedingly self-critical and soon withdrew the work. Yet many of the themes found their way 18 years later into *The Damnation of Faust.* Berlioz's formal conception, the way he treats the dramatic material, is quite original. This may be partly due to the problems he had had in getting his opera *Benvenuto Cellini* performed at the Grand Opéra in Paris. He decided to create new forms that could be performed outside opera houses. As Berlioz eventually returned to the Faust theme he took great liberties regarding the storyline and characterized the libretto as "inspired by Goethe." He even included his mighty adaptation of the Hungarian Rákóczy march merely because it was so impressive and had conquered even Hungarian audiences. For this and no other reason his Faust begins his adventures in the plains of that country. In replying to his critics Berlioz argued that composers should have the same rights as men of letters in setting events of their stories wherever they deemed suitable. Goethe himself had located the scenes of the second part of his Faust all over his mythical universe, including even Menelaus' palace in ancient Greece.

The Damnation of Faust is not intended as a coherent music drama. Rather, this *dramatic legend* is a series of scenes set to some of the most vibrant music of the Romantic era. As the composer has decided not to use opera-like recitative to explain how things develop; the story is highly elliptical and difficult to follow without previous knowledge or programme notes. At the beginning, we hear evocative sonorous images of nature in the full bloom of spring, young love at its most exuberant, and soldiers marching in their splendid shining armor. As his own youth and beauty appear to have faded away, Faust is prepared to end his day. He is interrupted by people praising Easter and the coming of spring. It is indicative of the difference between Goethe's and Berlioz's approaches that whereas Goethe's Faust says "the earth has me again," Berlioz's hero states that "heaven has won me back." Soon after this – immediately in Berlioz's legend – Méphistophélès appears. While Goethe's demon defines itself as the spirit who always denies, his French colleague announces himself as the very spirit of life and promises Faust happiness and pleasures, "all that the wildest desire can dream of." The impetuous romantic that he is, Faust immediately accepts the offer without so much as asking about the terms of this bargain. As this remarkably short scene indicates, Berlioz is not interested in developing Faust as a character or symbolic figure. As the composer did not intend his dramatic legend to be staged, he could even afford to leave his protagonist a mere onlooker in many scenes. Only in the Marguerite scene does Faust momentarily become a dramatic force. He is consumed by his desire for the girl, and she is prepared to relinquish everything for her love.

The only scene that refers to the second part of the tragedy is Faust's splendid *Invocation to Nature* which serves as a moment of repose before his inescapable fall into the abyss in this rather truncated moral universe. Meanwhile, Marguerite is about to be executed after having caused her mother's death with a potion in an attempt to keep her from wakening up to the sounds of their night of love. Only now Méphistophélès extorts Faust into signing a pact in exchange for his help in rescuing Marguerite. There is a sense that he has been tricked in that his fate is sealed by his willingness to make good his evils rather than the actual evil deeds he has committed. Or perhaps his real sin is his total inability to think of anything in a longer perspective. His character is neatly summarized in his words as he decides to accept Méphistophélès' offer: "What is tomorrow when I suffer now?" Here the plot and the character are closer to Marlowe's version of *Faust* than Goethe's.

Marguerite is granted divine grace as, according to the chorus of celestial spirits, she is "an artless soul that love led astray." This has clearly been her fate all along, as can be heard in the words of the chorus of peasants during *The Ride to the Abyss*: after having prayed for Santa Maria and Santa Magdalena, they also appeal to Santa Margarita. Pointedly enough, Faust himself uses this form of her name in his ecstasy of the first vision of her as evoked by Méphistophélès – and, of course, this is how the heavenly voice hails her in order to invite her to join the celestial sphere. This is a far cry from Goethe's in some ways dubious but at least richly multidimensional moral vision. There is no notion of sexuality or any other form of human endeavor as a creative force. In Berlioz's somewhat idiosyncratic theology all this seems to imply that male sexuality, touched by the spirit, leads to perdition, whereas female spirituality, having innocently touched sexuality, leads to salvation. But then again, Berlioz was an extraordinary musical dramaturge and not a theologian.

In his *Faust* Berlioz does not use music dramatic devices such as motivic repetition in creating connections between events or characters. But he does employ the tritone interval, the standard means of referring to the Devil or devilish influences since the Middle Ages. He does it even in such an unlikely situation as Marguerite's "The King of Thule" ballad, as if to indicate that Méphistophélès' influence is already seeping into her imagination. And in a typically Romantic fashion – epitomized in Wagner's *Tristan and Isolde* – the fleeting tonal cadenza in Faust's evocation of nature serves as a musical image of unquenchable yearning. All in all, Berlioz captures something of the richness of Goethe's vision in his almost shameless employment of his astonishing capacity for melodic innovation, his use of harmonies ranging from the most exquisite to some of the boldest ever heard, as well as his talent for splendid orchestration. Even with its typically nineteenth-century moralistic framework *The Damnation of Faust* serves as a warning of how all the beautiful, enticing things that the earth can offer might lead a sensitive soul into egoistic pursuit of pleasure and emotional satisfaction at the cost of becoming blind to the plight of those he exploits in fulfilling his desires.

Schumann: *Scenes from Goethe's Faust*

Robert Schumann started working on his *Faust* in 1844. He contemplated writing an opera, but then opted for an oratorio. He began by composing first the Chorus Mysticus of the second part of the tragedy, a sequence which epitomizes Goethe's philosophy but contains no plot development. Schumann worked on this project intermittently over several years. Two scenes set to passages from the second part were premiered under the title *Fausts Verklärung* (Faust's Transfiguration) in Dresden during the celebrations of the first centenary of Goethe's birth. The performance on the 28th of August in 1849 was a great success. Franz Liszt praised the work as a successful way "to group the various forms of vocal and instrumental music usual in works for the concert hall around the oratorio, which requires a less animated plot than an opera, and, instead of the dramatic interrelations stipulated by the representation on the stage, to let the episodes of the narrative follow one another, transferring the centre of interest alternatively from the orchestra to the choir and then back again" (Liszt, *Dörnröschen*, 1856, qtd. in Stegman, 1982, 11). The statement is indicative of how Liszt's own thinking, partly influenced by Berlioz's, was developing regarding programme music.

Encouraged by this success, Schumann composed more scenes mainly from the first part but also a few from the second part. The work, known in its entirety as *Scenes from Goethe's Faust*, was premiered in 1862. It is the most episodic of all the musical adaptations of *Faust*. On its own it can hardly be said to be a narrative work at all. From the first part of Goethe's tragedy it includes only the seduction scene and two scenes related to Gretchen's agony. The seduction scene is an amalgam of different parts of Goethe's work and Schumann has made Gretchen sound somewhat flirtatious. There is nothing that would explain the next scene, her agony facing the image of Mater Dolorosa. Almost as if to intensify the mood, the scene is followed by another one in the cathedral in which Gretchen is mercilessly pestered by evil spirits. The scene is made powerful by the choir singing the "dies irae" from the Requiem.

From the second part of the tragedy Schumann has included, first of all, the marvelous opening scene in which Faust is found resting on flower-bedecked grass as the sun rises. The spirit Ariel sings. This is the highpoint of the work, vocally powerful and well orchestrated. Schumann then moves straight to the conclusion of the story, into a scene in which four allegorical figures, Want, Guilt, Necessity, and Care, are looking for Faust. Care finds him and deprives him of his sight. Yet, for Faust, this is a moment of enlightenment. Schumann has given this scene a truly enticing atmosphere. With greater enthusiasm than ever Faust engages in his construction project – only to be tricked by Mephistopheles, who is having his lemurs dig Faust's grave. Faust has a vision of a better world, dies, and is laid in his grave. This and the preceding scene are by far the finest of Schumann's scenes. His *lied*-like style functions perfectly in gauging at least some of Faust's spiritual depths. This Faust may not be quite as torn by conflicting pursuits as Goethe's hero, but he now radiates human grandeur, peace after having found a spiritual centre. The music evokes beautiful calm as Mephistopheles gently buries him. Schumann has left out the ending of the scene in which celestial hosts deprive Mephistopheles of his victory – an absolutely crucial scene in Goethe's scheme of things. Furthermore, apart form isolated delights such as Doktor Marianus' "Hier ist die Aussicht frei," Schumann's treatment of the final scene falls curiously flat. The choral sections, particularly the concluding "Alles Vergängliche," appear clumsily naïve.

Schumann's *Faust Scenes* is symptomatic of the composer's weakness in constructing large scale music dramatic structures. Thus it would be pointless to try to summarize how Goethe's ideas are treated in this work. Yet, the idea of composing only a few selected scenes without even a pretence of a narrative line is an interesting solution to the problem of treating Goethe's immense work in music. Liszt suggested that in its lack of a dramatic line the oratorio is closer to the epic of antiquity than to drama. It is not conducive to depicting passionate conflicts, developing characters, or achieving dramatic turning points. But even considering this, one can not help wishing that Schumann would have selected the scenes more judiciously and reworked the scenes taken from the second part of the tragedy.

Liszt: *A Faust Symphony*

Franz Liszt is yet another nineteenth-century artist who kept on returning to the Faust theme. Berlioz had acquainted him with Goethe's tragedy in 1830. In 1858–62 Liszt composed *Two Episodes from Lenau's Faust* which he titled *Der nächtliche Zug* (Nocturnal Procession) and *Der Tanz in der*

Dorfschenke (Dance in the Inn) – the latter is known as *Mephisto Waltz 1*. Eventually Goethe's work inspired Liszt to compose one his greatest masterpieces. However, it was only after he had settled down in Weimar, Goethe's home city, that he started thinking about what he could achieve with this material. Undoubtedly the performance of Schumann's *Faust Scenes* in 1849 provided him with further inspiration. In 1852 he invited Berlioz to conduct his *The Damnation of Faust* in Weimar and that same year he himself conducted Wagner's *Faust Overture* (Watson, 1979, 127, 139).

Liszt began working on this work of symphonic proportions in the summer of 1854 and completed the work in eight months. Three years later he revised the work and added the final chorus set to the final words of Goethe's tragedy. He dedicated his masterpiece to Berlioz (Walker, 1989, 326–8). The complete title is *A Faust Symphony in Three Character Pictures for Tenor, Male Chorus, and Orchestra*. This crystallizes the core idea of Liszt's treatment of the material. In an article on Berlioz's *Harold Symphony*, which appeared at the same time, Liszt proposed that instrumental music and programme music in particular, as opposed to opera or oratorio, were suited to give form to "Those modern poems which, for want of a better name, we shall call *philosophical epopoeias*, among [which] Goethe's *Faust* is the colossus."

> In the modern epopoeia she [nature] is rather celebrated than depicted; here her mysterious relations to the constitution of the human soul are riddled; here she almost ceases to be an object and intervenes in the development as though an active person, in order to curb man by her example, sharing his impressions, consoling him, lulling him to sleep with her dreams. (Strunk, 1965, 125)

Liszt thought that audiences in concert halls were more sophisticated than those in opera houses and that they would thus be able to appreciate the affects of the soul rather than just action (Liszt, 1996, 14–5). Programme music forced the composer to use the musical material to communicate the movements in this soul. The very form of the work was to emerge from a poetic idea, not from a detailed programme or story. The composer was to employ the extra-musical idea on such an abstract level as to be able to treat it in a purely musical fashion (Floros, 1980, 50).

The three movements of *A Faust Symphony* characterize the three central characters, Faust, Gretchen, and Mephistopheles respectively. The work concludes in a final apotheosis, the second major musical setting of "Alles Vergängliche," the concluding passage of the tragedy. Free from the constraints of an opera composer, Liszt has been able to treat the characters solely as aspects of human nature rather than individuals. Certain themes may well be associated with certain elements and even individual scenes in Goethe's tragedy. Thus, while the music appears to proceed according to a purely musical logic, particular themes, thematic developments, and intertwinement of the first movement can also be heard as a portrayal of a human tragedy about ceaseless quest, gnawing doubts, shameless arrogance, all embracing passions, and yearning for love. The music as a whole expresses the restlessness of Western man, his sensuality and his passions, his quest for knowledge, understanding, and, finally, for transcending his own limits. The lyrical second movement represents the drama of the fulfillment of love. It is an encounter with the more delicate and refined side of human nature – feminine as opposed to masculine, as Liszt and his age thought. It appears truly wonderful, but lacks the strength to curb the reckless hero. He continues his pursuits without considering the destruction he causes on his way until he turns into a parody of himself. In the third movement, all the themes that depicted him and made him appear grandiose in the first movement are distorted to the point of turning all that they represented into a grotesque joke. Moving on a general level of human experience, Liszt does not encounter the question of whether Faust is worthy of salvation. But the music does suggest that there has been something grand about the hero. This is made manifest in the love of Gretchen, who here stands for the eternal feminine. When finally the apotheosis opens up the possibility of experiencing life as something cosmically meaningful, the Gretchen themes reappear.

The way ideas are treated by means of metamorphoses of the musical material is in perfect accord with one of the most crucial ideas exemplified in the second part of *Faust*: the idea of ceaseless variations, thematic transformations, kaleidoscopic patterns generated by continuous change as the essence of the inseparable realms of nature and spirit. In this sense, Liszt has truly accomplished something in the order of Goethe's masterpiece.

Gounod: *Faust*

Faust retained his popularity in Paris for many years. In the 1840s and 1850s there appeared several adaptations in the boulevard theatres. They often relied on stage effects to gain popularity, and as volcanic eruptions were in fashion, in Adolphe d'Ennery's *Faust* the protagonist's adventures were extended as far as Pompeii – 79 B.C. (Huebner, 1990, 104). Compared to such exploits, Charles Gounod's *Faust* is a relatively respectful adaptation. The libretto was written by Jules Barbier on the basis of Michel Carré's play *Faust et Marguerite*. Nevertheless, once again Goethe's crucial idea, the perilous pact an aspiring human being makes with dubious forces in order to transcend material, natural, and spiritual limits, is completely absent. As in *The Damnation of Faust*, Gounod's opera contains only some of the most colorful scenes from the first part of Goethe's tragedy, set to equally catchy melodies. This time there is a unified plot leading into a magnificent finale as Marguerite ascends into heaven. But there is no redemption granted to the nobly ever-questing soul. As Berlioz and Liszt had realized, it could hardly have been otherwise in the context of the nineteenth-century commercial world of opera. Here both music and drama had to appeal to immediate sensations and elicit great emotions, not indulge in philosophical pondering.

Exploiting the material which Goethe had provided posed no problems to the French playwrights and librettists: there were plenty of scenes which could give rise to emotional supercharge and magnificent spectacle. Only a very little had to be added to make the story function as grand opera. Carré had included a lot of comic elements in his play, but Barbier put more emphasis on the tragic material. He included the infanticide for which Marguerite is condemned to death, which Carré had omitted, and expanded the tavern scene by having Siebel and Wagner force Méphistophélès to step back by forming a cross with their swords. This addition is indicative of the change that once again was made to Goethe's thinking: the genuinely metaphysical was reduced to the quasireligious. But at least the opera is less moralistic in tone than Berlioz's *Damnation*. All that Faust asks in exchange for promising to serve Méphistophélès down below is his youth. It is not made clear why Faust does not remain with Marguerite after the seduction. He does not appear to be a seducer or a power thirsty hedonist like Marlowe's hero. Neither is he a fundamentally restless Goethean spirit. He just happens to disappear after the seduction, while she, now pregnant, looses her reputation. Méphistophélès provokes a duel between Marguerite's brother Valentin and Faust, resulting in the brother's death. Among Carré's most ingenious additions was to have Valentin at his moment of death condemn her sister in such a fierce manner that even the bystanders are shocked. He thus becomes an emblem of unrelenting, blind vengeance.

It appears that the librettist and the composer were not all that interested in Faust. Instead, Marguerite emerges as much more the central figure, and the team actually contemplated naming the work after her. She first appears only briefly as late as the second act, but in the third and forth acts her "King of Thule" ballad, the jewel aria, and the spinning song are the main solo numbers. Also, her voice soars above everything else in the concluding trio. Faust has his moments, the third act cavatina in particular, but toward the end he appears to be merely the catalyzer of Marguerite's fate. Méphistophélès is a colorful but nevertheless fairly standard demon figure. Marguerite's centrality is apparent also in the most cruelly imposing scene of the opera. After being rejected by her brother and fellow men, she begs in agony for forgiveness from God. But Méphistophélès informs her that she will not be pardoned and the choir sings, "Where shall I find a protector, when the innocent are not free from fear?" Of the other major Faust composers, only Schumann has set this formidable scene. In accordance with Goethe, he has evil spirits torment the girl. These may easily be thought of as her bad conscience. It is more difficult to think of Méphistophélès in these terms, so he is merely being cruel without any kind of divine mandate to offer such opinions. At the very end it turns out that Marguerite will be redeemed, not because of presumed innocence as in Berlioz's *Damnation*, but because of divine grace. The point is made massively manifest in an awesome choral statement, accompanied by majestic organ music. Arguably, Gounod's *Faust* actually goes against Christian moralizing. It is symptomatic of the final concerns of the librettist and the composer that it is left open what happens to Faust. According to the last stage direction: "The walls of the prison have opened. The soul of Marguerite rises to Heaven. Faust falls to his kneels and prays. Méphistophélès is half struck down by the Archangel's shining sword."

It is pointless to disparage Gounod's *Faust* for not reaching the metaphysical heights of Goethe's masterpiece. The composer and the librettist had no such ambitions. They were professionals at the heights of their careers and produced one of the most successful operas ever composed – 1000 performances in Paris by 1894, 2000 by 1934. *Faust* was also the inaugural work at the opening of the New York Metropolitan opera in 1883. As an operatic adaptation of the first part of Goethe's Faust it may be considered unsurpassable.

Boito: *Mefistofele*

Arrigo Boito's *Mefistofele* was a serious attempt at creating a music dramatic work that would span the majestic arch of Goethe's work within a coherent plot – albeit not without substantial cuts. The work grew to such immense proportions that having it performed and taken seriously was a daunting task of truly Faustian proportions. Part of the problem was that the Italian audience was not interested in mythological and fantastic subjects; nor were they appreciative of the idea of an agonized protagonist such as Faust. Even after the Italian unification, which took place in 1867–70, they favored stories about great national heroes. And as Boito's music sounded to Italian ears most Wagnerian, the premiere of *Mefistofele* in 1868 became one of the great scandals of the history of the La Scala opera house. Boito withdrew the work, revisited it, and had the new versions successfully premiered in Bologna in 1875.

The title was probably chosen so as to distinguish the work from Gounod's still new and highly popular work rather than to reflect a change of emphasis in the treatment of the material. Nevertheless, Mefistofele does have an impressive role, more akin to Goethe's conception than in any other musical adaptation. He, too, introduces himself as "the Spirit that forever negates all." He also sneers, which is made manifest in what is probably the greatest stage whistle in the history of opera, first at the celestial choirs and then in his grand aria as he appears to Faust.

Boito begins with a prologue in heaven which he expands into shattering sonorous proportions. However, it has a very different function than the corresponding scene in Goethe's tragedy. There this encounter is preceded by the Dedication and the Prelude on the Stage. This is highly significant as the main story is thus given a triple frame, implying that the absolute can only open up for us through representations. This idea, as well as the equally crucial passage from the masculine principle manifested by the Lord to the feminine principle epitomized by Mater Gloriosa, is missing. Nor is anything left of Goethe's philosophy of nature. But once this has been pointed out, one can not help but admire Boito's ability to adapt so much of the tremendous poetic work into a normal length opera.

As the story begins, Boito's Faust is a good Christian, completely satisfied by life. In contrast to Berlioz's curious and Gounod's sensuous Faust, both of whom are adventurous spirits, this man is a philosopher. Mefistofele makes a bet with the Lord – represented by the Chorus Mysticus, which in Goethe's work appears only in the final scene – about being able to seduce Faust by exploiting his unquenchable thirst for knowledge. Faust is prepared to die and go to hell if only he could experience the satisfaction of a moment of peace endowed by full knowledge of both the world and his own soul. In Italy Boito may have been accused of being a Wagnerian, but even here he does not relinquish the Italian operatic tradition of beautiful melodic line. Far from being dramatic, the key scene of making this second bet sounds more like romantic yearning than a dramatic climax. Thus Faust does not really appear like a true Goethean hero ever bent on hot pursuit of knowledge; this quest is almost imposed on him. Possibly Boito may have thought of Mefistofele as Faust's alter ego, his evil side. He often parodies Faust's utterances, as he parodied the

Chorus Mysticus in the prologue. The idea may well derive from Liszt's *A Faust Symphony.*

Somewhat like Schumann, Boito selected certain scenes from almost the entire length of Goethe's tragedy, and like Gounod he forged them into a reasonably coherent story – although some of the ellipses in the storyline are almost as big as in Berlioz's *Damnation of Faust.* The ellipses may here be justified either dramatically as Mefistofele's magic tricks or dramatically as contrasts between scenes – Elena (Helen of Troy) appears in the scene following the one where Margherita perishes (there is an act division). The parallel is emphasized by having the same soprano perform both roles. We first hear the crazed Margherita, condemned to death, sing a delightful aria (sic), in which she tells about the horrible cell in which she is imprisoned, accused of matricide and infanticide. Assisted by Mefistofele's magic, Faust appears but is not able to persuade her to escape. She is saved by a celestial host, but as she is lost to Faust, he now attempts the gain the favors of a mythical ideal woman in the form of Elena. This is as close as Boito's Faust will ever get to the eternal feminine. At the end of the fourth act, during an ecstatic love duet, the two fall into each other's embrace. An epilogue follows in which Faust is already an old man preparing for his death. He summarizes his life:

> I have tasted each mortal secret
> The real, the ideal
> The first love of a virgin
> The ripe passion of a goddess ... yes.
> But reality proved only sadness
> And the ideal a mere dream ...

At his dying moment, Faust has a vision of a better world in which men are governed by wise laws. Boito's Faust is not saved by the eternal feminine or because he has remained faithful to his quest. He is saved much more conventionally by being fundamentally a good Christian who just wants to be a good person among his fellow men. His evil deeds are thus effortlessly whitewashed. It has been suggested that Boito opted for this rather bland conclusion because of fear of censorship. Correspondingly, the music of the conclusion reaches nowhere near the magnificence of the prologue.

Mahler: *Symphony No. 8*

Gustav Mahler crystallized his understanding of the symphonic form in the famous statement, "a symphony should be like the world: it must embrace everything." This is most evident in his *Symphony No. 8*, which has elements of an oratorio, music drama, and a salvation mystery (Floros, 1977, 38). In this respect the work is, on a formal level, much like the second part of Goethe's *Faust*, and the second (and final) movement is actually a setting of the final scene of the second part of Goethe's tragedy. However, instead of depicting the pursuits of humanity as exemplified by a reckless male hero, Mahler creates his own cultural historical vision by using the medieval hymn "veni creator spiritus" (come creative spirit) as the text of the first movement. The two texts are put into counterpoint with one another by means of telling thematic connections. The first movement is in sonata form, whereas the second is based on free thematic development guided by poetic ideas in the manner of Liszt's *A Faust Symphony*. The overall scheme as it expresses philosophical ideas through organic development of the musical material in relation to the two texts can be heard as a realization of Goethe's idea of the fundamental unity of all being.

David Greene has suggested that the most prominent theme of the first theme group of the first movement expresses in its "uproarious exuberance" the playfulness of a soul filled by the creative spirit rather than the anxiety experienced by a soul in the quest of fulfillment. Thus already the first movement is about transcendent consciousness, expressing the state achieved at the conclusion of the tragedy, rather than the eternal yearning which is the theme of the tragedy as a whole. The second theme group, beginning with the words "imple superna gratia" (fill [our souls] with grace), in turn expresses spiritual fulfillment as the tender sensation of peace (Greene, 1984, 202–3). There is a brief reference to the frailty of our bodies, "infirma nostri corporis," referring at least implicitly to doubts and despair, but this is soon swept away by the tremendous statement "accende lumen sensibus" (kindle our senses with light) in brilliant E major, thematically related to the opening "veni" themes yet clearly manifesting ascension to a higher level of being. Gradually all oppositions of the thematic material are suspended and the work culminates in an ecstatic double choir. In full accordance with Goethe's philosophy, the creative spirit has illuminated the way to participating in the universal process of creation. This exemplifies how at least in a symbolic way mankind can reach a state of not being in opposition with nature and creation – or with itself, for that matter. As the concluding verses "Gloria Patri Domino" praise the Lord, this expresses the masculine principle of creation which is to be complemented by the feminine in the second movement.

Many themes of the first movement reappear in the second so that references to the spiritual are paralleled with the celebration of nature. Perhaps most tellingly, the shattering "accende lumen" culmination of the first movement is reflected in the evocative whisperings of the *Choir and Echo* at the opening of the second movement, thus indicating that the mysterious forces of nature are consubstantial with the creative spirit. Also Pater Profundus' paean to nature as a manifestation of almighty Love is illuminated by the "accende" theme.

The overall movement is from depths and darkness to ever brighter heights. Yet, because of the musical recurrences ascension to every new sphere evokes the sensation of something familiar, as if the wonderful thing in some form or shape had always been there. The effect is amplified by the dexterous way in which a new sequence might impatiently begin before the previous one has finished – as when Doktor Marianus' ecstatic praise of Mater Gloriosa begins while the Blessed Boys are still singing. His voice fully bursts with the words "Höchste Herrscherin der Welt" (Most exalted mistress of the world) in glorious E major – as in the "accende lumen" in the first movement. All this can be thought of as a musical image of eternal becoming, where several levels of being are simultaneously manifest and illuminated by love. Toward the end of the symphony this notion reaches its peak in the appearance of Mater Gloriosa – the eternal feminine in her maternal glory. This passage has been characterized as an "aria for the orchestra" (Mitchell, 1985, 581). It is marvelously translucent and tender, orchestrated for strings, harp, and harmonium. The bridge between mundane and celestial love is completed as Gretchen intercedes in favor of "Der früh Geliebte" (The love of long ago), whom we may identify as Faust, or rather, ever questing mankind – in this state of overabundant love there is no more division into individuals. Through her sacrifice Gretchen exemplifies love that unites Faust with the divine process of creation. Significantly, the Gloriosa theme is first heard sung in her words "Neige, neige, du ohnegleiche" (Incline, incline, though unparalleled). Later on she sings her pleading "er ahnet kaum das frische Leben" (hardly conscious of the new life) on Faust's behalf to the first movement "imple superna gratia" theme. The symphony concludes with themes which derive from the "accende" and Mater Gloriosa themes, and which now resound as expressions of boundless joy.

Works Cited

Brown, Jane K. 1986. *Goethe's Faust: The German Tragedy*. Ithaca and London: Cornell University Press.

Floros, Constantin 1980. "Die Faust Symphonie von Franz Liszt." *Musik Konzepte* 12, München Edition, 42–87.

Floros, Constantin 1977. *Gustav Mahler, vol II – Mahler und die Symphonik des 19. Jahrhunderts in neuer Deutung.* Wiesbaden: Breitkopf & Härtel.

Goethe, Johann Wolfgang, von. *Faust.* Translated by Bayard Taylor (1870) 1946.

Greene, David B. 1984. *Mahler – Consciousness and Temporality.* New York: Gordon and Branch Science Publishers.

Heller, Erich 1959. *The Disinherited Mind.* New York: Meridian Books.

Huebner, Steven 1990. *The Operas of Charles Gounod.* Oxford: Clarendon Press.

Mitchell, Donald 1985. *Songs and Symphonies of Life and Death.* London: Faber and Faber.

Neumann, Michael 1985. *Das Ewig-Weibliche in Goethes "Faust."* Heidelberg: Carl Winter Universitätsverlag.

Reed, T. J. 1980. *The Classical Centre – Goethe and Weimar 1775–1832.* London: Croom Helm.

Stegmann, Michael 1982. "Eine kühne und schöne Idee." Notes on EMI-Classics recording CDMB 69450, (1982).

Strunk, Oliver (ed.) 1965. *Source Readings in Music History (V): The Romantic Era.* New York: W. W. Norton & Company.

Walker, Alan 1989. *Franz Liszt – The Weimar Years 1848–1861*, vol. 2. London and Boston: Faber and Faber.

Watson, Derek 1979. *Richard Wagner – A Biography.* London: J. M. Dent & Sons Ltd.

The Damnation of Faust

Hector Berlioz

Première Partie

Plaines de Hongrie

Scène 1

FAUST, *seul dans les champs, au lever du soleil*
Le vieil hiver a fait place au printemps;
La nature s'est rajeunie;
Des cieux la coupole infinie
Laisse pleuvoir mille feux éclatants.
Je sens glisser dans l'air la brise matinale;
De ma poitrine ardente un souffle pur s'exhale.
J'entends autour de moi le réveil des oiseaux,
Le long bruissement des plantes et des eaux …
Oh! qu'il est doux de vivre au fond des solitudes,
Loin de la lutte humaine et loin des multitudes!

*De lointaines rumeurs agrestes et guerrières commencent
à troubler le calme de la scène pastorale.*

RONDE DES PAYSANS

CHŒUR DES PAYSANS
Les bergers quittent leurs troupeaux;
Pour la fête ils se rendent beaux;
Fleurs des champs et rubans sont leur parure;
Sous les tilleuls, les voilà tous,
Dansant, sautant comme des fous.
Ha! ha! ha! ha!
Landerira!
Suivez donc la mesure!
Tra la la la la!
Ho! ho! ho!

FAUST
Quels sont ces cris? quel est ce bruit lointain?

CHŒUR
Tra la la la! Ho! ho! ho!

Part 1

Plains of Hungary

Scene 1

FAUST, *alone in the fields, at sunrise*
Old winter has made way for spring;
Nature has grown young again.
The immense dome of heaven pours down
A glittering rain of light.
I feel the morning breeze stir the air.
From my ardent breast a pure breath breaks.
All around me I hear birds waking,
The steady rustle of plants and streams.
Oh, how sweet it is to live in utter solitude,
Far from human strife and the multitudes of men!

*Distant sounds of rustic life and of war begin to disturb
the calm of the landscape.*

PEASANTS' ROUND DANCE

CHORUS OF PEASANTS
The shepherds leave their flocks;
They're dressing up for the feast;
Ribbons and wild flowers are their attire.
See them all, under the lime trees,
Dancing, leaping like madmen.
Ha! ha! ha! ha!
Fa la la la!
Follow the beat of the dance.
Tra la la la la!
Ho! ho! ho!

FAUST
What are those cries, what is that distant sound?

CHORUS
Tra la la la! Ho! ho! ho!

FAUST

Ce sont des villageois, au lever du matin
Qui dansent en chantant sur la verte pelouse.
De leurs plaisirs ma misère est jalouse.

CHŒUR

Ils passaient tous comme l'éclair,
Et les robes volaient en l'air;
Mais bientôt on fut moins agile:
Le rouge leur montait au front,
Et l'un sur l'autre dans le rond,
Ha! ha! ha! *etc.*

Landerira!
Tours tombaient à la file,
Ha! ha! ha! ha! Landerira!
"Ne me touchez donc pas ainsi!"
– "Paix! ma femme n'est point ici!
Profitons de la circonstance!"
Dehors il l'emmena soudain,
Et tout allait, allait son train,
Ha! ha! ha! ha! Landerira!
La musique et la danse.
Tra la la la!
Ho! ho! ho!

Scène 2

Une autre partie de la plaine; une armée qui s'avance.

FAUST

Mais d'un éclat guerrier les campagnes se parent.
Ah! les fils du Danube aux combats se préparent!
Avec quel air fier et joyeux
Ils portent leur armure!
Et quel feu dans leurs yeux!
Tout cœur frémit à leur chant de victoire;
Le mien seul reste froid, insensible à la gloire.

MARCHE HONGROISE

Les troupes passent; Faust s'éloigne.

FAUST

It is villagers, who have risen at daybreak
To dance and sing on the green sward.
My wretchedness grudges them their delights.

CHORUS

They all went by like lightning
And their dresses flew in the air;
But presently they grew clumsy,
Their faces were on fire,
And one by one in the ring,
Ha! ha! ha! *etc.*

Fa la la la!
They all fell down in a row.
Ha! ha! ha! ha! Fa la la la!
"Don't touch me like that!"
– "Don't worry, my wife's not here,
Let's take your chance."
He snatched her from the circle,
And everything took its course.
Ha! ha! ha! ha! Fa la la la!
Music and dancing.
Tra la la la!
Ho! ho! ho!

Scene 2

Another part of the plain; an army advancing.

FAUST

But the plains flash with a warlike gleam.
Ah, the sons of the Danube prepare for combat.
With what joy and price
They wear their armour.
With what fire their eyes blaze.
All hearts throb to their victory song;
Mine alone remains cold, indifferent to glory.

HUNGARIAN MARCH

The troops pass; Faust moves off.

Deuxième Partie

Nord de l'Allemagne

Scène 3

FAUST, *seul dans son cabinet de travail*
Sans regrets j'ai quitté les riantes campagnes
Où m'a suivi l'ennui.
Sans plaisir je revois nos altières montagnes;
Dans ma vieille cité je reviens avec lui.
Oh! je souffre, je souffre! et la nuit sans étoiles,
Qui vient d'étendre au loin son silence et ses voiles,
Ajoute encor à mes sombres douleurs.
Ô terre! pour moi seul tu n'as donc pas de fleurs!
Par le monde, où trouver ce qui manque à ma vie?
Je chercherais en vain, tout fuit mon âpre envie!
Allons! il faut finir! …
Mais je tremble … pourquoi
Trembler devant l'abîme entr'ouvert devant moi?
Ô coupe trop longtemps à mes désirs ravie,
Viens, viens, noble cristal! verse-moi le poison
Qui doit illuminer ou tuer ma raison!

Il porte la coupe à ses lèvres.

CHANT DE LA FÊTE DE PÂQUES

CHŒUR
Christ vient de ressusciter!

FAUST
Qu'entends-je?

CHŒUR
Quittant du tombeau
Le séjour funeste.
Au parvis céleste
Il monte plus beau.
Vers les gloires immortelles
Tandis qu'il s'élance à grands pas,
Ses disciples fidèles
Languissent ici-bas.
Hélas! c'est ici qu'il nous laisse

Part 2

North Germany

Scene 3

FAUST, *alone in his study*
Without regret I left the smiling countryside;
There too my ennui pursued me.
Without pleasure I see again our proud mountains;
I return to my ancient city with my burden still.
Oh how I suffer – and the starless night
Which has just spread its veil of silence over the world
Intensifies my brooding melancholy.
Earth, for me alone do you bear no flowers?
Where in all the world can I find what my life lacks?
Vainly would I search: everything flies my yearning grasp.
Come, it's time to end ...
Yet I tremble ... Why
Tremble before the abyss that already yawns before me?
Oh cup too long denied to my desires,
Come, noble crystal, give me the poison
That must illuminate my reason or destroy it!

He lifts the cup to his lips.

EASTER HYMN

CHORUS
Christ has risen!

FAUST
What do I hear?

CHORUS
Leaving the dark confines
Of the tomb,
He rises transfigured
To the courts of heaven.
While He strides
Towards eternal glory,
His faithful disciples
Languish here below.
Alas, He leaves us here

Sous les traits brûlants du malheur.
Ô divin Maître! ton bonheur
Est cause de notre tristesse!
Ô divin Maître! tu nous laisses
Sous les traits brûlants du malheur.

FAUST
Ô souvenirs!

CHŒUR
Christ vient de ressusciter!
Hosanna!

FAUST
Ô mon âme tremblante!
Sur l'aile de ces chants
Vas-tu voler aux cieux?
La foi chancelante
Revient, me ramenant
La paix des jours pieux,
Mon heureuse enfance,
La douceur de prier,
La pure jouissance
D'errer et de rêver
Par les vertes prairies,
Aux clartés infinies
D'un soleil de printemps!
Ô baiser de l'amour céleste
Qui remplissais mon cœur de doux pressentiments,
Et chassais tout désir, tout désir funeste!

CHŒUR
Quittant du tombeau
Le séjour funeste,
Au parvis céleste
Il monte plus beau.
Vers les gloires immortelles
Tandis qu'il s'élance à grands pas,
Ses disciples fidèles
Languissent ici-bas,
Mais croyons-en sa parole éternelle.
Nous le suivrons un jour,
Au céleste séjour

Under the burning arrows of adversity.
Oh, divine Master, Thy bliss
Is cause of our sorrow.
Oh divine Master, Thou leavest us
Under the burning arrows of adversity.

FAUST
Oh memories!

CHORUS
Christ has risen!
Hosanna!

FAUST
Oh my fluttering soul,
Will you soar to heaven
On the wings of this song?
My wavering beliefs, renewed,
Return, bringing me the peace
Of my days of faith,
My happy childhood,
The tenderness of prayer,
The pure delight
Of wandering, dreamlike,
Through the green meadows
In the infinite light
Of a springtime sun.
Oh kiss of divine love
That filled my heart with sweet presentiments
And banished all fatal desires!

CHORUS
Leaving the dark confines
Of the tomb,
He rises transfigured
To the courts of heaven.
While He strides
Towards eternal glory,
His faithful disciples
Languish here below.
But let us believe His eternal word:
One day we shall follow Him
To the heavenly home

Où sa voix nous appelle.
Hosanna! Hosanna! Hosanna!

FAUST
Hélas! doux chants du ciel, pourquoi dans sa poussière
Réveiller le maudit? Hymnes de la prière,
Pourquoi soudain venir ébranler mon dessein?
Vos suaves accords refraîchissent mon sein.
Chants plus doux que l'aurore,
Retentissez encore!
Mes larmes ont coulé, le ciel m'a reconquis.

Scène 4

MÉPHISTOPHÉLÈS, *apparaissant brusquement*
Ô pure émotion! Énfant du saint parvis!
Je t'admire, docteur! Les pieuses volées
De ces clochers d'argent
Ont charmé grandement
Tes oreilles troublées!

FAUST
Qui donc es-tu? toi, dont l'ardent regard
Pénètre ainsi que l'éclat d'un poignard,
Et qui, comme la flamme,
Brûle et dévore l'âme!

MÉPHISTOPHÉLÈS
Vraiment, pour un docteur, la demande est frivole.
Je suis l'esprit de vie, et c'est moi qui console.
Je te donnerai tout: le bonheur, le plaisir,
Tout ce que peut rêver le plus ardent désir.

FAUST
Eh bien! pauvre démon, fais-moi voir tes merveilles!

MÉPHISTOPHÉLÈS
Certes! j'enchanterai tes yeux et tes oreilles.
Au lieu de t'enfermer, triste comme le ver
Qui ronge tes bouquins, viens! suis-moi! change d'air!

FAUST
J'y consens.

Where His voice summons us.
Hosanna! Hosanna! Hosanna!

FAUST
Alas, gentle hymns of heaven, why awake
The cursed wretch in his dust? Songs of prayer,
Why have you come to shake my purpose?
Your tender tones refresh my heart.
Songs sweeter than the dawn,
Play on!
My tears have flowed, heaven has won me back.

Scene 4

MEPHISTOPHELES, *suddenly appearing*
Oh innocent emotion! Child of the precincts!
My congratulations, doctor: the pious pealing
Of those silver bells
Has marvellously charmed
Your troubled ears.

FAUST
Who are you, whose fierce glance
Pierces like the point of a dagger
And, like a flame
Burns and consumes the soul?

MEPHISTOPHELES
Really, for a learned man the question is not serious.
I am the spirit of life, the consoler of men.
I'll give you everything: happiness, pleasure,
All that the wildest desire can dream of.

FAUST
Very well, my poor demon, show me your tricks.

MEPHISTOPHELES
Done! I'll delight your eyes and ears.
Instead of shutting yourself up, dreary as the worms
That gnaw your old books, come, follow me – a change of air.

FAUST
I consent.

MÉPHISTOPHÉLÈS
Partons donc pour connaître la vie,
Et laisse le fatras de ta philosophie!

Ils disparaissent dans les airs.

Scène 5

Le cave d'Auerbach à Leipzig

CHŒUR DE BUVEURS

CHŒUR
A boire encor! du vin
Du Rhin!

MÉPHISTOPHÉLÈS
Voici, Faust, un séjour de folle compagnie.
Ici vins et chansons réjouissent la vie.

CHŒUR
Oh! qu'il fait bon, quand le ciel tonne,
Rester près d'un bol enflammé,
Et se remplir comme une tonne,
Dans un cabaret enfumé!
J'aime le vin et cette eau blonde
Qui fait oublier le chagrin.
Quand ma mère me mit au monde
J'eus un ivrogne pour parrain.
Oh! qu'il fait bon, quand le ciel tonne, *etc.*

UNE PARTIE DU CHŒUR
Qui sait quelque plaisante histoire?
En riant le vin est meilleur.

UNE PARTIE DU CHŒUR
A toi, Brander!

UNE PARTIE DU CHŒUR
Il n'a plus de mémoire.

BRANDER
J'en sais une, et j'en suis l'auteur.

CHŒUR
Eh bien donc, vite!

MEPHISTOPHELES
Come, we'll get to know life
And leave behind your useless philosophy.

They vanish into the air.

Scene 5

Auerbach's cellar in Leipzig

CHORUS OF DRINKERS

CHORUS
More drink! Some wine!
Some Rhenish!

MEPHISTOPHELES
Here, Faust, a den of mad companions;
Here life is gladdened with wine and song.

CHORUS
Oh, it's good when the skies thunder
To sit by a bowl of fiery drink
And fill yourself like a barrel
In a smoky tavern.
I love wine and that pale spirit
That makes you forget your troubles.
When my mother brought me into the world
She gave me a drunkard for godfather.
Oh, it's good when the skies thunder, *etc.*

PART OF THE CHORUS
Who knows a good story?
Wine is better when you laugh.

PART OF THE CHORUS
Brander, it's your turn.

PART OF THE CHORUS
He's past remembering anything.

BRANDER
I know one, I wrote it myself.

CHORUS
Well, out with it.

BRANDER
Puisqu'on m'invite,
Je vais vous chanter du nouveau.

CHŒUR
Bravo! bravo!

CHANSON DE BRANDER

BRANDER
Certain rat, dans une cuisine
Établi comme un vrai frater,
S'y traitait si bien que sa mine
Eût fait envie au gros Luther.
Mais un beau jour le pauvre diable,
Empoisonné, sauta dehors,
Aussi triste, aussi misérable
Que s'il eût eu l'amour au corps!

CHŒUR
Que s'il eût eu l'amour au corps!

BRANDER
Il courait devant et derrière;
Il grattait, reniflait, mordait,
Parcourait la maison entière;
La rage à ses maux ajoutait,
Au point qu'à l'aspect du délire
Qui consumait ses vains efforts
Les mauvais plaisants pouvaient dire:
Ce rat a bien l'amour au corps!

CHŒUR
Ce rat a bien l'amour au corps!

BRANDER
Dans le fourneau le pauvre sire
Crut pourtant se cacher très bien;
Mais il se trompait, et le pire,
C'est qu'on l'y fit rôtir enfin.
La servante, méchante fille,
De son malheur rit bien alors. –
Ah! disait-elle, comme il grille!
Il a vraiment l'amour au corps!

BRANDER
Since you press me,
I'll sing you a new one.

CHORUS
Bravo, bravo!

BRANDER'S SONG

BRANDER
A rat once in a kitchen
Had set itself up like a real monk.
It did itself so well that the sight of it
Would have moved the fat Luther to envy.
But one fine day the poor devil
Ate poison, and leaped out
Just as wretched and frantic
As if it had been on heat.

CHORUS
As if it had been on heat!

BRANDER
It ran up and down,
Scratched, snuffled, gnawed,
And rushed all over the house.
Its rage only made it suffer worse,
Until at the sight of the frenzy
Which exhausted its useless efforts,
The cruel wits could say:
"That rat's really on heat."

CHORUS
"That rat's really on heat."

BRANDER
The poor brute thought that the oven
Would make a good refuge;
But is was wrong; and the worst of it was
That it was quite roasted in the end.
The nasty kitchen maid
Laughed at its fate.
"Ah-ha," she said, "look how it's singed!
It's on heat all right."

CHŒUR
Il a vraiment l'amour au corps!
Requiescat in pace. Amen.

BRANDER
Pour l'amen une fugue! une fugue! un choral!
Improvisons un morceau magistral.

MÉPHISTOPHÉLÈS, *bas à Faust*
Écoute bien ceci: nous allons voir, docteur,
La bestialité dans toute sa candeur.

FUGUE SUR LE THÈME DE LA CHANSON DE BRANDER

BRANDER, CHŒUR
Amen.

MÉPHISTOPHÉLÈS
Vrai Dieu, messieurs, votre fugue est forte belle,
Et telle
Qu'à l'entendre on se croit aux saints lieux!
Souffrez qu'on vous le dise:
Le style en est savant, vraiment religieux;
On ne saurait exprimer mieux
Les sentiments pieux
Qu'en terminant ses prières l'Eglise
En un seul mot résume. Maintenant,
Puis-je à mon tour riposter par un chant
Sur un sujet non moins touchant
Que le vôtre?

CHŒUR
Ah ça! mais se moque-t-il de nous?
Quel est cet homme? Quel est cet homme?
Oh! qu'il est pâle, et comme
Son poil est roux!
N'importe! Volontiers! Autre chanson! A vous! à vous!

CHANSON DE MÉPHISTOPHÉLÈS

MÉPHISTOPHÉLÈS
Une puce gentille
Chez un prince logeait.
Comme sa propre fille,
Le brave homme l'aimait.

CHORUS
"It's on heat all right!"
Requiescat in pace. Amen.

BRANDER
For the amen a fugue, a fugue, a chorale;
Let's improvise a first-rate number.

MEPHISTOPHELES, *in a low voice to Faust*
Attend carefully, professor; we'll see
Brutality in all its innocence.

FUGUE ON THE THEME OF BRANDER'S SONG

BRANDER, CHORUS
Amen.

MEPHISTOPHELES
By heaven, gentlemen, your fugue is very fine;
To hear it
One would suppose one was in some holy place.
If you'll allow me to say so,
Its style is learned, truly religious;
One could not express better
Those pious sentiments
Which the Church, to conclude its prayers,
Sums up in a single word. Now,
May I cap it
With another, on a subject
No less touching than yours?

CHORUS
What's this, is he making fun of us?
Who is this man? Who is this man?
Ah, how pale he is,
What red hair he's got!
No matter! All right – another song! Your turn!

MEPHISTOPHELES' SONG

MEPHISTOPHELES
A delightful flea
Once lodged with a prince;
The good man loved it
As his own daughter,

Et, l'histoire l'assure,
Par son tailleur, un jour,
Lui fit prendre mesure
Pour un habit de cour.

L'insecte plein de joie,
Dès qu'il se vit paré
D'or, de velours, de soie,
Et de croix décoré,
Fit venir de province
Ses frères et ses sœurs
Qui, par ordre du prince,
Devinrent grands seigneurs.

Mais ce qui fut bien pire,
C'est que les gens de cour,
Sans en oser rien dire,
Se grattaient tout le jour.
Cruelle politique!
Ah! plaignons leur destin.
Et dès qu'une nous pique,
Ecrasons-la soudain!

CHŒUR
Bravo! ha! ha! bravo! bravissimo!
Ecrasons-la, oui, écrasons-la soudain!

FAUST
Assez! fuyons ces lieux où la parole est vile,
La joie ignoble et le geste brutal!
N'as tu d'autres plaisirs, un séjour plus tranquille
A me donner, toi, mon guide infernal?

MÉPHISTOPHÉLÈS
Ah, ceci te déplait? Suis-moi.

Ils partent.

And, so history assures us,
One day had it
Measured by his tailor
For a court dress.

The insect, overjoyed
At the sight of itself
Dressed in gold, velvet, and silk
And decorated with a cross,
Sent for its brothers and sisters
From the country,
And by order of the prince
They became grandees.

But the tragedy of it was
That the courtiers
Dared not say anything,
But scratched all day long.
Cruel politics!
Ah, let us bewail their fate,
And as soon as one bites us,
Squash it on the spot!

CHORUS
Bravo, ha! ha! bravo! bravissimo!
Squash it, yes, squash it on the spot!

FAUST
Enough, let's leave this place where speech is vile,
Joy base and action brutal.
Have you no other pleasures, a gentler place
To give me, my satanic guide?

MEPHISTOPHELES
Oh, don't you like it? Then follow me.

They leave.

Scène 6

Bosquets et prairies du bord de l'Elbe

AIR DE MÉPHISTOPHÉLÈS

MÉPHISTOPHÉLÈS
Voici des roses,
De cette nuit écloses.
Sur ce lit embaumé,
Ô mon Faust bien-aimé,
Repose!
Dans un voluptueux sommeil
Où glissera sur toi plus d'un baiser vermeil,
Où des fleurs pour ta couche ouvriront leurs corolles,
Ton oreille entendra de divines paroles.
Écoute! écoute!
Les Esprits de la terre et de l'air
Commencent pour ton rêve un suave concert.

SONGE DE FAUST

CHŒUR DE GNOMES ET DE SYLPHES
Dors! heureux
Faust. Bientôt sous un voile
D'or et d'azur tes yeux
Vont se fermer;
Au front des cieux
Va briller ton étoile;
Songes d'amour vont enfin te charmer.

De sites ravissants
La campagne se couvre,
Et notre œil y découvre
Des fleurs, des bois, des champs,
Et d'épaisses feuillées
Où de tendres amants
Promènent leurs pensées.

MÉPHISTOPHÉLÈS
Heureux Faust!
Bientôt, sous un voile
D'or et d'azur, tes yeux
Vont se fermer.

Scene 6

Groves and meadows by the Elbe

MEPHISTOPHELES' ARIA

MEPHISTOPHELES
Here are roses
New-blown tonight.
Here on this embalmed bed,
Oh my beloved Faust,
Rest yourself.
In a voluptuous sleep,
While crimson kisses steal upon you,
And flowers bloom for your couch,
Your ear will hear divine utterance.
Listen! Listen!
The spirits of earth and air
Begin soft music for your dream.

FAUST'S DREAM

CHORUS OF GNOMES AND SYLPHS
Sleep,
Happy Faust! Soon beneath a veil
Of gold and azure
Your eyes will close;
Your star will burn brightly
In the heavens.
Dreams of love will at last enchant you.

The countryside is covered
With exquisite places;
Our vision discovers
Flowers, woods, fields,
And secret groves
Where gentle lovers
Walk with their thoughts.

MEPHISTOPHELES
Happy Faust!
Soon beneath a veil
Of gold and azure
Your eyes will close.

CHŒUR
De sites ravissants
La campagne se couvre, *etc.*

Mais plus loin sont couverts
Les longs rameaux des treilles
De bourgeons, pampres verts,
Et de grappes vermeilles.

MÉPHISTOPHÉLÈS
Au front des cieux
Va briller ton étoile.

FAUST
Ah! sur mes yeux
Déjà s'étend un voile.

CHŒUR
Vois ces jeunes amants
Le long de la vallée,
Oublier les instants
Sous la fraîche feuillée.
Une beauté les suit,
Ingénue et pensive;
A sa paupière luit
Une larme furtive.

MÉPHISTOPHÉLÈS
Une beauté les suit.
Faust, elle t'aimera.

FAUST, *endormi*
Margarita!

CHŒUR, MÉPHISTOPHÉLÈS
Le lac étend ses flots
A l'entour des montagnes;
Dans les vertes campagnes
Il serpente en ruisseaux.

CHŒUR
Là, de chants d'allégresse
La rive retentit. Ha!
D'autres chœurs là sans cesse
La danse nous ravit.

CHORUS
The countryside is covered
With exquisite places, *etc.*

Farther off, the long boughs
Are thick with vines,
Green clusters
And purple grapes.

MEPHISTOPHELES
Your star will burn brightly
In the heavens.

FAUST
Ah! over my eyes
Already falls a veil.

CHORUS
See those young lovers
Along the valley,
Forgetting time
Under the green arches.
A lovely girl follows them,
Artless and melancholy;
On her eyelid glistens
A shy tear.

MEPHISTOPHELES
A lovely girl follows them.
Faust, she will love you.

FAUST, *asleep*
Margarita!

CHORUS, MEPHISTOPHELES
The lake spreads its waters
Around the mountains;
In the green countryside
It winds in streams.

CHORUS
There, songs of joy
Echo from the bank. Ha!
There the dancing of other troupes
Endlessly delights us.

Les uns gaiement s'avancent
Autour des coteaux verts. Ha!
De plus hardis s'élancent
Au sein des flots amers.

FAUST, *rêvant*
Margarita, ô Margarita!

CHŒUR, MÉPHISTOPHÉLÈS
Le lac étend ses flots, *etc.*

CHŒUR
Partout l'oiseau timide,
Cherchant l'ombre et le frais,
S'enfuit d'un vol rapide.

MÉPHISTOPHÉLÈS
Le charme opère; il est à nous.

CHŒUR
Au milieu des marais,
Tous, pour goûter la vie.

FAUST
Margarita!

CHŒUR
Tous cherchent dans les cieux
Une étoile chérie
Qui s'alluma pour eux.
C'est elle,
Si belle,
Qu'amour te destina.
Dors! dors!
Dors! dors! dors!

MÉPHISTOPHÉLÈS
C'est bien, c'est bien, jeunes esprits,
Je suis content de vous.
Bercez, bercez son sommeil enchanté!

CHŒUR
Dors, heureux Faust, dors! dors!

Some gaily advance
Over the green slopes. Ha!
The boldest plunge
Into the chilly stream.

FAUST, *dreaming*
Margarita! Oh, Margarita!

CHORUS, MEPHISTOPHELES
The lake spreads its waters, *etc.*

CHORUS
Everywhere timid birds
Seek the cool shade
And flee with rapid wings

MEPHISTOPHELES
The charm's working, he's ours.

CHORUS
To the midst of the marshes.
Everyone, in search of life,

FAUST
Margarita!

CHORUS
Everyone seeks in the skies
A cherished star
Which shines for him.
It is she,
So fair,
That love destined for you.
Sleep! Sleep!
Sleep! Sleep! Sleep!

MEPHISTOPHELES
It is well, my young elves;
I am pleased with you.
Rock gently his enchanted sleep.

CHORUS
Sleep, happy Faust, sleep! sleep!

BALLET DES SYLPHES

Les esprit de l'air se balancent quelque temps autour de Faust endormi et disparaissent peu à peu.

Scène 7

FAUST, *s'éveillant en sursaut*
Margarita!
Qu'ai-je vu?
Quelle céleste image! quel ange
Au front mortel!
Où le trouver?
Vers quel autel
Traîner à ses pieds ma louange?

MÉPHISTOPHÉLÈS
Eh bien! il faut me suivre encor
Jusqu'à cette alcôve embaumée
Où repose ta bien-aimée.
A toi seul ce divin trésor!
Des étudiants voici la joyeuse cohorte
Qui va passer devant sa porte.
Parmi ces jeunes fous, au bruit de leurs chansons,
Vers ta beauté nous parviendrons;
Mais contiens tes transports et suis bien mes leçons.

CHŒUR DE SOLDATS ET CHANSON D'ÉTUDIANTS

CHŒUR DE SOLDATS
Villes entourées
De murs et remparts,
Fillettes sucrées,
Aux malins regards,
Victoire certaine
Près de vous m'attend.
Si grande est la peine,
Le prix est plus grand.
Aux sons des trompettes,
Les braves soldats
S'élancent aux fêtes
Ou bien aux combats.
Fillettes et villes

DANCE OF THE SYLPHS

The spirits of the air hover awhile around
the sleeping Faust then vanish one by one.

Scene 7

FAUST, *waking with a start*
Margarita!
What have I seen?
What heavenly vision, what angel
With mortal countenance!
Where can I find her?
At what altar
Lay my homage at her feet?

MEPHISTOPHELES
All right, then, you must follow me once more,
To that perfumed bower
Where lies your beloved.
This heavenly treasure is for you alone.
Here's a jovial crowd of students
Which will be passing by her door.
Among these young fools, to the sound of their songs,
We'll make our way to your beauty.
But contain your raptures and follow my instructions carefully.

SOLDIERS' CHORUS AND STUDENTS' SONG

CHORUS OF SOLDIERS
Towns girdled
With walls and ramparts,
Demure girls
With sly looks,
Certain victory
Over you will be mine.
The effort is great
But the prize is greater.
At the trumpets' sound
Brave soldiers
Hurl themselves
Into pleasure or battle.
Young girls and towns

Font les difficiles;
Bientôt tout se rend.
Si grande est la peine,
Le prix est plus grand.
Villes entourées, *etc.*

CHŒUR D'ÉTUDIANTS

* Jam nox stellata velamina pandit.
Nunc, nunc bibendum et amandum est.
Vita brevis fugaxque voluptas,
Gaudeamus igitur, gaudeamus!
Nobis sub ridente luna,
Per urbem quaerentes puellas eamus!
Ut cras, fortunati Caesares, dicamus:
Veni, vidi, vici!
Gaudeamus, gaudeamus, gaudeamus igitur!

Chœur de soldats et chanson d'étudiants ensemble

CHŒUR DE SOLDATS
Villes entourées
De murs et remparts, *etc.*

CHŒUR DES ÉTUDIANTS, FAUST, MÉPHISTOPHÉLÈS
Jam nox stellata velamina pandit, *etc.*

---

* Déjà la nuit étend ses voiles étoilés;
    C'est l'heure de boire et d'aimer.
    La vie est brève et le plaisir fugitif!
    Réjouissons-nous donc, réjouissons-nous.
    Pendant que la lune nous sourit,
    Allons par la ville cherchant les jeunes filles,
    Pour que demain, heureux Césars, nous disions:
    "Je suis venu, j'ai vu, j'ai vaincu!"
    Réjouissons-nous donc, réjouissons-nous!

Put up resistance;
But soon they all surrender.
The effort is great
But the prize greater.
Towns girdled, *etc.*

CHORUS OF STUDENTS
* Jam nox stellata velamina pandit.
Nunc, nunc bibendum et amandum est.
Vita brevis fugaxque voluptas,
Gaudeamus igitur, gaudeamus!
Nobis sub ridente luna,
Per urbem quaerentes puellas eamus!
Ut cras, fortunati Caesares, dicamus:
Veni, vidi, vici!
Gaudeamus, gaudeamus, gaudeamus igitur!

Soldiers' Chorus and Students' Song together

CHORUS OF SOLDIERS
Towns girdled
With walls and ramparts, *etc.*

CHORUS OF STUDENTS, FAUST, MEPHISTOPHELES
Jam nox stellata velamina pandit, *etc.*

---

* Already night draws its starry veil.
Now's the time to drink and make love.
Life is short, pleasure fleeting;
So let's enjoy ourselves.
While the moon winks down at us,
Let's roam the town looking for girls,
So that tomorrow, happy Caesars, we can say:
I came, I saw, I conquered!
So let's enjoy ourselves.

Troisième Partie

Tambours et trompettes sonnant la retraite.

Chambre de Marguerite, le soir.

Scène 8

AIR DE FAUST

FAUST
Merci, doux crépuscule! Oh! sois le bienvenu!
Éclaire enfin ces lieux, sanctuaire inconnu,
Où je sens à mon front glisser comme un beau rêve,
Comme le frais baiser d'un matin qui se lève!
C'est de l'amour, c'est de l'amour, j'espère …
Oh! comme on sent ici
S'envoler le souci!
Que j'aime ce silence, et comme je respire
Un air pur!
Ô jeune fille! ô ma charmante!
Ô ma trop idéale amante!
Quel sentiment j'éprouve en ce moment fatal!

Que j'aime à contempler ton chevet virginal!
Quel air pur je respire!
Seigneur! Seigneur!
Après ce long martyre,
Que de bonheur!

*Faust, marchant lentement, examine avec une curiosité passionnée
l'intérieur de la chambre de Marguerite.*

Scène 9

MÉPHISTOPHÉLÈS, *accourant*
Je l'entends!
Sous ces rideaux de soie
Cache-toi.

FAUST
Dieu! mon cœur se brise dans la joie!

Part 3

Drums and trumpets sounding Retreat.

Marguerite's room, evening.

Scene 8

FAUST'S ARIA

FAUST
Thanks, gentle twilight, you are welcome.
Reveal to me at last this secret sanctuary
Where I feel peace steal over me like a dream,
Like the caress of the fresh morning air:
It is of love, it is of love, I hope ...
Oh, how one feels
Cares vanish in this place!
How I adore this silence and breathe
A pure serenity!
Oh sweet girl, my enchanting one,
My too longed for lover!
What feelings possess me in this moment of destiny!

What delight to look upon your maiden bed!
What pure tranquillity I breathe!
God! God!
After my long martyrdom
What happiness!

*Faust walks slowly about Marguerite's room, examining it with
passionate curiosity.*

Scene 9

MEPHISTOPHELES, *rushing in*
I can hear her.
Hide
Behind these silk curtains.

FAUST
God, my heart is bursting for joy!

MÉPHISTOPHÉLÈS
Profite des instants. Adieu, modère-toi
Ou tu la perds.

Il cache Faust derrière les rideaux.

Bien! mes follets et moi,
Nous allons vous chanter un bel épithalame.

FAUST
Oh, calme-toi,
Mon âme!

Scène 10

*Entre Marguerite, une lampe à la main; Faust caché,
Méphistophélès sort.*

MARGUERITE
Que l'air est étouffant!
J'ai peur comme une enfant!
C'est mon rêve d'hier qui m'a toute troublée …
En songe je l'ai vu, lui, mon futur amant,
Qu'il était beau!
Dieu! j'étais tant aimée! j'étais tant aimée!
Et combien je l'aimais!
Nous verrons-nous jamais
Dans cette vie?
Folie!

LE ROI DE THULÉ (chanson gothique)

Marguerite chante en tressant ses cheveux.

Autrefois un roi de Thulé
Qui jusqu'au tombeau fut fidèle,
Reçut, à la mort de sa belle,
Une coupe d'or ciselé.
Comme elle ne le quittait guère,
Dans les festins les plus joyeux,
Toujours une larme légère
A sa vue humectait ses yeux.

Ce prince, à la fin de sa vie,
Lègue ses villes et son or,

MEPHISTOPHELES
Take your chance. Farewell, and keep calm
Or you will lose her.

He conceals Faust behind the arras.

Good. Now my will o' the wisp and I
Will sing you both a fine nuptial song.

FAUST
Be still,
My soul!

Scene 10

Marguerite enters, a lamp in her hand; Faust hidden.
Mephistopheles goes out.

MARGUERITE
How heavy the air is;
I'm as frightened as a child.
The dream I had last night has quite upset me ...
While I slept I saw him, my future lover.
How handsome he was!
God, how I was loved,
And how I loved him!
Shall we ever see one another
In this life?
What madness!

THE KING OF THULE (Ballad)

Marguerite sings as she braids her hair.

Once a king of Thule
Who kept faith until the grave
Received, at his fair one's death,
A cup of carved gold.
At the most joyful feasts
It hardly ever left his hand,
And ever at the sight of it
A tear moistened his eye.

This prince, at the end of his life,
Bequeaths his cities and his gold,

Excepté la coupe chérie
Qu'à la main il conserve encor.
Il fait, à sa table royale,
Asseoir ses barons et ses pairs,
Au milieu de l'antique salle
D'un château que baignaient les mers.

Le buveur se lève et s'avance
Auprès d'un vieux balcon doré.
Il boit, et soudain sa main lance
Dans les flots le vase sacré.
Le vase tombe; l'eau bouillonne,
Puis se calme aussitôt après.
Le vieillard pâlit et frissonne:
Il ne boira plus désormais.
Autrefois un roi … de Thulé …
Jusqu'au tombeau … fut fidèle …
Ah! *(profond soupir)*

Scène 11

Cour de la maison de Marguerite.

ÉVOCATION

MÉPHISTOPHÉLÈS
Esprits des flammes inconstantes,
Accourez! j'ai besoin de vous.
Accourez! accourez!
Follets capricieux, vos lueurs malfaisantes
Vont charmer une enfant et l'amener à nous.
Au nom du diable, en danse!
Et vous, marquez bien la cadence,
Ménétriers d'enfer, ou je vous éteins tous.

MENUET DES FOLLETS

Scène 12

MÉPHISTOPHÉLÈS, *faisant le mouvement d'un homme
qui joue de la vielle.*
Maintenant
Chantons à cette belle une chanson morale,
Pour la perdre plus sûrement.

But not the cherished cup
Which he still keeps in his hand.
He seats his barons and his peers
At the royal table
In the middle of the antique hall
Of a castle washed by the sea.

The drinker rises and goes
To an ancient gilded balcony.
He drinks, then suddenly his hand flings
The holy goblet into the waves.
The goblet sinks, the water seethes,
Then is calm a moment later.
The old man grows pale and shivers.
He will never drink again.
Once a king ... of Thule ...
Kept faith ... until the grave ...
Ah! *(deep sigh)*

Scene 11

The courtyard of Marguerite's house.

EVOCATION

MEPHISTOPHELES
Spirits of fickle flame,
Come quickly, I have need of you.
Come quickly!
Wayward will o' the wisps, your dubious gleam
Is going to bewitch a young girl and lead her to us.
Dance in the Devil's name!
And you, minstrels of hell,
Keep time, or I'll put out all your lights!

MINUET OF THE WILL O' THE WISPS

Scene 12

MEPHISTOPHELES, *with the gesture of a man playing a hurdy-gurdy*
Now
Let's sing the fair one a moral song,
To damn her the more surely.

SÉRÉNADE DE MÉPHISTOPHÉLÈS
(avec chœur de follets)

Devant la maison.
De celui qui t'adore,
Petite Louison,
Que fais tu dès l'aurore?
Au signal du plaisir,
Dans la chambre du drille
Tu peux bien entrer fille,
Mais non fille en sortir …
Devant la maison, *etc.*

CHŒUR
Que fais-tu, que fais-tu?

MÉPHISTOPHÉLÈS, CHŒUR
avec un éclat de rire strident.
Ha!

MÉPHISTOPHÉLÈS
Il te tend les bras,
Près de lui tu cours vite,
Bonne nuit, hélas!
Ma petite, bonne nuit, bonne nuit!

CHŒUR
Bonne nuit! bonne nuit!

MÉPHISTOPHÉLÈS
Près du moment fatal –

MÉPHISTOPHÉLÈS, CHŒUR
Fais grande résistance,
S'il ne t'offre d'avance
Un anneau conjugal.
Il te tend les bras, *etc.*
Ha!

MÉPHISTOPHÉLÈS
Chut! disparaissez!

Les follets s'abîment.

MEPHISTOPHELES' SERENADE
(with chorus of will o' the wisps)

Before the house
Of him who adores you,
Little Louisa,
What have you been doing since dawn?
When pleasure calls,
Into this fine fellow's room
You may enter a maid
But you'll not come out one …
Before the house, *etc.*

CHORUS
What have you been doing?

MEPHISTOPHELES, CHORUS
with a burst of harsh laughter
Ha!

MEPHISTOPHELES
He welcomes you with open arms,
And you rush to him.
Good night, alas,
Good night, little one, good night!

CHORUS
Good night, good night!

MEPHISTOPHELES
As the fatal moment approaches –

MEPHISTOPHELES, CHORUS
Put up a strong resistance
If he doesn't first offer you
A wedding ring.
He welcomes you with open arms, *etc.*
Ha!

MEPHISTOPHELES
Sh! Vanish!

The will o' the wisps sink into the ground.

Silence!
Allons voir roucouler nos tourtereaux.

Scène 13

Chambre de Marguerite

MARGUERITE, *apercevant Faust.*
Grands dieux!
Que vois-je? Est-ce bien lui?
Dois-je en croire mes yeux?

TRIO ET CHŒUR

FAUST
Ange adoré, dont la céleste image
Avant de te connaître illuminait mon cœur,
Enfin je t'aperçois, et du jaloux nuage
Qui te cachait encor mon amour est vainqueur.
Marguerite, je t'aime!

MARGUERITE
Tu sais mon nom? Moi-même
J'ai souvent dit le tien:
(timidement)
Faust!

FAUST
Ce nom est le mien;
Un autre le sera, s'il te plaît davantage.

MARGUERITE
En songe je t'ai vu –

FAUST
En songe –

MARGUERITE
– tel que je te revois.

FAUST
– tu m'as vu?

MARGUERITE
Je reconnais ta voix,
Tes traits, ton doux langage!

Silence!
Let's go and see our turtle doves cooing.

Scene 13

Marguerite's room

MARGUERITE, *catching sight of Faust*
Great gods!
What do I see! Is it really he?
Can I believe my eyes?

TRIO AND CHORUS

FAUST
Beloved angel, whose image divine
Lit up my heart before I ever knew you,
I behold you at last; my love has driven away
The jealous mists that still hid you from me.
Marguerite, I love you.

MARGUERITE
You know my name? I too
Have often spoken yours:
(timidly)
Faust!

FAUST
That name is mine, but it will be
Any other that pleases you more.

MARGUERITE
In dreams I saw you –

FAUST
In dreams –

MARGUERITE
– just as I see you now.

FAUST
You saw me?

MARGUERITE
I recognise your voice,
Your features, your gentle words!

FAUST
Et tu m'aimais?

MARGUERITE
Je ... t'attendais!

FAUST
Marguerite adorée!

MARGUERITE
Ma tendresse inspirée
Etait d'avance à toi.

FAUST
Marguerite est à moi!

MARGUERITE
Mon bien-aimé, ta noble et douce image,
Avant de te connaître, illuminait mon cœur.
Enfin je t'aperçois, et du jaloux nuage
Qui te cachait encor ton amour est vainqueur.

FAUST
Ange adoré, dont la céleste image, *etc.*

Marguerite, ô tendresse!
Cède à l'ardente ivresse
Qui vers toi m'a conduit!

MARGUERITE
Je ne sais quelle ivresse
Dans ses bras me conduit.

FAUST, *avec élan*
Marguerite, ô tendresse, *etc.*

MARGUERITE
Je ne sais quelle ivresse,
Brûlante, enchanteresse,
Dans tes bras me conduit.
Quelle langueur s'empare de mon être!

FAUST
Au vrai bonheur
Dans mes bras tu vas naître.
Viens!

FAUST
And you loved me?

MARGUERITE
I ... was waiting for you.

FAUST
Beloved Marguerite!

MARGUERITE
My love divined you
And was already yours.

FAUST
Marguerite is mine!

MARGUERITE
My beloved, your sweet and noble image
Lit up my heart before I ever knew you;
I behold you at last; your love has driven away
The jealous mists that still hid you from me.

FAUST
Beloved angel, whose image divine, *etc.*

Marguerite, my love,
Yield to the burning passion
That has led me to you!

MARGUERITE
I know not what passion
Leads me to his arms.

FAUST, *rapturously*
Marguerite, my love, *etc.*

MARGUERITE
I know not what passion,
Devouring, bewitching,
Leads me to your arms.
What languor seizes my whole being!

FAUST
In my arms
You will be born again to true happiness!
Come!

MARGUERITE
Dans mes yeux des pleurs ...
Tout s'efface ... je meurs ...
Tout s'efface ...

FAUST
Viens!

MARGUERITE
Ah! je meurs!

Scène 14

MÉPHISTOPHÉLÈS, *entrant brusquement*
Allons, il est trop tard!

MARGUERITE
Quel est cet homme?

FAUST
Un sot!

MÉPHISTOPHÉLÈS
Un ami!

MARGUERITE
Son regard
Me déchire le cœur!

MÉPHISTOPHÉLÈS
Sans doute je dérange ...

FAUST
Qui t'a permis d'entrer?

MÉPHISTOPHÉLÈS
Il faut sauver cet ange!
Déjà tous les voisins, éveillés par nos chants,
Accourent, désignant la maison aux passants.
En raillant Marguerite, ils appellent sa mère.
La vieille va venir ...

FAUST
Que faire?

MARGUERITE
In my eyes are tears ...
Everything's growing faint ... I'm dying ...
Everything's growing faint ...

FAUST
Come!

MARGUERITE
Ah! I'm dying!

Scene 14

MEPHISTOPHELES, *bursting in*
Quick! It's too late.

MARGUERITE
What man is this?

FAUST
A fool!

MEPHISTOPHELES
A friend!

MARGUERITE
His glance
Tears my heart!

MEPHISTOPHELES
Forgive me if I intrude ...

FAUST
Who said you could come in?

MEPHISTOPHELES
We must save this angel.
Already all the neighbours, roused by our songs,
Are hurrying here, pointing out the house to the passers-by.
They're jeering at Marguerite and calling to her mother.
The old woman will be here ...

FAUST
What shall we do?

MÉPHISTOPHÉLÈS
Il faut partir.

FAUST
Damnation!

MÉPHISTOPHÉLÈS
Vous vous verrez demain; la consolation
Est bien près de la peine.

MARGUERITE
Oui, demain, bien-aimé!
Dans la chambre prochaine
Déjà j'entends du bruit.

FAUST
Adieu donc, belle nuit
A peine commencée!
Adieu, festin d'amour
Que je m'étais promis!

MÉPHISTOPHÉLÈS
Partons, voilà le jour!

FAUST
Te reverrai-je encor, heure trop fugitive,
Où mon âme au bonheur allait enfin s'ouvrir!
Où mon âme, *etc.*

CHŒUR DE VOISINES, *dans la rue*
Holà, mère Oppenheim!
Vois ce que fait ta fille!

MÉPHISTOPHÉLÈS
La foule arrive.

CHŒUR
L'avis n'est pas hors de saison:
Un galant est dans ta maison —

MÉPHISTOPHÉLÈS
Hâtons-nous de partir!

CHŒUR
— et tu verras dans peu s'accroître ta famille.
Holà!

MEPHISTOPHELES
We must leave.

FAUST
Damnation!

MEPHISTOPHELES
You'll meet again tomorrow; after pain
Soon comes consolation.

MARGUERITE
Yes, tomorrow, beloved.
I can already hear a noise
In the next room.

FAUST
Farewell then, sweet night
So lately begun,
Farewell, feast of love
That I had promised myself!

MEPHISTOPHELES
Let's be off, daylight is here!

FAUST
Shall I see you again, brief hour
When my soul at last was about to open to happiness?
When my soul, *etc.*

CHORUS OF NEIGHBOURS *in the street*
Hey there, Mother Oppenheim,
Look what your daughter's up to!

MEPHISTOPHELES
The crowd's arriving.

CHORUS
The advice is timely;
A gallant's in your house –

MEPHISTOPHELES
Make haste to be gone!

CHORUS
– you'll soon see an addition to the family.
Hey there!

MARGUERITE
Ciel!

CHŒUR
Holà!

MARGUERITE
Ciel! entends-tu ces cris?
Devant Dieu, je suis morte
Si l'on te trouve ici!

MÉPHISTOPHÉLÈS
Viens! on frappe à la porte.

FAUST
Oh fureur!

MÉPHISTOPHÉLÈS
Oh sottise!

MARGUERITE
Adieu! adieu! Par le jardin
Vous pouvez échapper.

FAUST
Ô mon ange, à demain!

MÉPHISTOPHÉLÈS
A demain, à demain!

FAUST
Je connais donc enfin
Tout le prix de la vie,
Le bonheur m'apparaît;
Il m'appelle et je vais le saisir.

MÉPHISTOPHÉLÈS
Je puis donc te traîner dans la vie,
Fier esprit! Le moment approche
Où je vais te saisir.

MARGUERITE
Ô mon Faust!

MARGUERITE
Heavens!

CHORUS
Hey there!

MARGUERITE
Heavens! Do you hear those shouts?
Before God, I'm lost
If they find you here.

MEPHISTOPHELES
Come! They're knocking at the door.

FAUST
Fury!

MEPHISTOPHELES
Nonsense!

MARGUERITE
Farewell, farewell! You can escape
By the garden.

FAUST
Till tomorrow, my angel!

MEPHISTOPHELES
Tomorrow, tomorrow!

FAUST
So at last I know
Life's prize and value.
Happiness is revealed to me;
It calls me, and I shall seize it.

MEPHISTOPHELES
So I have you in my grasp,
Proud spirit; the time is near
When I shall seize you.

MARGUERITE
Oh my Faust!

FAUST
L'amour s'est emparé
De mon âme ravie;
Il comblera bientôt
Mon dévorant désir.

MÉPHISTOPHÉLÈS
Sans combler ton dévorant désir
L'amour en t'enivrant
Doublera ta folie,
Et le moment approche
Où je vais te saisir.

MARGUERITE
Je te donne ma vie.
L'amour s'est emparé
De mon âme ravie.
Il m'entraîne vers toi.
Te perdre, c'est mourir.

Ô mon Faust bien aimé,
Je te donne ma vie, *etc.*

FAUST
Je connais donc tout le prix, *etc.*

MÉPHISTOPHÉLÈS
Je puis donc à mon gré
Te traîner dans la vie;
Fier esprit, le moment approche
Où je vais te saisir, *etc.*

CHŒUR
Un galant est dans ta maison,
Et tu verras dans peu s'accroître ta famille.

MARGUERITE
Te perdre, c'est mourir!

FAUST
Il comblera bientôt, *etc*

MÉPHISTOPHÉLÈS
Le moment approche, *etc.*

FAUST
Love has taken possession
Of my ecstatic soul;
Soon it will gratify
My consuming desire.

MEPHISTOPHELES
Without gratifying your consuming desire,
Love, by infatuating you,
Will redouble your madness,
And the time is near
When I shall seize you.

MARGUERITE
I give my life to you.
Love has taken possession
Of my ecstatic soul.
It draws me to you;
To lose you is to die.

Oh my beloved Faust,
I give my life to you, *etc.*

FAUST
So I know life's prize, *etc.*

MEPHISTOPHELES
So I have you in my grasp
And can do what I want with you;
Proud spirit, the time is near
When I shall seize you, *etc.*

CHORUS
A gallant's in your house;
You'll soon see an addition to the family.

MARGUERITE
To lose you is to die.

FAUST
Soon it will gratify, *etc.*

MEPHISTOPHELES
The time is near, *etc.*

CHŒUR
Holà, mère Oppenheim, etc.
Ah! ah! ah! ah!

Quatrième Partie

Scène 15

ROMANCE

MARGUERITE, *seule*
D'amour l'ardente flamme
Consume mes beaux jours.
Ah! la paix de mon âme
A donc fui pour toujours!

Son départ, son absence
Sont pour moi le cercueil,
Et, loin de sa présence,
Tout me paraît en deuil.

Alors ma pauvre tête
Se dérange bientôt;
Mon faible cœur s'arrête,
Puis se glace aussitôt.

Sa marche que j'admire,
Son port si gracieux,
Sa bouche au doux sourire,
Le charme de ses yeux,

Sa voix enchanteresse
Dont il sait m'embraser,
De sa main la caresse,
Hélas! et son baiser,

D'une amoureuse flamme,
Consument mes beaux jours!
Ah! la paix de mon âme
A donc fui pour toujours!

Je suis à ma fenêtre,
Ou dehors, tout le jour:
C'est pour le voir paraître
Ou hâter son retour.

CHORUS
Hey there, Mother Oppenheim, *etc.*
Ha! ha! ha! ha!

Part 4

Scene 15

ROMANCE

MARGUERITE, *alone*
The burning flame of love
Consumes my youth away.
Ah, peace has fled
From my soul for ever.

His departure, his absence
Are like the grave for me,
And far away from him
All life seems in mourning.

So my poor head
Soon loses its senses;
My feeble heart stops beating
And turns to ice.

His walk that I marvel at,
His graceful bearing,
His mouth with its gentle smile,
The charm of his eyes,

His bewitching voice
With which he can set me on fire,
The caress of his hand,
And, alas, his kiss,

Consume my life away
In amorous fires.
Ah, peace has fled
For ever from my soul.

All day I'm at my window
Or outside,
In case I may see him appear,
Or hasten his return.

Mon cœur bat et se presse
Dès qu'il le sent venir.
Au gré de ma tendresse
Puis je le retenir!

Ô caresses de flamme!
Que je voudrais un jour
Voir s'exhaler mon âme
Dans ses baisers d'amour!

CHŒUR DE SOLDATS, *dans le lointain*
Au son des trompettes
Les braves soldats
S'élancent aux fêtes
Ou bien aux combats.

MARGUERITE
Bientôt la ville entière
Au repos va se rendre.

CHŒUR
Si grande est la peine,
Le prix est plus grand.

MARGUERITE
Clairons, tambours du soir
Déjà se font entendre
Avec des chants joyeux,
Comme au soir où l'amour
Offrit Faust à mes yeux.

CHŒUR D'ÉTUDIANTS, *plus loin*
* Jam nox stellata velamina pandit.

MARGUERITE
Il ne vient pas!

CHŒUR
** Per urbem quaerentes puellas eamus.

---

  * Déjà la nuit étend ses voiles étoilés.
** Allons par la ville cherchant les jeunes filles.

My heart beats faster
When it feels him near.
Would that I could keep him here
Just by the power of my love!

Oh caress of fire!
If only one day
I could see my very soul sigh out
In the flame of his kisses!

CHORUS OF SOLDIERS, *in the distance*
At the trumpets' sound
Brave soldiers
Hurl themselves
Into pleasure or battle.

MARGUERITE
Soon all the town
Will be going to its rest.

CHORUS
The effort is great
But the prize is greater.

MARGUERITE
Already the sound of the evening trumpets
And drums is heard,
With cheerful songs,
As on the evening when love
Brought Faust to me.

CHORUS OF STUDENTS, *farther away*
* Jam nox stellata velamina pandit.

MARGUERITE
He comes not!

CHORUS
** Per urbem quaerentes puellas eamus.

---

  * Already night draws its starry veil.
 ** Let's roam the town looking for girls.

MARGUERITE
Il ne vient pas!
Hélas!

Scène 16

Forêts et Cavernes

INVOCATION À LA NATURE

FAUST
Nature immense, impénétrable et fière,
Toi seule donnes trêve à mon ennui sans fin.
Sur ton sein tout-puissant je sens moins ma misère,
Je retrouve ma force, et je crois vivre enfin.
Oui, soufflez ouragans, criez, forêts profondes,
Croulez, rochers, torrents précipitez vos ondes!
A vos bruits souverains ma voix aime à s'unir.
Forêts, rochers, torrents, je vous adore! mondes
Qui scintillez, vers vous s'élance le désir
D'un cœur trop vaste et d'une âme altérée,
D'un bonheur qui la fuit.

Scène 17

RÉCITATIF ET CHASSE

MÉPHISTOPHÉLÈS, *gravissant les rochers*
A la voûte azurée
Aperçois-tu, dis-moi, l'astre d'amour constant?
Son influence, ami, serait fort nécessaire;
Car tu rêves ici, quand cette pauvre enfant,
Marguerite –

FAUST
Tais-toi!

MÉPHISTOPHÉLÈS
Sans doute il faut me taire,
Tu n'aimes plus!
Pourtant en un cachot traînée,
Et pour un parricide à la mort condamnée –

MARGUERITE
He comes not!
Alas!

Scene 16

Forests and Caves

INVOCATION TO NATURE

FAUST
Nature, vast, unfathomable, proud,
You alone give pause to my unending ennui;
On your omnipotent breast I feel my misery less keenly,
I regain my strength and believe in life at last.
Yes, blow, hurricanes! Roar, you mighty forests,
Crash down, you rocks, and torrents, hurl headlong your waters!
My voice delights to mingle with your majestic sounds.
Forests, rocks, torrents, I worship you!
Glittering worlds above, to you the longing
Of a heart too vast and a soul insatiable
Cries out for the happiness it cannot seize.

Scene 17

RECITATIVE AND HUNT

MEPHISTOPHELES, *climbing up the rocks*
Tell me, do you perceive in the azure vault
Love's steadfast star? My friend,
You should need its influence badly;
While you dream here, – that poor child,
Marguerite –

FAUST
Hold your tongue!

MEPHISTOPHELES
No doubt I should hold my tongue,
You no longer love her.
But, dragged off to a dungeon
And condemned to death as a parricide –

FAUST
Quoi!

MÉPHISTOPHÉLÈS
J'entends des chasseurs qui parcourent les bois.

FAUST
Achève! Qu'as-tu dit?
Marguerite en prison?

MÉPHISTOPHÉLÈS, *posément*
Certaine liqueur brune, un innocent poison,
Qu'elle tenait de toi pour endormir sa mère
Pendant vos noctures amours
A causé tout le mal!
Caressant sa chimère,
T'attendant chaque soir, elle en usait toujours.
Elle en a tant usé
Que la vieille en est morte.
Tu comprends maintenant?

FAUST
Feux et tonnerre!

MÉPHISTOPHÉLÈS
En sorte
Que son amour pour toi la conduit –

FAUST, *avec fureur*
Sauve-la,
Sauve-la, misérable!

MÉPHISTOPHÉLÈS
Ah! je suis le coupable!
On vous reconnaît là,
Ridicules humains!
N'importe!
Je suis le maître encor de t'ouvrir cette porte!
Mais qu'as-tu fait pour moi
Depuis que je te sers?

FAUST
Qu'exiges-tu?

FAUST
What!

MEPHISTOPHELES
I hear huntsmen moving through the woods.

FAUST
Go on! What did you say?
Marguerite in prison?

MEPHISTOPHELES, *calmly*
A certain brown liquid, a harmless poison
Which she had from you to keep her mother quiet
During your nights of love
Has caused all the trouble!
Caressing her idle dream,
Waiting for you each night, she used the drug
Constantly: to such an extent
That the old woman died of it.
Now do you understand?

FAUST
Thunder and lightning!

MEPHISTOPHELES
So her love for you
Is taking her –

FAUST, *frantically*
Save her,
Save her, you wretch!

MEPHISTOPHELES
Ah, so I am to blame!
How like you,
Ludicrous humans.
No matter:
I still have power to open this door for you.
But what have you done for me
Since I served you?

FAUST
What do you require?

MÉPHISTOPHÉLÈS
De toi?
Rien qu'une signature
Sur ce vieux parchemin,
Je sauve Marguerite à l'instant,
Si tu jures
Et signes ton serment
De me servir demain!

FAUST
Eh, que me fait demain quand je souffre à cette heure!
Donne!
Il signe.
Voilà mon nom!
Vers sa sombre demeure
Volons donc maintenant!
Ô douleur insensée!
Marguerite, j'accours!

MÉPHISTOPHÉLÈS
A moi, Vortex! Giaour!
Sur ces deux noirs chevaux, prompts comme la pensée,
Montons, et au galop!
La justice est pressée.

Scène 18

LA COURSE À L'ABÎME

Faust et Méphistophélès galopant sur deux chevaux noirs.

FAUST
Dans mon cœur retentit sa voix
Désespérée;
Ô pauvre abandonnée!

CHŒUR DES PAYSANS, *agenouillés devant une croix champêtre*
Sancta Maria, ora pro nobis.
Sancta Magdalena, ora pro nobis.

FAUST
Prends garde à ces enfants,
A ces femmes priant
Au pied de cette croix!

MEPHISTOPHELES
From you?
Merely a signature
On this old parchment.
I'll save Marguerite at once
If you swear
And seal your oath
To serve me tomorrow.

FAUST
What is tomorrow to me when I suffer now?
Give it to me!
He signs.
There is my name.
Let's fly now
To her gloomy dwelling!
Oh grief past bearing!
Marguerite, I'm coming!

MEPHISTOPHELES
Here, Vortex, Giaour!
On these two black steeds, swift as thought,
Let's mount and be off at a gallop:
Justice will not wait.

Scene 18

THE RIDE TO THE ABYSS

Faust and Mephistopheles galloping on two black horses.

FAUST
Her despairing voice
Rings in my heart.
Oh poor abandoned girl!

CHORUS OF PEASANTS, *kneeling at a wayside cross*
Sancta Maria, ora pro nobis.
Sancta Magdalena, ora pro nobis.

FAUST
Be careful of those children,
Those women praying
At the foot of that cross!

MÉPHISTOPHÉLÈS
Eh! qu'importe! en avant!

CHŒUR
Sancta Margarita – Ah! *(cri d'effroi)*

Les femmes et les enfants se dispersent, épouvantés.

FAUST
Dieux!
Un monstre hideux
En hurlant
Nous poursuit.

MÉPHISTOPHÉLÈS
Tu rêves.

FAUST
Quel essaim de grands oiseaux de nuit!
Quels cris affreux!
Ils me frappant de l'aile!

MÉPHISTOPHÉLÈS, *retenant son cheval*
Le glas des trépassés sonne déjà pour elle.
As-tu peur? retournons!

Ils s'arrêtent.

FAUST
Non! je l'entends! courons!

Les chevaux redoublent de vitesse.

MÉPHISTOPHÉLÈS, *excitant son cheval*
Hop! hop! hop!

FAUST
Regarde autour de nous
Cette ligne infinie de squelettes dansant!
Avec quel rire horrible
Ils nous saluent en passant!

MÉPHISTOPHÉLÈS
Hop! hop! Pense à sauver sa vie
Et ris-toi des morts!
Hop! hop!

MEPHISTOPHELES
What? What of it? Ride on!

CHORUS
Sancta Margarita – Ah! *(with a scream of fear)*

The women and children scatter in terror.

FAUST
Gods!
A hideous beast,
Baying,
Is pursuing us.

MEPHISTOPHELES
You're dreaming.

FAUST
Huge night birds swarm round me,
Uttering terrible shrieks,
Beating me with their wings!

MEPHISTOPHELES, *reining his horse*
The death-knell is already sounding for her.
Are you afraid? Turn back, then.

They stop.

FAUST
No! I can hear it! Hurry!

The horses redouble their pace.

MEPHISTOPHELES, *urging on his horse*
Hup! hup! hup!

FAUST
About us see that endless line
Of skeletons dancing!
With what horrid laughter
They greet us as they pass!

MEPHISTOPHELES
Hup! hup! Think about saving her life,
And scorn the dead!
Hup! hup!

FAUST, *de plus en plus épouvanté et haletant*
Nos chevaux frémissent,
Leurs crins se hérissent,
Ils brisent leurs mors.
Je vois onduler
Devant nous la terre;
J'entends le tonnerre
Sous nos pieds rouler.

MÉPHISTOPHÉLÈS
Hop! hop! hop!

FAUST
Il pleut du sang!

MÉPHISTOPHÉLÈS, *d'une voix tonnante*
Cohortes infernales,
Sonnez vos trompes triomphales!
Il est à nous!

FAUST
Horreur! Ah!

MÉPHISTOPHÉLÈS
Je suis vainqueur!

Ils tombent dans un gouffre.

Scène 19

PANDAEMONIUM *(Chœur en langue inconnue)*

CHŒUR DES DÉMONS ET DES DAMNÉES
Has! Irimiru Karabrao! Has! Has! Has!

LES PRINCES DES TÉNÈBRES
De cette âme si fière
A jamais es-tu maître
Et vainqueur, Méphisto?

MÉPHISTOPHÉLÈS
J'en suis maître à jamais.

LES PRINCES DES TÉNÈBRES
Faust a donc librement signé
L'acte fatal qui le livre à la flamme?

FAUST, *more and more horror-struck and breathless*
The horses are shuddering,
Their manes are bristling,
They are breaking their bridles.
I can see the earth
Writhe before us;
I hear the thunder
Roll beneath our feet.

MEPHISTOPHELES
Hup! hup! hup!

FAUST
It's raining blood!

MEPHISTOPHELES, *with a voice of thunder*
Cohorts of hell,
Sound your triumphal trumpets –
He is ours!

FAUST
Horror! Ah! –

MEPHISTOPHELES
I am victorious!

They fall into a chasm.

Scene 19

PANDEMONIUM (Chorus in an unknown tongue)

CHORUS OF DEMONS AND THE DAMNED
Has! Irimiru Karabrao! Has! Has! Has!

THE PRINCES OF DARKNESS
Mephisto, are you master
And lord over this proud soul
For ever and ever?

MEPHISTOPHELES
I am master for ever and ever.

THE PRINCES OF DARKNESS
Then Faust freely signed
The fatal deed which consigns him to the flames?

MÉPHISTOPHÉLÈS
Il signa librement.

CHŒUR
Has! Has!

Les démons portent Méphistophélès en triomphe.

CHŒUR
Tradioun marexil fir tru dinxé burrudixé.
Fory my dinkorlitz,
O mérikariu! O mévixé! Mérikariba!
O mérikariu! o mi dara caraibo lakinda, merondor dinkorlitz,
Merondor dinkorlitz, merondor.
Tradioun marexil,
Tradioun burrudixé,
Trudinxe caraibo
Fir ome vixe merondor
Mit aysko, merondor, mit aysko! oh! oh!

Les démons dansent autour de Méphistophélès.

Diff! diff! merondor, merondor aysko!
Has! has! Satan! has! has! Belphégor!
Has! has! Méphisto!
Has! has! Kroïx!
Diff! diff! Astaroth!
Diff! diff! Belzébuth!
Belphégor! Astaroth! Méphisto!
Sat, sat rayk ir kimour.
Has! has! Méphisto!
Has! has! Méphisto!
Has! has! has!
Irimiru karabrao.

Scène 20

ÉPILOGUE SUR LA TERRE

QUELQUES VOIX
Alors, l'Enfer se tut.
L'affreux bouillonnement
De ses grands lacs de flammes,
Les grincements de dents

MEPHISTOPHELES
He freely signed.

CHORUS
Has! Has!

The demons bear Mephistopheles in triumph.

CHORUS
Tradioun marexil fir tru dinxé burrudixé.
Fory my dinkorlitz,
O mérikariu! O mévixé! Mérikariba!
O mérikariu! o mi dara caraibo lakinda, merondor dinkorlitz,
Merondor dinkorlitz, merondor.
Tradioun marexil,
Tradioun burrudixé,
Trudinxe caraibo
Fir ome vixe merondor
Mit aysko, merondor, mit aysko! oh! oh!

The demons dance round Mephistopheles

Diff! diff! merondor, merondor aysko!
Has! has! Satan! has! has! Belphégor!
Has! has! Méphisto!
Has! has! Kroïx!
Diff! diff! Astaroth!
Diff! diff! Belzébuth!
Belphégor! Astaroth! Méphisto!
Sat, sat rayk ir kimour.
Has! has! Méphisto!
Has! has! Méphisto!
Ha! has! has!
Irimiru karabrao.

Scene 20

EPILOGUE ON EARTH

A FEW VOICES
Then Hell fell silent.
Only the dreadful bubbling
Of its great lakes of fire
And the gnashing of teeth

De ses tourmenteurs d'âmes
Se firent seul entendre;
Et, dans ses profondeurs,
Un mystère d'horreur
S'accomplit.

PETIT CHŒUR
Oh terreurs!

Scène 21

LE CIEL

Séraphins inclinés devant le Très Haut

CHŒUR D'ESPRITS CÉLESTES
Laus! Laus! Hosanna! Hosanna!
Elle a beaucoup aimé, Seigneur.

UNE VOIX
Margarita!

APOTHÉOSE DE MARGUERITE

CHŒUR
Remonte au ciel, âme naïve
Que l'amour égara;
Viens revêtir ta beauté primitive
Qu'une erreur altéra.
Viens! les vierges divines,

CHŒUR D'ESPRITS CÉLESTES
ET CHŒUR D'ENFANTS
Viens! les vierges divines
Tes sœur, les Séraphines,
Sauront tarir les pleurs
Que t'arrachent encor les terrestres douleurs.
Conserve l'espérance,
Et souris au bonheur!
Viens, Margarita!

UNE VOIX
Margarita!

Of those who tortured souls
Could then be heard;
And in its depths
A frightful mystery
Was performed.

SEMI CHORUS
Oh dread!

Scene 21

HEAVEN

Seraphim bowing before the Most High

CHORUS OF CELESTIAL SPIRITS
Praise! Praise! Hosanna! Hosanna!
Lord, she greatly loved.

A VOICE
Marguerite!

MARGUERITE'S APOTHEOSIS

CHORUS
Rise up again to Heaven, artless soul
That love led astray;
Put on again your first beauty
Which a fault corrupted.
Come, the heavenly virgins,

CHORUS OF CELESTIAL SPIRITS
AND CHORUS OF CHILDREN
Come, the heavenly virgins
Your sisters, the Seraphim,
Will dry the tears
That earthly sorrows still exact.
Hope on,
And smile on your blessings.
Come, Marguerite!

A VOICE
Marguerite!

CHŒUR
Viens, Margarita!
Viens! viens! viens! viens!

FIN

CHORUS
Come, Marguerite!
Come! Come! Come! Come!

END

Faust
An Opera in Five Acts

Founded on Goethe's Poem by Jules Barbier and Michel Carré
Music by Charles Gounod

Ouverture

Acte Premier

Le Cabinet de Faust

(Faust, seul. Sa lampe est près de s'éteindre. Il est assis devant une table chargée de parchemins. Un livre est ouvert devant lui.)

Scène 1

FAUST
Rien! … – En vain j'interroge, en mon ardente veille,
La nature et le Créateur;
Pas une voix ne glisse à mon oreille
Un mot consolateur!
J'ai langui triste et solitaire,
Sans pouvoir briser le lien
Qui m'attache encore à la terre! …
Je ne vois rien! – Je ne sais rien! …

(Il ferme le livre et se lève. Le jour commence à naître.)

Le ciel pâlit! – Devant l'aube nouvelle
La sombre nuit
S'évanouit! …

(avec désespoir)

Encore un jour! – encore un jour qui luit! …
O mort, quand viendras-tu m'abriter sous ton aile?

(saisissant une fiole sur la table)

Eh bien! puisque la mort me fuit,
Pourquoi n'irais-je pas vers elle? …
Salut! ô mon dernier matin!
J'arrive sans terreur au terme du voyage;
Et je suis, avec ce breuvage,

Orchestral Introduction

Act I

Faust's Study

(Night. Faust discovered, alone. He is seated at a table covered with books and parchments; an open book lies before him. His lamp is flickering in the socket.)

Scene 1

FAUST
No! In vain hath my soul aspired, with ardent longing,
All to know, – all in earth and heaven.
No light illumines the visions, ever thronging
My brain; no peace is given,
And I linger, thus sad and weary,
Without power to sunder the chain
Binding my soul to life always dreary.
Nought do I see! Nought do I know!

(He closes the book and rises. Day begins to dawn.)

Again 'tis light!
On its westward course flying,
The somber night vanishes.

(despairingly)

Again the light of a new day!
O death! when will thy dusky wings
Above me hover and give me – rest?

(seizing a flask on the table)

Well, then! Since death thus evades me,
Why should I not go in search of him?
Hail, my final day, all hail!
No fears my heart assail;
On earth my days I number;

Le seul maître de mon destin!

(Il verse le contenu de la fiole dans une coupe de cristal. Au moment où il va porter la coupe à ses lèvres, des voix de jeunes filles se font entendre au dehors.)

CHOEUR DE JEUNES FILLES
Paresseuse fille
Qui sommeille encor!
Déjà le-jour brille
Sous son manteau d'or.
Déjà l'oiseau chante
Ses folles chansons;
L'aube caressante
Sourit aux moissons;
Le ruisseau murmure,
La fleur s'ouvre au jour,
Toute la nature
S'éveille à l'amour!

FAUST
Vains échos de la joie humaine.
Passez, passez votre chemin! …
O coupe des aïeux, qui tant fois fus pleine,
Pourquoi trembles-tu dans ma main?

(Il porte de nouveau la coupe à ses lèvres.)

CHOEUR DES LABOUREURS

(dehors)

Aux champs l'aurore nous rappelle;
A peine voit-on l'hirondelle,
Qui vole et plonge d'un coup d'aîle
Dans le profondeur du ciel bleu!
Le temps est beau, la terre est belle,
Béni soit Dieu!

JEUNES FILLES ET LABOUREURS
Béni soit Dieu!

FAUST *(reposant la coupe)*
Dieu!

(Il se laisse retomber dans son fauteuil.)

For this draught immortal slumber
Will secure me, and care dispel!

(Pours liquid from the flask into a crystal goblet. Just as he is about to raise it to his lips, the following chorus is heard, without.)

CHORUS OF MAIDENS

Why thy eyes so lustrous
Hidest thou from sight?
Bright Sol now is scatt'ring
Beams of golden light;
The nightingale is warbling
Its carol of love;
Rosy tints of morning
Now gleam from above;
Flow'rs unfold their beauty
To the scented gale;
Nature all awakens –
Of love tells its tale.

FAUST

Hence, empty sounds of human joys
Flee far from me.
O goblet, which my ancestors
So many times have filled,
Why tremblest thou in my grasp?

(Again raising the goblet to his lips.)

CHORUS OF LABORERS

(without)

The morn into the fields doth summon us,
The swallow hastes away!
Why tarry, then?
To labor let's away! to work let's on,
The sky is bright, the earth is fair,
Our tribute, then, let's pay to heav'n.

CHORUS OF MAIDEN AND LABORERS
Praises to God!

FAUST *(setting down the cup)*
God! God!

(He sinks into a chair.)

Mais ce Dieu, que peut-il pour moi!

(se levant)

Me rendra-t'il l'amour, l'espérance et la foi?

(avec rage)

Maudites soyez-vous, ô voluptés humaines!
Maudites soient les chaînes
Qui me font ramper ici-bas!
Maudit soit tout ce qui nous leurre,
Vain espoir qui passe avec l'heure,
Rêves d'amour ou de combats!
Maudit soit le bonheur, maudites la science,
La prière et la foi!
Maudite sois-tu, patience!
A moi, Satan! à moi!

Scène 2

MÉPHISTOPHÉLÈS

(apparaissant)

Me voici! … D'où vient ta surprise?
Ne suis-je pas mis à ta guise?
L'épée au côté, la plume au chapeau,
L'escarcelle pleine, un riche manteau
Sur l'épaule; – en somme
Un vrai gentilhomme!
Eh bien! que me veux-tu, docteur!
Parle, voyons! … Te fais-je peur?

FAUST
Non.

MÉPHISTOPHÉLÈS
Doutes-tu ma puissance? …

FAUST
Peut-être!

MÉPHISTOPHÉLÈS
Mets-la donc à l'épreuve! …

FAUST
Va-t'en!

But this God, what will he do for me?

(rising)

Will he return to me youth, love, and faith?

(with rage)

Cursed be all of man's vile race!
Cursed be the chains which bind him in his place!
Cursed be visions false, deceiving!
Cursed the folly of believing!
Cursed be dreams of love or hate!
Cursed be souls with joy elate.
Cursed be science, prayer, and faith!
Cursed my fate in life and death!
Internal king, arise!

Scene 2

MEPHISTOPHELES

(suddenly appearing)

Here am I! So, I surprise you?
Satan, sir, at your service!
A sword at my side; on my hat a gay feather; –
A cloak o'er my shoulder; and altogether,
Why, gotten up quite in the fashion!
But come, Doctor Faust, what is your will?
Behold! Speak! Are you afraid of me?

FAUST
No.

MEPHISTOPHELES
Do you doubt my power?

FAUST
Perhaps.

MEPHISTOPHELES
Prove it, then.

FAUST
Begone!

MÉPHISTOPHÉLÈS
Fi! – c'est là ta reconnaissance!
Apprends de moi qu'avec Satan
L'on en doit user d'autre sorte,
Et qu'il n'était pas besoin
De l'appeler de si loin
Pour le mettre ensuite à la porte!

FAUST
Et que peux-tu pour moi?

MÉPHISTOPHÉLÈS
Tout. – Mais dis-moi d'abord
Ce que tu veux; – est-ce de l'or?

FAUST
Que ferais-je de la richesse?

MÉPHISTOPHÉLÈS
Bon! je vois où le bât te blesse!
Tu veux la gloire?

FAUST
Plus encor!

MÉPHISTOPHÉLÈS
La puissance!

FAUST
Non! je veux un trésor
Qui les contient tous! … je veux la jeunesse!
A moi les plaisirs,
Les jeunes maîtresses!
A moi leurs caresses!
A moi leurs désirs!
A moi l'énergie
Des instincts puissants,
Et la folle orgie
Du cœur et des sens!
Ardente jeunesse,
A moi tes désirs!
A moi ton ivresse!
A moi tes plaisirs! …

MEPHISTOPHELES
Fie! Fie! Is this your politeness!
But learn, my friend, that with Satan
One should conduct in a different way.
I've entered your door with infinite trouble.
Would you kick me out the very same day?

FAUST
Then what will you do for me?

MEPHISTOPHELES
Anything in the world! All things. But
Say first what you would have.
Abundance of gold?

FAUST
And what can I do with riches?

MEPHISTOPHELES
Good. I see where the show pinches.
You will have glory.

FAUST
Still wrong.

MEPHISTOPHELES
Power, then.

FAUST
No. I would have a treasure
Which contains all. I wish for youth.
Oh, I would have pleasure,
And love, and caresses,
For youth is the season
When joy most impresses.
One round of enjoyment,
One scene of delight,
Should be my employment
From day-dawn till night.
Oh, I would have pleasure,
And love, and caresses;
If youth you restore me,
My joys I'll renew!

MÉPHISTOPHÉLÈS
Fort bien! je puis contenter ton caprice.

FAUST
Et que te donnerai-je en retour?

MÉPHISTOPHÉLÈS
Presque rien:
Ici, je suis à ton service,
Mais là-bas tu seras au mien.

FAUST
Là-bas? …

MÉPHISTOPHÉLÈS
Là-bas.

(lui présentant un parchemin)

Allons, signe. – Eh quoi! ta main tremble!
Que faut-il pour te décider?
La jeunesse t'appelle; ôse la regarder! …

(Il fait un geste. Au fond du théâtre s'ouvre et laisse voir Marguerite assise devant son rouet et filant.)

FAUST
O merveille! …

MÉPHISTOPHÉLÈS
Eh bien! que t'en semble?

(prenant le parchemin)

FAUST
Donne! …

(Il signe.)

MÉPHISTOPHÉLÈS
Allons donc!

(Prenant la coupe restée sur la table.)

Et maintenant,
Maître, c'est moi qui te convie
A vider cette coupe où fume en bouillonnant
Non plus la mort, non plus le poison; – mais la vie!

MEPHISTOPHELES
'Tis well – all thou desirest I can give thee.

FAUST
Ah! but what must I give in return?

MEPHISTOPHELES
'Tis but little:
In this world I will be thy slave,
But down below thou must be mine.

FAUST
Below?

MEPHISTOPHELES
Below.

(unfolding a scroll)

Come, write, What! does thy hand tremble?
Whence this dire trepidation?
'Tis youth that now awaits thee – Behold!

(At a sign from Mephistopheles, the scene opens and discloses Marguerite, spinning.)

FAUST
Oh, wonder!

MEPHISTOPHELES
Well, how do you like it?

(taking parchment)

FAUST
Give me the scroll!

(Signs.)

MEPHISTOPHELES
Come on then! And now, master,

(Taking cup from the table.)

I invite thee to empty a cup,
In which there is neither poison nor death
But young and vigorous life.

FAUST
(prenant la coupe et se tournant vers Marguerite)
A toi, fantôme adorable et charmant! ...

(Il vide la coupe et se trouve métamorphosé en jeune et élégant seigneur. La vision disparaît.)

MÉPHISTOPHÉLÈS
Viens!

FAUST
Je la reverrai?

MÉPHISTOPHÉLÈS
Sans doute.

FAUST
Quand?

MÉPHISTOPHÉLÈS
Aujourd'hui.

FAUST
C'est bien!

MÉPHISTOPHÉLÈS
En route!

FAUST
A moi les plaisirs,
Les jeunes maîtresses!
A moi leurs caresses!
A moi leurs désirs! *etc.*

MÉPHISTOPHÉLÈS
A toi les plaisirs,
Les jeunes maîtresses!
A toi leurs caresses!
A toi leurs désirs! *etc.*

(Ils sortent. – La toile tombe.)

FAUST
(taking cup and turning toward Marguerite)
O beautiful, adorable vision! I drink to thee!

(He drinks the contents of the cup, and is transformed into a young and handsome man. The vision disappears.)

MEPHISTOPHELES
Come, then.

FAUST
Say, shall I again behold her?

MEPHISTOPHELES
Most surely!

FAUST
When?

MEPHISTOPHELES
This very day!

FAUST
'Tis well.

MEPHISTOPHELES
Then let's away.

FAUST
'Tis pleasure I covet,
'Tis beauty I crave;
I sigh for its kisses,
Its love I demand! *etc.*

MEPHISTOPHELES
'Tis pleasure you covet,
'Tis beauty you crave;
You sigh for its kisses,
Its love you demand! *etc.*

(Exeunt. The curtain falls.)

Acte Deuxième

La Kermesse

(Une des portes de la ville. A gauche un caborte à l'enseigne du Bacchus.)

Scène 1

ÉTUDIANTS

Vin ou bière	Sans vergogne,
Bière ou vin,	Coup sur coup,
Que mon verre	Un ivrogne
Soit plein!	Boit tout!

WAGNER

Jeune adepte	Que ta gloire,
De tonneau	Tes amours,
N'en excepte	Soient de boire
Que l'eau!	Toujours!

ÉTUDIANTS

Jeune adepte	Que ta gloire,
De tonneau	Tes amours,
N'en excepte	Soient de boire
Que l'eau!	Toujours!

(Ils trinquent et boivent.)

SOLDATS

Filles ou forteresses,
C'est tout un, morbleu!
Vieux burgs, jeunes maîtresses
Sont pour nous un jeu!
Celui qui sait s'y prendre
Sans trop de façon,
Les oblige à se rendre
En payant rançon!

BOURGEOIS

Aux jours de dimanche et de fête,
J'aime à parler guerre et combats;
Tandis que les peuples là-bas
Se cassent la tête.

Act II

The Fair

(One of the city gates. To the left, an Inn, bearing the sign of the god Bacchus.)

Scene 1

STUDENTS
Wine or beer, now, which you will!
So the glass quick you fill!
And replenish at our need:
At our bouts we drink with speed!

WAGNER
Now, young tipplers at the cask,
Don't refuse what I ask –
Drink to glory! drink to love!
Drain the sparkling glass!

STUDENTS
We young tipplers at the cask
Won't refuse what you ask –
Here's to glory! here's to love!
Drain the sparkling glass!

(They drink.)

SOLDIERS
Castles, hearts, or fortresses,
Are to us all one.
Strong towers, maids with fair tresses,
By the brave are won;
He, who hath the art to take them,
Shows no little skill;
He, who knows the way to keep them,
Hath more wisdom still.

CITIZENS
On holy-days and feast-days,
I love to talk of war and battles.
While the toiling crowds around
Worry their brains with affairs,

Je vais m'asseoir sur les côteaux
Qui sont voisins de la rivière.
Et je vois passer les bateaux
En vidant mon verre!

(Bourgeois et Soldats remontent vers le fond du théâtre.)
(Un groupe de jeunes filles entre en scène.)

LES JEUNES FILLES

(regardant de côté)

Voyez ces hardis compères
Qui viennent là-bas;
Ne soyons pas trop sévères,
Retardons le pas.

(Elles gagnent la droite de théâtre. Un second chœur d'étudiants entre à leur suite.)

DEUXIÈME CHOEUR D'ÉTUDIANTS

Voyez ces mines gaillardes
Et ces airs vainqueurs!
Amis, soyons sur nos gardes,
Tenons bien nos cœurs!

CHOEUR DE MATRONES

(observant les étudiants et les jeunes filles)

Voyez après ces donzelles
Courir ces messieurs!
Nous sommes aussi bien qu'elles,
Sinon beaucoup mieux!

(Ensemble.)

MATRONES

(aux jeunes filles)

Vous voulez leur plaire
Nous le voyons bien.

ÉTUDIANTS

Vin ou bière,
Bière ou vin,
Que mon verre
Soit plein!

I stroll calmly to this retreat
On the banks of the gliding river,
And behold the boats which pass
While I leisurely empty my glass.

(Citizens and soldiers go to back of stage.)
(A group of young girls enters.)

GIRLS

(glancing aside)

Merry fellows come this way,
Yes, they now advance;
Let us, then, our steps delay,
Just to take one glance.

(They go to right of stage. A second chorus of students enters after them.)

STUDENTS

Sprightly maidens now advance,
Watch their conquering airs;
Friends be guarded, lest a glance
Take you unawares.

MATRONS

(watching the students and young girls)

Behold the silly damsels,
And the foolish young men;
We were once as young as they are,
And as pretty again.

(All join in the following chorus, each singing as follows.)

MATRONS

(to the Maidens)

Ye strive hard to please,
Your object is plain.

STUDENTS

Beer or wine, wine or beer,
Nought care I, with heart of cheer.

SOLDATS
Pas de beauté fière!
Nous savons leur plaire
En un tour de main!

BOURGEOIS
Vidons un verre
De ce bon vin!

JEUNES FILLES
De votre colère
Nous ne craignons rien!

JEUNES ÉTUDIANTS
Voyez leur colère,
Voyez leur maintien!

(Les étudiants et les soldats séparent les femmes en riant. Tous les groupes s'éloignent et disparaissent.)

Scène 2

VALENTIN

(paraissant au fond; il tient une petite médaille à la main)

O sainte médaille,
Qui me viens de ma sœur,
Au jour de la bataille,
Pour écarter la mort, reste là sur mon cœur!

WAGNER
Ah! voici Valentin qui nous cherche sans doute!

VALENTIN
Un dernier coup, messieurs, et mettons-nous en route!

WAGNER
Qu'as-tu donc? … quels regrets attristent nos adieux?

VALENTIN
Comme vous, pour longtemps, je vais quitter ces lieux;
J'y laisse Marguerite, et, pour veiller sur elle,

SOLDIERS
On, then, let's on;
Brave soldiers are we,
To conquest we'll on.

CITIZENS
Come, neighbor! In this fine weather
Let us empty a bottle together!

MAIDENS
They wish to please us, but 'tis in vain!
If you are angry, little you'll gain.

YOUNG STUDENTS
They are bright little maidens, 'tis plain;
We'll contrive their favor to gain.

(The soldiers and students, laughing, separate the women. All the groups depart.)

Scene 2

VALENTINE

(advancing from the back of the stage and holding in his hand a small silver medal)

O sacred medallion,
    Gift of my sister dear
    To ward off danger and fear,
As I charge with my brave battalion,
    Rest thou upon my heart.

WAGNER
Here comes Valentine, in search of us, doubtless.

VALENTINE
Let us drain the parting cup, comrades,
It is time we were on the road.

WAGNER
What sayst thou?
Why this sorrowful farewell?

VALENTINE
Like you, I soon must quit these scenes,
Leaving behind me Marguerite.

Ma mère n'est plus là!

SIEBEL
Plus d'un ami fidèle
Saura te remplacer a ses côtés!

VALENTIN
(lui serrant la main)
Merci!

SIEBEL
Sur moi tu peux compter!

ÉTUDIANTS
Compte sur nous aussi.

Cavatine de Valentin

VALENTIN
Avant de quitter ces lieux,
Sol natal de mes aïeux,
A toi, Seigneur et Roi des Cieux,
Ma sœur je confie.
Daigne de tout danger
Toujours la protéger,
Cette sœur si chérie.
Délivré d'une triste pensée,
J'irai chercher la gloire au sein des ennemis,
Le premier, le plus brave au fort de la mêlée,
J'irai combattre pour mon pays.
Et si vers lui Dieu me rappelle,
Je veillerai sur toi fidèle,
O Marguerite!

WAGNER
Allons, amis! point de vaines alarmes!
A ce bon vin ne mêlons pas de larmes!
Buvons, trinquons, et qu'un joyeux refrain
Nous mette en train!

Alas! my mother no longer lives,
To care for and protect her.

SIEBEL
More than one friend hast thou
Who faithfully will thy place supply.

VALENTINE
(taking his hand)
My thanks!

SIEBEL
On me you may rely.

STUDENTS
In us thou surely mayst confide.

Valentine's Cavatina

VALENTINE
Even bravest heart may swell
In the moment of farewell.
Loving smile of sister kind,
Quiet home I leave behind.
Oft shall I think of you
Whene'er the wine-cup passes round,
When alone my watch I keep.
But when danger to glory shall call me,
I still will be first in the fray,
As blithe as a knight in his bridal array.
Careless what fate shall befall me
When glory shall call me.

WAGNER
Come on, friends! No tears nor vain alarms;
Quaff we good wine, to the success of our arms!
Drink, boys, drink!
In a joyous refrain
Bid farewell, till we meet again.

ÉTUDIANTS
Buvons, trinquons, et qu'un joyeux refrain
Nous mette en train!

WAGNER

(montant sur un escabeau)

Un rat plus poltron que brave,
Et plus laid que beau,
Logeait au fond d'une cave,
Sous un vieux tonneau;
Un chat …

Scène 3

MÉPHISTOPHÉLÈS

(paraissant tout à coup au milieu des étudiants et interrompant Wagner)

Pardon!

WAGNER
Hein?

MÉPHISTOPHÉLÈS
   Parmi vous, de grâce
Permettez-moi de prendre place!
Que votre ami d'abord achève sa chanson!
Moi, je vous en promets plusieurs de ma façon!

WAGNER

(descendant de son escabeau)

Une seule suffit, pourvu qu'elle soit bonne!

MÉPHISTOPHÉLÈS
Je ferai de mon mieux pour n'ennuyer personne!

I
Strophes du veau d'or

Le veau d'or est toujours debout;
On encense
Sa puissance

STUDENTS
We'll drink! Fill high!
Once more in song our voices
Let us raise.

WAGNER

(mounting on a table)

A rat, more coward than brave,
And with an exceedingly ugly head,
Lodged in a sort of hole or cave,
Under an ancient hogshead.
A cat –

Scene 3

MEPHISTOPHELES

(appearing suddenly among the students and interrupting Wagner)

Good sir!

WAGNER
What?

MEPHISTOPHELES
If it so please ye I should wish
To mingle with ye a short time.
If your good friend will kindly end this song.
I'll tell ye a few things well worth the hearing.

WAGNER

(coming down from the table)

One will suffice, but let that one be good!

MEPHISTOPHELES
My utmost I will do
Your worships not to bore.

I
The Song of the Golden Calf

Calf of Gold! aye in all the world
To your mightiness they proffer,
Incense at your fane they offer

D'un bout du monde à l'autre bout!
Pour fêter l'infâme idole,
Rois et peuples confondus,
Au bruit sombre des écus
Dansent une ronde folle
Autour de son piédestal! …
Et Satan conduit le bal!

II

Le veau d'or est vainqueur des dieux;
Dans son gloire
Dérisoire
Le monstre abjecte insulte aux cieux!
Il contemple, ô rage étrange!
A ses pieds le genre humain
Se ruant, le fer en main,
Dans le sang et dans la fange
Où brille l'ardent métal! …
Et Satan conduit le bal!

TOUS
Et Satan conduit le bal!

La scène des épées

CHOEUR
Merci de ta chanson!

VALENTIN
(à part)
Singulier personnage!

WAGNER
(tendant un verre à Méphistophélès)
Nous ferez vous l'honneur de trinquer avec nous?

MÉPHISTOPHÉLÈS
Volontiers! …
(Saisissant la main de Wagner et l'examinant.)
Ah! voici qui m'attriste pour vous!
Vous voyez cette ligne?

From end to end of all the world.
And in honor of the idol
Kings and peoples everywhere
To the sound of jingling coins
Dance with zeal in festive circle,
Round about the pedestal.
Satan, he conducts the ball.

II

Calf of Gold, strongest god below!
To his temple overflowing
Crowds before his vile shape bowing,
The monster dares insult the skies.
With contempt he views around him
All the vaunted human race,
As they strive in abject toil,
As with souls debased they circle
Round about the pedestal.
Satan, he conducts the ball.

ALL
Satan, he conducts the ball.

The Scene of the Swords

CHORUS
A strange story this of thine.

VALENTINE
(aside)
And stranger still is he who sings it.

WAGNER
(Offering a cup to Mephistopheles)
Will you honor us by partaking of wine?

MEPHISTOPHELES
With pleasure. Ah!
(Taking Wagner by the hand, and scrutinizing his palm.)
Behold what saddens me to view.
See you this line?

WAGNER
Eh bien?

MÉPHISTOPHÉLÈS
Fâcheux présage!
Vous vous ferez tuer en montant à l'assaut!

SIEBEL
Vous êtes donc sorcier?

MÉPHISTOPHÉLÈS
Tout juste autant qu'il faut
Pour lire dans ta main que le ciel te condamne
A ne plus toucher une fleur
Sans qu'elle se fane!

SIEBEL
Moi?

MÉPHISTOPHÉLÈS
Plus de bouquets à Marguerite! …

VALENTIN
Ma sœur! …
Qui vous a dit son nom?

MÉPHISTOPHÉLÈS
Prenez garde, mon brave!
Vous vous ferez tuer par quelqu'un que je sais!

(prenant le verre des mains de Wagner)

A votre santè! …

(jetant le contenu du verre, après y avoir trempé ses lèvres)

Peuh! que ton vin est mauvais! …
Permettez-moi de vous en offrir de ma cave!

(Frappant sur le tonneau, surmonté d'un Bacchus, qui sert d'enseigne au cabaret.)

Holà! seigneur Bacchus! à boire! …

(Le vin jaillit du tonneau. Aux étudiants.)

Approchez-vous!
Chacun sera servi selon ses goûts!
A la santé que tout à l'heure
Vous portiez, mes amis, à Marguerite!

WAGNER
Well?

MEPHISTOPHELES
A sudden death it presages, –
You will be killed in mounting to th' assault!

SIEBEL
You are then a sorcerer!

MEPHISTOPHELES
Even so. And your own hand shows plainly
To what fate condemns. What flower you would gather
Shall wither in the grasp.

SIEBEL
I?

MEPHISTOPHELES
No more bouquets for Marguerite.

VALENTINE
My sister! How knew you her name?

MEPHISTOPHELES
Take care, my brave fellow!
Some one I know is destined to kill you.

(taking the cup)

Your health, gentlemen!

(throwing away the cup's contents after having tasted it)

Pah! What miserable wine!
Allow me to offer you some from my cellar!

(Jumps on the table, and strikes on a little cask surmounted by the effigy of the god Bacchus, which serves as a sign to the Inn.)

What ho! thou god of wine, now give us drink!

(Wine gushes forth from the cask, and Mephistopheles fills his goblet.)

Approach, my friends!
Each one shall be served to his liking.
To your health, now and hereafter!
To Marguerite!

VALENTIN

(lui arrachant le verre des mains)

Assez! ...

Si je ne te fais taire à l'instant, que je meure!

(Le vin s'enflamme dans la vasque placée au-dessous du tonneau.)

WAGNER ET LES ÉTUDIANTS

Holà! ...

(Ils tirent leurs épées.)

MÉPHISTOPHÉLÈS

Pourquoi trembler, vous qui me menacez?

(Il tire un cercle autour de lui avec son épée. – Valentin s'avance pour l'attaquer. – Son épée se brise.)

VALENTIN

Mon fer, ô surprise!

Dans les airs se brise! ...

VALENTIN, WAGNER, SIEBEL ET LES ÉTUDIANTS

(forçant Méphistophélès à reculer et lui présentant la garde de leurs épées)

De l'enfer qui vient émousser

Nos armes!

Nous ne pouvons pas repousser

Les charmes!

Mais puisque tu brises le fer,

Regarde! ...

C'est une croix qui, de l'enfer,

Nous garde!

(Ils sortent.)

Scène 4

MÉPHISTOPHÉLÈS

(remettant son épée au fourreau)

Nous nous retrouverons, mes amis! – Serviteur!

VALENTINE

(seizing the cup from his hands)

Enough! If I do not silence him,
And that instantly, I will die.

(The wine bursts into flame.)

WAGNER AND STUDENTS
Hola!

(They draw their swords.)

MEPHISTOPHELES
Ah, ha! Why do you tremble so, you who menace me?

(He draws a circle around him with his sword. Valentine attacks; his sword is broken.)

VALENTINE
My sword, O amazement!
Is broken asunder.

ALL

(forcing Mephistopheles to retire by holding toward him the cross-shaped handles of their swords)

Gainst the powers of evil our arms assailing,
Strongest earthly might is unavailing.
But thou canst not charm us,
Look hither!
While this blest sign we wear
Thou canst not harm us.

(Exeunt.)

Scene 4

MEPHISTOPHELES

(replacing his sword)

We'll meet anon, good sirs, – adieu!

FAUST

(entrant en scène)

Qu'as-tu donc?

MÉPHISTOPHÉLÈS

Rien! – A nous deux, cher docteur!
Qu'attendez-vous de moi? par où commencerai-je?

FAUST

Où se cache la belle enfant
Que ton art m'a fait voir? – Est-ce un vain sortilège?

MÉPHISTOPHÉLÈS

Non pas! mais contre nous sa vertu la protège;
Et le ciel même la défend!

FAUST

Qu'importe? je le veux! viens! conduis-mois vers elle!
Ou je me sépare de toi!

MÉPHISTOPHÉLÈS

Il suffit ... je tiens trop à mon nouvel emploi
Pour vous laisser douter un instant de mon zèle!
Attendons! ... Ici même, à ce signal joyeux,
La belle et chaste enfant va paraître à vos yeux!

Scène 5

(Les étudiants et les jeunes filles, bras dessus, bras dessus, et précédés par des joueurs de violon, envahissent la scène. Ils sont suivis par les bourgeois qui ont paru au commencement de l'acte.)

Les Mêmes, Étudiants, Jeunes Filles, Bourgeois, puis Siebel et Marguerite.

CHOEUR

(marquant la mesure en marchant)

Ainsi que la brise légère
Soulève en épais tourbillons
La poussière
Des sillons,

FAUST

(enters)

Why, what has happened?

MEPHISTOPHELES
Oh, nothing! let us change the subject!
Say, Doctor, what would you of me?
With what shall we begin?

FAUST
Where bides the beauteous maid
Thine art did show to me?
Or was't mere witchcraft?

MEPHISTOPHELES
No, but her virtue doth protect her from thee.
And heaven itself would keep her pure.

FAUST
It matters not!
Come, lead me to her,
Or I straightway abandon thee.

MEPHISTOPHELES
Then I'll comply! 'twere pity you should think
So meanly of the magic power which
I possess.
Have patience! and to this joyous tune,
Right sure am I, the maiden will appear.

Scene 5

(Students, with Maidens on their arms, preceded by Musicians, take possession of the stage. Burghers in the rear, as at the commencement of the act.)

Students, Maidens, Burghers, etc., afterwards Siebel and Marguerite.

CHORUS

(marking waltz time with their feet)

As the wind that sportively plays,
At first will light dust only raise,
Yet, at last, becomes a gale,
So our dancing and our singing,

Que la valse nous entraîne!
Faites retentir la plaine
De l'éclat de nos chansons!

(Les Musiciens montent sur les bancs; la valse commence.)

MÉPHISTOPHÉLÈS

(à Faust)

Vois ces filles
Gentilles!
Ne veux-tu pas
Aus plus belles
D'entre elles
    Offrir ton bras?

FAUST
Non! fais trêve
A ce ton moqueur!
Et laisse mon cœur
A son rêve! …

SIEBEL

(rentrant en scène)

C'est par ici que doit passer
Marguerite!

QUELQUES JEUNES FILLES

(s'approchant de Siebel)

Faut-il qu'une fille à danser
Vous invite?

SIEBEL
Non! … non! je ne veux pas valser! …

CHOEUR
Ainsi que la brise légère
Soulève en épais tourbillons
La poussière
Des sillons,
Que la valse nous entraîne!
Faites retentir la plaine
De l'éclat de nos chansons! …

(Marguerite paraît.)

Soft at first, then loudly ringing,
Will resound o'er hill and dale.

(The Musicians mount upon the table, and dancing begins.)

MEPHISTOPHELES

(to Faust)

See those lovely young maidens.
Will you not ask of them
To accept you?

FAUST
No! desist from thy idle sport,
And leave my heart free to reflection.

SIEBEL

(entering)

Marguerite this way alone can arrive.

SOME OF THE MAIDENS

(approaching Siebel)

Pray seek you a partner to join in
the dance?

SIEBEL
No: it has no charm for me.

CHORUS
As the wind that sportively plays,
At first will light dust only raise,
Yet, at last, becomes a gale,
So our dancing and our singing,
Soft at first, then loudly ringing,
Will resound o'er hill and dale.

(Marguerite enters.)

FAUST

Ah! … la voici … c'est elle! …

MÉPHISTOPHÉLÈS

Eh bien, abordez-la!

SIEBEL

(apercevant Marguerite et faisant un pas vers elle)

Marguerite! …

MÉPHISTOPHÉLÈS

(se retournant et se trouvant face à face avec Siebel)

Plaît-il! …

SIEBEL

(à part)

Maudit homme! encor là! …

MÉPHISTOPHÉLÈS

(d'un ton milleux)

Eh quoi! mon ami! vous voilà! …

(en riant)

Ah, vraiment, mon ami!

(Siebel recule devant Méphistophélès, qui lui fait faire ainsi le tour du théâtre en passant derrière le groupe des danseurs.)

FAUST

(abordant Marguerite qui traverse la scène)

Ne permettrez-vous pas, ma belle demoiselle,
Qu'on vous offre le bras pour faire le chemin?

MARGUERITE

Non, monsieur! je ne suis demoiselle, ni belle,
Et je n'ai pas besoin qu'on me donne la main.

(Elle passe devant Faust et s'éloigne.)

FAUST

(la suivant des yeux)

Par le ciel! que de grâce … et quelle modestie!
O belle enfant, je t'aime! …

FAUST

It is she! behold her!

MEPHISTOPHELES

'Tis well! now, then, approach!

SIEBEL

(perceiving Marguerite and approaching her)

Marguerite!

MEPHISTOPHELES

(turning round and finding himself face to face with Siebel)

What say you?

SIEBEL

(aside)

Malediction! here again!

MEPHISTOPHELES

(coaxingly)

What, here again, dear boy?

(laughing)

Ha, ha! a right good jest!

(Siebel retreats before Mephistopheles, who then compels him to make a circuit of the stage, passing behind the dancers.)

FAUST

(approaching Marguerite, who crosses the stage)

Will you not permit me, my fairest demoiselle,
To offer you my arm, and clear for you the way?

MARGUERITE

No, sir. I am no demoiselle, neither am I fair;
And I have no need to accept your offered arm.

(Passes Faust and retires.)

FAUST

(gazing after her)

What beauty! What grace! What modesty!
O lovely child, I love thee! I love thee!

SIEBEL

(redescendant en scène sans avoir vu ce qui vient de se passer)

Elle est partie!

(Il va pour s'élancer sur la trace de Marguerite; mais, se trouvant de nouveau face à face avec Méphistophélès, il lui tourne le dos et s'éloigne par le fond du théâtre.)

MÉPHISTOPHÉLÈS

(à Faust)

Eh bien?

FAUST

On me repousse! …

MÉPHISTOPHÉLÈS

(en riant)

Allons! à tes amours
Je vois qu'il faut prêter secours! …

(Il s'éloigne avec Faust du même côté que Marguerite.)

QUELQUES JEUNES FILLES

(s'adressant à trois ou quatre d'entre elles qui ont observé la rencontre de Faust et de Marguerite)

Qu'est-ce donc! …

DEUXIÈME GROUPE DE JEUNES FILLES
Marguerite,
Qui de ce beau seigneur refuse la conduite! …

ÉTUDIANTS

(se rapprochant)

Valsons encor!

JEUNES FILLES
Valsons toujours!

SIEBEL

(coming forward, without having seen what has occurred)

She has gone!

(He is about to hurry after Marguerite, when he suddenly finds himself face to face with Mephistopheles – he hastily turns away and leaves the stage.)

MEPHISTOPHELES

(to Faust)

Well, Doctor!

FAUST
Well. She has repulsed me.

MEPHISTOPHELES

(laughing)

Ay, truly, I see, in love,
You know not how to make the first move.

(He retires with Faust, in the direction taken by Marguerite.)

SOME OF THE MAIDENS

(who have noticed the meeting between Faust and Marguerite)

What is it?

OTHERS
Marguerite. She has refused the escort
Of yonder elegant gentleman.

STUDENTS

(approaching)

Waltz again!

MAIDENS
Waltz always!

Acte Troisième

Le Jardin de Marguerite
(Au fond, un mur percé d'une petite porte. A gauche, un bosquet. A droite, un pavillon dont la fenêtre fait face au public. Arbres et massifs.)

Scène 1

Siebel, seul.
(Il est arrêté près d'un massif de roses et de lilas.)

Air de Siebel

SIEBEL

I

Faites-lui mes aveux, portez mes vœux,
Fleurs écloses près d'elle,
Dites-lui qu'elle est belle …
Que mon cœur nuit et jour
Languit d'amour!
Révélez à son âme
Le secret de ma flamme!
Qu'il s'exhale avec vous
Parfums plus doux! …
(Il cueille une fleur.)
Fanée! … hélas!
(Il jette la fleur avec dépit.)
Ce sorcier, que Dieu damne,
M'a porté malheur!
(Il cueille une autre fleur qui s'effeuille encore.)
Je ne puis sans qu'elle se fane
Toucher une fleur! …
Si je trempais mes doigts dans l'eau bénite? …
(Il s'approche du pavillon et trempe ses doigts dans un bénitier accroché au mur.)
C'est là que chaque soir vient prier Marguerite!
Voyons maintenant! voyons vite! …
(Il cueille deux ou trois fleurs.)
Elles se fanent? … Non! … Satan, je ris de toi …

Act III

Marguerite's Garden

(At the back a wall, with a little door. To the left a bower. On the right a pavilion, with a window facing the audience. Trees, shrubs, etc.)

Scene 1

Siebel, alone. (He enters through the little door at the back, and stops on the threshold of the pavilion, near a group of roses and lilies.)

The Flower Song

SIEBEL

I

Gently whisper to her of love, dear flow'r;
Tell her that I adore her,
And for me, oh, implore her,
For my heart feels alone for her
   love's pow'r.
Say in sighing I languish,
That for her, in my anguish
Beats alone, dearest flow'r,
My aching heart.

(Plucks flowers.)

Alas! they are wither'd!

(Throws them away.)

Can the accursed wizard's words be true?

(Plucks another flower, which, on touching his hand, immediately withers.)

"Thou shalt ne'er touch flower again
But it shall wither!"
I'll bathe my hand in holy water!

(Approaches the pavilion, and dips his fingers in a little font suspended to the wall.)

When day declines, Marguerite hither
Comes to pray, so we'll try again.

(Plucks more flowers.)

Are they wither'd? No! Satan, thou art conquer'd!

II

C'est en vous que j'ai foi;
Parlez pour moi!
Qu'elle puisse connaître
L'ardeur qu'elle a fait naître,
Et dont mon cœur troublé
N'a point parlé!
Si l'amour l'effarouche,
Que la fleur sur sa bouche
Sache au moins déposer
Un doux baiser! …

(Il cueille des fleurs pour former un bouquet et disparaît dans les massifs du jardin.)

Scène 2

FAUST

(entrant doucement en scène)

C'est ici?

MÉPHISTOPHÉLÈS
Suivez-moi!

FAUST
Que regardes-tu là?

MÉPHISTOPHÉLÈS
Siebel, votre rival.

FAUST
Siebel?

MÉPHISTOPHÉLÈS
Chut! … le voilà!

(Il se cache avec Faust dans un bosquet.)

SIEBEL

(rentrant en scène, avec un bouquet à la main)

Mon bouquet n'est-il pas charmant?

MÉPHISTOPHÉLÈS

(à part)

Charmant!

II

In these flowers alone I've faith,
For they will plead for me;
To her they will reveal
My hapless state.
The sole cause of my woe is she,
And yet she knows it not.
But in these flowers I've faith,
For they will plead for me.

(Plucks flowers in order to make a bouquet, and disappears amongst the shrubs.)

Scene 2

FAUST

(cautiously entering through the garden door)

We are here!

MEPHISTOPHELES
Follow me.

FAUST
Whom dost thou see?

MEPHISTOPHELES
Siebel, your rival.

FAUST
Siebel?

MEPHISTOPHELES
Hush! He comes.

(They enter the bower.)

SIEBEL

(entering with a bouquet in his hand)

My bouquet is charming indeed?

MEPHISTOPHELES

(aside)

It is indeed!

SIEBEL
Victoire!
Je lui raconterai demain toute l'histoire;
Et, si l'on veut savoir le secret de mon cœur,
Un baiser lui dira le reste!

MÉPHISTOPHÉLÈS

(à part)

Séducteur!

(Siebel attache le bouquet à la porte du pavillon et sort.)

Scène 3

MÉPHISTOPHÉLÈS
Attendez-moi là, cher docteur!
Pour tenir compagnie aux fleurs de votre élève,
Je vais vous chercher un trésor
Plus merveilleux, plus riche encor
Que tous ceux qu'elle voit en rêve!

FAUST
Laisse-moi!

MÉPHISTOPHÉLÈS
J'obéis! … daignez m'attendre ici.

(Il sort.)

Scène 4

Cavatine

FAUST

(seul)

Quel trouble inconnu me pénètre!
Je sens l'amour s'emparer de mon être.
O Marguerite! à tes pieds me voici!
Salut! demeure chaste et pure, où se devine
La présence d'une âme innocente et divine! …
Que de richesse en cette pauvreté!
En ce réduit, que de félicité! …

SIEBEL
Victory!
Tomorrow I'll reveal all to her.
I will disclose to her the secret
That lies concealed in my heart:
A kiss will tell the rest.

MEPHISTOPHELES

(aside, mockingly)

Seducer!

(Exit Siebel, after fastening bouquet to the door of the pavilion.)

Scene 3

MEPHISTOPHELES
Now attend, my dear doctor!
To keep company with the flowers of our friend,
I go to bring you a treasure,
Which outshines them beyond measure,
And of beauty past believing.

FAUST
Leave me!

MEPHISTOPHELES
I obey. Deign to await me here.

(Disappears.)

Scene 4

Cavatina

FAUST

(alone)

What new emotion penetrates my soul!
Love, a pure and holy love, pervades my being.
O Marguerite, behold me at thy feet!
All hail, thou dwelling pure and lowly,
Home of an angel fair and holy,
All mortal beauty excelling!
What wealth is here, a wealth outbidding gold,

O nature, c'est là que tu la fis si belle!
C'est là que cette enfant a grandi sous ton aile,
A dormi sous tes yeux?
Là que, de ton haleine enveloppant son âme,
Tu fis avec amour épanouir la femme
En cet ange des cieux!
Salut! demeure chaste et pure, où se devine
La présence d'une âme innocente et divine! ...

Scène 5

(Méphistophélès reparaît, une cassette sous le bras.)

MÉPHISTOPHÉLÈS
Alerte! la voilà! ... Si le bouquet l'emporte
Sur l'écrin, je consens à perdre mon pouvoir!

(Il ouvre l'écrin.)

FAUST
Fuyons! ... je veux ne jamais la revoir!

MÉPHISTOPHÉLÈS
Quel scrupule vous prend? ...

(Plaçant l'écrin sur le seuil du pavillon.)

Sur le seuil de la porte,
Voici l'écrin placé! ... venez! ... j'ai bon espoir!

(Il entraine Faust et disparaît avec lui dans le jardin. Marguerite entre par la porte du fond et descend en silence jusque sur le devant de la scène.)

Of peace, and love, and innocence untold!
Bounteous Nature! 'twas here by day thy love was taught her,
Thou here with kindly care didst o'er-shadow thy daughter
Through hours of night!
Here waving tree and flower
Made her an Eden bower
Of beauty and delight,
For one whose very birth
Brought down heaven to our earth.
All hail, thou dwelling pure and lowly,
Home of an angel fair and holy.

Scene 5

(Mephistopheles reappears carrying a casket under his arm.)

MEPHISTOPHELES
What ho! see here!
If flowers are more potent than bright jewels,
Then I consent to lose my power.

(Opens the casket and displays the jewels.)

FAUST
Let us fly; I ne'er will see her more.

MEPHISTOPHELES
What scruple now assails thee?

(Lays the casket on the threshold of the pavilion.)

See on yonder step,
The jewels snugly lie;
We've reason now to hope.

(Draws Faust after him, and disappears in the garden. Marguerite enters through the doorway at the back, and advances silently to the front.)

Scène 6

MARGUERITE

(seule)

Je voudrais bien savoir quel était ce jeune homme,
Si c'est un grand seigneur, et comment il se nomme?

(Elle s'assied dans le bosquet, devant son rouet, et prend son fuseau autour duquel elle prépare de la laine.)

I

Chanson du Roi de Thulé

"Il était un roi de Thulé,
Qui, jusqu'à la tombe fidèle,
Eut, en souvenir de sa belle,
Une coupe en or ciselé! ..."

(s'interrompant)

Il avait bonne grâce, à ce qu'il m'a semblé.

(reprenant sa chanson)

"Nul trésor n'avait plus de charmes!
Dans les grands jours il s'en servait,
Et chaque fois qu'il y buvait,
Ses yeux se remplissaient de larmes! ..."

II

(Elle se lève et fait quelques pas.)

"Quand il sentit venir la mort,
Etendu sur sa froide couche,
Pour la porter jusqu'à sa bouche
Sa main fit un suprême effort! ..."

(s'interrompant)

Je ne savais que dire, et j'ai rougi d'abord.

(reprenant sa chanson)

"Et puis, en l'honneur de sa dame,
Il but un dernière fois;

Scene 6

MARGUERITE

(alone)

Fain would I know the name
Of the fair youth I met;
Fain would I his birth
And station also know!

(Seats herself at her wheel in the arbor, and arranges the flax upon the spindle.)

I

The Ballad of the King of Thule

"Once there was a king of Thule,
Who was until death always faithful,
And in memory of his loved one
Caused a cup of gold to be made."

(breaking off)

His manner was so gentle! 'Twas true politeness.

(resuming the song)

"Never treasure prized he so dearly,
Naught else would use on festive days,
And always when he drank from it,
His eyes with tears would be o'erflowing."

II

(She rises, and takes a few paces.)

"When he knew that death was near,
As he lay on his cold couch smiling,
Once more he raised with greatest effort
To his lips the golden vase."

(breaking off)

I knew not what to say, my face red with blushes!

(resuming the song)

"And when he, to honor his lady,
Drank from the cup the last, last time,

La coupe trembla dans ses doigts.
Et doucement il rendit l'âme!"
Les grands seigneurs ont seuls des airs si résolus,
Avec cette douceur!

(elle se dirige vers le pavillon)

Allons! n'y pensons plus!
Cher Valentin, si Dieu m'écoute,
Je te reverrai! ... me voilà
Toute seule! ...

(Au môment d'entrer dans la pavillon, elle aperçoit le bouquet suspendu à la porte.)

Un bouquet!

(elle prend le bouquet)

C'est de Siebel, sans doute!
Pauvre garçon!

(apercevant la cassette)

Que vois-je là?
D'où ce riche coffret peut-il venir? ... Je n'ose
Y toucher, et pourtant ... – Voici la clef, je crois! ...
Si je l'ouvrais! ... ma main tremble! ... Pourquoi!
Je ne fais, en l'ouvrant, rien de mal, je suppose! ...

(Elle ouvre la cassette et laisse tomber le bouquet.)

Air des bijoux

O Dieu! que de bijoux! ... est-ce un rêve charmant
Qui m'éblouit, ou si je veille! –
Mes yeux n'ont jamais vu de richesse pareille! ...

(Elle place la cassette tout ouverte sur une chaise et s'agenouille pour se parer.)

Si j'osais seulement
Me parer un moment
De ces pendants d'oreille!

(Elle tire des boucles d'oreilles de la cassette.)

Voici tout justement,
Au fond de la cassette,

Soon falling from his trembling grasp,
Then gently passed his soul away."
Nobles alone can bear them with so bold a mien,
So tender, too, withal!

(she goes toward the pavilion)

I'll think of him no more! Good Valentine!
If Heav'n heeds my prayer, we shall meet again.
Meanwhile I am alone!

(Suddenly perceiving the bouquet attached to the door of the pavilion.)

Flowers!

(unfastens the bouquet)

They are Siebel's, surely!
Poor faithful boy!

(perceiving the casket)

But what is this?
From whom did this splendid casket come?
I dare not touch it –
Yet see, here is the key! – I'll take one look!
How I tremble – yet why? – can it be
Much harm just to look in a casket?

(Opens the casket and lets the bouquet fall.)

The Jewel Song

Oh, heaven! what jewels!
Can I be dreaming?
Or am I really awake?
Ne'er have I seen such costly things before!

(Puts down the casket on a rustic seat, and kneels down in order to adorn herself with the jewels.)

I should just like to see
How they'd look upon me
Those brightly sparkling ear-drops!

(Takes out the ear-rings.)

Ah! at the bottom of the casket is a glass:
I there can see myself! –

Un miroir! … comment
N'être pas coquette?

(Elle se pare des boucles d'oreilles, se lève et se regarde dans le miroir.)

Ah! je ris de me voir
Si belle en ce miroir! …
Est-ce toi, Marguerite?
Réponds-moi, réponds vite! –
Non! non! – ce n'est plus toi!
Ce n'est plus ton visage!
C'est la fille d'un roi,
Qu'on salue au passage!
Ah! s'il était ici!
S'il me voyait ainsi! …
Comme une demoiselle
Il me trouverait belle! …
Achevons la métamorphose!
Il me tarde encor d'essayer
Le bracelet et le collier.

(Elle se pare du collier d'abord, puis du bracelet. – Se levant.)

Dieu! c'est comme une main qui sur mon bras se pose!
Ah! je ris de me voir
Si belle en ce miroir!
Est-ce toi, Marguerite?
Réponds-moi, réponds vite! –
Non! non! – ce n'est plus toi!
Ce n'est plus ton visage!
C'est la fille d'un roi,
Qu'on salue au passage! …
Ah! s'il était ici!
S'il me voyait ainsi! …
Comme une demoiselle
Il me trouverait belle! …
Ah! s'il était ici! …

But am I not becoming vain?

(Puts on the ear-rings, rises, and looks at herself in the glass.)

Ah! I laugh, as I pass, to look into a glass;
Is it truly Marguerite, then?
Is it you?
Tell me true!
No, no, no, 'tis not you!
No, no, that bright face there reflected
Must belong to a queen!
It reflects some fair queen, whom I greet as I pass her.
Ah! could he see me now,
Here, deck'd like this, I vow,
He surely would mistake me,
And for noble lady take me!
I'll try on the rest.
The necklace and the bracelets
I fain would try!

(She adorns herself with the bracelets and necklace, then rises.)

Heavens! 'Tis like a hand
That on mine arm doth rest!
Ah! I laugh, as I pass, to look into a glass;
Is it truly Marguerite, then?
Is it you?
Tell me true!
No, no, no, 'tis not you!
No, no, that bright face there reflected
Must belong to a queen!
It reflects some fair queen, whom I greet as I pass her.
Ah! could he see me now,
Here, deck'd like this, I vow,
He surely would mistake me,
And for noble lady take me!

Scène 7

MARTHE

(entrant par le fond)

Seigneur Dieu! Que vois-je … comme vous voilà belle,
Mon ange! … – D'où vous vient ce riche écrin?

MARGUERITE

(avec confusion)

Hélas!
On l'aura par mégarde apporté!

MARTHE

Que non pas!
Ces bijoux sont à vous, ma chère demoiselle!
Oui! c'est là le cadeau d'un seigneur amoureux!

(soupirant)

Mon cher époux jadis était moins généreux!

Scène 8

(Méphistophélès et Faust entrent en scène.)

MÉPHISTOPHÉLÈS
Dame Marthe Schwerlein, s'il vous plaît?

MARTHE
Qui m'appelle?

MÉPHISTOPHÉLÈS
Pardon d'oser ainsi nous présenter chez vous!

(bas à Faust)

Vous voyez qu'elle a fait bel accueil aux bijoux?

(haut)

Dame Marthe Schwerlein?

Scene 7

MARTHA

(entering from the back)

Just heaven! what is't I see?
How fair you now do seem!
Why, what has happened?
Who gave to you these jewels?

MARGUERITE

(confused)

Alas! by some mistake
They have been hither brought.

MARTHA
Why so?
No, beauteous maiden,
These jewels are for you;
The gift are they of some enamor'd lord.

(sighing)

My husband, I must say,
Was of a less generous turn!

Scene 8

(Mephistopheles and Faust enter.)

MEPHISTOPHELES
Tell me, I pray, are you Martha Schwerlein?

MARTHA
Sir, I am!

MEPHISTOPHELES
Pray pardon me,
If thus I venture to present myself.

(aside, to Faust)

You see your presents
Are right graciously received.

(to Martha)

Are you, then, Martha Schwerlein?

MARTHE
Me voici?

MÉPHISTOPHÉLÈS
La nouvelle
Que j'apporte n'est pas pour vous mettre en gaîté: –
Votre mari, madame, est mort et vous salue!

MARTHE
Ah! ... grand Dieu! ...

MARGUERITE
Qu'est-ce donc?

MÉPHISTOPHÉLÈS
Rien! ...
(Marguerite baisse les yeux sous le regard de Méphistophélès, se hâte d'ôter le collier, le bracelet et les pendants d'oreilles et de les remettre dans la cassette.)

MARTHE
O calamité!
O nouvelle imprévue! ...

MARGUERITE
(à part)
Malgré moi mon cœur tremble et tressaille à sa vue!

FAUST
(à part)
La fièvre de mes sens se dissipe à sa vue!

MÉPHISTOPHÉLÈS
(à Marthe)
Votre mari, madame, est mort et vous salue!

MARTHE
Ne m'apportez-vous rien de lui?

MARTHA
Sir, I am.

MEPHISTOPHELES
The news I bring
Is of an unpleasant kind;
Your much-loved spouse is dead,
And sends you greeting.

MARTHA
Great Heaven!

MARGUERITE
Why, what has happened?

MEPHISTOPHELES
Stuff!

(Marguerite hastily takes off the jewels, and is about to replace them in the casket.)

MARTHA
Oh woe! oh, unexpected news!

MARGUERITE

(aside)

How beats my heart
Now he is near!

FAUST

(aside)

The fever of my love
Is lull'd when at her side!

MEPHISTOPHELES

(to Martha)

Your much-loved spouse is dead,
And sends you greeting!

MARTHA
Sent he nothing else to me?

MÉPHISTOPHÉLÈS

Rien! … et, pour le punir, il faut dès aujourd'hui
Chercher quelqu'un qui le remplace!

FAUST

(à Marguerite)

Pourquoi donc quitter ces bijoux?

MARGUERITE

Ces bijoux ne sont pas à moi! … Laissez de grâce!

MÉPHISTOPHÉLÈS

(à Marthe)

Que ne serait heureux d'échanger avec vous
La bague d'hyménée?

MARTHE

(á part)

Ah, bah!

(haut)

Plaît-il?

MÉPHISTOPHÉLÈS

(soupirant)

Hélas! cruelle destinée! …

Le quatuor

FAUST

(à Marguerite)

Prenez mon bras un moment!

MARGUERITE

(se défendant)

Laissez! … Je vous en conjure! …

MÉPHISTOPHÉLÈS

(de l'autre côté du théâtre, à Marthe)

Votre bras! …

MEPHISTOPHELES
No. We'll punish him for't;
Upon this very day
We'll find him a successor.

FAUST

(to Marguerite)

Wherefore lay aside these jewels?

MARGUERITE
Jewels are not made for me;
'Tis meet I leave them where they are.

MEPHISTOPHELES

(to Martha)

Who would not gladly unto
You present the wedding-ring!

MARTHA

(aside)

Indeed!

(to Mephistopheles)

You think so?

MEPHISTOPHELES

(sighing)

Ah me! ah, cruel fate!

The quartet

FAUST

(to Marguerite)

Pray lean upon mine arm!

MARGUERITE

(retiring)

Leave me, I humbly pray!

MEPHISTOPHELES

(offering his arm to Martha)

Take mine!

MARTHE

(à part)

Il est charmant!

(prenant son bras)

MÉPHISTOPHÉLÈS

(à part)

La voisine est un peu mûre!

(Marguerite abandonne son bras à Faust et s'éloigne avec lui. Méphistophélès et Marthe restent seuls en scène.)

MARTHE

Ainsi vous voyagez toujours?

MÉPHISTOPHÉLÈS

Dure nécessité, madame!

Sans ami, sans parents! … sans femme.

MARTHE

Cela sied encore aux beaux jours!

Mais plus tard, combien il est triste

De vieillir seul, en égoïste!

MÉPHISTOPHÉLÈS

J'ai frémi souvent, j'en conviens,

Devant cette horrible pensée!

MARTHE

Avant que l'heure en soit passée!

Digne seigneur, songez-y bien!

MÉPHISTOPHÉLÈS

J'y songerai!

MARTHE

Songez-y bien!

(Ils sortent. Entre Faust et Marguerite.)

FAUST

Eh quoi! toujours seule? …

MARTHA

(aside)

In sooth, a comely knight!

(taking his arm)

MEPHISTOPHELES

(aside)

The dame is somewhat tough!

(Marguerite yields her arm to Faust, and withdraws with him. Mephistopheles and Martha remain together.)

MARTHA

And so you are always traveling!

MEPHISTOPHELES

A hard necessity it is, madame!
Alone and loveless. Ah!

MARTHA

In youth it matters not so much,
But in late years 'tis sad indeed!
Right melancholy it is in solitude
Our olden age to pass!

MEPHISTOPHELES

The very thought doth make me shudder.
But still, alas! what can I do?

MARTHA

If I were you, I'd not delay,
But think on't seriously at once.

MEPHISTOPHELES

I'll think on't!

MARTHA

At once and seriously!

*(They withdraw.
Faust and Marguerite re-enter.)*

FAUST

Art always thus alone?

MARGUERITE
Mon frère
Est soldat; j'ai perdu ma mère;
Puis ce fut un autre malheur,
Je perdis ma petite sœur!
Pauvre ange! ... Elle m'était bien chère! ...
C'était mon unique souci;
Que de soins, hélas! ... que de peines!
C'est quand nos âmes en sont pleines
Que la mort nous les prend ainsi! ...
Sitôt qu'elle s'éveillait, vite
Il fallait que je fusse là! ...
Elle n'aimait que Marguerite!
Pour la voir, la pauvre petite,
Je reprendrais bien tout cela! ...

FAUST
Si le ciel, avec un sourire,
L'avait faite semblable à toi.
C'était un ange! ... Oui, je le crois! ...

MARGUERITE
Vous moquez-vous! ...

FAUST
Non! je t'admire!

MARGUERITE

(soupirant)

Je ne vous crois pas
Et de moi tout bas
Vous riez sans doute! ...
J'ai tort de rester
Pour vous écouter! ...
Et pourtant j'écoute! ...

FAUST
Laisse-moi ton bras! ...
Dieu ne m'a-t-il pas
Conduit sur ta route? ...
Pourquoi redouter,

MARGUERITE
My brother is at the wars,
My mother dear is dead!
By misadventure, too,
My dear sister have I lost.
Dear sister mine!
My greatest happiness was she.
Sad sorrows these;
When our souls with love are filled,
Death tears the loved one from us!
At morn, no sooner did she wake,
Than I was always at her side!
The darling of my life was she!
To see her once again.
I'd gladly suffer all.

FAUST
If heaven, in joyous mood,
Did make her like to thee,
An angel must she indeed have been!

MARGUERITE
Thou mock'st me!

FAUST
Nay, I do love thee!

MARGUERITE

(sighing)

Flatterer! thou mock'st me!
I believe thee not! thou seekest to deceive.
No longer will I stay, thy words to hear.

FAUST
Nay, I do love thee! Stay, oh stay!
Heaven hath with an angel crown'd my path.
Why fear'st thou to listen?

Hélas! d'êcouter? …
Mon cœur parle; écoute! …
(Méphistophélès et Marthe reparaissent.)

MARTHE

(à Méphistophélès)

Vous n'entendez pas,
Ou de moi tout bas
Vous riez sans doute!
Avant d'écouter,
Pourquoi vous hâter
De vous mettre en route?

MÉPHISTOPHÉLÈS

(à Marthe)

Ne m'accusez pas,
Si je dois, hélas!
Me remettre en route.
Faut-il attester
Qu'on voudrait rester
Quand on vous écoute?

(La nuit commence à tomber.)

MARGUERITE

(à Faust)

Retirez-vous! … voici la nuit.

FAUST

(passant son bras autour de la taille de Marguerite)

Chère âme!

MARGUERITE

Laissez-moi!

(Elle se dégage et s'enfuit.)

FAUST

(la poursuivant)

Quoi! méchante! … on me fuit!

It is my heart that speaks.

(Re-enter Mephistopheles and Martha.)

MARTHA

(to Mephistopheles)

Of what now are you thinking?
You heed me not – perchance you mock me.
Now list to what I say. –
You really must not leave us thus!

MEPHISTOPHELES

(to Martha)

Ah, chide me not, if my wanderings I resume.
Suspect me not; to roam I am compelled!
Need I attest how gladly I remain?
I hear but thee alone.

(Night comes on.)

MARGUERITE

(to Faust)

It grows dark, – you must away.

FAUST

(embracing her)

My loved one!

MARGUERITE
Ah! no more!
(Escapes.)

FAUST

(pursuing her)

Ah, cruel one, would'st fly?

MÉPHISTOPHÉLÈS

(à part, tandis que Marthe, dépitée, lui tourne le dos)

L'entretien devient trop tendre!
Esquivons nous!

(Il se cache derrière un arbre.)

MARTHE

(à part)

Comment m'y prendre?
Eh bien! il est parti! … Seigneur! …

(Elle s'éloigne.)

MÉPHISTOPHÉLÈS

Oui! Cours après moi! …
Ouf! cette vieille impitoyable
De force ou de gré, je crois,
Allait épouser le diable!

FAUST

(dans la coulisse)

Marguerite!

MARTHE

(dans la coulisse)

Cher seigneur!

MÉPHISTOPHÉLÈS

Serviteur!

Scène 9

(seul)

Il était temps! sous le feuillage sombre
Voici nos amoureux qui reviennent! …
C'est bien!
Gardons nous de troubler un si doux entretien!
O nuit, étends sur eux ton ombre!
Amour, ferme leur âme aux remords importuns!
Et vous, fleurs aux subtils parfums,

MEPHISTOPHELES

(aside, whilst Martha angrily turns her back to him)

The matter's getting serious,
I must away.

(Conceals himself behind a tree.)

MARTHA

(aside)

What's to be done? he's gone!
What ho, good sir!

(Retires.)

MEPHISTOPHELES
Yes, seek for me – that's right!
I really do believe
The aged beldame would
Actually have married Satan!

FAUST

(without)

Marguerite!

MARTHA

(without)

Good sir!

MEPHISTOPHELES
Your servant!

Scene 9

(alone)

'Twas high time!
By night, protected.
In earnest talk of love,
They will return! 'Tis well!
I'll not disturb
Their amorous confabulation!
Night, conceal them in thy darkest shade.
Love, from their fond hearts

Epanouissez-vous sous, cette main maudite!
Achevez de troubler le cœur de Marguerite! …

(Il s'éloigne et disparaît dans l'ombre.)

Scène 10

MARGUERITE
Il se fait tard! adieu!

FAUST

(la retenant)

Quoi! je t'implore en vain!
Attends! laisse ta main s'oublier dans la mienne!
Laisse-moi, laisse-moi contempler ton visage
Sous la pâle clarté
Dont l'astre de la nuit, comme dans un nuage,
Caresse ta beauté! …

MARGUERITE
O silence! ô bonheur! ineffable mystère!
Enivrante langueur!
J'écoute … Et je comprends cette voix solitaire
Qui chante dans mon cœur!

(dégageant sa main de celle de Faust)
Laissez un peu, de grâce! …
(Elle se penche et cueille une Marguerite.)

FAUST
Qu'est se donc?

MARGUERITE
Un simple jeu!
Laissez un peu!
(Elle effeuille la marguerite.)

Shut out all troublesome remorse.
And ye, O flowers of fragrance subtle,
This hand accurs'd
Doth cause ye all to open!
Bewilder the heart of Marguerite!

(Disappears amid the darkness.)

Scene 10

MARGUERITE
It groweth late, farewell!

FAUST

(holding her back)

I but implore in vain.
Let me thy hand take, and clasp it,
And behold but thy face once again,
Illum'd by that pale light,
From yonder moon that shines.
O'er thy beauteous features shedding
Its faint but golden ray.

MARGUERITE
Oh, what stillness reigns around,
Oh, ineffable mystery!
Sweetest, happiest feeling,
I list; a secret voice
Now seems to fill my heart.
Still its tone again resoundeth in my bosom.

(withdrawing her hand from Faust's)

Leave me awhile, I pray.

(Stoops and picks a daisy.)

FAUST
What is it thou doest?

MARGUERITE
This flower I consult.

(She plucks the petals of the daisy.)

FAUST

(à part)

Que dit ta bouche à voix basse? ...

MARGUERITE

Il m'aime! – Il ne m'aime pas! –
Il m'aime! – pas! – Il m'aime! – pas! – Il m'aime!

FAUST

Oui! ... crois en cette fleur éclose sous tes pas! ...
Qu'elle soit pour ton cœur l'oracle du ciel même! ...
Il t'aime! ... comprends-tu ce mot sublime et doux? ...
Aimer! porter en nous
Une ardeur toujours nouvelle! ...
Nous enivrer sans fin d'une joie éternelle!

FAUST ET MARGUERITE

Eternelle! ...

FAUST

O nuit d'amour ... ciel radieux! ...
O douces flammes! ...
Le bonheur silencieux
Vers les cieux
Dans nos deux âmes! ...

MARGUERITE

Je veux t'aimer et te chérir!
Parle encore!
Je t'appartiens! ... je t'adore! ...
Pour toi je veux mourir! ...

FAUST

Marguerite! ...

MARGUERITE

(se dégageant des bras de Faust)

Ah! ... partez! ...

FAUST

Cruelle! ...
Me séparer de toi! ...

FAUST

(aside)

What utters she in tones subdued?

MARGUERITE

He loves me! – no, he loves me not!
He loves me! – no! – He loves me!

FAUST

Yes, believe thou this flower,
The flower of love.
To thine heart let it tell
The truth it would teach, –
He loves thee! Know'st thou not
How happy 'tis to love?
The cherish in the heart a flame that never dies!
To drink forever from the fount of love!

BOTH

We'll love for ever!

FAUST

Oh, night of love! oh, radiant night!
The bright stars shine above;
Oh, joy, this is divine!
I love, I do adore thee!

MARGUERITE

Mine idol fond art thou!
Speak, speak again!
Thine, thine I'll be;
For thee I'll gladly die.

FAUST

Oh, Marguerite!

MARGUERITE

(suddenly tearing herself from Faust's arms)

Ah, leave me!

FAUST

Cruel one!

MARGUERITE
Je chancelle! …

FAUST
Ah! cruelle! …

MARGUERITE
Laissez-moi! …

FAUST
Tu veux que je te quitte!
Hélas! … vois ma douleur.
Tu me brises le cœur,
O Marguerite! …

MARGUERITE
Partez! oui, partez vite!
Je tremble! … hélas! … j'ai peur!
Ne brisez pas la cœur
De Marguerite!

FAUST
Par pitié …

MARGUERITE
Si je vous suis chère,
Par votre amour, par ces aveux
Que je devais taire,
Cédez à ma prière! …
Cédez à mes vœux!

(Elle tombe aux pieds de Faust.)

FAUST

(après un silence, la relevant doucement)

Divine pureté! …
Chaste innocence,
Dont la puissance
Triomphe de ma volonté! …
J'obéis! … Mais demain!

MARGUERITE
Oui, demain! .. dès l'aurore! …
Demain toujours! …

MARGUERITE
Fly hence! alas! I tremble!

FAUST
Cruel one!

MARGUERITE
Pray leave me!

FAUST
Would'st thou have me leave thee?
Ah! see'st thou not my grief?
Ah, Marguerite, thou breakest my heart!

MARGUERITE
Go hence! I waver! mercy, pray!
Fly hence! alas! I tremble!
Break not, I pray, thy Marguerite's heart!

FAUST
In pity –

MARGUERITE
If to thee I'm dear,
I conjure thee, by thy love,
By this fond heart,
That too readily its secret hath revealed,
Yield thee to my prayer, –
In mercy get thee hence!

(Kneels at the feet of Faust.)

FAUST

(after a few moments' silence, gently raising her)

O fairest child,
Angel so holy,
Thou shalt control me,
Shalt curb my will.
I obey; but at morn –

MARGUERITE
Yes, at morn,
Very early.

FAUST
Un mot encore! …
Répète-moi ce doux aveu! …
Tu m'aimes! …

MARGUERITE
Adieu! …

(Elle entre dans le pavillon.)

FAUST
Félicité du ciel … Ah … fuyons!

(Il s'élance vers la porte du jardin. Méphistophélès lui barre le passage.)

Scène 11

MÉPHISTOPHÉLÈS
Tête folle! …

FAUST
Tu nous écoutais.

MÉPHISTOPHÉLÈS
Par bonheur.
Vous auriez grand besoin, docteur,
Qu'on vous renvoyât à l'école.

FAUST
Laisse-moi.

MÉPHISTOPHÉLÈS
Daignez seulement
Écouter un moment
Ce qu'elle va conter aux étoiles, cher maître.
Tenez; elle ouvre sa fenêtre.

(Marguerite ouvre la fenêtre du pavillon et s'y appuie un moment en silence, la tête entre les mains.)

MARGUERITE
Il m'aime; … quel trouble en mon cœur!
L'oiseau chante! … le vent murmure! …
Toutes les voix de la nature
Me redisent en chœur:
Il t'aime! … – Ah! qu'il est doux de vivre! …

FAUST
One word at parting.
Repeat thou lovest me.

MARGUERITE
Adieu!

(Hastens towards the pavilion.)

FAUST
Adieu! Were it already morn!

(He rushes toward the garden door. Mephistopheles bars his way.)

Scene 11

MEPHISTOPHELES
Fool!

FAUST
You overheard us?

MEPHISTOPHELES
Happily. You have great need, learned doctor,
To be sent again to school.

FAUST
Leave me!

MEPHISTOPHELES
Deign first to listen for a moment,
To the speech she rehearses to the stars.
Dear master, delay. She opens her window.

(Marguerite opens the window of the pavilion, and remains with her head resting on her hand.)

MARGUERITE
He loves me! Wildly beats my heart!
The night-bird's song,
The evening breeze,
All nature's sounds together say,
"He loves thee!"

Le ciel me sourit; ... l'air m'enivre! ...
Est-ce de plaisir et d'amour
Que la feuille tremble et palpite? ...
Demain? ... – Ah! presse ton retour,
Cher bien-aimé! ... viens! ...

FAUST

(s'élançant vers la fenêtre et saisissant la main de Marguerite)

Marguerite! ...

MARGUERITE
Ah! ...

MÉPHISTOPHÉLÈS

(moquant)

Ho! ho!

(Marguerite rest un moment interdite et laisse tomber sa tête sur l'épaule de Faust; Méphistophélès ouvre la porte du jardin et sort en ricanant. La toile tombe.)

Acte Quatrieme

* Première Partie

La chambre de Marguerite

Scène 1

MARGUERITE
Elles ne sont plus là ...
Je riais avec elles
Autrefois – maintenant ...

---

* Editor's note: Part I of Act IV is reprinted with the kind permission of G. Schirmer Inc. London/New York, publisher of the G. Schirmer's Collection of Opera Librettos, in which C. Gounod's *Faust* was published, translated by Ruth and Thomas Martin. This section is scene I of Act III (pp. 14–16) in the G. Schirmer edition (1966).

Ah! sweet, sweet indeed
Now is this life to me!
Another world it seems;
The very ecstasy of love is this!
With tomorrow's dawn,
Haste thee, oh dear one,
Haste thee to return! Yes, come!

FAUST

(rushing to the window, and grasping her hand)

Marguerite!

MARGUERITE
Ah!

MEPHISTOPHELES

(Mockingly)

Ho! ho!

(Marguerite, overcome, allows her head to fall on Faust's shoulder. Mephistopheles opens the door of the garden, and departs, laughing derisively. The curtain falls.)

Act IV

* **Part I**

Marguerite's Room

Scene 1

MARGUERITE
They all have gone away –
Once I shared in their laughter,
Long ago – but no more …

CHOEUR DES FILLES *(en dehors)*
Le galant étranger s'enfuit
Et court encor!
Ah! ah! ah! ah! ah! ah!

MARGUERITE
Elles se cachaient!
Ah! cruelles!
Je ne trouvais pas d'outrage assez fort, jadis, pour les pêches des autres!
Un jour vient où l'on est sans pitié pour les nôtres!
Je ne suis que honte à mon tour.
Et pourtant – Dieu le sait,
Je n'étais pas infâme;
Tout ce qui t'entraîna, mon âme,
N'était que tendresse et qu'amour.
Il ne revient pas,
J'ai peur, je frissonne;
Je languis, hélas!
En vain l'heure sonne;
Il ne revient pas
Où donc peut-il être?
Seule à ma fenêtre
Je plonge là-bas
Mon regard, hélas! hélas!
Je n'ose me plaindre,
Il faut me contraindre!
Je pleure tout bas,
S'il pouvait connaître ma douleur!
Où donc peut-il être?
Il ne revient pas.
Oh! le voir, entendre
Le bruit de ses pas.
Mon cœur est si las,
Si las de l'attendre
Il ne revient pas!
Mon seigneur, mon maître!
S'il allait paraître,
Quelle joie!
Hélas! Où donc peut-il être?
Il ne revient pas.

GIRLS' VOICES *(off-stage)*
The gallant stranger ran away!
Where has he gone?
Ha ha ha ha ha ha!

MARGUERITE
They have gone away!
Ah, they scorn me!
Not so long ago I could not find words
    too strong for other people's vices, and
    today it is they who show me no pity.
In my turn I must suffer too.
But heaven knows,
I had no thought of evil;
My only wish, my only longing
Was love, tender love,
Good and true.
He does not return, I am lonely,
How I long and yearn,
I wait for him only,
He does not return.
O where does he wander?
Far into the distance
I gaze and I mourn
As I wait for him and yearn.
My grief, I must bear it,
With no one to share it.
No more can I sleep,
I wake and I weep.
All my grief and sorrow
Are to him unknown!
O where does he wander?
He does not return.
I wait for his step at the door,
My poor heart is sore,
So weary of waiting,
He does not return.
Gracious Lord, Almighty!
Could I see him before me,
I would be so happy!
Alas, o where does he wander,
He does not return.

Scène 2

SIEBEL

(s'approchant doucement de Marguerite)

Marguerite!

MARGUERITE

Siebel!

SIEBEL

Encor des pleurs.

etc.

MARGUERITE *(se levant)*

Hélas!

Vous seul ne me maudissez pas.

SIEBEL

Je ne suis qu'un enfant, mais j'ai le cœur d'un homme

Et je vous vengerai de son lâche abandon

Je le tuerai!

MARGUERITE

Qui donc?

SIEBEL

Faut-il que je le nomme?

L'ingrat qui vous trahit!

MARGUERITE

Non, taisez-vous!

SIEBEL

Pardon!

Vous l'aimez encore?

MARGUERITE

Oui! Toujours!

Mais ce n'est pas à vous de plaindre mon ennui,

J'ai tort, Siebel, de vous parler de lui.

Scene 2

SIEBEL

(Siebel enters hurriedly.)

Marguerite!

MARGUERITE

Siebel!

SIEBEL

In tears again!

MARGUERITE

Alas, the only faithful friend I have.

SIEBEL

I am still very young,
But a man in spirit,
And I swear I'll avenge
All the wrong he has done.
I'll strike him dead!

MARGUERITE

Whom?

SIEBEL

You ask me to name him,
The villain who betrayed you?

MARGUERITE

No, say no more.

SIEBEL

Forgive me. Then you still love him?

MARGUERITE

I do.
But I have no right to burden you like this.
I'm wrong, my friend,
To speak of him to you.

SIEBEL
Si le bonheur à sourire t'invite,
Joyeux alors je sens un doux émoi;
Si la douleur t'accable, Marguerite,
O Marguerite, je pleure alors,
Je pleure comme toi!
Comme deux fleurs sur une même tige,
Notre destin suivant le même cours,
De tes chagrins en frère je m'afflige,
O Marguerite, comme une sœur,
Je t'aimerai toujours!

MARGUERITE
Soyez béni, Siebel! votre amitié m'est douce!
Ceux dont la main cruelle me repousse,
N'ont pas fermé pour moi les portes du Saint-lieu!
J'y vais pour mon enfant et pour lui prier Dieu!

(Elle sort; Siebel la suit à pas lents.)

Deuxième Partie

Scène de l'église

(Quelques femmes traversent la scène et entrent dans l'église. Marguerite entre après elles et s'agenouille.)

MARGUERITE
Seigneur, daignez permettre à votre humble servante
De s'agenouiller devant vous!

MÉPHISTOPHÉLÈS
Non! … tu ne prieras pas …! Frappez-la d'épouvante!
Esprits du mal, accourez tous!

VOIX DE DEMONS INVISIBLES
Marguerite!

SIEBEL *(taking Marguerite's hand)*
When you are glad
And the sun is shining,
Then, Marguerite,
I am happy too.
But when in grief and mourning you are pining,
O Marguerite,
I weep and grieve with you.
As twin-stars wander in the sky together,
So we are destined to one common end.
I want to share your suffering forever,
O Marguerite,
I shall always love you as a friend.

MARGUERITE
May heaven smile on you.
For you are good to me.
All those who now disdain me as a sinner
Can still not bar the way
To God who will forgive.
I'll go. For my child and for him
I shall pray.

Part II

Interior of a Church

(Women enter the church and cross the stage. Marguerite enters after them, and kneels.)

MARGUERITE
O heaven!
Permit thy lowly handmaiden
To prostrate herself before thine altar.

MEPHISTOPHELES
No, thou shalt not pray!
Spirits of evil, haste ye at my call,
And drive this woman hence!

CHORUS OF DEMONS
Marguerite!

MARGUERITE
Qui m'appelle?

VOIX
Marguerite!

MARGUERITE
Je chancelle!
Je meurs! – Dieu bon! Dieu clément!
Est-ce déjà l'heure du châtiment?

(Méphistophélès parait derrière un pilier et se penche à l'oreille de Marguerite.)

MÉPHISTOPHÉLÈS
Souviens-toi du passé, quand sous l'aile des anges,
Arbitant ton bonheur,
Tu venais dans son temple, en chantant ses louanges,
Adorer le Seigneur!
Lorsque tu bégayais une chaste prière
D'une timide voix,
Et portais dans ton cœur les baisers de ta mère.
Et Dieu tout à la fois!
Écoute ces clameurs! c'est l'enfer qui t'appelle! …
C'est l'enfer qui te suit!
C'est l'éternel remords et l'angoisse éternelle
Dans l'éternelle nuit!

MARGUERITE
Dieu! quelle est cette voix qui me parle dans l'ombre?
Dieu tout puissant!
Quel voile sombre
Sur moi descend!

CHANT RELIGIEUX
Quand du Seigneur le jour luira,
Sa croix au ciel resplendira,
Et l'univers s'écroulera …

MARGUERITE
Hélas! … ce chant pieux est plus terrible encore! …

MARGUERITE
Who calls me?

CHORUS
Marguerite!

MARGUERITE
I tremble! – oh, heaven!
My last hour is surely nigh!

(The tomb opens and discloses Mephistopheles, who bends over to Marguerite's ear.)

MEPHISTOPHELES
Remember the glorious days
When an angel's wings
Protected thy young heart.
To church thou camest then to worship,
Nor hadtst thou then sinned 'gainst heaven.
Thy prayers then issued
From an unstained heart
And on the wings of faith
Did rise to the Creator.
Hear'st thou their call?
'Tis hell that summons thee!
Hell claims thee for its own!
Eternal pain, and woe, and tribulation,
Will be thy portion!

MARGUERITE
Heaven! what voice is this
That in the shade doth speak to me?
What mysterious tones are these!

RELIGIOUS CHORUS
When the last day shall have come,
The cross in heaven shall shine forth.
This world to dust shall crumble.

MARGUERITE
Ah me! more fearful still becomes their song.

MÉPHISTOPHÉLÈS
Non!
Dieu pour toi n'a plus de pardon!
Pour toi le ciel n'a plus d'aurore!

CHOEUR RELIGIEUX
Que dirai-je alors au Seigneur?
Où trouverai-je un protecteur,
Quand l'innocent n'est pas sans peur!

MARGUERITE
Ah! ce chant m'étouffe et m'oppresse!
Je suis dans un cercle de fer!

MÉPHISTOPHÉLÈS
Adieu les nuits d'amour et les jours pleins d'ivresse!
A toi malheur! A toi l'enfer!

MARGUERITE ET LE CHOEUR RELIGIEUX
Seigneur, accueillez la prière
Des cœurs malheureux!
Qu'un rayon de votre lumière
Descende sur eux!

MÉPHISTOPHÉLÈS
Marguerite!
Sois maudite! A toi l'enfer!

MARGUERITE
Ah!

(Il disparait.)

MEPHISTOPHELES
No pardon hath heaven left for thee!
For thee e'en heaven hath no more light!

RELIGIOUS CHORUS
What shall we say unto high heav'n?
Who shall protection find
When innocence such persecution meets?

MARGUERITE
A heavy weight my breast o'erpowers. –
I can no longer breathe!

MEPHISTOPHELES
Nights of love, farewell!
Ye days of joy, adieu!
Lost, lost for aye art thou!

MARGUERITE AND CHORUS
Heav'n! hear thou the prayer
Of a sad, broken heart!
A bright ray send thou
From the starry sphere
Her anguish to allay!

MEPHISTOPHELES
Marguerite, lost, lost art thou!

MARGUERITE
Ah!

(He disappears.)

Troisième Partie

La Rue

Scène 1

Chœur de soldats

CHOEUR
Déposons les armes;
Dans nos foyers enfin nous voici revenus.
Nos mères en larmes,
Nos mères et nos sœurs ne nous attendront plus.

Scène 2

VALENTIN

(apercevant Siebel)

Eh! parbleu! c'est Siebel!

SIEBEL
En effet, je …

VALENTIN
Viens vite!
Viens dans mes bras.

(Il l'embrasse)

Et Marguerite?

SIEBEL

(avec embarras)

Elle est à l'église, je crois.

VALENTIN
Oui, priant Dieu pour moi …
Chère sœur, tremblante et craintive,
Comme elle va prêter une oreille attentive
Au récit de nos combats!

CHOEUR
Oui, c'est plaisir dans les familles
De conter aux enfants qui frémissent tout bas,

Part III

The Street

Scene 1

The Soldier's Chorus

CHORUS
Our swords we will suspend
Over the paternal hearth;
At length we have returned.
Sorrowing mothers no longer
Will bewail their absent sons.

Scene 2

VALENTINE
(perceiving Siebel, who enters)
Ah, Siebel, is it thou?

SIEBEL
Yes, 'tis I, but ...

VALENTINE
Come, then, to my heart.

(embraces him)
And Marguerite?

SIEBEL
(confused)
Perhaps she's yonder at the church.

VALENTINE
She doubtless prays for my return.
Dear girl, how pleased
She'll be to hear me tell
My warlike deeds!

CHORUS
Yes, 'tis a joy for men victorious
To the children by the fire, trembling in our arms,

Aux vieillards, aux jeunes filles,
La guerre et ses combats.

Gloire immortelle
De nos aïeux,
Sois nous fidèle,
Mourons comme eux!
Et sous ton aile,
Soldats vainqueurs,
Dirige nos pas, enflamme nos cœurs!
Pour toi, mère patrie,
Affrontant le sort,
Tes fils, l'âme aguerrie,
Ont bravé la mort.
Ta voix sainte nous crie:
En avant, soldats!
Le fer à la main, courez aux combats!
Gloire immortelle
De nos aïeux,
Sois nous fidèle,
Mourons comme eux!
Et sous ton aile,
Soldats vainqueurs,
Dirige nos pas, enflamme nos cœurs!

Vers nos foyers
Hâtons le pas;
On nous attend, le paix est faite,
Plus de soupirs! ne tardons pas,
Ver nos foyer hâtons le pas.
Notre pays nous tend les bras,
L'amour nous rit, l'amour nous fête,
Et plus d'un cœur frémit tout bas
Au souvenir de nos combats.
Hâtons le pas,
Ne tardons pas.
Gloire immortelle, *etc.*

VALENTIN
Allons, Siebel! entrons dans la maison!
Le verre en main, tu me feras raison!

To old men, to shy young girls,
To talk of war's alarms!

Glory to those
Who in battle fall,
Their bright deeds
We can with pride recall.
May we, then,
Honor and fame acquire,
Their glorious deeds our hearts will inspire!
Who needs bidding to dare,
By a trumpet blown?
Who lacks pity to spare
When the field is won?
Who would fly from a foe
If alone or last,
And boast he was true, when peril had past?
Glory to those
Who in battle fall,
Their bright deeds
We can with pride recall.
May we, then,
Honor and fame acquire,
Their glorious deeds our hearts will inspire!

Now home again
We come, the long
And fiery strife of battle over;
Rest calls us after toil as hard
As ours beneath a wild and stranger sun.
Many a maiden fair is waiting there
To greet her truant soldier lover,
And many a heart will fail, and brow grow pale,
To hear the tale of cruel peril he has run.
We are at home,
At home at last.
Glory to those, *etc*

VALENTINE
Come, Siebel, we'll to my dwelling
And o'er a flask of wine hold converse.

SIEBEL

(vivement)

Non! n'entre pas!

VALENTIN

Pourquoi? … – tu détournes la tête?

Ton regard fuit le mien? … – Siebel, explique-toi!

SIEBEL

Eh bien! – non, je ne puis!

VALENTIN

Que veux-tu dire?

(Il se dirige vers la maison.)

SIEBEL

(l'arrêtant)

Arrête!

Sois clément, Valentin!

VALENTIN

(furieux)

Laisse-moi! laisse-moi!

(Il entre dans la maison.)

SIEBEL

Pardonne-lui!

(seul)

Mon Dieu! je vous implore!

Mon Dieu, protégez-la.

(Il s'éloigne)

Scène 3

(Méphistophélès et Faust entrent en scène; Méphistophélès tient une guitare à la main.)

(Faust se dirige vers la maison de Marguerite et s'arrête.)

MÉPHISTOPHÉLÈS

Qu'attendez-vous encore?

Entrons dans la maison.

SIEBEL

(excitedly)

Nay, enter not!

VALENTINE

Why not, I pray? – Thou turn'st away;
Thy silent glance doth seek the ground –
Speak, Siebel – what hath happened?

SIEBEL

No! I cannot tell thee!

VALENTINE

What mean'st thou?

(Rushing toward the house.)

SIEBEL

(withholding him)

Hold, good Valentine, take heart!

VALENTINE

(furious)

What is't thou mean'st!

(Enters the house.)

SIEBEL

Forgive her!

(alone)

Shield her, gracious Heaven!

(He leaves)

Scene 3

(Faust and Mephistopheles come on stage. Mephistopheles carries a guitar.)

(Faust goes towards Marguerite's house, but hesitates.)

MEPHISTOPHELES

Why tarry ye?
Let us enter the house.

FAUST
Tais-toi, maudit! … j'ai peur
De rapporter ici la honte et le malheur.

MÉPHISTOPHÉLÈS
A quoi bon la revoir, après l'avoir quitté?
Notre présence ailleurs serait bien mieux fêtée!
Le sabbat nous attend!

FAUST
Marguerite!

MÉPHISTOPHÉLÈS
Je vois
Que mes avis sont vains et que l'amour l'emporte!
Mais, pour vous faire ouvrir la porte,
Vous avez grand besoin du secours de ma voix!

(Faust, pensif, se tient à l'écart. Méphistophélès s'accompagne sur sa guitare.)

Sérénade de Méphistophélès

I

"Vous qui faites l'endormie,
N'entendez-vous pas,
O Catherine, ma mie,
Ma voix et mes pas …?"
Ainsi ton galant t'appelle,
Et ton cœur l'en croit!
N'ouvre ta porte, ma belle,
Que la bague au doigt!

II

"Catherine que j'adore,
Pourquoi refuser
A l'amant qui vous implore
Un si doux baiser? …"
Ainsi ton galant supplie,
Et ton cœur l'en croit!
Ne donne un baiser, ma mie,
Que la bague au doigt!

FAUST
Peace! I grieve to think that I
Brought shame and sorrow hither.

MEPHISTOPHELES
Why see her again, then, after leaving her?
Some other sight might be more pleasing.
To the sabbath let us on.

FAUST
Marguerite!

MEPHISTOPHELES
My advice, I know,
Availeth but little
Against thy stubborn will.
Doctor, you need my voice!

(Throwing back his mantle, and accompanying himself on the guitar.)

Mephistopheles' Serenade

I

Maiden, now in peace reposing,
From thy sleep awake,
Hear my voice with love imploring,
Wilt thou pity take?
But beware how thou confidest
Even in thy friend,
If not for thy wedding finger
He a ring doth send.

II

Yes, sweet maiden, I implore thee, –
Oh, refuse not this, –
Smile on him who doth adore thee,
Bless him with thy kiss.
But beware how thou confidest
Even in thy friend,
If not for thy wedding finger
He a ring doth send.

Scène 4

(Valentin sort de la maison.)

Trio du duel

VALENTIN
Que voulez-vous, messieurs?

MÉPHISTOPHÉLÈS
Pardon! mon camarade,
Mais ce n'est pas pour vous qu'était la sérénade!

VALENTIN
Ma sœur l'écouterait mieux que moi, je le sais!

(Il dégaine et brise la guitare de Méphistophélès d'un coup d'épée.)

FAUST
Sa sœur!

MÉPHISTOPHÉLÈS

(à Valentin)

Quelle mouche vous pique?
Vous n'aimez donc pas le musique?

VALENTIN
Assez d'outrage! … assez! …
A qui de vous dois-je demander compte
De mon malheur et de ma honte? …
Qui de vous deux doit tomber sous mes coupes? …

(Faust tire son épée.)

C'est lui! …

MÉPHISTOPHÉLÈS
Vous le voulez? … – Allons, docteur, à vous! …

VALENTIN
Redouble, ô Dieu puissant,
Ma force et mon courage!
Permets que dans son sang
Je lave mon outrage!

Scene 4

(Valentine rushes from the house.)

The Duel scene

VALENTINE
Good sirs, what want you here?

MEPHISTOPHELES
My worthy fellow, it was not to you
That we addressed our serenade!

VALENTINE
My sister, perhaps, would more gladly
hear it!

(Valentine draws his sword, and breaks Mephistopheles' guitar.)

FAUST
His sister!

MEPHISTOPHELES

(to Valentine)

Why this anger?
Do ye not like my singing?

VALENTINE
Your insults cease!
From which of ye must I demand
Satisfaction for this foul outrage?
Which of ye must I now slay?

(Faust draws his sword.)

'Tis he!

MEPHISTOPHELES
Your mind's made up, then!
On, then, doctor, at him, pray!

VALENTINE
Oh, heaven, thine aid afford,
Increase my strength and courage,
That in his blood my sword
May wipe out this fell outrage!

FAUST

(à part)

Terrible et frémissant,
Il glace mon courage!
Dois-je verser le sang
Du frère que j'outrage? …

MÉPHISTOPHÉLÈS

De son air menaçant,
De son aveugle rage,
Je ris! … mon bras puissant
Va détourner l'orage!

VALENTIN

(tirant de son sein la médaille que lui a donné Marguerite)

Et toi qui préservas mes jours,
Toi qui me viens de Marguerite,
Je ne veux plus de ton secours,
Médaille maudite! …

(Il jette la médaille loin de lui.)

MÉPHISTOPHÉLÈS

(à part)

Tu t'en repentiras!

VALENTIN

(à Faust)

En garde! … et défends-toi!

MÉPHISTOPHÉLÈS

(à Faust)

Serrez-vous contre moi! …
Et poussez seulement, cher docteur! … moi, je pare.

(Ils se combattent.)

VALENTIN
Ah!

(Valentin tombe.)

FAUST

(aside)

What fear is this unnerves my arm?
Why falters now my courage?
Dare I to take his life,
Who but resents an outrage?

MEPHISTOPHELES

His wrath and his courage
I laugh alike to scorn!
To horse, then, for his last journey
The youth right soon will take!

VALENTINE

(taking in his hand the medallion suspended round his neck)

Thou gift of Marguerite,
Which till now hath ever saved me,
I'll no more of thee – I cast thee hence!
Accursed gift, I throw thee from me!

(Throws it angrily away.)

MEPHISTOPHELES

(aside)

Thou'll repent it!

VALENTINE

(to Faust)

Come one, defend thyself!

MEPHISTOPHELES

(to Faust, in a whisper)

Stand near to me, and attack him only;
I'll take care to parry!

(They fight.)

VALENTINE
Ah!

(Falls.)

MÉPHISTOPHÉLÈS
Voici notre héros étendu sur le sable! …
Au large maintenant! au large! …

(Il entraine Faust. Arrivent Marthe et des bourgeois portant des torches.)

Scène 5

Mort de Valentin

(Valentin, Marthe, Bourgeois, puis Siebel et Marguerite.)

MARTHE ET LES BOURGEOIS
Par ici! …
Par ici, mes amis! on se bat dans la rue! … –
L'un d'eux est tombé là! – Regardez … le voici! …
Il n'est pas encore mort! … – on dirait qu'il remue! …
Vite, approchez! … il faut le secourir!

VALENTIN
(se soulevant avec effort)
Merci!
De vos plaintes, faites-moi grâce! …
J'ai vu, morbleu! la mort en face
Trop souvent pour en avoir peur! …
(Marguerite paraît au fond soutenue par Siebel.)

MARGUERITE
Valentin! … Valentin! …
(Elle écarte la foule et tombe à genoux près de Valentin.)

VALENTIN
Marguerite! ma sœur! …
(Il la repousse.)
Que me veux-tu? … va-t'en!

MARGUERITE
O Dieu! …

MEPHISTOPHELES
Behold our hero,
Lifeless on the ground!
Come, we must hence – quick fly!

(Exit, dragging Faust after him.)

Scene 5

Valentine's Death

(Enter Citizens, with lighted torches; afterwards Siebel and Marguerite.)

CHORUS
Hither, hither, come this way –
They're fighting here hard by!
See, one has fallen;
The unhappy man lies prostrate there.
Ah! he moves – yes, still he breathes;
Quick, then, draw nigh
To raise and succor him!

VALENTINE

(raising himself with great effort)

'Tis useless, cease these vain laments.
Too often have I gazed
On death, to heed it
When my own time hath come!

(Marguerite appears at the back, supported by Siebel.)

MARGUERITE
Valentine! ah, Valentine!

(advancing, and falling on her knees at Valentine's side)

VALENTINE
Marguerite!

(thrusting her from him)

What would'st thou here? – away!

MARGUERITE
O heav'n!

VALENTIN
Je meurs par elle! ...
J'ai sottement
Cherché querelle
A son amant!

LA FOULE
(à demi voix, montrant Marguerite)
Il meurt, frappé par son amant!

MARGUERITE
Douleur cruelle!
O châtiment! ...

SIEBEL
Grâce pour elle! ...
Soyez clément!

VALENTIN
(soutenu par ceux qui l'entourent)
Écoute-moi bien, Marguerite! ...
Ce qui doit arriver arrive à l'heure dite!
La mort nous frappe quand il faut,
Et chacun obéit aux volontés d'en haut! ...
– Toi! ... te voilà dans la mauvaise voie!
Tes blanches mains ne travailleront plus!
Tu renieras, pour vivre dans la joie,
Tous les devoirs et toutes les vertus!
Va! la honte t'accable
Le remords suit tes pas!
Mais enfin l'heure sonne!
Meurs! et si Dieu te pardonne,
Sois maudite ici-bas.

LA FOULE
O terreur, ô blasphème
A ton heure suprême, infortuné,
Songe, hélas, a toi-même,
Pardonne, si tu veux être un jour pardonné!

VALENTINE

For her I die! Poor fool!
I thought to chastise her seducer!

CHORUS

(in a low voice, pointing to Marguerite)

He dies, slain by her seducer!

MARGUERITE

Fresh grief is this! ah, bitter punishment.

SIEBEL

Have pity on her, pray!

VALENTINE

(supported by those around him)

Marguerite, give ear awhile;
That which was decreed
Hath duly come to pass.
Death comes at its good pleasure:
All mortals must obey its behest.
But for you intervenes an evil life!
Those white hands will never work more;
The labors and sorrows that others employ,
Will be forgotten in hours of joy.
Darest thou live, ingrate?
Darest thou still exist?
Go! Shame overwhelm thee! Remorse follow thee!
At length *thy* hour will sound.
Die! And if God pardons thee hereafter,
So may this life be a continual curse!

CHORUS

Terrible wish! Unchristian thought!
I thy last sad hour, unfortunate!
Think of thy own soul's welfare.
Forgive, if thou wouldst be forgiven.

VALENTIN
Marguerite! Sois maudite!
La mort t'attend sur ton grabat!
Moi je meurs de ta main
Et je tombe en soldat!

(Il meurt.)

LA FOULE
Que le Seigneur ait son âme
Et pardonne au pécheur.

Acte Cinquième

Première Partie

La Nuit de Walpurgis

(sur la montagne de Harz, scène de la fête des sorcières)

Scène 1

FEUX-FOLLETS
Dans les bruyères,
Dans les roseaux,
Parmis les pierres
Et sur les eaux,
De place en place,
Perçant la nuit
S'allume et passe
Un feu qui luit!
Alerte! Alerte!
De loin, de près,
Dans l'herbe verte,
Sous les cyprès,
Mouvantes flammes,
Rayons glacés,
Ce sont les âmes
Des trépassés!

(Faust et Méphistophélès paraissent sur la montagne.)

FAUST
Arrête!

VALENTINE
Marguerite; I curse you! Death awaits me.
I die by your hand; but I die a soldier.

(Dies.)

CHORUS
God receive thy spirit!
God pardon thy sins!

Act V

Part I

Walpurgis Night

(on the Harz Mountain, scene of the witches' Midsummer-night festival)

Scene 1

WILL-O-THE-WISPS
Afar and near,
On every side,
'Mid rocky ravines,
O'er waters wide,
From place to place
Glide through the gloom
Myriad lights.
O'er moss-grown tomb
Behold, behold them!
From every way,
Under cypress, 'mid herbs,
O'er meadows stray
Pale flames,
Peopling earth again,
For they are the souls
Of sinful men.

(Faust and Mephistopheles appear on the mountain.)

FAUST
Stay!

MÉPHISTOPHÉLÈS
N'as tu pas promis
De m'accompagner sans rien dire?

FAUST
Où sommes-nous?

MÉPHISTOPHÉLÈS
Dans mon empire!
Ici, docteur, tout m'est soumis!
Voici la nuit de Walpurgis.

CHOEUR
Voici la nuit de Walpurgis.
Hou, hou, hou, hou, hou, hou!

FAUST
Mon sang se glace!

MÉPHISTOPHÉLÈS
Attends! je n'ai qu'un signe à faire,
Pour qu'ici tout change et s'éclaire!

Scène 2

Sur l'ordre de Méphistophélès les montagnes ouvrent, un palais resplendissant paraît.
Des reines et des femmes sont assises au festin.)

MÉPHISTOPHÉLÈS
Jusqu'aux premiers feux de matin,
A l'abri des regards profanes,
Je t'offre une place, au festin
Des reines et des courtisanes.

CHOEUR
Que les coupes s'emplissent
Au nom des anciens dieux,
Que les airs retentissent
De nos accords joyeux!

MÉPHISTOPHÉLÈS
Reines de beauté
De l'antiquité,
Cléopâtre au doux yeux,

MEPHISTOPHELES
Hast thou not promised
To accompany me?

FAUST
But where are we?

MEPHISTOPHELES
In my empire! Here, Doctor,
All submit to my sway.
Behold the night of Walpurgis!

CHORUS
Behold the night of Walpurgis!
Hoo, hoo, hoo, hoo, hoo, hoo!

FAUST
My blood is frozen!

MEPHISTOPHELES
But wait! At a sign all will change,
all become clear to thee.

Scene 2

(At Mephistopheles' command the mountains open. A splendid palace appears. Queens and women are sitting at a feast.)

MEPHISTOPHELES
Until the first fires of morning,
Far from the reach of prying eyes,
I offer thee a place
At the feast of queens and courtesans.

CHORUS
Fill, fill the flowing cups,
In the names of our ancient gods.
Let the air resound
With our joyful clamors!

MEPHISTOPHELES
Queens of beauty!
Queens of antique realms!
Cleopatra of the tender eyes!

Laïs au front charmant,
Laissez-nous au banquet prendre place un moment.

(à Faust)

Allons! allons! pour guérir la fièvre
De ton cœur blessé,
Prends cette coupe, et que ta lèvre
Y puise l'oubli du passé!

CHOEUR
Que les coupes s'emplissent
Au nom des anciens dieux,
Que les airs retentissent
De nos accords joyeux!

Scène 3

Ballet

No. 1. Les Nubiennes
No. 2. Adagio
No. 3. Danse antique
No. 4. Variations de Cléopâtre
No. 5. Les Troyens
No. 6. Variations du Miroir
No. 7. Danse de Phryné

* FAUST
Vains remords! risible folie!
Il est temps que mon cœur oublie!
Donne et buvons, buvons jusqu'à la lie
Doux nectar, dans ton ivresse
Tiens mon cœur enseveli,
Ou'un baiser de feu caresse
Jusqu'au jour mon front pâli.

CHOEUR
O doux nectar!

---

* Editor's note: This section of Scène 3 reprinted with the permission of G.
Schirmer Inc. – see note p. 358.

Laïs of charming mien!
Allow us at your banquet to find place!

(to Faust)

Come! To heal the fever
Of thy wounded heart,
Drink thou.
It is the cup of forgetfulness.

CHORUS
Fill, fill the flowing cups,
In the names of our ancient gods.
Let the air resound
With our joyful clamors!

Scene 3

Ballet

No. 1. Dance of the Nubians
No. 2. Adagio
No. 3. Danse Antique
No. 4. Cleopatra's Dance
No. 5. The Women of Troy
No. 6. The Mirror Variations
No. 7. The Dance of Phryne

* FAUST
Vain remorse! I laugh at my folly!
Now's the time to forget your sorrow,
Come, let us sing and drink till to-morrow!
Golden nectar, brew that blesses,
Soothe my heart in tranquil bliss,
Shower me with warm caresses,
On my brow bestow your kiss!

CHORUS
Goddess of joy!

FAUST
Endors dans ton ivresse
Mon cœur enseveli!
Dans la coupe enchanteresse
Pour jamais je bois l'oubli!

MÉPHISTOPHÉLÈS ET CHOEUR
Dans la coupe enchanteresse
Pour jamais buvons l'oubli!

FAUST
Volupté, devant tes charmes
Se réveille le désir,
Laisse-nous loin des alarmes
Au passage te saisir!
Déesse, par tes charmes
Réveille le désir
Et noyons l'amour en larmes
Dans l'ivresse et le plaisir!

MÉPHISTOPHÉLÈS ET CHOEUR
Et noyons l'amour en larmes etc.

Scène 4

(Au comble de l'orgie paraît une vision de Marguerite, inaperçu de Faust, qui prend la coupe.)

MÉPHISTOPHÉLÈS
Que ton ivresse, ô volupté,
Étouffe le remords dans son cœur enchanté!

(Faust regard là-haut et voit Marguerite. Il repousse la coupe; le palais, le banquet et le courtisanes disparaissent.)

MÉPHISTOPHÉLÈS
Qu'as-tu donc?

FAUST
Ne la vois-tu pas? … là, devant nous!
Muette et blême!
Quel étrange ornement
Autour de ce beau cou!

FAUST
Bestow your healing graces
To dim my heat's regret,
In your tender warm embraces,
Magic cup, let me forget!

MEPHISTOPHELES AND CHORUS
In your tender warm embraces,
Magic cup, let us forget!

FAUST
Joyous love, your charms excite me
And awaken my desire.
How you beckon and invite me,
Set my senses all afire!
O Goddess, with your graces,
Enchant my heart tonight,
Drown the past in your embraces,
In an orgy of delight!

MEPHISTOPHELES AND CHORUS
Drown the past etc ...

Scene 4

(At the climax of the orgy there appears a vision of Marguerite, unseen by Faust, who seizes the cup.)

MEPHISTOPHELES
Let thy enchantments, Goddess of Joy,
Stifle the remorse in his enchanted heart.

(Faust looks upward and sees Marguerite. He throws away the cup; the palace, the banquet, and the courtesans disappear.)

MEPHISTOPHELES
Well! What now?

FAUST
There! Dost thou not see? Before us!
Speechless and pale!
What strange ornament
Encircles her fair neck?

MÉPHISTOPHÉLÈS
Vision!

FAUST
Un ruban rouge qu'elle cache!

MÉPHISTOPHÉLÈS
Magie!

FAUST
Un ruban rouge.
Étroit comme un tranchant de hache!

MÉPHISTOPHÉLÈS
Sortilège!

(La vision disparaît.)

FAUST
Marguerite! Je sens se dresser mes chexeux!
Je veux la voir! Viens, je le veux!

(L'épée à la main, Faust le train avec lui, forçant la route au milieu des monstres infernaux.)

Deuxième Partie

La scène de la prison et la fin

Scène 1

FAUST
Va t'en!

MÉPHISTOPHÉLÈS
Le jour va luire. – On dresse l'échafaud!
Décide sans retard Marguerite à te suivre.
Le geôlier dort. – Voici les clefs. – Il faut
Que ta main d'homme la délivre.

FAUST
Laisse-moi!

MÉPHISTOPHÉLÈS
J'obéis. Moi, je veille au dehors.

(Il sort.)

MEPHISTOPHELES
'Tis nought!

FAUST
A scarlet ribbon she's concealing!

MEPHISTOPHELES
Magic!

FAUST
A scarlet ribbon,
Fine as the edge of an axe!

MEPHISTOPHELES
Sorcery!

(The vision fades.)

FAUST
Marguerite! With horror my hair stands on end!
I must see her! Come, I command it!

(Sword in hand, Faust drags Mephistopheles with him, clearing a path through the infernal monsters.)

Part II

The Prison Scene and Finale

Scene 1

FAUST
Go! get thee hence!

MEPHISTOPHELES
The morn appears, black night is on the wing.
Quickly prevail upon Marguerite to follow thee.
The jailer soundly sleeps – here is the key,
Thine own hand now can open the door.

FAUST
Good! get thee gone!

MEPHISTOPHELES
As you will.
I will keep watch without.

(Exit.)

FAUST

Mon cœur est pénétré d'épouvante! – O torture,
O source de regrets et d'éternels remords!
C'est elle! – La voici, la douce créature
Jetée au fond d'une prison
Comme une vile criminelle!
Le désespoir égara sa raison!
Son pauvre enfant, ô Dieu! tué par elle!
Marguerite!

MARGUERITE

(s'eveillant)

Ah! c'est la voix du bien-aimé!

(Elle se lève.)

A son appel mon cœur s'est ranimé.

FAUST

Marguerite!

MARGUERITE

Au milieu de vos éclats de rire,
Démons qui m'entourez, j'ai reconnu sa voix!

FAUST

Marguerite!

MARGUERITE

Sa main, sa douce main m'attire!
Je suis libre! Il est là! je l'entends! je le vois.
Oui, c'est toi, je t'aime,
Les fers, la mort même
Ne me font plus peur!
Tu m'as retrouvée,
Me voilà sauvée!
C'est toi, je suis sur ton cœur!

FAUST

Oui, c'est moi, je t'aime,
Malgré l'effort même
Du démon moqueur,

FAUST

With grief my heart is wrung!
Oh, torture! oh, source of agony
And remorse eternal! Behold her there,
The good, the beauteous girl,
Cast like a criminal
Into this vile dungeon;
Grief must her reason have disturbed,
For, with her own hand, alas!
Her child she slew!
Oh, Marguerite!

MARGUERITE

(waking)

His voice did sure
Unto my heart resound.

(Rises.)

FAUST

Marguerite!

MARGUERITE

At that glad sound it wildly throbs again
Amid the mocking laugh of demons.

FAUST

Marguerite!

MARGUERITE

Now am I free. He is here. It is his voice.
Yes, thou art he whom I love.
Fetters, death, have no terrors for me;
Thou hast found me. Thou has returned.
Now am I saved! Now rest I on thy heart!

FAUST

Yes, I am here, and I love thee,
In spite of the efforts of yon mocking demon.

Je t'ai retrouvé,
Te voilà sauvée!
C'est moi, viens sur mon cœur!

MARGUERITE

(se dégageant doucement de ses bras)

Attends! … voici la rue
Où tu m'as vue
Pour la première fois! …
Où votre main osa presque effleurer mes doigts!
"– Ne permettrez-vous pas, ma belle demoiselle,
Qu'on vous offre le bras pour faire le chemin?"
"– Non, monsieur, je ne suis demoiselle ni belle,
Et je n'ai pas besoin qu'on me donne la main!"

FAUST
Oui, mon cœur se souvient!
Mais suis-moi, l'heure passe!

MARGUERITE
Et voici le jardin charmant,
Perfumé de myrte et de rose,
Où chaque soir discrètement
Tu pénétrais à la nuit close.

FAUST
Viens, Marguerite, fuyons!

MARGUERITE
Non, reste encore.

FAUST
O ciel, elle ne m'entend pas!

Scène 2

MÉPHISTOPHÉLÈS
Alerte! alerte! ou vous êtes perdus!
Si vous tardez encor, je ne m'en mêle plus!

MARGUERITE

(gently disengaging herself from his arms)

Stay! this is the spot
Where one day thou didst meet me.
Thine hand sought mine to clasp.
"Will you not permit me, my fairest demoiselle,
To offer you my arm, and clear for you the way?"
"No, sir. I am no demoiselle, neither am I fair;
And I have no need to accept your offered arm."

FAUST
Yes, my heart remembers!
But come, time is passing!

MARGUERITE
And the garden I love is here,
Odorous of myrtle and roses,
Where every eve thou camest in
With careful step, as night was falling.

FAUST
Come, Marguerite, let us fly!

MARGUERITE
No! stay a moment!

FAUST
O heav'n , she does not understand!

Scene 2

MEPHISTOPHELES
Away at once, while yet there's time!
If longer ye delay,
Not e'en my power can save ye.

MARGUERITE
Le démon! le démon! – Le vois-tu? ... Là ... dans l'ombre
Fixant sur nous son oeil de feu!
Que nous veut-il? – Chasse-le du saint lieu!

MÉPHISTOPHÉLÈS
Quittons ce lieu sombre,
Le jour est levé;
De leur pied sonore
J'entends nos chevaux frapper le pavé.

(cherchant à entraîner Faust)

Viens! sauvons-la. Peut-être il en est temps encore!

MARGUERITE
Mon Dieu, protégez-moi! – Mon Dieu, je vous implore!

(tombant à genoux)

Anges purs! anges radieux!
Portez mon âme au sein des cieux!
Dieu juste, à toi je m'abandonne!
Dieu bon, je suis à toi! – pardonne!

FAUST
Viens, suis-moi! je le veux!

MARGUERITE
Anges purs! anges radieux!
Portez mon âme au sein des cieux!
Dieu juste, à toi je m'abandonne!
Dieu bon, je suis à toi! – pardonne!
Anges purs, anges radieux!
Portez mon âme au sein des cieux!

MÉPHISTOPHÉLÈS ET FAUST
Hâtons-nous! L'heure sonne!
Hâtons-nous de quitter ces lieux,
Déjà le jour envahit les cieux!

(bruit au dehors)

FAUST
Marguerite!

MARGUERITE
See'st thou yon demon crouching in the shade?
His deadly glance is fixed on us;
Quick! drive him from these sacred walls.

MEPHISTOPHELES
Away! leave we this spot,
The dawn hath appeared;
Hear'st thou not the fiery chargers,
As with sonorous hoof they paw the ground?

(endeavoring to drag Faust with him)

Haste ye, then, – perchance there yet
Is time to save her!

MARGUERITE
O Heaven, I crave thy help!
Thine aid alone I do implore!

(kneeling)

Holy angels, in heaven bless'd,
My spirit longs with ye to rest!
Great Heaven, pardon grant, I implore thee,
For soon shall I appear before thee!

FAUST
Marguerite! Follow me, I implore!

MARGUERITE
Holy angels, in heaven bless'd,
My spirit longs with ye to rest!
Great Heaven, pardon grant, I implore thee,
For soon shall I appear before thee!

MEPHISTOPHELES AND FAUST
Let us hast! The hour is striking!
Let us haste, for the day is near;
See how the dawn reddens the skies!

(a noise without)

FAUST
O Marguerite!

MARGUERITE
Pourquoi ce regard menaçant?

FAUST
Marguerite!

MARGUERITE
Pourquoi ces mains rouges de sang?

(le repoussant)

Va! … tu me fais horreur!

(elle tombe sans mouvement)

MÉPHISTOPHÉLÈS
Jugée!

Scène 3

CHOEUR DES ANGES
Sauvée! Christ est ressuscité!
Christ vient de renaître!
Paix et félicité
Aux disciples du Maître!
Christ vient de renaître!
Christ est ressuscité!

(Les murs de la prison se sont ouverts. L'âme de Marguerite s'élève dans les cieux. Faust la suit des yeux avec désespoir; il tombe à genoux et prie. Méphistophélès est à demi renversé sous l'épée lumineuse de l'archange.)

Fin.

MARGUERITE
Why that glance with anger fraught?

FAUST
Marguerite!

MARGUERITE
What blood is that which stains thy hand!

(pushing him away)

Away! thy sight doth cause me horror!

(Falls.)

MEPHISTOPHELES
Condemned!

Scene 3

CHORUS OF ANGELS
Saved! Christ hath arisen!
Christ is born again!
Peace and felicity
To all disciples of the Master!
Christ is born again!
Christ hath arisen!

(The prison walls open. The soul of Marguerite rises toward heaven. Faust gazes despairingly after her, then falls on his knees and prays. Mephistopheles turns away, barred by the shining sword of an archangel.)

End of the Opera.

V 19th-Century American Fausts

Osman Durrani

The Faust legend enjoys a curiously close relationship to North America. It is simultaneously appropriate and inappropriate for an understanding of the American character. The English Faust chapbook was among the most popular books in Puritan areas. Invoices of Boston booksellers show that *The History of the Damnable Life and Deserved Death of Dr. John Faustus* outsold all books other than the Bible, hymnals, and a few school textbooks in seventeenth-century New England (Wright, 121–3). Many still follow Luther in seeing the devil as a real character who is constantly pitted against all that is good, and this belief lives on among several of today's political leaders, as recent talk of an 'Evil Empire' and an 'Axis of Evil' demonstrates. It is in the Puritan heartland of New England that many of America's most 'Faustian' works came into existence.

Nathaniel Hawthorne was familiar with such writings, in which there is ample evidence of the morbid fears that assailed the Puritan conscience in much the same way as they pitted themselves against Luther. Over one hundred years later, when Goethe's works became known in North America, they had great influence on the intellectual climate. Longfellow analysed them in depth at Harvard and planned to write a 'New England Faust' in which the old indigenous Puritan tradition would be enriched with Goethean wisdom. The age of witch hunts was over, but in the new conflicts between forces such as Calvinism and Unitarianism, *Faust* seemed to 'shadow forth the soul of the age', as Margaret Fuller put it, and to point a way forward. Hawthorne himself was quick to recognise the dangers of erecting a new temple of faith on the uncertain foundations of a misunderstood idealism imported from Germany (Fiedler, 125f; Long, 116f; Stein, 23–34).

Although no pacts as such are ever concluded in Hawthorne's stories and novels, they do examine the effect of the Faustian bargain on New England folk, who when tempted to go against God in private bring about their own fall and damnation. Fanshawe is an early example of such an obsession, intoxicated as he is by a dream of all-embracing knowledge and undying fame. In 'Peter Goldthwaithe's Treasure', the figure of 'Old Scratch' is introduced in situations that look back to Irving and forward to Benét; Peter wrecks his uncle's house in search of legendary treasure, only to find it in a form that is of no use. 'Dr. Heidegger's Experiment' ushers the reader into a combination of Faust's study and a witch's kitchen, complete with a magic mirror showing the doctor's deceased patient. A rejuvenation of sorts takes place, but such is the exuberance of the newly restored men that they destroy the very elixir that contained the gift of youth. Even those characters who resist, like Young Goodman Brown, have to learn the bitter truth at the heart of Puritan history: that their fathers and forefathers were in league with evil while posing as upright citizens. Here the devil can claim, 'I have been as well acquainted with your family as with ever a one among the Puritans; and that's no trifle to say. I helped your grandfather, the constable, when he lashed the Quaker woman so smartly through the streets of Salem; and it was I that brought your father a pitch-pine knot, kindled at my own hearth, to set fire to an Indian village, in King Philip's war. They were my good friends, both' (Hawthorne, 136). Brown, too, is ultimately destroyed by his desire for hidden knowledge.

Works Cited

Leslie A. Fiedler, *Love and Death in the American Novel.* London: Jonathan Cape, 1967.

Nathaniel Hawthorne, *Selected Tales and Sketches*, ed. Michael J. Colacurcio. New York: Penguin, 1987.

O. W. Long, 'Goethe and Longfellow', *Germanic Review* 7 (1932), 166f.

William Bysshe Stein, *Hawthorne's Faust: A Study of the Devil Archetype.* Gainesville, 1953. Rptd Hamden/CT: Archon Books, 1968.

Thomas G. Wright, *Literary Culture in New England.* New Haven: Yale University Press, 1920.

The Birthmark

Nathaniel Hawthorne

In the latter part of the last century there lived a man of science, an eminent proficient in every branch of natural philosophy, who not long before our story opens had made experience of a spiritual affinity more attractive than any chemical one. He had left his laboratory to the care of an assistant, cleared his fine countenance from the furnace smoke, washed the stain of acids from his fingers, and persuaded a beautiful woman to become his wife. In those days when the comparatively recent discovery of electricity and other kindred mysteries of Nature seemed to open paths into the region of miracle, it was not unusual for the love of science to rival the love of woman in its depth and absorbing energy. The higher intellect, the imagination, the spirit, and even the heart might all find their congenial aliment in pursuits which, as some of their ardent votaries believed, would ascend from one step of powerful intelligence to another, until the philosopher should lay his hand on the secret of creative force and perhaps make new worlds for himself. We know not whether Aylmer possessed this degree of faith in man's ultimate control over Nature. He had devoted himself, however, too unreservedly to scientific studies ever to be weaned from them by any second passion. His love for his young wife might prove the stronger of the two, but it could only be by intertwining itself with his love of science, and uniting the strength of the latter to his own.

Such a union accordingly took place, and was attended with truly remarkable consequences and a deeply impressive moral. One day, very soon after their marriage, Aylmer sat gazing at his wife with a trouble in his countenance that grew stronger until he spoke.

"Georgiana," said he, "has it never occurred to you that the mark upon your cheek might be removed?"

"No, indeed," said she, smiling; but perceiving the seriousness of his manner, she blushed deeply. "To tell you the truth it has been so often called a charm that I was simple enough to imagine it might be so."

"Ah, upon another face perhaps it might," replied her husband; "but never on yours. No, dearest Georgiana, you came so nearly perfect from the hand of Nature that this slightest possible defect, which we hesitate whether to term a defect or a beauty, shocks me, as being the visible mark of earthly imperfection."

"Shocks you, my husband!" cried Georgiana, deeply hurt; at first reddening with momentary anger, but then bursting into tears. "Then why did you take me from my mother's side? You cannot love what shocks you!"

To explain this conversation it must be mentioned that in the centre of Georgiana's left cheek there was a singular mark, deeply interwoven, as it were, with the texture and substance of her face. In the usual state of her complexion – a healthy though delicate bloom – the mark wore a tint of deeper crimson, which imperfectly defined its shape amid the surrounding rosiness. When she blushed it gradually became more indistinct, and finally vanished amid the triumphant rush of blood that bathed the whole cheek with its brilliant glow. But if any shifting motion caused her to turn pale there was the mark again, a crimson stain upon the snow, in what Aylmer sometimes deemed an almost fearful distinctness. Its shape bore not a little similarity to the human hand, though of the smallest pygmy size. Georgiana's lovers were wont to say that some fairy at her birth hour had laid her tiny hand upon the infant's cheek, and left this impress there in token of the magic endowments that were to give her such sway over all hearts. Many a desperate swain would have risked life for the privilege of pressing his lips to the mysterious hand. It must not be concealed, however, that the impression wrought by this fairy sign manual varied exceedingly, according to the difference of temperament in the beholders. Some fastidious persons – but they were exclusively of her own sex – affirmed that the bloody hand, as they chose to call it, quite destroyed the effect of Georgiana's beauty, and rendered her countenance even hideous. But it would be as reasonable to say that one of those small blue stains which sometimes occur in the purest statuary marble would convert the Eve of Powers to a monster. Masculine observers, if the birthmark did not heighten their admiration, contented themselves with wishing it away, that the world might possess one living specimen of ideal loveliness without the semblance of a flaw. After his marriage, – for he thought little or nothing of the matter before, – Aylmer discovered that this was the case with himself.

Had she been less beautiful, – if Envy's self could have found aught else to sneer at, – he might have felt his affection heightened by the prettiness of this mimic hand, now vaguely portrayed, now lost, now stealing forth again and glimmering to and fro with every pulse of emotion that throbbed within her heart; but seeing her otherwise so perfect, he found this one defect grow more and more intolerable with every moment of their united lives. It was the fatal flaw of humanity which Nature, in one shape or another, stamps ineffaceably on all her productions, either to imply that they are temporary and finite, or that their perfection must be wrought by toil and pain. The crimson hand expressed the ineludible gripe in which mortality clutches the highest and purest of earthly mould, degrading them into kindred with the lowest, and even with the very brutes, like whom their visible frames return to dust. In this manner, selecting it as the symbol of his wife's liability to sin, sorrow, decay, and death, Aylmer's sombre imagination was not long in rendering the birthmark a frightful object, causing him more trouble and horror than ever Georgiana's beauty, whether of soul or sense, had given him delight.

At all the seasons which should have been their happiest, he invariably and without intending it, nay, in spite of a purpose to the contrary, reverted to this one disastrous topic. Trifling as it at first appeared, it so connected itself with innumerable trains of thought and modes of feeling that it became the central point of all. With the morning twilight Aylmer opened his eyes upon his wife's face and recognized the symbol of imperfection; and when they sat together at the evening hearth his eyes wandered stealthily to her cheek, and beheld, flickering with the blaze of the wood fire, the spectral hand that wrote mortality where he would fain have worshipped. Georgiana soon learned to shudder at his gaze. It needed but a glance with the peculiar expression that his face often wore to change the roses of her cheek into a death-like paleness, amid which the crimson hand was brought strongly out, like a bass-relief of ruby on the whitest marble.

Late one night when the lights were growing dim, so as hardly to betray the stain on the poor wife's cheek, she herself, for the first time, voluntarily took up the subject.

"Do you remember, my dear Aylmer," said she, with a feeble attempt at a smile, "have you any recollection of a dream last night about this odious hand?"

"None! none whatever!" replied Aylmer, starting; but then he added, in a dry, cold tone, affected for the sake of concealing the real depth of his emotion, "I might well dream of it; for before I fell asleep it had taken a pretty firm hold of my fancy."

"And you did dream of it?" continued Georgiana, hastily; for she dreaded lest a gush of tears should interrupt what she had to say. "A terrible dream! I wonder that you can forget it. Is it possible to forget this one expression? – 'It is in her heart now; we must have it out!' Reflect, my husband; for by all means I would have you recall that dream."

The mind is in a sad state when Sleep, the all-involving, cannot confine her spectres within the dim region of her sway, but suffers them to break forth, affrighting this actual life with secrets that perchance belong to a deeper one. Aylmer now remembered his dream. He had fancied himself with his servant Aminadab, attempting an operation for the removal of the birthmark; but the deeper went the knife, the deeper sank the hand, until at length its tiny grasp appeared to have caught hold of Georgiana's heart; whence, however, her husband was inexorably resolved to cut or wrench it away.

When the dream had shaped itself perfectly in his memory, Aylmer sat in his wife's presence with a guilty feeling. Truth often finds its way to the mind close muffled in robes of sleep, and then speaks with uncompromising directness of matters in regard to which we practise an unconscious self-deception during our waking moments. Until now he had not been aware of the tyrannizing influence acquired by one idea over his mind, and of the lengths which he might find in his heart to go for the sake of giving himself peace.

"Aylmer," resumed Georgiana, solemnly, "I know not what may be the cost to both of us to rid me of this fatal birthmark. Perhaps its removal may cause cureless deformity; or it may be the stain goes as deep as life itself. Again: do we know that there is a possibility, on any terms, of unclasping the firm gripe of this little hand which was laid upon me before I came into the world?"

"Dearest Georgiana, I have spent much thought upon the subject," hastily interrupted Aylmer. "I am convinced of the perfect practicability of its removal."

"If there be the remotest possibility of it," continued Georgiana, "let the attempt be made at whatever risk. Danger is nothing to me; for life, while this hateful mark makes me the object of your horror and disgust, – life is a burden which I would fling down with joy. Either remove this dreadful hand, or take my wretched life! You have deep science. All the world bears witness of it. You have achieved great wonders. Cannot you remove this little, little mark, which I cover with the tips of two small fingers? Is this beyond your power, for the sake of your own peace, and to save your poor wife from madness?"

"Noblest, dearest, tenderest wife," cried Aylmer, rapturously, "doubt not my power. I have already given this matter the deepest thought – thought which might almost have enlightened me to create a being less perfect than yourself. Georgiana, you have led me deeper than ever into the heart of science. I feel myself fully competent to render this dear cheek as faultless as its fellow; and then, most beloved, what will be my triumph when I shall have corrected what Nature left imperfect in her fairest work! Even Pygmalion, when his sculptured woman assumed life, felt not greater ecstasy then mine will be."

"It is resolved, then," said Georgiana, faintly smiling. "And Aylmer, spare me not, though you should find the birthmark take refuge in my heart at last."

for that office by his great mechanical readiness, and the skill with which, while incapable of comprehending a single principle, he executed all the details of his master's experiments. With his vast strength, his shaggy hair, his smoky aspect, and the indescribable earthiness that incrusted him, he seemed to represent man's physical nature; while Aylmer's slender figure, and pale, intellectual face, were no less apt a type of the spiritual element.

"Throw open the door of the boudoir, Aminadab," said Aylmer, "and burn a pastil."

"Yes, master," answered Aminadab, looking intently at the lifeless form of Georgiana; and then he muttered to himself, "If she were my wife, I'd never part with that birthmark."

When Georgiana recovered consciousness she found herself breathing an atmosphere of penetrating fragrance, the gentle potency of which had recalled her from her deathlike faintness. The scene around her looked like enchantment. Aylmer had converted those smoky, dingy, sombre rooms, where he had spent his brightest years in recondite pursuits, into a series of beautiful apartments not unfit to be the secluded abode of a lovely woman. The walls were hung with gorgeous curtains, which imparted the combination of grandeur and grace that no other species of adornment can achieve; and as they fell from the ceiling to the floor, their rich and ponderous folds, concealing all angles and straight lines, appeared to shut in the scene from infinite space. For aught Georgiana knew, it might be a pavilion among the clouds. And Aylmer, exluding the sunshine, which would have interfered with his chemical processes, had supplied its place with perfumed lamps, emitting flames of various hue, but all uniting in a soft, impurpled radiance. He now knelt by his wife's side, watching her earnestly, but without alarm; for he was confident in his science, and felt that he could draw a magic circle round her within which no evil might intrude.

"Where am I? Ah, I remember," said Georgiana, faintly; and she placed her hand over her cheek to hide the terrible mark from her husband's eyes.

"Fear not, dearest!" exclaimed he. "Do not shrink from me! Believe me, Georgiana, I even rejoice in this single imperfection, since it will be such a rapture to remove it."

"Oh, spare me!" sadly replied his wife. "Pray do not look at it again. I never can forget that convulsive shudder."

In order to soothe Georgiana, and, as it were, to release her mind from the burden of actual things, Aylmer now put in practice some of the light and playful secrets which science had taught him among its profounder lore. Airy figures, absolutely bodiless ideas, and forms of unsubstantial

Her husband tenderly kissed her cheek – her right cheek – not t
which bore the impress of the crimson hand.

The next day Aylmer apprised his wife of a plan that he had form
whereby he might have opportunity for the intense thought and consta
watchfulness which the proposed operation would require; while Geo
giana, likewise, would enjoy the perfect repose essential to its succes
They were to seclude themselves in the extensive apartments occupie
by Aylmer as a laboratory, and where, during his toilsome youth, he ha
made discoveries in the elemental powers of Nature that had roused th
admiration of all the learned societies in Europe. Seated calmly in thi
laboratory, the pale philosopher had investigated the secrets of the highest cloud region and of the profoundest mines; he had satisfied himself
of the causes that kindled and kept alive the fires of the volcano; and had
explained the mystery of fountains, and how it is that they gush forth,
some so bright and pure, and others with such rich medicinal virtues,
from the dark bosom of the earth. Here, too, at an earlier period, he had
studied the wonders of the human frame, and attempted to fathom the
very process of which Nature assimilates all her precious influences from
earth and air, and from the spiritual world, to create and foster man, her
masterpiece. The latter pursuit, however, Aylmer had long laid aside in
unwilling recognition of the truth – against which all seekers sooner or
later stumble – that our great creative Mother, while she amuses us with
apparently working in the broadest sunshine, is yet severely careful to
keep her own secrets, and, in spite of her pretended openness, shows us
nothing but results. She permits us, indeed, to mar, but seldom to mend,
and, like a jealous patentee, on no account to make. Now, however,
Aylmer resumed these half-forgotten investigations; not, of course, with
such hopes or wishes at first suggested them; but because they involved
much physiological truth and lay in the path of his proposed scheme for
the treatment of Georgiana.

As he led her over the threshold of the laboratory, Georgiana was cold
and tremulous. Aylmer looked cheerfully into her face, with intent to reas-
sure her, but was so startled with the intense glow of the birthmark upon
the whiteness of her cheek that he could not restrain a strong convulsive
shudder. His wife fainted.

"Aminadab! Aminadab!" shouted Aylmer, stamping violently on the
floor.

Forthwith there issued from an inner apartment a man of low stature,
but bulky frame, with shaggy hair hanging about his visage, which wa
grimed with the vapors of the furnace. This personage had been Aylmer'
underworker during his whole scientific career, and was admirably fitte

beauty came and danced before her, imprinting their momentary foot-steps on beams of light. Though she had some indistinct idea of the method of these optical phenomena, still the illusion was almost perfect enough to warrant the belief that her husband possessed sway over the spiritual world. Then again, when she felt a wish to look forth from her seclusion, immediately, as if her thoughts were answered, the procession of external existence flitted across the screen. The scenery and the figures of actual life were perfectly represented, but with that bewitching, yet indescribable difference which always makes a picture, an image, or a shadow so much more attractive than the original. When wearied of this, Aylmer bade her cast her eyes upon a vessel containing a quantity of earth. She did so, with little interest at first; but was soon startled to per-ceive the germ of a plant shooting upward from the soil. Then came the slender stalk; the leaves gradually unfolded themselves; and amid them was a perfect and lovely flower.

"It is magical!" cried Georgiana. "I dare not touch it."

"Nay, pluck it," answered Aylmer, – "pluck it, and inhale its brief per-fume while you may. The flower will wither in a few moments and leave nothing save its brown seed vessels; but thence may be perpetuated a race as ephemeral as itself."

But Georgiana had no sooner touched the flower than the whole plant suffered a blight, its leaves turning coal-black as if by the agency of fire.

"There was too powerful a stimulus," said Aylmer, thoughtfully.

To make up for this abortive experiment, he proposed to take her por-trait by a scientific process of his own invention. It was to be effected by rays of light striking upon a polished plate of metal. Georgiana assented; but, on looking at the result, was affrighted to find the features of the por-trait blurred and indefinable; while the minute figure of a hand appeared where the cheek should have been. Aylmer snatched the metallic plate and thew it into a jar of corrosive acid.

Soon, however, he forgot these mortifying failures. In the intervals of study and chemical experiment he came to her flushed and exhausted, but seemed invigorated by her presence, and spoke in glowing language of the resources of his art. He gave a history of the long dynasty of the alchem-ists, who spent so many ages in quest of the universal solvent by which the golden principle might be elicited from all things vile and base. Aylmer appeared to believe that, by the plainest scientific logic, it was altogether within the limits of possibility to discover this long-sought medium; "but," he added, "a philosopher who should go deep enough to acquire the power would attain too lofty a wisdom to stoop to the exercise of it." Not less singular were his opinions in regard to the elixir vitae. He more than intimated that it was at his option to concoct a liquid that should prolong life for years, perhaps interminably; but that it would produce a discord in Nature which all the world, and chiefly the quaffer of the immortal nostrum, would find cause to curse.

"Aylmer, are you in earnest?" asked Georgiana, looking at him with amazement and fear. "It is terrible to possess such power, or even to dream of possessing it."

"Oh, do not tremble, my love," said her husband, "I would not wrong either you or myself by working such inharmonious effects upon our lives; but I would have you consider how trifling, in comparison, is the skill requisite to remove this little hand."

At the mention of the birthmark, Georgiana, as usual, shrank as if a redhot iron had touched her cheek.

Again Aylmer applied himself to his labors. She could hear his voice in the distant furnace room giving directions to Aminadab, whose harsh, uncouth, misshappen tones were audible in response, more like the grunt or growl of a brute then human speech. After hours of absence, Aylmer reappeared and proposed that she should now examine his cabinet of chemical products and natural treasurers of the earth. Among the former he showed her a small vial, in which, he remarked, was contained a gentle yet most powerful fragrance, capable of impregnating all the breezes that blow across a kingdom. They were of inestimable value, the contents of that little vial; and, as he said so, he threw some of the perfume into the air and filled the room with piercing and invigorating delight.

"And what is this?" asked Georgiana, pointing to a small crystal globe containing a gold-colored liquid. "It is so beautiful to the eye that I could imagine it the elixir of life."

"In one sense it is," replied Aylmer; "or, rather, the elixir of immortality. It is the most precious poison that ever was concocted in this world. By its aid I could apportion the lifetime of any mortal at whom you might point your finger. The strength of the dose would determine whether he were to linger out years, or drop dead in the midst of a breath. No king on his guarded throne could keep his life if I, in my private station, should deem that the welfare of millions justified me in depriving him of it."

"Why do you keep such a terrific drug?" inquired Georgiana in horror.

"Do not mistrust me, dearest," said her husband, smiling; "its virtuous potency is yet greater than its harmful one. But see! here is a powerful cosmetic. With a few drops of this in a vase of water, freckles may be washed away as easily as the hands are cleansed. A stronger infusion would take the blood out of the cheek, and leave the rosiest beauty a pale ghost."

"Is it with this lotion that you intend to bathe my cheek?" asked Georgiana, anxiously.

"Oh, no," hastily replied her husband; "this is merely superficial. Your case demands a remedy that shall go deeper."

In his interviews with Georgiana, Aylmer generally made minute inquiries as to her sensations and whether the confinement of the rooms and the temperature of the atmosphere agreed with her. These questions had such a particular drift that Georgiana began to conjecture that she was already subjected to certain physical influences, either breathed in with the fragrant air or taken with her food. She fancied likewise, but it might be altogether fancy, that there was a stirring up of her system – a strange, indefinite sensation creeping through her veins, and tingling, half painfully, half pleasurable, at her heart. Still, whenever she dared to look into the mirror, there she beheld herself pale as a white rose and the crimson birthmark stamped upon her cheek. Not even Aylmer now hated it so much as she.

To dispel the tedium of the hours which her husband found it necessary to devote to the processes of combination and analysis, Georgiana turned over the volumes of his scientific library. In many dark old tomes she met with chapters full of romance and poetry. They were the works of the philosophers of the middle ages, such as Albertus Magnus, Cornelius Agrippa, Paracelsus, and the famous friar who created the prophetic Brazen Head. All these antique naturalists stood in advance of their centuries, yet were imbued with some of their credulity, and therefore were believed, and perhaps imagined themselves to have acquired from the investigation of Nature a power above Nature, and from physics a sway over the spiritual world. Hardly less curious and imaginative were the early volumes of the Transactions of the Royal Society, in which the members, knowing little of the limits of natural possibility, were continually recording wonders or proposing methods whereby wonders might be wrought.

But to Georgiana the most engrossing volume was a large folio from her husband's own hand, in which he had recorded every experiment of his scientific career, its original aim, the methods adopted for its development, and its final success or failure, with the circumstances to which either event was attributable. The book, in truth, was both the history and emblem of his ardent, ambitious, imaginative, yet practical and laborious life. He handled physical deatils as if there were nothing beyond them; yet spiritualized them all, and redeemed himself from materialism by his strong and eager aspiration towards the infinite. In his grasp the veriest clod of earth assumed a soul. Georgiana, as she read, reverenced Aylmer and loved him more profoundly than ever, but with a less entire dependence on his judgment than heretofore. Much as he had accomplished, she could not but observe that his most splendid successes were almost invariably failures, if compared with the ideal at which he aimed. His brightest diamonds were the merest pebbles, and felt to be so by himself, in comparison with the inestimable gems which lay hidden beyond his reach. The volume, rich with achievements that had won renown for its author, was yet as melancholy a record as ever mortal hand had penned. It was the sad confession and continual exemplification of the shortcomings of the composite man, the spirit burdened with clay and working in matter, and of the despair that assails the higher nature of finding itself so miserably thwarted by the earthly part. Perhaps every man of genius in whatever sphere might recognize the image of his own experience in Aylmer's journal.

So deeply did these reflections affect Georgiana that she laid her face upon the open volume and burst into tears. In this situation she was found by her husband.

"It is dangerous to read in a sorcerer's books," said he with a smile, though his countenance was uneasy and displeased. "Georgiana, there are pages in that volume which I can scarcely glance over and keep my senses. Take heed lest it prove as detrimental to you."

"It has made me worship you more than ever," said she.

"Ah, wait for this one success," rejoined he, "then worship me if you will. I shall deem myself hardly unworthy of it. But come, I have sought you for the luxury of your voice. Sing to me, dearest."

So she poured out the liquid music of her voice to quench the thirst of his spirit. He then took his leave with a boyish exuberance of gayety, assuring her that her seclusion would endure but a little longer, and that the result was already certain. Scarcely had he departed when Georgiana felt irresistibly impelled to follow him. She had forgotten to inform Aylmer of a symptom which for two or three hours past had begun to excite her attention. It was a sensation in the fatal birthmark, not painful, but which induced a restlessness throughout her system. Hastening after her husband, she intruded for the first time into the laboratory.

The first thing that struck her eye was the furnace, that hot and feverish worker, with the intense glow of its fire, which by the quantities of soot clustered above it seemed to have been burning for ages. There was a distilling apparatus in full operation. Around the room were retorts, tubes, cylinders, crucibles, and other apparatus of chemical research. An electrical machine stood ready for immediate use. The atmosphere felt oppressively close, and was tainted with gaseous odors which had been tormented forth by the processes of science. The severe and homely simplicity of the apartment, with its naked walls and brick pavement, looked strange, accustomed as Georgiana had become to the fantastic elegance of her boudoir. But what chiefly, indeed almost solely, drew her attention, was the aspect of Aylmer himself.

He was pale as death, anxious and absorbed, and hung over the furnace as if it depended upon his utmost watchfulness whether the liquid which it was distilling should be the draught of immortal happiness or misery. How different from the sanguine and joyous mien that he had assumed for Georgiana's encouragement!

"Carefully now, Aminadab; carefully, thou human machine; carefully, thou man of clay!" muttered Aylmer, more to himself than his assistant. "Now, if there be a thought too much or too little, it is all over."

"Ho! ho!" mumbled Aminadab. "Look, master! look!"

Aylmer raised his eyes hastily, and at first reddened, then grew paler than ever, on beholding Georgiana. He rushed towards her and seized her arm with a gripe that left the print of his fingers upon it.

"Why do you come hither? Have you no trust in your husband?" cried he, impetuously. "Would you throw the blight of that fatal birthmark over my labors? It is not well done. Go, prying woman, go!"

"Nay, Aylmer," said Georgiana with the firmness of which she possessed no stinted endowment, "it is not you that have a right to complain. You mistrust your wife; you have concealed the anxiety with which you watch the development of this experiment. Think not so unworthily of me, my husband. Tell me all the risk we run, and fear not that I shall shrink; for my share in it is far less than your own."

"No, no, Georgiana!" said Aylmer, impatiently; "it must not be."

"I submit," replied she calmly. "And, Aylmer, I shall quaff whatever draught you bring me; but it will be on the same principle that would induce me to take a dose of poison if offered by your hand."

"My noble wife," said Aylmer, deeply moved, "I knew not the height and depth of your nature until now. Nothing shall be concealed. Know, then, that this crimson hand, superficial as it seems, has clutched its grasp into your being with a strength of which I had no previous conception. I have already administered agents powerful enough to do aught except to change your entire physical system. Only one thing remains to be tried. If that fail us we are ruined."

"Why did you hesitate to tell me this?" asked she.

"Because, Georgiana," said Aylmer, in a low voice, "there is danger."

"Danger? There is but one danger – that this horrible stigma shall be left upon my cheek!" cried Georgiana. "Remove it, remove it, whatever be the cost, or we shall both go mad!"

"Heaven knows your words are too true," said Aylmer, sadly. "And now, dearest, return to your boudoir. In a little while all will be tested."

He conducted her back and took leave of her with a solemn tenderness which spoke far more than his words how much was now at stake. After his departure Georgiana became rapt in musings. She considered the character of Aylmer, and did it completer justice than at any previous moment. Her heart exulted, while it trembled, at his honorable love – so pure and lofty that it would accept nothing less than perfection nor miserably make itself contented with an earthlier nature than he had dreamed off. She felt how much more precious was such a sentiment than that meaner kind which would have borne with the imperfection for her sake, and have been guilty of treason to holy love by degrading its perfect idea to the level of the actual; and with her whole spirit she prayed that, for a single moment, she might satisfy his highest and deepest conception. Longer than one moment she well knew it could not be; for his spirit was ever on the march, ever ascending, and each instant required something that was beyond the scope of the instant before.

The sound of her husband's footsteps aroused her. He bore a crystal goblet containing a liquor colorless as water, but bright enough to be the draught of immortality. Aylmer was pale; but it seemed rather the consequence of a highly-wrought state of mind and tension of spirit than of fear or doubt.

"The concoction of the draught has been perfect," said he, in answer to Georgiana's look. "Unless all my science have deceived me, it cannot fail."

"Save on your account, my dearest Aylmer," observed his wife, "I might wish to put off this birthmark of mortality by relinquishing mortality itself in preference to any other mode. Life is but a sad possession to those who have attained precisely the degree of moral advancement at which I stand. Were I weaker and blinder it might be happiness. Were I stronger, it might be endured hopefully. But, being what I find myself, methinks I am of all mortals the most fit to die."

"You are fit for heaven without tasting death!" replied her husband. "But why do we speak of dying? The draught cannot fail. Behold its effect upon this plant."

On the window seat there stood a geranium diseased with yellow blotches, which had overspread all its leaves. Aylmer poured a small quantity of the liquid upon the soil in which it grew. In a little time, when the roots of the plant had taken up the moisture, the unsightly blotches began to be extinguished in a living verdure.

"There needed no proof," said Georgiana, quietly. "Give me the goblet. I joyfully stake all upon your word."

"Drink, then, thou lofty creature!" exclaimed Aylmer, with fervid admiration. "There is no taint of imperfection on thy spirit. Thy sensible frame, too, shall soon be all perfect."

She quaffed the liquid and returned the goblet to his hand.

"It is grateful," said she with a placid smile. "Methinks it is like water from a heavenly fountain; for it contains I know not what of unobtrusive fragrance and deliciousness. It allays a feverish thirst that had parched me for many days. Now, dearest, let me sleep. My earthly senses are closing over my spirit like the leaves around the heart of a rose at sunset."

She spoke the last words with a gentle reluctance, as if it required almost more energy than she could command to pronounce the faint and lingering syllables. Scarcely had they loitered through her lips ere she was lost in slumber. Aylmer sat by her side, watching her aspect with the emotions proper to a man the whole value of whose existence was involved in the process now to be tested. Mingled with this mood, however, was the philosophic investigation characteristic of the man of science. Not the minutest symptom escaped him. A heightened flush of the cheek, a slight irregularity of breath, a quiver of the eyelid, a hardly perceptible tremor through the frame, – such were the details which, as the moments passed, he wrote down in his folio volume. Intense thought had set its stamp upon every previous page of that volume, but the thoughts of years were all concentrated upon the last.

While thus employed, he failed not to gaze often at the fatal hand, and not without a shudder. Yet once, by a strange and unaccountable impulse, he pressed it with his lips. His spirit recoiled, however, in the very act; and Georgiana, out of the midst of her deep sleep, moved uneasily and murmured as if in remonstrance. Again Aylmer resumed his watch. Nor was it without avail. The crimson hand, which at first had been strongly visible upon the marble paleness of Georgiana's cheek, now grew more faintly outlined. She remained not less pale than ever; but the birthmark, with every breath that came and went, lost somewhat of its former distinctness. Its presence had been awful; its departure was more awful still. Watch the stain of the rainbow fading out of the sky, and you will know how that mysterious symbol passed away.

"Ah, clod! ah, earthly mass!" cried Aylmer, laughing in a sort of frenzy, "you have served me well! Matter and spirit – earth and heaven – have both done their part in this! Laugh, thing of the senses! You have earned the right to laugh."

"By Heaven! it is well-nigh gone!" said Aylmer to himself, in almost irrepressible ecstasy. "I can scarcely trace it now. Success! success! And now it is like the faintest rose color. The lightest flush of blood across her cheek would overcome it. But she is so pale!"

He drew aside the window curtain and suffered the light of natural day to fall into the room and rest upon her cheek. At the same time he heard a gross, hoarse chuckle, which he had long known as his servant Aminadab's expression of delight.

These exclamations broke Georgiana's sleep. She slowly unclosed her eyes and gazed into the mirror which her husband had arranged for that purpose. A faint smile flitted over her lips when she recognized how barely perceptible was now that crimson hand which had once blazed forth with such disastrous brilliance as to scare away all their happiness. But then her eyes sought Aylmer's face with a trouble and anxiety that he could by no means account for.

"My poor Aylmer!" murmured she.

"Poor? Nay, richest, happiest, most favored!" exclaimed he. "My peerless bride, it is successful! You are perfect!"

"My poor Aylmer," she repeated, with a more than human tenderness, "you have aimed loftily; you have done nobly. Do not repent that with so high and pure a feeling, you have rejected the best the earth could offer. Aylmer, dearest Aylmer, I am dying!"

Alas! it was too true! The fatal hand had grappled with the mystery of life, and was the bond by which an angelic spirit kept itself in union with a mortal frame. As the last crimson tint of the birthmark – that sole token of human imperfection – faded from her cheek, the parting breath of the now perfect woman passed into the atmosphere, and her soul, lingering a moment near her husband, took its heavenward flight. Then a hoarse, chuckling laugh was heard again! Thus ever does the gross fatality of earth exult in its invariable triumph over the immortal essence which, in this dim sphere of half development, demands the completeness of a higher state. Yet, had Aylmer reached a profounder wisdom, he need not thus have flung away the happiness which would have woven his mortal life of the selfsame texture with the celestial. The momentary circumstance was too strong for him; he failed to look beyond the shadowy scope of time, and, living once for all in eternity, to find the perfect future in the present.

Ethan Brand
A Chapter from an Abortive Romance

Nathaniel Hawthorne

Bartram the lime-burner, a rough, heavy-looking man, begrimed with charcoal, sat watching his kiln at nightfall, while his little son played at building houses with the scattered fragments of marble, when, on the hillside below them, they heard a roar of laughter, not mirthful, but slow, and even solemn, like a wind shaking the boughs of the forest.

"Father, what is that?" asked the little boy, leaving his play, and pressing betwixt his father's knees.

"Oh, some drunken man, I suppose," answered the lime-burner; "some merry fellow from the bar-room in the village, who dared not laugh loud enough within doors lest he should blow the roof of the house off. So here he is, shaking his jolly sides at the foot of Graylock."

"But, father," said the child, more sensitive then the obtuse, middle-aged clown, "he does not laugh like a man that is glad. So the noise frightens me!"

"Don't be a fool, child!" cried his father, gruffly. "You will never make a man, I do believe; there is too much of your mother in you. I have known the rustling of a leaf startle you. Hark! Here comes the merry fellow now. You shall see that there is no harm in him."

Bartram and his little son, while they were talking thus, sat watching the same lime-kiln that had been the scene of Ethan Brand's solitary and meditative life, before he began his search for the Unpardonable Sin. Many years, as we have seen, had now elapsed, since that portentous night when the IDEA was first developed. The kiln, however, on the mountain-side, stood unimpaired, and was in nothing changed since he had thrown his dark thoughts into the intense glow of its furnace, and melted them, as it were, into the one thought that took possession of his life. It was a rude, round, towerlike structure about twenty feet high, heavily built of rough stones, and with a hillock of earth heaped about the larger part of its circumference; so that the blocks and fragments of marble might be drawn by cart-loads, and thrown in at the top. There was an opening at the bottom of the tower, like an oven-mouth, but large enough to admit a man in a stooping posture, and provided with a massive iron door. With the smoke and jets of flame issuing from the chinks and crevices of this door, which seemed to give admittance into the hellside, it resembled nothing so much as the private entrance to the infernal regions, which the shepherds of the Delectable Mountains were accustomed to show to pilgrims.

There are many such lime-kilns in that tract of country, for the purpose of burning the white marble which composes a large part of the substance of the hills. Some of them, built years ago, and long deserted, with weeds growing in the vacant round of the interior, which is open to the sky, and grass and wild-flowers rooting themselves into the chinks of the stones, look already like relics of antiquity, and may yet be overspread with the lichens of centuries to come. Others, where the lime-burner still feeds his daily and nightlong fire, afford points of interest to the wanderer among the hills, who seats himself on a log of wood or a fragment of marble, to hold a chat with the solitary man. It is a lonesome, and, when the character is inclined to thought, may be an intensely thoughtful occupation; as it proved in the case of Ethan Brand, who had mused to such strange purpose, in days gone by, while the fire in this very kiln was burning.

The man who now watched the fire was of a different order, and troubled himself with no thoughts save the very few that were requisite to this business. At frequent intervals, he flung back the clashing weight of the iron door, and, turning his face from the insufferable glare, thrust in huge logs of oak, or stirred the immense brands with a long pole. Within the furnace were seen the curling and riotous flames, and the burning marble, almost molten with the intensity of heat; while without, the reflection of the fire quivered on the dark intricacy of the surrounding forest, and showed in the foreground a bright and ruddy little picture of the hut, the spring beside its door, the athletic and coal-begrimed figure of the lime-burner, and the half-frightened child, shrinking into the protection of his father's shadow. And when, again, the iron door was closed, then reappeared the tender light of the half-full moon, which vainly strove to trace out the indistinct shapes of the neighboring mountains; and, in the upper sky, there was a flitting congregation of clouds, still faintly tinged with the rosy sunset, though thus far down into the valley the sunshine had vanished long and long ago.

The little boy now crept still closer to his father, as footsteps were heard ascending the hill side, and a human form thrust aside the bushes that clustered beneath the trees.

"Halloo! who is it?" cried the lime-burner, vexed at his son's timidity, yet half infected by it. "Come forward, and show yourself, like a man, or I'll fling this chunk of marble at your head!"

"You offer me a rough welcome," said a gloomy voice, as the unknown man drew nigh. "Yet I neither claim nor desire a kinder one, even at my own fireside."

To obtain a distincter view, Bartram threw open the iron door of the kiln, whence immediately issued a gush of fierce light, that smote full upon the stranger's face and figure. To a careless eye there appeared nothing very remarkable in his aspect, which was that of a man in a coarse, brown, country-made suit of clothes, tall and thin, with the staff and heavy shoes of a wayfarer. As he advanced, he fixed his eyes – which were very bright – intently upon the brightness of the furnace, as if he beheld, or expected to behold, some object worthy of note within it.

"Good evening, stranger," said the lime-burner; "whence come you, so late in the day?"

"I come from my search," answered the wayfarer; "for, at last, it is finished."

"Drunk! – or crazy!" muttered Bartram to himself. "I shall have trouble with the fellow. The sooner I drive him away, the better."

The little boy, all in a tremble, whispered to his father, and begged him to shut the door of the kiln, so that there might not be so much light; for that there was something in the man's face which he was afraid to look at, yet could not look away from. And, indeed, even the lime-burner's dull and torpid sense began to be impressed by an indescribable something in that thin, rugged, thoughtful visage, with the grizzled hair hanging wildly about it, and those deeply sunken eyes, which gleamed like fires within the entrance of a mysterious cavern. But, as he closed the door, the stranger turned towards him, and spoke in a quiet, familiar way, that made Bartram feel as if he were a sane and sensible man, after all.

"Your task draws to an end, I see," said he. "This marble has already been burning three days. A few hours more will convert the stone to lime."

"Why, who are you?" exclaimed the lime-burner. "You seem as well acquainted with my business as I am myself."

"And well I may be," said the stranger; "for I followed the same craft many a long year, and here, too, on this very spot. But you are a newcomer in these parts. Did you never hear of Ethan Brand?"

"The man that went in search of the Unpardonable Sin?" asked Bartram, with a laugh.

"The same," answered the stranger. "He has found what he sought, and therefore he comes back again."

"What! then you are Ethan Brand himself?" cried the lime-burner, in amazement. "I am a newcomer here, as you say, and they call it eighteen years since you left the foot of Graylock. But, I can tell you, the good folks still talk about Ethan Brand, in the village yonder, and what a strange errand took him away from his lime-kiln. Well, and so you have found the Unpardonable Sin?"

"Even so!" said the stranger, calmly.

"If the question is a fair one," proceeded Bartram, "where might it be?"
Ethan Brand laid his finger on his own heart.

"Here!" replied he.

And then, without mirth in his countenance, but as if moved by an in-
voluntary recognition of the infinite absurdity of seeking throughout the
world for what was the closest of all things to himself, and looking into
every heart, save his own, for what was hidden in no other breast, he
broke into a laugh of scorn. It was the same slow, heavy laugh, that almost
appalled the lime-burner when it heralded the wayfarer's approach.

The solitary mountain-side was made dismal by it. Laughter, when out
of place, mistimed, or bursting forth from a disordered state of feeling,
may be the most terrible modulation of the human voice. The laughter of
one asleep, even if it be a little child, – the madman's laugh, – the wild,
screaming laugh of a born idiot, – are sounds that we sometimes tremble
to hear, and would always willingly forget. Poets have imagined no utterance of fiends or hobgoblins so fearfully appropriate as a laugh. And even
the obtuse lime-burner felt his nerves shaken, as this strange man looked
inward at his own heart, and burst into laughter that rolled away into the
night, and was indistinctly reverberated among the hills.

"Joe," said he to his little son, "scamper down to the tavern in the village, and tell the jolly fellows there that Ethan Brand has come back, and
that he has found the Unpardonable Sin!"

The boy darted away on his errand, to which Ethan Brand made no ob-
jection, nor seemed hardly to notice it. He sat on a log of wood, looking
steadfastly at the iron door of the kiln. When the child was out of sight,
and his swift and light footsteps ceased to be heard treading first on the
fallen leaves and then on the rocky mountain-path, the lime-burner began
to regret his departure. He felt that the little fellow's presence had been a
barrier between his guest and himself, and that he must now deal, heart to
heart, with a man who, on his own confession, had committed the one
only crime for which Heaven could afford no mercy. That crime, in its indistinct blackness, seemed to overshadow him. The lime-burner's own
sins rose up within him, and made his memory riotous with a throng of
evil shapes that asserted their kindred with the Master Sin, whatever it
might be, which it was within the scope of man's corrupted nature to con-
ceive and cherish. They were all of one family; they went to and fro between his breast and Ethan Brand's, and carried dark greetings from one
to the other.

Then Bartram remembered the stories which had grown traditionary
in reference to this strange man, who had come upon him like a shadow
of the night, and was making himself at home in his old place, after so

long absence, that the dead people, dead and buried for years, would have had more right to be at home, in any familiar spot, than he. Ethan Brand, it was said, had conversed with Satan himself in the lurid blaze of this very kiln. The legend had been matter of mirth heretofore but looked grisly now. According to this tale, before Ethan Brand departed on his search, he had been accustomed to evoke a fiend from the hot furnace of the lime-kiln, night after night, in order to confer with him about the Unpardonable Sin; the man and the fiend each laboring to frame the image of some mode of guilt which could neither be atoned for nor forgiven. And, with the first gleam of light upon the mountain-top, the fiend crept in at the iron door, there to abide the intensest element of fire until again summoned forth to share in the dreadful task of extending man's possible guilt beyond the scope of Heaven's else infinite mercy.

While the lime-burner was struggling with the horror of these thoughts, Ethan Brand rose from the log, and flung open the door of the kiln. The action was in such accordance with the idea in Bartram's mind, that he almost expected to see the Evil One issue forth, red-hot, from the raging furnace.

"Hold! hold!" cried he, with a tremulous attempt to laugh; for he was ashamed of his fears, although they overmastered him. "Don't, for mercy's sake, bring out your Devil now!"

"Man!" sternly replied Ethan Brand, "what need have I of the Devil? I have left him behind me, on my track. It is with such half-way sinners as you that he busies himself. Fear not, because I open the door. I do but act by old custom, and am going to trim your fire, like a lime-burner, as I was once."

He stirred the vast coals, thrust in more wood, and bent forward to gaze into the hollow prison-house of the fire, regardless of the fierce glow that reddened upon his face. The lime-burner sat watching him, and half-suspected this strange guest of a purpose, if not to evoke a fiend, at least to plunge bodily into the flames, and thus vanish from the sight of man. Ethan Brand, however, drew quickly back, and closed the door of the kiln.

"I have looked," said he, "into many a human heart that was seven times hotter with sinful passions than yonder furnace is with fire. But I found not there what I sought. No, not the Unpardonable Sin!"

"What is the Unpardonable Sin?" asked the lime-burner; and then he shrank farther from his companion, trembling lest his question should be answered.

"It is a sin that grew within my own breast," replied Ethan Brand, standing erect, with a pride that distinguished all enthusiasts of his stamp. "A sin that grew nowhere else! The sin of an intellect that triumphed over the sense of brotherhood with man and reverence for God, and sacrificed everything to its own mighty claims! The only sin that deserves a recompense of immortal agony! Freely, were it to do again, would I incur the guilt. Unshrinkingly I accept the retribution!"

"The man's head is turned," muttered the lime-burner to himself. "He may be a sinner like the rest of us, – nothing more likely, – but I'll be sworn, he is a madman too."

Nevertheless, he felt uncomfortable at his situation, alone with Ethan Brand on the wild mountain-side, and was right glad to hear the rough murmur of tongues, and the footsteps of what seemed a pretty numerous party, stumbling over the stones and rustling through the underbrush. Soon appeared the whole lazy regiment that was wont to infest the village tavern, comprehending three or four individuals who had drunk flip beside the bar-room fire through all the winters, and smoked their pipes beneath the stoop through all the summers, since Ethan Brand's departure. Laughing boisterously, and mingling all their voices together in unceremonious talk, they now burst into the moonshine and narrow streaks of firelight that illuminated the open space before the lime-kiln. Bartram set the door ajar again, flooding the spot with light, that the whole company might get a fair view of Ethan Brand, and he of them.

There, among other old acquaintances, was a once ubiquitous man, now almost extinct, but whom we were formerly sure to encounter at the hotel of every thriving village throughout the country. It was the stage-agent. The present specimen of the genus was a wilted and smoke-dried man, wrinkled and red-nosed, in a smarthy cut, brown, bobtailed coat, with brass buttons, who, for a length of time unknown, had kept his desk and corner in the bar-room, and was still puffing what seemed to be the same cigar that he had lighted twenty years before. He had great fame as a dry joker, though, perhaps, less on account of any intrinsic humor than from a certain flavor of brandy-toddy and tobacco-smoke, which impregnated all his ideas and expressions, as well as his person. Another well-remembered, though strangely altered, face was that of Lawyer Giles, as people still called him in courtesy; an elderly ragamuffin, in his soiled shirt-sleeves and tow-cloth trousers. This poor fellow had been an attorney, in what he called his better days, a sharp practitioner, and in great vogue among the village litigants; but flip, and sling, and toddy, and cocktails, imbibed at all hours, morning, noon, and night, had caused him to slide from intellectual to various kinds of degrees of bodily labor, till at last, to adopt his own phrase, he slid into a soap-vat. In other words, Giles was now a soap-boiler, in a small way. He had come to be but the fragment of a human being, a part of one foot having been chopped off by an axe, and an entire hand torn away by the devilish grip of a steam-engine. Yet, though the corporeal hand was gone, a spiritual member remained; for, stretching forth the stump, Giles steadfastly averred that he felt an invisible thumb and fingers with as vivid a sensation as before the real ones were amputated. A maimed and miserable wretch he was; but one, nevertheless, whom the world could not trample on, and had no right to scorn, either in this or any previous stage of his misfortunes, since he had still kept up the courage and spirit of a man, asked nothing in charity, and with his one hand – and that the left one – brought a stern battle against want and hostile circumstances.

Among the throng, too, came another personage, who, with certain points of similarity to Lawyer Giles, had many more of difference. It was the village doctor; a man of some fifty years, whom, at an earlier period of his life, we introduced as paying a professional visit to Ethan Brand during the latter's supposed insanity. He was now a purple-visaged, rude, and brutal, yet half-gentlemanly figure, with something wild, ruined, and desperate in his talk, and in all the details of his gesture and manners. Brandy possessed this man like an evil spirit, and made him as surly and savage as a wild beast, and as miserable as a lost soul; but there was supposed to be in him such wonderful skill, such native gifts of healing, beyond any which medical science could impart, that society caught hold of him, and would not let him sink out of its reach. So, swaying to and fro upon his horse, and grumbling thick accents at the bedside, he visited all the sick-chambers for miles about among the mountain towns, and sometimes raised a dying man, as it were, by miracle, or quite as often, no doubt, sent his patient to a grave that was dug many a year too soon. The doctor had an everlasting pipe in his mouth, and, as somebody said, in allusion to his habit of swearing, it was always alight with hell-fire.

These three worthies pressed forward, and greeted Ethan Brand each after his own fashion, earnestly inviting him to partake of the contents of a certain black bottle, in which, as they averred, he would find something far better worth seeking than the Unpardonable Sin. No mind, which has wrought itself by intense and solitary meditation into a high state of enthusiasm, can endure the kind of contact with low and vulgar modes of thought and feeling to which Ethan Brand was now subjected. It made him doubt – and, strange to say, it was a painful doubt – whether he had indeed found the Unpardonable Sin, and found it within himself. The whole question on which he had exhausted life, and more than life, looked like a delusion.

"Leave me," he said bitterly, "ye brute beasts, that have made yourselves so, shrivelling up our souls with fiery liquors! I have done with you.

Years and years ago, I groped into your hearts and found nothing there for my purpose. Get ye gone!"

"Why, you uncivil scoundrel," cried the fierce doctor, "is that the way you respond to the kindness of your best friends? Then let me tell you the truth. You have no more found the Unpardonable Sin than yonder boy Joe has. You are but a crazy fellow, – I told you so twenty years ago, – neither better nor worse than a crazy fellow, and the fit companion of old Humphrey, here!"

He pointed to an old man, shabbily dressed, with long white hair, thin visage, and unsteady eyes. For some years past this aged person had been wandering about among the hills, inquiring of all travellers whom he met for his daughter. The girl, it seemed, had gone off with a company of circus-performers, and occasionally tidings of her came to the village, and fine stories were told of her glittering appearance as she rode on horseback in the ring, or performed marvellous feats on the tight-rope.

The white-haired father now approached Ethan Brand, and gazed unsteadily into his face.

"They tell me you have been all over the earth," said he, wringing his hands with earnestness. "You must have seen my daughter, for she makes a grand figure on the world, and everybody goes to see her. Did she send any word to her old father, or say when she was coming back?"

Ethan Brand's eye quailed beneath the old man's. That daughter, from whom he so earnestly desired a word of greeting, was the Esther of our tale, the very girl whom, with such old and remorseless purpose, Ethan Brand had made the subject of a psychological experiment, and wasted, absorbed, and perhaps annihilated her soul, in the process.

"Yes," murmured he, turning away from the hoary wanderer, "it is no delusion. There is an Unpardonable Sin!"

While these things were passing, a merry scene was going forward in the area of cheerful light, beside the spring and before the door of the hut. A number of the youth of the village, young men and girls, had hurried up the hill-side, impelled by curiosity to see Ethan Brand, the hero of so many a legend familiar to their children. Finding nothing, however, very remarkable in his aspect, – nothing but a sunburnt wayfarer, in plain garb and dusty shoes, who sat looking into the fire as if he fancied pictures among the coals, – these young people speedily grew tired of observing him. As it happened, there was other amusement at hand. An old German Jew travelling with a diorama on his back, was passing down the mountain-road towards the village just as the party turned aside from it, and, in hopes of eking out the profits of the day, the showman had kept them company in the lime-kiln.

"Come, old Dutchman," cried one of the young men, "let us see your pictures, if you can swear they are worth looking at!"

"Oh yes, Captain," answered the Jew, – whether as a mater, of courtesy or craft, he styled everybody Captain, – "I shall show you, indeed, some very superb pictures!"

So, placing his box in a proper position, he invited the young men and girls to look through the glass orifices of the machine, and proceeded to exhibit a series of the most outrageous scratchings and daubings, as specimens of the fine arts, that ever an itinerant showman had the face to impose upon his circle of spectators. The pictures were worn out, moreover, tattered, full of cracks and wrinkles, dingy and tobacco-smoke, and otherwise in a most pitiable condition. Some purported to be cities, public edifices, and ruined castles in Europe; others represented Napoleon's battles and Nelson's sea-fights; and in the midst of these would be seen a gigantic, brown, hairy hand, – which might have been mistaken for the Hand of Destiny, though, in truth, it was only the showman's, – pointing its forefinger to various scenes of the conflict, while its owner gave historical illustrations. When, with much merriment at its abominable deficiency of merit, the exhibition was concluded, the German bade little Joe put his head into the box. Viewed through the magnifying-glasses, the boy's round, rosy visage assumed the strangest imaginable aspect of an immense Titanic child, the mouth grinning broadly, and the eyes and every other feature overflowing with fun at the joke. Suddenly, however, that merry face turned pale, and its expression changed to horror, for this easily impressed and excitable child had become sensible that the eye of Ethan Brand was fixed upon him through the glass.

"You make the little man to be afraid, Captain," said the German Jew, turning up the dark and strong outline of his visage from his stooping posture. "But look again, and, by chance, I shall cause you to see somewhat that is very fine, upon my word!"

Ethan Brand gazed into the box for an instant, and then starting back, looked fixedly at the German. What had he seen? Nothing, apparently; for a curious youth, who had peeped in almost at the same moment, beheld only a vacant space of canvas.

"I remember you now," muttered Ethan Brand to the showman.

"Ah, Captain," whispered the Jew of Nuremburg, with a dark smile, "I find it to be a heavy matter in my show-box, – this Unpardonable Sin? By my faith, Captain, it has wearied my shoulders, this long day, to carry it over the mountain."

"Peace," answered Ethan Brand, sternly, "or get thee into the furnace yonder!"

The Jew's exhibition had scarcely concluded, when a great, elderly dog – who seemed to be his own master, as no person in the company laid claim to him – saw fit to render himself to the object of public notice. Hitherto, he had shown himself a very quiet, well-disposed old dog, going round from one to another, and, by way of being sociable, offering his rough head to be patted by any kindly hand that would take so much trouble. But now, all of a sudden, this grave and venerable quadruped, of his own mere motion, and without the slightest suggestion from anybody else, began to run round after his tail, which, to heighten the absurdity of the proceeding, was a great deal shorter than it should have been. Never was seen such headlong eagerness in pursuit of an object that could not possibly be attained; never was heard such a tremendous outbreak of growling, snarling, barking, and snapping, – as if one end of the ridiculous brute's body were at deadly and most unforgivable enmity with the other. Faster and faster, round about went the cur; and faster and still faster fled the unapproachable brevity of this tail; and louder and fiercer grew his yells of rage and animosity; until, utterly exhausted, and so far from the goal as ever, the foolish old dog ceased his performance as suddenly as he had begun it. The next moment he was as mild, quiet, sensible, and respectable in his deportment, as when he first scraped acquaintance with the company.

As may be supposed, the exhibition was greeted with universal laughter, clapping of hands, and shouts of encore, to which the canine performer responded by wagging all there was to wag of his tail, but appeared totally unable to repeat his very successful effort to amuse the spectators.

Meanwhile, Ethan Brand has resumed his seat upon the log, and moved, it might be, by a perception of some remote analogy between his own case and that of this self-pursuing cur, he broke into the awful laugh, which, more than any other token, expressed the condition of his inward being. From that moment, the merriment of the party was at an end; they stood aghast, dreading lest the inauspicious sound should be reverberated around the horizon, and that mountain would thunder it to mountain, and so the horror be prolonged upon their ears. Then, whispering one to another that it was late, – that the moon was almost down, – that the August night was growing chill, – they hurried homewards, leaving the lime-burner and little Joe to deal as they might with their unwelcome guest. Save for these three human beings, the open space on the hill-side was a solitude, set in a vast gloom of forest. Beyond that darksome verge, the firelight glimmered on the stately trunks and almost black foliage of pines, intermixed with the lighter verdure of sapling oaks, maples and poplars, while here and there lay the gigantic corpses of dead trees, decaying on the leaf-strewn soil. And it seemed to little Joe – a timorous and imaginative child – that the silent forest was holding its breath until some fearful thing should happen.

Ethan Brand thrust more wood into the fire, and closed the door of the kiln; then looking over his shoulder at the lime-burner and his son, he bade, rather than advised, them to retire to rest.

"For myself, I cannot sleep," said he. "I have matters that it concerns me to meditate upon. I will watch the fire, as I used to do in the old time."

"And call the Devil out of the furnace to keep you company, I suppose," muttered Bartram, who had been making intimate acquaintance with the black bottle above mentioned. "But watch, if you like, and call as many devils as you like! For my part, I shall be all the better for a snooze. Come, Joe!"

As the boy followed his father into the hut, he looked back at the wayfarer, and the tears came into his eyes, for his tender spirit had an intuition of the bleak and terrible loneliness in which this man had enveloped himself.

When they had gone, Ethan Brand sat listening to the crackling of the kindled wood, and looking at the little spirts of fire that issued through the chinks of the door. These trifles, however, once so familiar, had but the slightest hold of his attention, while deep within his mind he was reviewing the gradual but marvellous change that had been wrought upon him by the search to which he had devoted himself. He remembered how the night dew had fallen upon him, – how the dark forest had whispered to him, – how the stars had gleamed upon him, – a simple and loving man, watching his fire in the years gone by, and ever musing as it burned. He remembered with what tenderness, with what love and sympathy for mankind, and what pity for human guilt and woe, he had first begun to contemplate those ideas which afterwards became the inspiration of his life; with what reverence he had then looked into the heart of man, viewing it as a temple originally divine, and, however desecrated, still to be held sacred by a brother; with what awful fear he had deprecated the success of his pursuit, and prayed that the Unpardonable Sin might never be revealed to him. Then ensued that vast intellectual development, which, in its progress, disturbed the counterpoise between his mind and heart. The Idea that possessed his life had operated as a means of education; it had gone on cultivating his powers to the highest point of which they were susceptible; it had raised him from the level of an unlettered laborer to stand on a star-lit eminence, whither the philosophers of the earth, laden with the lore of universities, might vainly strive to clamber after him. So much for the intellect! But where was the heart? That, indeed, had withered, – had contracted, – had hardened, – had perished! It had ceased to partake of the universal throb. He had lost his hold of the magnetic chain of humanity. He was no longer a brother-man, opening the chambers or the dungeons of our common nature by the key of holy sympathy, which gave him a right to share in all its secrets; he was now a cold observer, looking on mankind as the subject of his experiment, and, at length, converting man and woman to be his puppets, and pulling the wires that moved them to such degrees of crime as were demanded for his study.

Thus Ethan Brand became a fiend. He began to be so from the moment that his mortal nature had ceased to keep the pace of improvement with his intellect. And now, as his highest effort and inevitable development, – as the bright and gorgeous flower, and rich, delicious fruit of his life's labor, – he had produced the Unpardonable Sin!

"What more have I to seek? what more to achieve?" said Ethan Brand to himself. "My task is done, and well done!"

Starting from the log with a certain alacrity in his gait and ascending the hillock of earth that was raised against the stone circumference of the lime-kiln, he thus reached the top of the structure. It was a space of perhaps ten feet across, from edge to edge, presenting a view of the upper surface of the immense mass of broken marble with which the kiln was heaped. All these innumerable blocks and fragments of marble were red-hot and vividly on fire, sending up great spouts of blue flame, which quivered aloft and danced madly, as within a magic circle, and sank and rose again, with continual and multitudinous activity. As the lonely man bent forward over this terrible body of fire, the blasting heat smote up against his person with a breath that, it might be supposed, would have scorched and shrivelled him up in a moment.

Ethan Brand stood erect, and raised his arms on high. The blue flames played upon his face, and imparted the wild and ghastly light which alone could have suited its expression; it was that of a fiend on the verge of plunging into his gulf of intensest torment.

"O Mother Earth," cried he, "who are no more my Mother, and into whose bosom this frame shall never be resolved! O mankind, whose brotherhood I have cast off, and trampled thy great heart beneath my feet! O stars of heaven, that shone on me of old, as if to light me onward and upward! – farewell all, and forever. Come, deadly element of Fire, – henceforth my familiar friend! Embrace me, as I do thee!"

That night the sound of a fearful peal of laughter rolled heavily through the sleep of the lime-burner and his little son; dim shapes of horror and anguish haunted their dreams, and seemed still present in the rude hovel, when they opened their eyes to the daylight.

"Up, boy, up!" cried the lime-burner, staring about him. "Thank Heaven, the night is gone, at last; and rather than pass such another, I would watch my lime-kiln, wide awake, for a twelvemonth. The Ethan Brand, with his humbug of an Unpardonable Sin, has done me no such mighty favor, in taking my place!"

He issued from the hut, followed by little Joe, who kept fast hold of his father's hand. The early sunshine was already pouring its gold upon the mountaintops, and though the valleys were still in shadow, they smiled cheerfully in the promise of the bright day that was hastening onward. The village, completely shut in by hills, which swelled away gently about it, looked as if it had rested peacefully in the hollow of the great hand of Providence. Every dwelling was distinctly visible; the little spires of the two churches pointed upwards, and caught a fore-glimmering of bright-ness from the sun-gilt skies upon their gilded weathercocks. The tavern was astir, and the figure of the old, smoke-dried stage-agent, cigar in mouth, was seen beneath the stoop. Old Graylock was glorified with a golden cloud upon his head. Scattered likewise over the breasts of the sur-rounding mountains, there were heaps of hoary mist, in fantastic shapes, some of them far down into the valley, others high up towards the sum-mits, and still others, of the same family of mist or cloud, hovering in the gold radiance of the upper atmosphere. Stepping from one to another of the clouds that rested on the hills, and thence to the loftier brotherhood that sailed in air, it seemed almost as if a mortal man might thus ascend into the heavenly regions. Earth was so mingled with sky that it was a day-dream to look at it.

To supply that charm of the familiar and homely, which Nature so readily adopts into a scene like this, the stage-coach was rattling down the mountain-road, and the driver sounded his horn, while Echo caught up the notes, and intertwined them into a rich and varied and elaborate har-mony, of which the original performer could lay claim to little share. The great hills played a concert among themselves, each contributing a strain of airy sweetness.

Little Joe's face brightened at once.

"Dear father," cried he, skipping cheerily to and fro, "that strange man is gone, and the sky and the mountains all seem glad of it!"

"Yes," growled the lime-burner, with an oath, "but he has let the fire go down, and no thanks to him if five hundred bushels of lime are not spoiled. If I catch the fellow hereabouts again, I shall feel like tossing him into the furnace!"

With his long pole in his hand, he ascended to the top of the kiln. After a moment's pause, he called to his son.

"Come up here, Joe!" said he.

So little Joe ran up the hillock, and stood by his father's side. The marble was all burnt into perfect, snow-white lime. But on its surface, in the midst of the circle, – snow-white too, and thoroughly converted into lime, – lay a human skeleton, in the attitude of a person who, after long toil, lies down to long repose. Within the ribs – strange to say – was the shape of a human heart.

"Was the fellow's heart made of marble?" cried Bartram, in some perplexity at this phenomenon. "At any rate, it is burnt into what looks like special good lime; and, taking all the bones together, my kiln is half a bushel the richer for him."

So saying, the rude lime-burner lifted his pole, and, letting if fall upon the skeleton, the relics of Ethan Brand were crumbled into fragments.

Moby-Dick (excerpts)

Herman Melville

The Quarter-Deck (Chapter 36)

It was not a great while after the affair of the pipe, that one morning shortly after breakfast, Ahab, as was his wont, ascended the cabin-gang-way to the deck. There most sea-captains usually walk at that hour, as country gentlemen, after the same meal, take a few turns in the garden.

Soon his steady, ivory stride was heard, as to and fro he paced his old rounds, upon planks so familiar to his tread, that they were all over dented, like geological stones, with the peculiar mark of his walk. Did you fixedly gaze, too, upon that ribbed and dented brow; there also, you would see still stranger foot-prints – the foot-prints of his one unsleeping, ever-pacing thought.

But on the occasion in question, those dents looked deeper, even as his nervous step that morning left a deeper mark. And, so full of his thought was Ahab, that at every uniform turn that he made, now at the main-mast and now at the binnacle, you could almost see that thought turn in him as he turned, and pace in him as he paced; so completely possessing him, indeed, that it all but seemed to inward mould of every outer movement.

"D'ye mark him, Flask?" whispered Stubb; "the chick that's in him pecks the shell. 'Twill soon be out."

The hours wore on; – Ahab now shut up within his cabin; anon, pacing the deck, with the same intense bigotry of purpose[1] in his aspect.

It drew near the close of day. Suddenly he came to a halt by the bul-warks, and inserting his bone leg into the auger-hole there, and with one hand grasping a shroud, he ordered Starbuck to send everbody aft.

"Sir!" said the mate, astonished at an order seldom or never given on ship-board except in some extraordinary case.

"Send everybody aft," repeated Ahab. "Mast-heads, there! come down!"

When the entire ship's company were assembled, and with curious and not wholly unapprehensive faces, were eyeing him, for he looked not un-like the weather horizon when a storm is coming up, Ahab, after rapidly glancing over the bulwarks, and then darting his eyes among the crew, started from his stand-point; and as though not a soul were nigh him re-

---

[1] Intense single-mindedness of purpose.

sumed his heavy turns upon the deck. With bent head and half-slouched hat he continued to pace, unmindful of the wondering whispering among the men; till Stubb cautiously whispered to Flak, that Ahab must have summoned them there for the purpose of witnessing a pedestrian feat. But this did not last long. Vehemently pausing, he cried: –

"What do ye do when ye see a whale, men?"

"Sing out for him!" was the impulsive rejoinder from a score of clubbed voices.

"Good!" cried Ahab, with a wild-approval in his tones; observing the hearty animation into which his unexpected question had so magnetically thrown them.

"And what do ye next, men?"

"Lower away, and after him!"

"And what tune is it ye pull to, men!"

"A dead whale or a stove boat!"

More and more strangely and fiercely glad and approving, grew the countenance of the old man at every shout; while the mariners began to gaze curiously at each other, as if marvelling how it was that they themselves became so excited at such seemingly purposeless questions.

But, they were all eagerness again, as Ahab, now half-revolving in his pivot-hole, with one hand reaching high up a shroud, and tightly, almost convulsively grasping it, addressed them thus: –

"All ye mast-headers have before now heard me give orders about a white whale. Look ye! d'ye see the Spanish ounce of gold?" – holding up a broad bright coin to the sun – "it is a sixteen dollar piece, men, – a doubloon. D'ye see it? Mr. Starbuck, hand me yon top-maul."

While the mate was getting the hammer, Ahab, without speaking, was slowly rubbing the gold piece against the skirts of his jacket, as if to heighten its lustre, and without using any words was meanwhile lowly humming to himself, producing a sound so strangely muffled and inarticulate that it seemed the mechanical humming of the wheels of his vitality in him.

Receiving the top-maul from Starbuck, he advanced towards the mainmast with the hammer uplifted in one hand, exhibiting the gold with the other, and with a high raised voice exclaiming: "Whosoever of ye raises me a white-headed whale with a wrinkled brow and a crooked jaw; whosoever of ye raises me that white-headed whale, with three holes punctured in his starboard fluke – look ye, whosoever of ye raises me that same white whale, he shall have this gold ounce, my boys!"

"Huzza! huzza!" cried the seamen, as with swinging tarpaulins they hailed the act of nailing the gold to the mast.

"It's a white whale, I say," resumed Ahab, as he threw down the top-maul; "a white whale. Skin your eyes for him, men; look sharp for white water; if ye see but a bubble, sing out."

All this while Tashtego, Daggoo, and Queequeg had looked on with even more intense interest and surprise than the rest, and at the mention of the wrinkled brow and crooked jaw they had started as if each was separately touched by some specific recollection.

"Captain Ahab," said Tashtego, "that white whale must be the same that some call Moby Dick."

"Moby Dick?" shouted Ahab. "Do ye know the white whale then, Tash?"

"Does he fan-tail a little curious, sir, before he goes down?" said the Gay-Header deliberately.

"And has he a curious spout, too," said Daggoo, "very bushy, even for a parmacetty, and mighty quick, Captain Ahab?"

"And he have one, two, tree – oh! good many iron in him hide, too, Captain," cried Queequeg disjointedly, "all twiske-tee betwisk, like him – him –" faltering hard for a word, and screwing his hand round and round as though uncorking a bottle – "like him – him –"

"Corkscrew!" cried Ahab, "aye, Queequeg, the harpoons lie all twisted and wrenched in him; aye, Daggoo, his spout is a big one, like a whole shock of wheat, and white as a pile of our Nantucket wool after the great annual sheep-shearing; aye, Tashtego, and he fan-tails like a split jib in a squall. Death and devils! men, it is Moby Dick ye have seen – Moby Dick – Moby Dick!"

"Captain Ahab," said Starbuck, who, with Stubb and Flask, had thus far been eyeing his superior with increasing surprise, but at last seemed struck with a thought which somewhat explained all the wonder. "Captain Ahab, I have heard of Moby Dick – but it was not Moby Dick that took off thy leg?"

"Who told thee that?" cried Ahab; then pausing. "Aye, Starbuck; aye, my hearties all round; it was Moby Dick that dismasted me; Moby Dick that brought me to this dead stump I stand on now. Aye, aye," he shouted with a terrific, loud, animal sob, like that of a heart-stricken moose; "Aye, aye! it was that accursed white whale that razeed me; made a poor pegging lubber of me for ever and a day!" Then tossing both arms, with measureless imprecations he shouted out: "Aye, aye! and I'll chase him round Good Hope, and round the Horn, and round the Norway Maelstrom, and round perdition's flames before I give him up. And this is what ye have shipped for, men! to chase that white whale on both sides of land, and over all sides of earth, till he spouts black blood and rolls fin out. What say ye, men, will ye splice hands on it, now? I think ye do look brave."

"Aye, aye!" shouted the harpooneers and seamen, running closer to the excited old man: "A sharp eye for the White Whale; a sharp lance for Moby Dick!"

"God bless ye," he seemed to half sob and half shout. "God bless ye, men. Steward! go draw the great measure of grog. But what's this long face about, Mr. Starbuck; wilt thou not chase the white whale? art not game for Moby Dick?"

"I am game for his crooked jaw, and for the jaws of Death too, Captain Ahab, if it fairly comes in the way of the business we follow; but I came here to hunt whales, not my commander's vengeance. How many barrels will thy vengeance yield thee even if thou gettest it, Captain Ahab? it will not fetch thee much in our Nantucket market."

"Nantucket market! But come closer, Starbuck; thou requirest a little lower layer. If money's to be the measure, man, and the accountants have computed their great counting-house the globe, by girdling it with guineas, one to every three part of an inch; then, let me tell thee, that my vengeance will fetch a great premium *here!*"

"He smites his chest," whispered Stubb, "what's that for? methinks it rings most vast, but hollow."

"Vengeance on a dumb brute!" cried Starbuck, "that simply smote thee from blindest instinct! Madness! To be enraged with a dumb thing, Captain Ahab, seems blasphemous."

"Hark ye yet again, – the little lower layer. All visible objects, man, are but as pasteboard masks. But in each event – in the living act, the undoubted deed – there, some unknown but still reasoning thing puts forth the mouldings of its features from behind the unreasoning mask. If man will strike, strike through the mask! How can the prisoner reach outside except by thrusting through the wall? To me, the white whale is that wall, shoved near to me. Sometimes I think there's naught beyond. But 'tis enough. He tasks me; he heaps me; I see in him outrageous strength, with an inscrutable malice sinewing it. That inscrutable thing is chiefly what I hate; and be the white whale agent, or be the white whale principal, I will wreak that hate upon him. Talk not to me of blasphemy, man; I'd strike the sun if it insulted me. For could the sun do that, then could I do the other; since there is ever a sort of fair play herein, jealousy presiding over all creations. But not my master, man, is even that fair play. Who's over me? Truth hath no confines. Take off thine eye! more intolerable than fiends' glarings is a doltish stare! So, so; thou reddenest and palest; my heat has melted thee to anger-glow. But look ye, Starbuck, what is said in heat, that thing unsays itself. There are men from whom warm words are small indignity. I meant not to incense thee. Let it go. Look! see yonder Turkish cheeks of spotted tawn – living, breathing pictures painted by the sun. The Pagan leopards – the unrecking and unworshipping things, that live, and seek, and give no reasons for the torrid life they feel! The crew, man, the crew! Are they not one and all with Ahab, in this matter of the whale? See Stubb! he laughs! See yonder Chilean! he snorts to think of it. Stand up amid the general hurricane, thy one tost sapling cannot, Starbuck! And what is it? Reckon it. 'Tis but to help strike a fin; no wondrous feat for Starbuck. What is it more? From this one poor hunt, then, the best lance out of all Nantucket, surely he will not hang back, when every foremast-hand has clutched a whetstone? Ah! constrainings seize thee; I see! the billow lifts thee! Speak, but speak! – Aye, aye! thy silence, then, *that* voices thee. *(Aside)* Something shot from my dilated nostrils, he has inhaled it in his lungs. Starbuck now is mine; cannot oppose me now, without rebellion."

"God keep me! – keep us all!" murmured Starbuck, lowly.

But in his joy at the enchanted, tacit acquiescence of the mate, Ahab did not hear his foreboding invocation; nor yet the low laugh from the hold; nor yet the presaging vibrations of the winds in the cordage; nor yet the hollow flap of the sails against the masts, as for a moment their hearts sank in. For again Starbuck's downcast eyes lighted up with the stubborness of life; the subterranean laugh dies away; the winds blew on; the sails filled out; the ship heaved and rolled as before. Ah, ye admonitions and warnings! why stay ye not when ye come? But rather are ye predictions that warnings, ye shadows! Yet not so much predictions from without, as verifications of the foregoing things within. For with little external to constrain us, the innermost necessities in our being, these still drive us on.

"The measure! the measure!" cried Ahab.

Receiving the brimming pewter, and turning to the harpooners, he ordered them to produce their weapons. Then ranging them before him near the capstan, with their harpoons in their hands, while his three mates stood at his side with their lances, and the rest of the ship's company formed a circle round the group; he stood for an instant searchingly eyeing every man of his crew. But those wild eyes met his, as the bloodshot eyes of the prairie wolves meet the eye of their leader, ere he rushes on at their head in the trail of the bison; but, alas! only to fall into the hidden snare of the Indian.

"Drink and pass!" he cried, handing the heavy charged flagon to the nearest seaman. "The crew alone now drink. Round with it, round! Short draughts – long swallows, men; 'tis hot as Satan's hoof. So, so; it goes round excellently. It spiralizes in ye; forks out at the serpent-snapping eye. Well done; almost drained. That way it went, this way it comes. Hand it me – here's a hollow! Men, ye seem the years; so brimming life is gulped and gone. Steward, refill!

"Attend now, my braves. I have mustered ye all round this capstan; and ye mates, flank me with your lances, and ye harpooneers, stand there with your irons; and ye, stout mariners, ring me in, that I may in some sort revive a noble custom of my fisherman fathers before me. O men, you will yet see that – Ha! boy, come back? bad pennies come not sooner. Hand it me. Why, now, this pewter had run brimming again, wert not thou St. Vitus' imp – away, thou ague?

"Advance, ye mates! Cross your lances full before me. Well done! Let me touch the axis." So saying, with extended arm, he grasped the three level, radiating lances at their crossed centre; while so doing, suddenly and nervously twitched them; meanwhile, glancing intently from Starbuck to Stubb; from Stuff to Flask. It seemed as though, by some nameless, interior volition, he would fain have shocked into them the same fiery emotion accumulated within the Leyden jar of his own magnetic life. The three mates quailed before his strong, sustained, and mystic aspect. Stubb and Flask looked sideways from him; the honest eye of Starbuck fell downright.

"In vain!" cried Ahab; "but, maybe, 'tis well. For did ye three but once take the full-forced shock, then mine own electric thing, *that* had perhaps expired from out me. Perchance, too, it would have dropped ye dead. Perchance ye need it not. Down lances! And now, ye mates, I do appoint ye three cup-bearers to my three pagan kinsmen there – yon three most honorable gentlemen and noblemen, my valiant harpooneers. Disdain the task? What, when the great Pope washes the feet of beggars, using his tiara for ewer? Oh, my sweet cardinals! your own condescension, *that* shall bend ye to it. I do not order ye; ye will it. Cut your seizings and draw the poles, ye harpooneers!"

Silently obeying the order, the three harpooneers now stood with the detached iron part of their harpoons, some three feet long, held, barbs up, before them.

"Stab me not with that keen steel! Cant them; cant them over! know ye not the goblet end? Turn up the socket! So, so; now, ye cup-bearers, advance. The irons! take them; hold them while I fill!" Forthwith, slowly going from one officer to the other, he brimmed the harpoon sockets with the fiery waters from the pewter.

"Now, three to three, ye stand. Commend the murderous chalices! Bestow them, ye who are now made parties to this indissoluble league. Ha!

Starbuck! but the deed is done! Yon ratifying sun now waits to sit upon it. Drink, ye harpooneers! drink and swear, ye men that man the deathful whaleboat's bow – Death to Moby Dick! God hunt us all, if we do not hunt Moby Dick to his death!" The long, barbed steel goblets were lifted; and to cries and maledictions against the white whale, the spirits were simultaneously quaffed down with a hiss. Starbuck paled, and turned, and shivered. Once more, and finally, the replenished pewter went the rounds among the frantic crew; when, waving his free hand to them, they all dispersed; and Ahab retired within his cabin.

Moby Dick (Chapter 41)

I, Ishmael, was one of that crew; my shouts had gone up with the rest; my oath had been welded with theirs; and stronger I shouted, and more did I hammer and clinch my oath, because of the dread in my soul. A wild, mystical, sympathetical feeling was in me; Ahab's quenchless feud seemed mine. With greedy ears I learned the history of that murderous monster against whom I and all the others had taken our oaths of violence and revenge.

For some time past, though at intervals only, the unaccompanied, secluded White Whale had haunted those uncivilized seas mostly frequented by the Sperm Whale fisherman. But not all of them knew of his existence; only a few of them, comparatively, had knowingly seen him; while the number who as yet had actually and knowingly given battle to him, was small indeed. For, owing to the large number of whale-cruisers; the disorderly way they were sprinkled over the entire watery circumference, many of them adventurously pushing their quest along solitary latitudes, so as seldom or never for a whole twelvemonth or more on a stretch, to encounter a single news-telling sail of any sort; the inordinate length of each separate voyage; the irregularity of the times of sailing from home; all these, with other circumstances, direct and indirect, long obstructed the spread through the whole world-wide whaling-fleet of the special individualizing tidings concerning Moby Dick. It was hardly to be doubted, that several vessels reported to have encountered, at such or such a time, or on such or such a meridian, a Sperm Whale of uncommon magnitude and malignity, which whale, after doing great mischief to his assailants, had completely escaped them; to some minds it was not an unfair presumption, I say, that the whale in question must have been no other than Moby Dick. Yet as of late the Sperm Whale fishery been marked by various and not unfrequent instances of great ferocity, cunning, and malice in the monster attacked; therefore it was, that those who by accident ignorantly gave battle to Moby Dick; such hunters, perhaps, for the most part, were content to ascribe the peculiar terror he bred, more, as it were, to the perils of the Sperm Whale fishery at large, then to the individual cause. In that way, mostly, the disastrous encounter between Ahab and the whale had hitherto been popularly regarded.

And as for those who, previously hearing of the White Whale, by chance caught sight of him; in the beginning of the thing they had every one of them, almost, as boldly and fearlessly lowered for him, as for any other whale of that species. But at length, such calamities did ensue in these assaults – not restricted to sprained wrists and ancles, broken limbs, or devouring amputations – but fatal to the last degree of fatality; those repeated disastrous repulses, all accumulating and piling their terrors upon Moby Dick; those things had gone far to shake the fortitude of many brave hunters, to whom the story of the White Whale had eventually come.

Nor did wild rumors of all sorts fail to exaggerate, and still the more horrify the true histories of these deadly encounters. For not only do fabulous rumors naturally grow out of the very body of all surprising terrible events, – as the smitten tree gives birth to its fungi; but, in maritime life, far more than in that of terra firma, wild rumors abound, wherever there is any adequate reality for them to cling to. And as the sea surpasses the land in this matter, so the whale fishery surpasses every other sort of maritime life, in the wonderfulness and fearfulness of the rumors which sometimes circulate there. For not only are whalemen as a body unexempt from that ignorance and superstitiousness hereditary to all sailors; but of all sailors, they are by all odds the most directly brought into contact with whatever is appallingly astonishing in the sea; face to face they not only eye its greatest marvels, but, hand to jaw, give battle to them. Alone, in such remotest waters, that though you sailed a thousand miles, and passed a thousand shores, you would not come to any chiselled hearthstone, or aught hospitable beneath that part of the sun; in such latitudes and longitudes, pursuing too such a calling as he does, the whaleman is wrapped by influences all tending to make his fancy pregnant with many a mighty birth.

No wonder, then, that ever gathering volume from the mere transit over the widest watery spaces, the outblown rumors of the White Whale did in the end incorporate with themselves all manner of morbid hints, and half-formed foetal suggestions of supernatural agencies, which eventually invested Moby Dick with new terrors unborrowed from anything that visibly appears. So that in many cases such a panic did he finally strike, that few who by those rumors, at least, had heard of the White

Whale, few of those hunters were willing to encounter the perils of his jaw.

But there were still other and more vital practical influences at work. Not even at the present day has the original prestige of the Sperm Whale, as fearfully distinguished from all other species of the leviathan, died out of the minds of the whalemen as a body. There are those this day among them, who, though intelligent and courageous enough in offering battle to the Greenland or Right whale, would perhaps – either from professional inexperience, or incompetency, or timidity, decline a contest with the Sperm Whale; at any rate, there are plenty of whalemen, especially among those whaling nations not sailing under the American flag, who have never hostilely encountered the Sperm Whale, but whose sole knowledge of the leviathan is restricted to the ignoble monster primitively pursued in the North; seated on their hatches, these men will hearken with a childish fire-side interest and awe, to the wild, strange tales of Southern whaling. Nor is the pre-eminent tremendousness of the great Sperm Whale anywhere more feelingly comprehended, than on board of those prows which stem him.

And as if the now tested reality of his might had in former legendary times thrown its shadow before it; we find some book naturalists – Olassen and Povelson – declaring the Sperm Whale not only to be a consternation to every other creature in the sea, but also to be so incredibly ferocious as continually to be athirst for human blood. Nor even down to so late a time as Cuvier's, were these or almost similar impressions effaced. For in his Natural History, the Baron himself affirms that at sight of the Sperm Whale, all fish (sharks included) are "struck with the most lively terrors," and "often in the precipitancy of their flight dash themselves against the rocks with such violence as to cause instantaneous death." And however the general experiences in the fishery may amend such reports as these; yet in their full terribleness, even to the bloodthirsty item of Povelson, the superstitious belief in them is, in some vicissitudes of their vocation, revived in the minds of the hunters.

So that overawed by the rumors and portents concerning him, not a few of the fishermen recalled, in reference to Moby Dick, the earlier days of the Sperm Whale fishery, when it was oftentimes hard to induce long practised Right whalemen to embark in the perils of this new and daring warfare; such men protesting that although other leviathans might be hopefully pursued, yet to chase and point lance at such an apparition as the Sperm Whale was not for mortal man. That to attempt it, would be inevitably to be torn into a quick eternity. On this head, there are some remarkable documents that may be consulted.

Nevertheless, some there were, who even in the face of these things were ready to give chase to Moby Dick; and a still greater number who, chancing only to hear of him distantly and vaguely, without the specific details of any certain calamity, and without superstitious accompaniments, were sufficiently hardy not to flee from the battle if offered.

One of the wild suggestings referred to, as at last coming to be linked with the White Whale in the minds of the superstitiously inclined, was the unearthly conceit that Moby Dick was ubiquitous; that he had actually been encountered in opposite latitudes at one and the same instant of time.

Nor, credulous as such minds must have been, was this conceit altogether without some faint show of superstitious probability. For as the secrets of the currents in the sea have never yet been divulged, even to the most erudite research; so the hidden ways of the Sperm Whale when beneath the surface remain, in great part, unaccountable to his pursuers; and from time to time have originated the most curious and contradictory speculations regarding them, especially concerning the mystic modes whereby, after sounding to a great depth, he transports himself with such vast swiftness to the most widely distant points.

It is a thing well known to both American and English whaleships, and also a thing placed upon authoritative record years ago by Scoresby, that some whales have been captured far north in the Pacific, in whose bodies have been found the barbs of harpoons darted in the Greenland seas. Nor is it to be gainsaid, that in some of these instances it has been declared that the interval of time between the two assaults could not have exceeded very many days. Hence, by inference, it has been believed by some whalemen, that the Nor' West Passage, so long a problem to man, was never a problem to the whale. So that here, in the real living experience of living men, the prodigies related in old times of the inland Strello mountain in Portugal (near whose top there was said to be a lake in which the wrecks of ships floated up to the surface), and that still more wonderful story of the Arethusa fountain near Syracuse (whose waters were believed to have come from the Holy Land by an underground passage), these fabulous narrations are almost fully equalled by the realities of the whaleman.

Forced into familiarity, then, with such prodigies as these; and knowing that after repeated, intrepid assaults, the White Whale had escaped alive; it cannot be much matter of surprise that some whalemen should go still further in their superstitions; declaring Moby Dick not only ubiquitous, but immortal (for immortality is but ubiquity in time); that though groves of spears should be planted in his flanks, he would still swim unharmed; or if needed he should ever be made to spout thick blood, such a sight would be but a ghastly deception; for again in unensanguined billows hundreds of leagues away, his unsullied jet would once more be seen.

But even stripped of these supernatural surmisings, there was enough in the earthly make and incontestable character of the monster to strike the imagination with unwonted power. For, it was not so much his uncommon bulk that so much distinguished him from other Sperm Whales, but, as was elsewhere thrown out – a peculiar snow-white wrinkled forehead, and a high, pyramidical white hump. These were his prominent features; the tokens whereby, even in the limitless, uncharted seas, he revealed his identity, at a long distance, to those who knew him.

The rest of his body was so streaked, and spotted, and marbled with the same shrouded hue, that, in the end, he had gained his distinctive appellation of the White Whale; a name, indeed, literally justified by his vivid aspect, when seen gliding at high noon through a dark blue sea, leaving a milky-way wake of creamy foam, all spangled with golden gleamings.

Nor was it his unwonted magnitude, nor his remarkable hue, nor yet his deformed lower jaw, that so much invested the whale with natural terror, as that unexampled, intelligent malignity which, according to specific accounts, he had over and over again evinced in his assaults. More than all, his treacherous retreats struck more of dismay than perhaps aught else. For, when swimming before his exulting pursuers, with every apparent symptom of alarm, he had several times been known to turn round suddenly, and, bearing down upon them, either stave their boats to splinters, or drive them back in consternation to their ship.

Already several fatalities had attended his chase. But though similar disasters, however little bruited ashore, were by no means unusual in the fishery; yet, in most instances, such seemed the White Whale's infernal aforethought of ferocity, that every dismembering or death that he caused, was not wholly regarded as having been inflicted by an unintelligent agent.

Judge, then, to what pitches of inflamed, distracted fury the minds of his more desperate hunters were impelled, when amid the chips of chewed boats, and the sinking limbs of torn comrades, they swam out of the white curds of the whale's direful wrath into the serene, exasperating sunlight, that smiled on, as if at a birth or a bridal.

His three boats stove around him, and oars and men both whirling in the eddies; one captain, seizing the line-knife from his broken prow, had dashed at the whale, as an Arkansas duellist at his foe, blindly seeking with a six inch blade to reach the fathom-deep life of the whale. The captain was Ahab. And then it was, that suddenly sweeping his sickle-shaped lower jaw beneath him, Moby Dick had reaped away Ahab's leg, as a mower a blade of grass in the field. No turbaned Turk, no hired Venetian or Malay, could have smote him with more seeming malice. Small reason was there to doubt, then, that ever since that almost fatal encounter, Ahab had cherished a wild vindictiveness against the whale, all the more fell for that in his frantic morbidness he at last came to identify with him, not only all his bodily woes, but all his intellectual and spiritual exasperations. The White Whale swam before him as the monomaniac incarnation of all those malicious agencies which some deep men feel eating in them, till they are left living on with half a heart and half a lung. That intangible malignity which has been from the beginning; to whose dominion even the modern Christians ascribe one-half of the world; which the ancient Ophites of the east reverenced in their statue devil; – Ahab did not fall down and worship it like them; but deliriously transferring its idea to the abhorred white whale, he pitted himself, all mutilated, against it. All that most maddens and torments; all that stirs up the lees of things; all truth with malice in it; all that cracks the sinews and cakes the brain; all the subtle demonisms of life and thought; all evil, to crazy Ahab, were visibly personified, and made practically assailable in Moby Dick. He piled upon the whale's white hump the sum of all the general rage and hate felt by his whole race from Adam down; and then, as if his chest had been a mortar, he burst his hot heat's shell upon it.

It is not probable that this monomania in him took its instant rise at the precise time of his bodily dismemberment. Then, in darting at the monster, knife in hand, he had but given loose to a sudden, passionate, corporal animosity; and when he received the stroke that tore him, he probably but felt the agonizing bodily laceration, but nothing more. Yet, when by this collision forced to turn towards home, and for long months of days and weeks, Ahab and anguish lay stretched together in one hammock, rounding in mid winter that dreary, howling Patagonian Cape; then it was, that his torn body and gashed soul bled into one another; and so interfusing, made him mad. That it was only then, on the homeward voyage, after the encounter, that the final monomania seized him, seems all but certain from the fact that, at intervals during the passage, he was a raving lunatic; and, though unlimbed of a leg, yet such vital strength yet lurked in his Egyptian chest, and was moreover intensified by his delirium, that his mates were forced to lace him fast, even there, as he sailed, raving in his hammock. In a strait-jacket, he swung to the mad rockings of the gales. And, when running into more sufferable latitudes, the ship, with mild stun'sails spread, floated across the tranquil tropics, and, to all appearances, the old man's delirium seemed left behind him with the Cape Horn swells, and he came forth from his dark den into the blessed light and air; even then, when he bore that firm, collected front, however pale, and issued his calm orders once again; and his mates thanked God and direful madness was now gone; even then, Ahab, in his hidden self, raved on. Human madness is oftentimes a cunning and most feline thing. When you think it fled, it may have but become tranfigured into some still subtler form. Ahab's full lunacy subsided not, but deepeningly contracted; like the unabated Hudson, when that noble Northman flows narrowly, but unfathomably through the Highland gorge. But, as in his narrow-flowing monomania, not one jot of Ahab's broad madness had been left behind; so in that broad madness, not one jot of his great natural intellect had perished. That before living agent, now became the living instrument. If such a furious trope may stand, his special lunacy stormed his general sanity, and carried it, and turned all its concentred cannon upon its own mad mark; so that far from having lost his strength, Ahab, to that one end, did now possess a thousand fold more potency than ever he had sanely brought to bear upon any one reasonable object.

This is much; yet Ahab's larger, darker, deeper part remains unhinted. But vain to popularize profundities, and all truth is profound. Winding far down from within the very heart of this spiked Hotel de Cluny[2] where we here stand – however grand and wonderful, now quit it; – and take your way, ye nobler, sadder souls, to those vast Roman halls of Thermes; where far beneath the fantastic towers of man's upper earth, his root of grandeur, his whole awful essence sits in bearded state; an antique buried beneath antiquities, and throned on torsoes! So with a broken throne, the great gods mock that captive king; so like a Caryatid, he patient sits, upholding on his frozen brow the piled entablatures of ages. Wind ye down there, ye prouder, sadder souls! question that proud, sad king! A family likeness! aye, he did beget ye, ye young exiled royalties; and from your grim sire only will the old State-secret come.

Now, in his heart, Ahab had some glimpse of this, namely: all my means are sane, my motive and my object mad. Yet without power to kill, or change, or shun the fact; he likewise knew that to mankind he did long dissemble; in some sort, did still. But that thing of his dissembling was only subject to his perceptibility, not to his will determinate. Nevertheless, so well did he succeed in that dissembling, that when with ivory leg he stepped ashore at last, no Nantucketer thought him otherwise than but naturally grieved, and that to the quick, with the terrible casualty which had overtaken him.

---

[2] A late medieval building in Paris (also called Palais des Thermes beneath which were the ruins of ancient Roman baths *(thermae)*).

The report of his undeniable delirium at sea was likewise popularly ascribed to a kindred cause. And so too, all the added moodiness which always afterwards, to the very day of sailing in the Pequod on the present voyage, sat brooding on his brow. Nor is it so very unlikely, that far from distrusting his fitness for another whaling voyage, on account of such dark symptoms, the calculating people of that prudent isle were inclined to harbor the conceit, that for those very reasons he was all the better qualified and set on edge, for a pursuit so full of rage and wildness as the bloody hunt of whales. Gnawed within and scorched without, with the infixed, unrelenting fangs of some incurable idea; such an one, could he be found, would seem the very man to dart his iron and lift his lance against the most appalling of all brutes. Or, if for any reason thought to be corporeally incapacitated for that, yet such an one would seem superlatively competent to cheer and howl on his underlings to the attack. But be all this as it may, certain it is, that with the mad secret of his unabated rage bolted up and keyed in him, Ahab had purposely sailed upon the present voyage with the one only and all-engrossing object of hunting the White Whale. Had any of his old acquaintances on shore but half dreamed of what was lurking in him then, how soon would their aghast and righteous souls have wrenched the ship from such a fiendish man! They were bent on profitable cruises, the profit to be counted down in dollars from the mint. He was intent on an audacious, immitigable, and supernatural revenge.

Here, then, was this grey-headed, ungodly old man, chasing with curses a Job's whale round the world, at the head of a crew, too, chiefly made up of mongrel renegades, and castaways, and cannibals – morally enfeebled also, by the incompetence of mere unaided virtue of right-mindedness in Starbuck, the invulnerable jollity of indifference and recklessness in Stubb, and the pervading mediocrity in Flask. Such a crew, so officered, seemed specially picked and packed by some infernal fatality to help him to his monomaniac revenge. How it was that they so aboundingly responded to the old man's ire – by what evil magic their souls were possessed, that at times his hate seemed almost theirs; the White Whale as much their insufferable foe as his; how all this came to be – what the White Whale was to them, or how to their unconscious understandings, also, in some dim, unsuspected way, he might have seemed the gliding great demon of the seas of life, – all this to explain, would be to dive deeper than Ishmael can go. The subterranean miner that works in us all, how can one tell whither leads his shaft by the ever shifting, muffled sound of his pick? Who does not feel the irresistible arm drag? What skiff in tow of a seventy-four can stand still? For one, I gave myself up to the

abandonment of the time and the place; but while yet all arush to encounter the whale, could see naught in that brute but the deadliest ill.

Ahab's Boat and Crew. Fedallah (Chapter 50)

Among whale-wise people it has often been argued whether, considering
the paramount importance of his life to the success of the voyage, it
is right for a whaling captain to jeopardize that life in the active perils of
the chase. So Tamerlane's soldiers often argued with tears in their eyes,
whether that invaluable life of his ought to be carried into the thickest of
the fight.

But with Ahab the question assumed a modified aspect. Considering
that with two legs man is but a hobbling wight in all times of danger; considering that the pursuit of whales is always under great and extraordinary
difficulties; that every individual moment, indeed, then comprises a peril;
under these circumstances is it wise for any maimed man to enter a whaleboat in the hunt? As a general thing, the joint-owners of the Pequod must
have plainly thought not.

Ahab well knew that although his friends at home would think little of
his entering a boat in certain comparatively harmless vicissitudes of the
chase, for the sake of being near the scene of action and giving his orders
in person, yet for Captain Ahab to have a boat actually apportioned to
him as a regular headsman in the hunt – above all for Captain Ahab to be
supplied with five extra men, as that same boat's crew, he well knew that
such generous conceits never entered the heads of the owners of the Pequod. Therefore he had not solicited a boat's crew from them, nor had he
in any way hinted his desires on that head. Nevertheless he had taken private measures of his own touching all that matter. Until Archy's published
discovery, the sailors had little foreseen it, though to be sure when, after
being a little while out of port, all hands had concluded the customary
business of fitting the whaleboats for service; when some time after this
Ahab was now and then found bestirring himself in the matter of making
thole-pins with his own hands for what was thought to be one of the spare
boats, and even solicitously cutting the small wooden skewers, which
when the line is running out are pinned over the groove in the bow: when
all this was observed in him, and particularly his solicitude in having an
extra coat of sheathing in the bottom of the boat, as if to make it better
withstand the pointed pressure of his ivory limb: and also the anxiety he
evinced in exactly shaping the thigh board, or clumsy cleat, as it is sometimes called, the horizontal piece in the boat's bow for bracing the knee
against in darting or stabbing at the whale; when it was observed how

often he stood up in that boat with his solitary knee fixed in the semi-cir-
cular depression in the cleat, and with the carpenter's chisel gouged out a
little here and straightened it a little there; all these things, I say, have awa-
kened much interest and curiosity at the time. But almost everybody supposed that this particular preparative heedfulness in Ahab must only be
with a view to the ultimate chase of Moby Dick; for he had already revealed his intention to hunt that mortal monster in person. But such a
supposition did by no means involve the remotest suspicion as to any
boat's crew being assigned to that boat.

Now, with the subordinate phantoms, what wonder remained soon
waned away; for in a whaler wonders soon wane. Besides, now and then
such unaccountable odds and ends of strange nations come up from the
unknown nooks and ash-holes of the earth to man these floating outlaws
of whalers; and the ships themselves often pick up such queer castaway
creatures found tossing about the open sea on planks, bits of wreck, oars,
whaleboats, canoes, blown-off Japanese junks, and what not; that Beelzebub himself might climb up the side and step down into the cabin to chat
with the captain, and it would not create any unsubduable excitement in
the forecastle.

But be all this as it may, certain it is that while the subordinate phantoms soon found their place among the crew, though still as it were somehow distinct from them, yet that hair-turbaned Fadallah remained a
muffled mystery to the last. Whence he came in a mannerly world like
this, by what sort of unaccountable tie he soon evinced himself to be
linked with Ahab's peculiar fortunes; nay, so far as to have some sort of a
half-hinted influence; Heaven knows, but it might have been even authority over him; all this none knew. But one cannot sustain an indifferent
air concerning Fedallah. He was such a creature as civilized, domestic
people in the temperate zone only see in their dreams, and that but dimly;
but the like of whom now and then glide among the unchanging Asiatic
communities, especially the Oriental isles to the east of the continent –
those insulated, immemorial, unalterable countries, which even in these
modern days still preserve much of the ghostly aboriginalness of earth's
primal generations, when the memory of the first man was a distinct recollection, and all men his descendants, unknowing whence he came, eyed
each other as real phantoms, and asked of the sun and the moon why they
were created and to what end; when though, according to Genesis, the angels indeed consorted with the daughters of men, the devils also, add the
uncanonical Rabbins, indulged in mundane amours.

The Try-Works (Chapter 96)

Besides her hoisted boats, an American whaler is outwardly distinguished by her try-works. She presents the curious anomaly of the most solid masonry joining with oak and hemp in constituting the completed ship. It is as if from the open field a brick-kiln were transported to her planks.

The try-works are planted between the foremost and main-mast, the most roomy part of the deck. The timbers beneath are of a peculiar strength, fitted to sustain the weight of an almost solid mass of brick and mortar, some ten feet by eight square, and five in height. The foundation does not penetrate the deck, but the masonry is firmly secured to the surface by ponderous knees of iron bracing it on all sides, and screwing it down to the timbers. On the flanks it is cased with wood, and at top completely covered by a large, sloping, battened hatchway. Removing this hatch we expose the great try-pots, two in number, and each of several barrels' capacity. When not in use, they are kept remarkably clean. Sometimes they are polished with soapstone and sand, till they shine within like silver punch-bowls. During the nightwatches some cynical old sailors will crawl into them and coil themselves away there for a nap. While employed in polishing them – one man in each pot, side by side – many confidential communications are carried on, over the iron lips. It is a place also for profound mathematical meditation. It was in the left hand try-pot of the Pequod, with the soapstone diligently circling round me, that I was first indirectly struck by the remarkable fact, that in geometry all bodies gliding along the cycloid, my soapstone for example, will descend from any point in precisely the same time.

Removing the fire-board from the front of the try-works, the bare masonry of that side is exposed, penetrated by the two iron mouths of the furnaces, directly underneath the pots. These mouths are fitted with heavy doors of iron. The intense heat of the fire is prevented from communicating itself to the deck, by means of a shallow reservoir extending under the entire inclosed surface of the works. By a tunnel inserted at the rear, this reservoir is kept replenished with water as fast as it evaporates. There are no external chimneys; they open direct from the rear wall. And here let us go back for a moment.

It was about nine o'clock at night that the Pequod's try-works were first started on this present voyage. It belonged to Stubb to oversee the business.

"All ready there? Off hatch, then, and start her. You cook, fire the works." This was an easy thing, for the carpenter had been thrusting his shavings into the furnace throughout the passage. Here be it said that in a whaling voyage the first fire in the try-works has to be fed for a time with wood. After that no wood is used, except as a means of quick ignition to the staple fuel. In a word, after being tried out, the crisp, shrivelled blubber, now called scraps or fritters, still contains considerable of its unctuous properties. These fritters feed the flames. Like a plethoric burning martyr, or a self-consuming misanthrope, once ignited, the whale supplies his own fuel and burns by his own body. Would that he consumed his own smoke? for his smoke is horrible to inhale, and inhale it you must, and not only that, but you must live in it for the time. It has an unspeakable, wild, Hindoo odor about it, such as may lurk in the vacinity of funereal pyres. It smells like the left wing of the day of judgment; it is an argument for the pit.

By midnight the works were in full operation. We were clear from the carcase; sail had been made; the wind was freshening; the wild ocean darkness was intense. But that darkness was licked up by the fierce flames, which at intervals forked forth from the sooty flues, and illuminated every lofty rope in the rigging, as with the famed Greek fire. The burning ship drove on, as if remorselessly commissioned to some vengeful deed. So the pitch and sulphur-freighted brigs of the bold Hydriote, Canaris,[3] issuing from their midnight harbors, with broad sheets of flame for sails, bore down upon the Turkish frigates, and folded them in conflagrations.

The hatch, removed from the top of the works, now afforded a wide hearth in front of them. Standing on this were the Tartarean shapes of the pagan harpooneers, always the whale-ship's stokers. With huge pronged poles they pitched hissing masses of blubber into the scalding pots, or stirred up the fires beneath, till the snaky flames darted, curling, out of the doors to catch them by the feet. The smoke rolled away in sullen heaps. To every pitch of the ship there was a pitch of the boiling oil, which seemed all eagerness to leap into their faces. Opposite the mouth of the work, on the further side of the wide wooden hearth, was the windlass. This served for a sea-sofa. Here lounged the watch, when not otherwise employed, looking into the red heat of the fire, till their eyes felt scorched in their heads. Their tawny features, now all begrimed with smoke and sweat, their matted beards, and the contrasting barbaric brilliancy of their teeth, all these were strangely revealed in the capricious emblazonings of the works. As they narrated to each other their unholy adventures, their tales of terror told in words of mirth; as their uncivilized laughter forked upwards out of them, like the flames from the furnace; as to and fro, in their front, the harpooneers wildly gesticulated with their

---

[3] The Greek hero who developed this fire-ship strategy in 1822, during the Greek war for independence.

huge pronged forks and dipper; as the wind howled on, and the sea leaped, and the ship groaned and dived, and yet steadfastly shot her red hell further and further into the blackness of the sea and the night, and scornfully champed the white bone in her mouth, and viciously spat round her on all sides; then the rushing Pequod, freighted with savages, and laden with fire, and burning a corpse, and plunging into that blackness of darkness, seemed the material counterpart of her monomaniac commander's soul.

So seemed it to me, as I stood at her helm, and for long hours silently guided the way for this fire-ship on the sea. Wrapped, for that interval, in darkness myself, I but the better saw the redness, the madness, the ghastliness of others. The continual sight of the fiend shapes before me, capering half in smoke and half in fire, these at last begat kindred visions in my soul, so soon as I began to yield to that unaccountable drowsiness which ever would come over me at a midnight helm.

But that night, in particular, a strange (and ever since inexplicable) thing occurred to me. Starting from a brief standing sleep, I was horribly conscious of something fatally wrong. The jaw-bone tiller smote my side, which leaned against it; in my ears was the low hum of sails, just beginning to shake in the wind; I thought my eyes were open; I was half conscious of putting my fingers to the lids and mechanically stretching them still further apart. But, spite of all this, I could see no compass before me to steer by; though it seemed but a minute since I had been watching the card, by the steadly binnacle lamp illuminating it. Nothing seemed before me but a jet gloom, now and then made ghastly by flashes of redness. Uppermost was the impression, that whatever swift, rushing thing I stood on was not so much bound to any haven ahead as rushing from all havens astern. A stark, bewildered feeling, as of death, came over me. Convulsively my hands grasped the tiller, but with the crazy conceit that the tiller was, somehow, in some enchanted way, inverted. My God! what is the matter with me? thought I. Lo! in my brief sleep I had turned myself about, and was fronting the ship's stern, with my back to her prow and the compass. In an instant I faced back, just in time to prevent the vessel from flying up into the wind, and very probably capsizing her. How glad and how greatful the relief from this unnatural hallucination of the night, and the fatal contingency of being brought by the lee!

Look not too long in the face of the fire, O man! Never dream with thy hand in the helm! Turn not thy back to the compass; accept the first hint of the hitching tiller; believe not the artificial fire, when its redness makes all things look ghastly. To-morrow, in the natural sun, the skies will be bright; those who glared like devils in the forking flames, the morn will show in far other, at least gentler, relief; the glorious, golden, glad sun, the only true lamp – all others but liars!

Nevertheless the sun hides not Virginia's Dismal Swamp, nor Rome's accursed Campagna, nor wide Sahara, nor all the millions of miles of deserts and of griefs beneath the moon. The sun hides not the ocean, which is the dark side of the earth, and which is two thirds of this earth. So, therefore, the mortal man who hath more of joy than sorrow in him, that mortal man cannot be true – not true, or undeveloped. With books the same. The truest of all men was the Man of Sorrows, and the truest of all books is Solomon's, and Ecclesiastes is the fine hammered steel of woe. "All is vanity." ALL. This wilful world hath not got hold of unchristian Solomon's wisdom yet. But he who dodges hospitals and jails, and walks fast crossing grave-yards, and would rather talk of operas then hell; calls Cowper, Young, Pascal, Rousseau, poor devils all of sick men; and throughout a care-free lifetime swears by Rabelais as passing wise, and therefore jolly; – not that man is fitted to sit down on tomb-stones, and break the green damp mould with unfathomably wondrous Solomon.

But even Solomon, he says, "the man that wandereth out of the way of understanding shall remain" (i.e. even while living) "in the congregation of the dead." Give not thyself up, then, to fire, lest it invert thee, deaden thee; as for the time it did me. There is a wisdom that is woe; but there is a woe that is madness. And there is a Catskill eagle in some souls that can alike dive down into the blackest gorges, and soar out of them again and become invisible in the sunny spaces. And even if he for ever flies within the gorge, that gorge is in the mountains; so that even in his lowest swoop the mountain eagle is still higher than other birds upon the plain, even though they soar.

The Forge (Chapter 113)

With matted beard, and swathed in a bristling shark-skin apron, about midday, Perth was standing between his forge and anvil, the latter placed upon an iron-wood log, with one hand holding a pike-head in the coals, and with the other at his forge's lungs, when Captain Ahab came along, carrying in his hand a small rusty-looking leathern bag. While yet a little distance from the forge, moody Ahab paused; till at last, Perth, withdrawing his iron from the fire, began hammering it upon the anvil – the red mass sending off the sparks in thick hovering flights, some of which flew close to Ahab.

"Are these thy Mother Carey's chicken, Perth? they are always flying in thy wake; birds of good omen, too, but not to all; – look here, they burn; but thou – thou liv'st among them without a scorch."

"Because I am scorched all over, Captain Ahab," answered Perth, resting for a moment on his hammer; "I am past scorching; not easily can'st thou scorch a scar."

"Well, well; no more. Thy shrunk voice sounds too calmly, sanely woeful to me. In no Paradise myself, I am impatient of all misery in others that is not mad. Thou should'st go mad, blacksmith; say, why dost thou not go mad? How can'st thou endure without being mad? Do the heavens yet hate thee, that thou can'st not go mad? – What wert thou making there?"

"Welding an old pike-head, sir; there were seams and dents in it."

"And can'st thou make it all smooth again, blacksmith, after such hard usage as it had?"

"I think so, sir."

"And I suppose thou can'st smooth almost any seams and dents; never mind how hard the metal, blacksmith?"

"Aye, sir, I think I can; all seams and dents but one."

"Look ye here, then," cried Ahab, passionately advancing, and leaning with both hands on Perth's shoulder; "look ye here – *here* – can ye smooth out a seam like this, blacksmith," sweeping one hand across his ribbed brow; "if thou could'st, blacksmith, glad enough would I lay my head upon thy anvil, and feel thy heaviest hammer between my eyes. Answer! Can'st thou smooth this seam?"

"Oh! that is the one, sir! Said I not all seams and dents but one?"

"Aye, blacksmith, it is the one; aye, man, it is unsmoothable; for though thou only see'st it here in my flesh, it has worked down into the bone of my skull – *that* is all wrinkles! But, away with child's play; no more gaffs and pikes to-day. Look ye here!" jingling the leathern bag as if it were full of gold coins. "I, too, want a harpoon made; one that a thousand yoke of fiends could not part, Perth; something that will stick in a whale like his own fine-bone. There's the stuff," flinging the pouch upon the anvil. "Look ye, blacksmith, these are the gathered nail-stubs of the steel shoes of racing horses."

"Horse-shoe stubs, sir? Why, Captain Ahab, thou hast here, then, the best and stubbornest stuff we blacksmiths ever work."

"I know it, old man; these stubs will weld together like glue from the melted bones of murderers. Quick! forge me the harpoon. And forge me first, twelve rods for its shank; then wind, and twist, and hammer these twelve together like the yarn and strands of a tow-line. Quick! I'll blow the fire."

When at last the twelve rods were made, Ahab tried them, one by one, by spiralling them, with his own hand, round a long, heavy iron bolt, "A flaw!" rejected the last one. "Work that over again, Perth."

This done, Perth was about to begin welding the twelve into one, when Ahab stayed his hand, and said he would weld his own iron. As, then, with regular, gasping hems, he hammered on the anvil, Perth passing to him the glowing rods, one after the other, and the hard pressed forge shooting up its intense staight flame, the Parsee passed silently, and bowing over his head towards the fire, seemed invoking some curse or some blessing on the toil. But, as Ahab looked up, he slid aside.

"What's that bunch of lucifers dodging about there for?" muttered Stubb, looking on from the forecastle. "That Parsee smells fire like a fusee; and smells of it himself, like a hot musket's powder-pan."

At last the shank, in one complete rod, received its final heat; and as Perth, to temper it, plunged it all hissing into the cask of water near by, the scalding steam shot up into Ahab's bent face.

"Would'st thou brand me, Perth?" wincing for a moment with the pain; "have I been but forging my own branding-iron, then?"

"Pray God, not that; yet I fear something, Captain Ahab. Is not this harpoon for the White Whale?"

"For the white fiend! But now for the barbs; thou must make them thyself, man. Here are my razors – the best of steel; here, and make the barbs sharp as the needle-sleet of the Icy Sea."

For a moment, the old blacksmith eyed the razors as though he would fain not use them.

"Take them, man, I have no need for them; for I now neither shave, sup, nor pray till – but here – to work!"

Fashioned at last into an arrowy shape, and welded by Perth to the shank, the steel soon pointed the end of the iron; and as the blacksmith was about giving the barbs their final heat, prior to tempering them, he cried to Ahab to place the water-cask near.

"No, no – no water for that; I want it of the true death-temper. Ahoy, there! Tashtego, Queequeg, Daggoo! What say ye, pagans! Will ye give me as much blood as will cover this barb?" holding it high up. A cluster of dark nods replied, Yes. Three punctures were made in the heathen flesh, and the White Whale's barbs were then tempered.

"Ego non baptizo te in nomine patris, sed in nomine diaboli,"[4] deliriously howled Ahab, as the malignant iron scorchingly devoured the baptismal blood.

---

[4] "... *sed in nomine diaboli!*" "I do not baptize you in the name of the Father, but in the name of the devil."

Now, mustering the spare poles from below, and selecting one of hickory, with the bark still investing it, Ahab fitted the end of the socket of the iron. A coil of new tow-line was then unwound, and some fathoms of it taken to the wildlass, and stretched to a great tension. Pressing his foot upon it, till the rope hummed like a harp-string, then eagerly bending over it, and seeing no strandings, Ahab exclaimed, "Good! and now for the seizings."

At one extremity the rope was unstranded, and the separate spread yarns were all braided and woven round the socket of the harpoon; the pole was then driven hard up into the socket; from the lower end the rope was traced half way along the pole's length, and firmly secured so, with intertwistings of twine. This done, pole, iron, and rope – like the Three Fates – remained inseparable, and Ahab moodily stalked away with the weapon; the sound of his ivory leg, and the sound of the hickory pole, both hollowly ringing along every plank. But ere he entered his cabin, a light, unnatural, half-bantering, yet most piteous sound was heard. Oh, Pip! thy wretched laugh, thy idle but unresting eye; all thy strange mummeries not unmeaningly blended with the black tragedy of the melancholy ship, and mocked it!

The Hat (Chapter 130)

And now that at the proper time and place, after so long and wide a preliminary cruise, Ahab, – all other whaling waters swept – seemed to have chased his foe into an ocean-fold, to slay him the more securely there; now, that he found himself hard by the very latitude and longitude where his tormenting wound had been inflicted; now that a vessel had been spoken which on the very day preceeding had actually encountered Moby Dick; – and now that all his successive meetings with various ships contrastingly concurred to show the demoniac indifference with which the white whale tore his hunters, whether sinning or sinned against; now it was that there lurked a something in the old man's eyes, which it was hardly sufferable for feeble souls to see. As the unsetting polar star, which through the livelong, arctic, six months' night sustains its piercing, steady, central gaze; so Ahab's purpose now fixedly gleamed down upon the constant midnight of the gloomy crew. It domineered above them so, that all their bodings, doubts, misgivings, fears, were fain to hide beneath their souls, and not sprout forth a single spear or leaf.

In this foreshadowing interval too, all humor, forced or natural, vanished. Stubb no more strove to raise a smile; Starbuck no more strove to check one. Alike, joy and sorrow, hope and fear, seemed ground to finest dust, and powdered, for the time, in the clamped mortar of Ahab's iron soul. Like machines, they dumbly moved about the deck, ever conscious that the old man's despot eye was on them.

But did you deeply scan him in his more secret confidential hours; when he thought no glance but one was on him; then you would have seen that even as Ahab's eyes so awed the crew's, the inscrutable Parsee's glance awed his; or somehow, at least, in some wild way, at times affected it. Such an added, gliding strangeness began to invest the thin Fedallah now; such ceaseless shudderings shook him; that the men looked dubious at him; half uncertain, as it seemed, whether indeed he were a mortal substance, or else a tremulous shadow cast upon the deck by some unseen being's body. And that shadow was always hovering there. For not by night, even, had Fedallah ever certainly been known to slumber, or go below. He would stand still for hours: but never sat or leaned; his wan but wonderous eyes did plainly say – We two watchmen never rest.

Nor, at any time, by night or day could the mariners now step upon the deck, unless Ahab was before them; either standing in his pivot-hole, or exactly pacing the planks between two undeviating limits, – the mainmast and the mizen; or else they saw him standing in the cabin-scuttle, – his living foot advanced upon the deck, as if to step; his hat slouched heavily over his eyes; so that however motionless he stood, however the days and nights were added on, that he had not swung in his hammock; yet hidden beneath that slouching hat, they could never tell unerringly whether, for all this, his eyes were really closed at times; or whether he was still intently scanning them; no matter, though he stood so in the scuttle for a whole hour on the stretch, and the unheeded night-damp gathered in beads of dew upon the stone-carved coat and hat. The clothes that the night had wet, the next day's sunshine dried upon him; and so, day after day, and night after night; he went no more beneath the planks; whatever he wanted from the cabin that thing he sent for.

He ate in the same open air; that is, his two only meals, – breakfast and dinner: supper he never touched; nor reaped his beard; which darkly grew all gnarled, as unearthed roots of trees blown over, which still grew idly on at naked base, though perished in the upper verdure. But though his whole life was now become one watch on deck; and though the Parsee's mystic watch was without intermission at his own; yet these two never seemed to speak – one man to the other – unless at long intervals some passing unmomentous matter made it necessary. Though such a potent spell seemed secretly to join the twain; openly, and to the awe-struck crew, they seemed pole-like asunder. If by day they chanced to speak one word; by night, dumb men were both, so far as concerned the slightest verbal interchange. At times, for longest hours, without a single hail, they stood far parted in the starlight; Ahab in his scuttle, the Parsee by the mainmast; but still fixedly gazing upon each other; as if in the Parsee Ahab saw his fore-thrown shadow, in Ahab the Parsee his abandoned substance.

And yet, somehow, did Ahab – in his own proper self, as daily, hourly, and every instant, commandingly revealed to his subordinates, – Ahab seemed an independent lord; the Parsee but his slave. Still again both seemed yoked together, and an unseen tyrant driving them: the lean shade siding the solid rib. For be this Parsee what he may, all rib and keel was solid Ahab.

At the first faintest glimmering of the dawn, his iron voice was heard from aft – "Man the mast-heads!" – and all through the day, till after sunset and after twilight, the same voice every hour, at the striking of the helmsman's bell, was heard – "What d'ye see? – sharp! sharp!"

But when three or four days had slided by, after meeting the children-seeking Rachel; and no spout had yet been seen; the monomaniac old man seemed distrustful of his crew's fidelity; at least, of nearly all except the Pagan harpooneers; he seemed to doubt, even, whether Stubb and Flask might not willingly overlook the sight he sought. But if these suspicions were really his, he sagaciously refrained from verbally expressing them, however his actions might seem to hint them.

"I will have the first sight of the whale myself," – he said. "Aye! Ahab must have the doubloon!" and with his own hands he rigged a nest of basketed bowlines; and sending a hand aloft, with a single sheaved block, to secure to the main-mast head, he received the two ends of the down-ward-reeved rope; and attaching one to his basket prepared a pin for the other end, in order to fasten it at the rail. This done, with that end yet in his hand and standing beside the pin, he looked round upon his crew, sweeping from one to the other; pausing his glance long upon Daggoo, Queequeg, Tashtego; but shunning Fedallah; and then settling his firm relying eye upon the chief mate, said, – "Take the rope, sir – I give it into thy hands, Starbuck." Then arranging his person in the basket, he gave the word for them to hoist him to his perch, Starbuck being the one who secured the rope at last; and afterwards stood near it. And thus, with one hand clinging round the royal mast, Ahab gazed abroad upon the sea for miles and miles, – ahead, astern, this side, and that, – within the wide expanded circle commanded at so great a height.

When in working with his hands at some lofty almost isolated place in the rigging, which chances to afford no foothold, the sailor at sea is hoisted upon to that spot, and sustained there by the rope; under these circumstances, its fastened end on deck is always given in strict charge to some one man who has the special watch of it. Because in such a wilderness of running rigging, whose various different relations aloft cannot always be infallibly discerned by what is seen of them at the deck; and when the deck-ends of these ropes are being every few minutes cast down from the fastenings, it would be but a natural fatality, if, unprovided with a constant watchman, the hoisted sailor should by some carelessness of the crew be cast adrift and fall all swooping to the sea. So Ahab's proceedings in this matter were not unusual; the only strange thing about them seemed to be, that Starbuck, almost the one only man who had ever ventured to oppose him and anything in the slightest degree approaching to decision – one of those too, whose faithfulness on the look-out he had seemed to doubt somewhat; – it was strange, that this was the very man he should select for his watchman; freely giving his whole life into such an otherwise distrusted person's hands.

Now, the first time Ahab was perched aloft; ere he had been there ten minutes; one of those red-billed savage sea-hawks which so often fly incommodiously close round the manned mast-heads of whalemen in these latitudes; one of these birds came wheeling and screaming round his head in a maze of untrackably swift circlings. Then it darted a thousand feet straight up into the air; then spiralized downwards, and went eddying again round his head.

But with his gazed fixed upon the dim and distant horizon, Ahab seemed not to mark this wild bird; nor, indeed, would any one else have marked it much, it being no uncommon circumstance; only now almost the last heedful eye seemed to see some sort of cunning meaning in almost every sight.

"Your hat, your hat, sir!" suddenly cried the Sicilian seaman, who being posted at the mizen-mast head, stood directly behind Ahab, though somewhat lower than his level, and with a deep gulf of air dividing them. But already the sable wing was before the old man's eyes; the long hooked bill at his head: with a scream, the black hawk darted away with his prize.

An eagle flew thrice round Tarquin's head, removing his cap to replace it, and thereupon Tanaquil, his wife, declared that Tarquin would be king of Rome. But only by the replacing of the cap was that omen accounted good. Ahab's hat was never restored; the wild hawk flew on and on with it; far in advance of the prow: and at last disappeared; while from the point of that disappearance, a minute black spot was dimly discerned, falling from that vast height into the sea.

VI Faust in the 20th and 21st Centuries

The Faust Theme in Twentieth-Century Opera

Steven R. Cerf

The myth of Faust, the savant given a chance at a new beginning, has had a singular effect on twentieth-century artists: more than merely stimulating their inventive and imaginative facilities, it has pricked their aesthetic consciences, causing them to reexamine many of their basic creative premises, almost as if they felt compelled to emulate their hero by themselves beginning anew. Thus it is not surprising that the spirit of a new beginning marks each of the four major twentieth-century operatic treatments of the Faust story. Each of the four was planned, in effect, as a "reform opera" – as much an aesthetic manifesto as a work of art – indeed, Busoni, Eisler, Pousseur, and Stravinsky, in their encounters with the Faust theme, found themselves redefining the whole concept of lyric theater. Rather than passively ignoring Romantic operatic conventions, they sought either to repudiate them decisively or to transform them past recognition. In fact, all four of their Faust projects, when unveiled were regarded as significant departures not only from the Romantic tradition, but from the contemporary mainstream as well.

Perhaps the boldest step of redefinition that these artists took was to distance themselves from Goethe's dramatic poem – in particular from the quintessentially Romantic *Faust*, Part I, which had proved so fertile a lyric source for nineteenth-century composers such as Berlioz, Gounod and Boito. Judged by conventional operatic wisdom, of course, this step must have seemed suicidal, since Goethe's *Faust* has so many of the elements that make for operatic success: a foredoomed love affair, a hero in conflict with himself, a villain of suave charm and real menace, an aura of the supernatural, and, at the end, a veritable deus ex machina providing salvation. Yet, however risky, the rejection of Goethe was essential for any composer who wished to go beyond Romanticism. Moreover, the Goethe dramatic poem, owing to its very operatic congeniality, is fatally easy for a composer to trivialize; indeed, Gounod has frequently been accused of doing so, especially in German speaking lands, where his opera is referred to – often belittlingly – as *Margarethe*, in order to distinguish it from Goethe's "more significant" *Faust*. The four composers under discussion fortunately had no temptation to fall into this trap. Departing emphatically from the previous century's treatment of the Faust story, each reappraised the myth in an innovative modernistic structure that demanded acceptance on its own terms.

In *A Dictionary of Literary Terms*, J. A. Cuddon has succinctly defined modernism as

> "a very comprehensive term applied to international tendencies and move-ments in all the creative arts since the latter end of the nineteenth century. Professor Frank Kermode has made a distinction between palaeo-modernism and neo-modernism. Palaeo-modernism refers to early manifestations of new movements concluding, perhaps, ca. 1914–1920, while neo-modernism refers to movements (like Surrealism) since that time."[1]

Without a doubt, Busoni's setting of *Doktor Faust* and Eisler's libretto for his intended *Johann Faustus*-opera, the music for which he never com-pleted, conform with Kermode's term of palaeo-modernism, whereas Pousseur's *Votre Faust* and Stravinsky's *Rake's Progress* fit under the rubric of neo-modernism or post-modernism, as it might be called today. By turning both to the centuries-old Faust puppet play and chapbook for their chief librettistic sources, Busoni and Eisler sought to reflect the kin-ship between their respective contemporary periods (1915–24; 1948) and sixteenth-century Germany, which was a new age of individual examin-ation and responsibility. Pousseur and Stravinsky, on the other hand, through their parodic and montagelike allusions to previous treatments of Faust achieved a post-modernistic multiplicity of perspective which allowed both them and their audiences a new freedom for exploration.

At first glance, it would appear that the three most famous nineteenth-century operatic treatments of Faust are very different in nature. Hector Berlioz in his *légende dramatique* of 1846, *La Damnation de Faust*, concen-trates on Faust's dreams and yearnings; Charles Gounod in his highly ac-cessible 1859 opera focuses on Marguerite as Romantic heroine and vic-tim; and Arrigo Boito in his 1868 opera, *Mefistofele*, emphasizes the satanic powers of his eponymous protagonist. The four tableaux that comprise Berlioz' work all illustrate different episodes from Faust's adventures: (1) his admiration of the soldierly life, (2) his yearning for Marguerite, (3) his courtship of her, and (4) his desperate attempt to save her. In the Gounod opera, it is Marguerite from her opening cantilena phrases to her ardent intoning of the final trio, who embodies the lyric focal point of the opera – the roles that correspond to hers in the *Damnation* and *Mefistofele* pale by comparison. And it is Mefistofele whose overwhelming presence domi-

---

[1] Cuddon (1982), p. 399.

nates the action not only in Boito's prologue and epilogue, but throughout the work.

This difference in emphases aside, the three lyric works share strikingly similar librettistic and musical concerns: (1) their libretti, more or less, follow the plot line of the first part of Goethe's *Faust* and (2) the three major roles in each respective work are assigned to singers in roughly the same vocal categories.[2]

In the "Vorspiel auf dem Theater," the clown alludes to the most human dimension of the first part of *Faust*, namely what has come to be known as the "Gretchen Tragödie." It is precisely this love interest – the romantic strand of the first part of *Faust* – that made the dramatic poem seem so "operatic" to the three above-mentioned composers and their respective librettists. As a consequence, the tenor voice was assigned to each Faust – the tenor being the most popular and youngest sounding of all male voices, having been automatically used for Romantic heroes of all descriptions. To the bass went the role of all three Mephistos – for the simple reason that it is the bass who was associated in nineteenth-century opera with the villain; in this case, the bass or the lowest vocal register being synonymous with subterranean regions and demonic motives. And it was to the soprano (or high mezzo-soprano, in the case of Berlioz) that the role of Margarete was given. Precisely because of such pat operatic conformity within the Romantic Faust canon, twentieth-century composers treating this theme felt the acute need to depart from such conventions.

In three pieces on aesthetics written at different times while at work on *Doktor Faust*, Ferruccio Busoni (1866–1924) enunciated the artistic principles that would eventually give his opera its particular modernistic character. In his "Entwurf einer neuen Ästhetik der Tonkunst" (1913), the composer described his real need to depart from the veristic tendencies in Italian opera of the last decades of the nineteenth century. Busoni believed that opera must go out of its way to include such highly stylized spectacles as those of the ceremony and of the supernatural, since these have always been recognized as music's special domain, even in spoken drama. As a non-mimetic artist, the composer wants the audience to realize that it is viewing a fictional event.

In this manner, opera as a revitalized happening can accomplish what it does best and provide a heightened state of aesthetic experience rather

---

[2] To be sure, Boito adapts portions of Part Two of *Faust* for the fourth act and the epilogue of his opera, but the major portion of *Mefistofele* revolves around *Faust*, Part One.

than ludicrously attempting to compete with the spoken drama which in fact conveys events of mimetic import.

In the verses spoken by the poet in front of the curtain toward the beginning of the opera, Busoni waxes autobiographical. After confession that he was originally drawn to the Don Juan myth, but rejected setting it to music because of the supremacy of Mozart's *Don Giovanni*, Busoni, who served both as librettist and composer for *Doktor Faust*, avows that he, unlike his nineteenth-century predecessors, chooses not to associate himself with Goethe's genius, but will hark back instead to Goethe's sixteenth-century sources. Busoni made it clear that the puppet play offered him an historical milieu which lent its protagonist a measure of artistic distance while preserving immanence. What was of prime importance for the composer was a setting, the Renaissance, that would boldly highlight the representative mythic *and* the uniquely human dimensions of his protagonist. By turning to the puppet play, Busoni has joined a tradition, hundreds of years old, without automatically being compared with Goethe.

The major librettistic differences between *Doktor Faust* and the nineteenth-century Faust operas can be found in three separate but interlocking areas: (1) Busoni's opera contains only references to the Gretchen-Episode – this love interest is replaced by the more cold-blooded courting of the Duchess of Parma, (2) Busoni's Mephistopheles, unlike his Italian and French counterparts, undergoes a significant transformation in the course of the opera, and (3) Faust's avowals, in the final scene of the work, are self-referential by nature, that is they reflect Busoni's own autobiographical concerns as an artist.

No Gretchen or Marguerite is present in *Doctor Faust*, as the drama unfolds after her episode in Faust's life has run its course. By denying Faust his Goethean love interest (after all the Gretchen episode was Goethe's contribution to the Faust myth) and replacing it with the Duchess of Parma episode, the source for which appears in the puppet play,[3] Busoni removes the humanistic patina that Faust had acquired during the Romantic Era, at the same time enhancing Faust's image as a magister obsessed by power and the supernatural. It is not by accident that the central scenes within the first tableau of the "Hauptspiel" revolve around Faust's abilities to evoke the visions of Solomon and the Queen of Sheba, Samson and Delilah, and Salome and John the Baptist – in each instance their faces appear similar to those of the Duchess and Faust (*DF* 163–74). It is in fact Faust's virtuosity in this scene, his feat or ability to gain the total af-

---

[3] Beaumont (1985 a), p. 320.

fection of the Duchess of Parma on her wedding day that Busoni emphasizes; and it is precisely this exhibition of power for power's sake in which
the magician Faust revels, a kind of empty artistic virtuosity, that will be
severely called into question by the protagonist in the concluding scene of
the opera.[4]

Busoni's Mephistopheles exerts increasingly less power over Faust as
the opera unfolds. In the first half of the work, Mephisto appears as an all-
powerful evil force. However, in the second half of the opera "as Faust
begins to comprehend the true nature of his mission, Mephisto domi-
nates no longer."[5] To be sure, he announces the death of the Duchess
of Parma while presenting Faust with their dead child (*DF* 234–35) and
conjures up Helena (*DF* 248–53) in the second tableau of the "Hauptspiel," but these actions are carried out without the dramatic force of
his earlier appearances. And Faust's insights before Helena in the same
episode are expressed only after Mephisto has departed (*DF* 258–74).
By the conclusion, as Busoni himself stated, Mephisto has left the realm
of the demonic.[6] As Helena's features appear superimposed on the figure
of Christ on the Crucifix – a direct allusion to the puppet play – Mephisto,
now a nightwatchman, stands silently as a passive bystander.[7]

The frank autobiographical allusions in the libretto of *Doktor Faust*
contribute to the modernistic self-referential nature of the work. The
transformation that Faust undergoes by the end of the opera when he re-
jects magic in the final scene of the work reflects Busoni's unswerving desire towards the end of his life to condemn virtuosity for its own sake:

> It takes Faust a long time to understand the true purpose of his strangely won
> freedom. As Busoni pointed out, the scenes of magic at the court of Parma are
> in fact 'time-wasting' and we can read into Faust's exaggeratedly sensational
> entrance and his cheap fairground tricks an elaborate allegory on the unhappy,
> empty life of a travelling virtuoso. But not until the final scene where, by
> destroying the book, Faust has already abandoned his magic, does he realize
> that his freedom can bring him beyond the power of God or the Devil.[8]

---

[4] For the thoughts contained in this paragraph as well as a number of other ideas
throughout this article, I am profoundly indebted to my former Bowdoin College colleague, Benjamin Folkman, now a contributing program annotator of
the New York Philharmonic Orchestra.

[5] Beaumont (1985 a), p. 321.

[6] Letter of Ferruccio Busoni to Gerda Busoni, March 31, 1915, in: *Briefe an seine
Frau* (1935), pp. 319–20.

[7] Beaumont (1985 a), p. 322.

[8] Ibid., pp. 322–23.

It is then in the realm of the future that both Busoni and his Faust seek that independent artistic will which will allow them to create unencumbered by the constraints of the past.

Busoni was without a doubt the greatest virtuoso pianist of his day. He was able to perform works at any speed and both his control of dynamics and his pedaling were unique. Because of his own wizardry, it is understandable that he would be drawn to the magical powers of Faust for his final and most ambitious work.[9] Yet, it was the emptiness of pyrotechnical brilliance for its own sake that Busoni rejected both in his own life and in his adaptation of Faust.

Two modernistic musical aspects of Busoni's *Faust*-opera are the unique vocal categories the composer assigned his three leads and the disparate musical forms and structures of varying styles and lengths he employed. By assigning Faust to a "Heldenbariton" – his range reminds the listener of that of Wagner's Wotan – Busoni underlies the philosophical-heroic qualities of his protagonist. Much of Faust's orchestrally accompanied recitative phrasing called for throughout the opera is easily understood because of the comprehensible middle vocal range employed. Mephisto is cast not as a bass, but as a tenor, and a very high and piercing one at that: his astonishing entrance as the sixth evil spirit, which takes him to a high C, immediately reflects his nasty, yet penetratingly insinuating manner (*DF* 58–66): his extremely high tessitura throughout reflects the vast unreality he represents.

At first glance the disparate types of scenes containing as they do purely orchestral music, or individual arias and monologues, or choral passages, or ensembles sung by varying constellations of soloists – all of disproportionate length – seem to be fragmentary and unbalanced. Nor is there a leitmotivic structural system present in the score that would unite musical themes in a post-Wagnerian manner. No, the unifying musical theme – it becomes clear from Antony Beaumont's exhaustive analysis of the opera – comes, as does the story line of the work, in part from Busoni's own life, in this case from his own musical œuvre.[10] By consistently incorporating a variety of his own previous musical compositions, both long and short, older and newer, etc. into the score of *Doktor Faust*, Busoni left no doubt as to the self-referential nature of his final and most ambitious stage work. It is, in fact, Busoni himself who is the quester hero, Faust, in search of infinitely new realms of artistic accomplishment.

9 Luening (1980), pp. 168–69.

10 Beaumont (1985 a), pp. 308–54.

Although Hanns Eisler (1898–1962) completed his own libretto for *Johann Faustus*, because of political pressure he was able to set little of the text to music. Nonetheless, the significance of his undertaking should briefly be considered. Though his political and social concerns were different from Busoni's aesthetic interest, both composer-librettists shared that single-minded modernistic creed, a belief in a radical break from nineteenth-century operatic convention. As in Busoni's opera, so in *Johann Faustus*, the romantic emphasis of nineteenth-century opera is replaced by the pivotal intellectual and emotional transformation undergone exclusively by the title hero.

In 1948 Eisler read Thomas Mann's novel, *Doktor Faustus*, which had just appeared, and was so impressed by Mann's modern-day treatment of the Faust chapbook that he too turned to this sixteenth-century source.[11] Eisler's Faustus betrays his peasant roots, because of his own materialistic obsessions, but, at last gains insight into his obligation to maintain an acute sense of social responsibility. Like Mann's fictional composer, Adrian Leverkühn,[12] Eisler's Faustus confesses that he had sacrificed his own humanity – to devasting end results – because of his selfish goals.

The political pressures placed on Eisler by the East German Communist Party prevented him from continuing to set his libretto to music. It was the Party Secretary himself, Walter Ulbricht, who personally levelled a public attack on Eisler's project in 1953; it seems such figures from Classical German literature as Goethe's Faust were to be set up by the Party as exemplars – whereas Eisler's Faust was too human, too full of foibles.[13] As a result, Eisler was forced to suspend plans to set his text to music. However, today Eisler's libretto stands intact, sans music to be sure, but as a total twentieth-century librettistic adaptation with its own vitality, and in turn, integrity.

The full title of the Michael Butor (*1926)/Henri Pousseur (*1929) collaboration, *Votre Faust, fantasie variable, genre opéra*, immediately conjures up the dominant neo-modernistic or post-modernistic attributes of both the opera's libretto and its score. Unlike Busoni and Eisler, Butor and Pousseur no longer are single-minded in their attitude of departing from eighteenth and nineteenth-century Faust treatments. Although in one respect they show an auto-referentiality akin to that of their twentieth-century predecessors – their Faust is after all a kind of Everyman composer – both librettist and composer seek to go outside themselves exploiting the

---

[11] Schebera (1981), p. 154.

[12] Mann (1974), pp. 658–66.

[13] Maue (1981), pp. 60–78.

pluralism of the Faust theme throughout its four-hundred-year existence. In so doing, they frame their unique contribution within an integrated encyclopedic fabric of allusion.

By entitling their work *Votre Faust*, Butor and Pousseur stress the accessible qualities of their protagonist, while actively encouraging the transferral of the Faust myth from the private domain of the exclusive artist to the public arena of the audience's collectivity. In this variable fantasy, it is the audience, not the authors, who decide on the outcome of crucial scenes. By insisting that the audience vote, the librettist and composer are in effect taking as their subject the heterogeneity of the composite tradition in which they are working.[14]

In Butor's libretto, the main character does not possess either the magistral distance of Busoni's Faust or the potential to lead within society as Eisler's Johann Faustus. Instead, he becomes entangled in an all too human set of events that a contemporary audience not only can identify with, but must decide the outcome of:

> *Votre Faust* has six main characters, Henri the composer, the Director who asks Henri to write a Faust and offers to support him while he does so, no matter how long the project might take, Maggy, Henri's girl friend, Greta her sister, the Opera singer and Richard, Henri's friend. The Director makes his proposition to Henri in the first act and is the cause of Maggy being taken to prison. From then on what happens depends on the opinion of the audience who have first to vote on whether or not Maggy should be released and then later have opportunities to intervene and reverse their first decision. In the second part of the opera Greta is substituted for Maggy by the Director and the relationship may or may not prosper. Henri goes to the fair to see a performance of the old Faust puppet play and afterwards begins to travel. At the end Henri may or may not break his contract with the Director.
>
> The structure of the opera turns on the visit to the Faust play. There the roles of the characters are clarified and so is the fact that they tend to be puppets in another's hands. Henri is identified with Faust though he remains in the audience (hence the real audience's participation is indicated too), Richard plays Faust's valet Guignol and Greta goes on stage to play Guignol's wife. All are masked. The Director arrives just in time to help Greta off the stage. It is evident that he is Mephistopheles.

In effect, because of the audience participation, Butor requires from his opera goers what he demands from the readers of his imaginative prose – literally, active involvement. Throughout the libretto, allusions to a

---

[14] Many of the creators' own thoughts concerning *Votre Faust* can be found in the following compilation of working text of the opera and series of interviews with Butor and Pousseur: *Votre Faust* (1968).

number of previous treatments of the Faust story can be gleaned: Maggy's adventure parallels Goethe's "Gretchen Tragödie," Henri, like Mann's Adrian Leverkühn is a composer, Marlowe's *Doctor Faustus* is cited, and "Valéry's Faust and Lust [from *Mon Faust*] are also there in the relationship established between the Devil and literature: the Director is responsible for Henri's libretto."[15]

Although any number of musical allusions to operas by Monteverdi, Mozart, Donizetti, Wagner, Bizet, and Offenbach appear in Pousseur's score, the composer includes no allusions to any previous operatic treatment of Faust: thus he reflects both Henri's reluctance to set the myth to music and his desire to stake out on his own. On the surface, the score appears to be merely a pastiche of older works, however, this highly original serial composition represents, in fact, the single greatest breakthrough, in an almost Faustian manner, for the Belgian composer:

> "Working with quotations in *Votre Faust* left a permanent mark on Pousseur's music, in that the exploitation of the 'harmonic energy thrown out' by earlier serial music became a principal interest."[16]

Luciano Berio in his discussion of the score as "an eloquent retrospective comment on the inner coherence of Pousseur's development" singled out Pousseur's use of Wagnerian allusions throughout the opera whenever Henri contemplates composing his *Faust* – Wagnerian chromaticism symbolizing the task of a modern composer to create. Berio most clearly articulates the uniqueness of Pousseur's post-modernist musical montage within the composer's own œuvre:

> "In reality, the main personage in *Votre Faust* is the history of music, not out of the old Faustian urge to use the past but out of the desire and need to deal with realities wherever they may be."[17]

Unfortunately, the by and large negative reviews *Votre Faust* received at its premiere on January 15, 1969 attest to the inability of an actual audience to intervene during the performance. Although the audience was told that any of its members could say "no" at any time during the performance and thus alter the direction of the plot, the only people who availed themselves of this opportunity were professional French-speaking actors posted at different places in the Piccola Scala to interrupt at previously

---

[15] Waelti-Walters (1977), pp. 82–83.

[16] Vanhulst (1980), p. 171.

[17] Berio (1974), p. 589.

agreed-upon moments.[18] Though the seriousness of Butor and Pousseur cannot be questioned – it took them almost a decade to complete their work – the difficulty surrounding audience interaction with an unfamiliar serial opera which includes extensive passages in a variety of languages has made this work almost impossible to perform. Whereas Busoni's *Faust* has enjoyed increasingly frequent performances (in the nineteen-eighties alone there have been critically acclaimed productions in London, Bologna, and Berlin), the recondite qualities of *Votre Faust* have prevented its further exposure to the actual opera-going public. An overriding irony surrounds *Votre Faust*: although its characters represented by both singers and spoken actors are highly accessible individuals, the difficult nature of the opera in which they appear – its score with all of its alternate versions, weighs over twenty pounds – makes the work itself highly inaccessible to the general public.

Though not strictly a Faust-opera in the exclusive sense as the other three twentieth-century works under discussion, *The Rake's Progress* (1951) by Igor Stravinsky certainly is deserving of brief consideration in this article. The libretto by W. H. Auden (1907–1973) and Chester Kallman (1921–1975), though primarily inspired by the set of eight engravings by Hogarth with the same name, includes a new Faustian dimension missing in Hogarth's set: the relationship between devil and protagonist. In their post-modernistic librettistic conflation Auden and Kallman center the plot of their work around the three wishes accorded by a Mephistophelian Nick Shadow to an almost anti-Faustian Tom Rakewell (unlike the traditional Faust whose tragic flaw is overweening ambition, Tom Rakewell's tragic flaw is lack of ambition). However, the twist in this Faust adaptation – in part because of its Hogarthian-inspired setting – is that it is the tenor Tom who becomes mad by the end of the opera, not the soprano, the Gretchen-like Anne Truelove. In fact, it is Tom's fourth wish for Anne's presence – a wish not foreseen by Nick – that saves Tom toward the conclusion of the graveyard-scene. This Faustian image of redemption through love is yet a further thematic element not present in Hogarth. Once again, as thirty-five years before with his chamber-work *L'Histoire du Soldat* (1918), Stravinsky brought his lean, anti-Romantic music to bear on the Faust theme.

Because of space restrictions a number of twentieth-century operas, such as A. Benjamin's *The Devil Take Her* (1931),[19] H. U. Engelmann's

---

[18] Tomasi (1969), pp. 134–36, and Brunner (1969), pp. 36–37.
[19] Cuddon (1982), p. 269.

Dr. Fausts Höllenfahrt (1951), N. V. Bentzon's *Faust III* (1964),[20] and J. Berg's *Dr. Johannes Faust* (1967)[21] could not be incorporated into the foregoing discussion. However, two composers who tackled the Faust myth in a novel way should at least be mentioned. The fact that Hermann Reutter (*1900) composed both *Dr. Johannes Faust* (1936) and *Don Juan and Faust* (1950) confers the unique distinction to him of possibly being the only recognized composer who set two different full-length operatic adaptations of Faust to music. Although the plot of the earlier opera, which the composer revised in 1955, has a strikingly similar plot to that of Busoni's *Doktor Faust*, his second opera, based on Grabbe's nineteenth-century play of the same name, juxtaposes the two most significant centuries-old European mythic figures. *The Devil and Daniel Webster* (1939), the folk-opera by the American composer Douglas Moore (1893–1969), centers around the persuasive defense of a contrite Faust figure, in this case a State Senator from New Hampshire, by the humane, expert debater, Daniel Webster. Moore's highly tuneful and truly accessible one-act work, with its folk-dancing, spirited choruses, and spoken prose text, linking the musical numbers, stands in marked contradistinction to the remarkably experimental and often arcane modernistic and post-modernistic operatic Faust versions considered in this article.

Works Cited

Achberger, Karen: *Literatur als Libretto.* Heidelberg 1980.

Beaumont, Antony: *Busoni the Composer.* Bloomington (Ind.) 1985 [1985a].

- "Doktor Faust: Ferruccio Busonis unvollendetes Meisterwerk," in: *Oper und Operntext*, hrsg. v. Jens Malte Fischer. Heidelberg 1985, S. 209–225 [1985b].

Berio, Luciano: "Henri Pousseur," in: *A Dictionary of Contemporary Music*, hrsg. v. John Vinton. New York 1974.

Brunner, Gerhard: "Kein Faust für Milanesen," in: *Opern-Welt* Nr. 4 (April) 1969, S. 36–37.

Busoni, Ferruccio: *Doktor Faust* (Piano Score). Leipzig 1925.

- *Über die Möglichkeiten der Oper und über die Partitur des "Doktor Faust".* Leipzig 1926.

- *Briefe an seine Frau*, hrsg. v. Friedrich Schnapp. Zürich 1935.

- "Von der Zukunft der Musik," in: *Wesen und Einheit der Musik*, hrsg. v. Joachim Herrmann. Berlin 1956.

Butor, Michel/Pousseur, Henri: *Votre Faust.* Paris 1968.

Cuddon, John A.: *A Dictionary of Literary Terms.* New York 1982.

Eisler, Hanns: *Johann Faustus.* Berlin 1983.

---

[20] Achberger (1980), p. 248 and p. 267.
[21] "Faust" (1979), p. 162.

"Faust" in: *The Concise Oxford Dictionary of Opera*, hrsg. v. Harold Rosenthal und John Warrack. London 1979.

Goethe, Johann Wolfgang v.: *Faust. Erster Teil.* Hamburg 1967 (Goethe, *Werke, Kommentare und Register.* 14 Bde., hrsg. v. Erich Trunz, Bd. 3).

Luening, Otto: *The Odyssey of an American Composer.* New York 1980.

Mann, Thomas: *Doktor Faustus.* Frankfurt 1974. (Mann, *Gesammelte Werke*, 13 Bde., hrsg. v. H. Bürgin, Bd. 6).

Maue, Karl-Otto: *Hanns Eislers "Johann Faustus" und das Problem des Erbes.* Göppingen 1981.

Schebera, Jürgen: *Hanns Eisler.* Berlin 1981.

Tomasi, Gioacchino Lanza: "'Votre Faust' an der Mailänder Piccola Scala gescheitert," in: *Melos* 36 (1969), S. 134–136.

Vanhulst, Henri: "Henri Pousseur," in: *The New Grove Dictionary of Music and Musicians*, 20 Bde., hrsg. v. Stanely Sadie, Bd. 15. London 1980.

Waelti-Walters, Jennifer: *Michel Butor: A study of his view of the world and a panorama of his work*, 1954–1974. Victoria (B.C.) 1977.

Wassermann, Jakob: *In memoriam Ferruccio Busoni.* Berlin 1925.

My Faust (excerpt)

Paul Valéry

Faust

Listen. I must tell you that your reputation in the world isn't quite so grand as it used to be.

Mephisto

You think so?

Faust

I'm certain. Oh, I don't mean your annual returns, or even your bonuses. I mean your credit, consideration, dignity ....

Mephisto

Maybe, maybe ....

Faust

You are no longer a terror. Hell is relegated now to the final curtain. You don't haunt men's minds nowadays. True, there are a few amateurs, a few backward areas ... But your methods are out-of-date, your physical make-up is comic ....

Mephisto

Could you be having an idea of rejuvenating me, maybe?

Faust

Why not? Everyone should have his turn.

Mephisto

Tempter! ...

Faust

I really do want to freshen you a little. And it would make a diversion for me. We could exchange functions.

Mephisto

This is beyond me. You have the audacity to suppose that I need *you?*

Faust

I know what I am saying. You are locked in Eternity, my dear Devil, you are nothing but a mind. And so you are without thought. You don't know how to disbelieve, how to look for what you haven't got. Fundamentally you are very simple. Like a tiger who is all beast of prey, nothing but a ravening instinct .... You don't even suspect that there are many things in the world besides Good and Evil. I won't explain. You wouldn't be able to understand me ....

Mephisto
No one has ever talked to me this way before ...

Faust
... Wait! Let me go on! While you have been sitting back in your lazy eternity, relying on methods dating from the Year One, man's mind – sharpened with your help! – has begun to attack Creation on its underside .... Think of this: within the very heart of matter, beyond the brink of their own reality, they've discovered old CHAOS itself.

Mephisto
CHAOS ... The one I knew? It isn't possible ....

Faust
It would be easy to show you ...

Mephisto
CHAOS, you say?

Faust
Yes, Chaos, the original one, the very first unutterable confusion, when space, time, light, possibilities, and essences were all in a state of yet-to-be.

Mephisto
They've rediscovered it. CHAOS! ... And I was an Archangel!

Faust
And in a groping way they begin to touch the very sources of life. Listen: they are no longer led astray by speculation. They've finished with that. They realize that intellect alone can only lead to error, that it must be absolutely subject to experiment. Their whole science is now founded on a fool-proof system. Discussion is a mere accessory .... And listen to this: what they discover in this way is utterly unlike what used to be imagined. Nothing is left now, neither truth nor fable, of what belonged to the old days.

Mephisto
Terrible ....

Faust
So it does begin to affect you ... Think, Satan, think: this extraordinary tranformation can affect you in your own redoubtable Person. The fate of Evil itself is at stake .... It may even, you know, mean the end of the soul.

The soul which impressed itself in each mind as an all-powerful sense of some incomparable and indestructible value, an inexhaustible will and power to enjoy, to suffer, to be oneself against all the odds of change, the soul has now sunk in value. The individual is dying. He is drowning in numbers. The accumulation of human beings is effacing all distinction. There's only a hairsbreadth of difference now between vice and virtue; the two are melted into the mass which is called "human material." Death now is just one of the statistical properties of this frightful living substance. Its … *classic* meaning and dignity are disappearing. And the immortality of the soul necessarily follows the same fate as death, which gave it its definition, its infinite significance and value ….

Mephisto
This is hideous!

Faust
It's the way it is. I'm not coloring it with any prejudice of mine. But I had to explain how things are, to win you over.

Mephisto
Go on …. After an affront like that, you can take my horns. Anyway, you'll soon be having a pair of your own, Professor ….

Faust
This is no time for joking. Let me finish. Are you quite sure, my dear Devil, that there's an eternal guarantee for your preeminence, sure there's no one Up There who thinks your official zeal may be slackening, your methods getting rusty, your returns diminishing? … Yours is the most important post of all in the administration of Supreme Justice. But maybe you no longer quite inspire the confidence you did. There's no decree that they won't ever find anyone … worse than you ….

Mephisto
My dear man, the First Archangel is irreplaceable …. True, I fell, but I fell from the top. *(For an instant he is suffused with a violet brillance.)*

Faust
No doubt …. But you'll understand me when you are better acquainted with mortals as they are now. The whole system of which you were a linchpin is falling to pieces. Confess that even you feel lost, unstuck as it were, among this new crowd of human beings who do evil without knowing or caring, who have no notion of Eternity, who risk their lives ten times a day playing with their new machines, who have created countless marvels your magic never dreamt of, and have put them in the reach of

any child, any fool ... And the said marvels have sped up development beyond belief ....

Mephisto
Can they make gold?

Faust
They soon will. Anyhow gold is dying out. They can get metals a hundred thousand times more precious.

Mephisto
What about the golden calf? ...

Faust
Won't be worth its weight in veal, presently.

Mephisto
Can they raise the dead?

Faust
They haven't the slightest wish to.

Mephisto
Why not? It used to be the great idea.

Faust
They feel that everyone should have his turn. New entrants would cause too much competition.

Mephisto
Ah, they know a lot now .... I'm half-afraid they've understood. It's serious ....

Faust
Poor Devil!

Mephisto
Ah, yes .... And poor people, too! Evil used to be such a lovely thing ...

Faust in the Nuclear Age

Osman Durrani

In recent times, several types of scientist, including those who clone life-forms and those who unleash radioactive chain-reactions, have made themselves vulnerable to the accusation of attempting to play God. Few scientists have done more to underline the Faustian responsibilities and Mephistophelean threats to scientific research than Freeman Dyson, sometime Professor of Physics at the Institute for Advanced Study in Princeton, who pays tribute to the influence of Goethe's drama on his thinking in 'The Redemption of Faust', a chapter of his autobiography *Disturbing the Universe* (Dyson (1979), 11–18). He was to acknowledge that he and others like John Robert Oppenheimer, under whom he studied, were guilty of service to a modern devil: 'The Faustian bargain is when you sell your soul to the devil in exchange for knowledge and power. That, of course, in a way, is what Oppenheimer did' (Dyson (1981), 14). The devil may offer the ability to lift a thousand tons of rock into the sky, or, as in I. A. Richards' play *Tomorrow Morning, Faustus*, the instrument of seduction may be nothing more than a tempting research grant argued over in the Board Room of the 'Futurity Foundation'. The connection between the German intellectuals who were expelled in 1939 and those who perfected the engines of destruction is cogently made in Karl Shapiro's poem 'The Progress of Faust', where it is precisely the expulsion of a 'backwardly tolerant' Faustus that leads to Germany's defeat ('the breaching of the Rhine').

Shapiro breaks new ground in depicting Faustus as a victim, not as a symbol or originator of Fascism, but his legacy to the world is far from beneficial; he is now implicated in the American weapons programme, which was based, as many have acknowledged, on Nazi Germany's rocket-building technology. The Faust that tried to be as God, the Faust that strove for mastery of the elements whatever the cost to his moral well-being, is still with us. Yet the case, once made, is apt to be overstated. Not every searching scientist is a clone of the magus. Rolf Hochhuth's recent play about Hermann Oberth describes the physicist as 'Hitler's Doctor Faustus' on the basis of his research into propulsion systems. John Cornwell's study *Hitler's Scientists. Science, War and the Devil's Pact* of 2003 draws the same parallel. The thousands of doctors, engineers, physicists – in short, any trained professional who aided and abetted the Führer's plans to subjugate Europe – were by definition involved in a Faustian pact with the Nazis, and all scientists who ignored the evil consequences of their discoveries deluded themselves if they pleaded that science could remain morally neutral. The threat has not gone away: 'The Faustian bargains lurk within routine grant applications, the pressure to publish for the sake of tenure and the department's budget, the treatment of knowledge as a commodity that can be owned, bought and sold' (Cornwell, 462). In *Newsweek*, Michael Hirsh arraigns Swiss bankers who made profits out of the war for concluding a 'Faustian bargain' ('Secret bankers for the Nazis', 24 June 1996, 50 f.). The list is endless and understandable in the circumstances.

Works Cited

John Cornwell, *Hitler's Scientists. Science, War and the Devil's Pact*. London: Viking, 2003.

Freeman Dyson, *Disturbing the Universe*. New York: Harper and Row, 1979.

– *The Day after Trinity: J. Robert Oppenheimer and the Atomic Bomb*. Kent/Ohio: Transcript Library, 1981.

I. A. Richards, *Tomorrow Morning, Faustus! An Infernal Comedy*. London: Routledge and Kegan Paul, 1962.

The Progress of Faust

Karl Shapiro

He was born in Deutschland, as you would suspect,
And graduated in magic from Cracow
In Fifteen Five. His portraits show a brow
Heightened by science. The eye is indirect,
As of bent light upon a crooked soul,
And that he bargained with the Prince of Shame
For pleasures intellectually foul
Is known by every court that lists his name.

His frequent disappearances are put down
To visits in the regions of the damned
And to the periodic deaths he shammed,
But, unregenerate and in Doctor's gown,
He would turn up to lecture at the fair
And do a minor miracle for a fee.
Many a life he whispered up the stair
To teach the black art of anatomy.

He was as deaf to angels as an oak
When, in the fall of Fifteen Ninety-four,
He went to London and crashed through the floor
In mock damnation of the playgoing folk.
Weekending with the scientific crowd,
He met Sir Francis Bacon and helped draft
"Colours of Good and Evil" and read aloud
An obscene sermon at which no one laughed.

He toured the Continent for a hundred years
And subsidized among the peasantry
The puppet play, his tragic history;
With a white glove he boxed the devil's ears
And with a black his own. Tired of this,
He published penny poems about his sins,
In which he placed the heavy emphasis
On the white glove which, for a penny, wins.

Some time before the hemorrhage of the Kings
Of France, he turned respectable and taught;
Quite suddenly everything that he had thought

Seemed to grow scholars' beards and angels' wings.
It was the Overthrow. On Reason's throne
He sat with the fair Phrygian on his knees
And called all universities his own,
As plausible a figure as you please.

Then back to Germany as the sages' sage
To preach comparative science to the young
Who came from every land in a great throng
And knew they heard the master of the age.
When for a secret formula he paid
The devil another fragment of his soul,
The scholars wept, and several even prayed
That Satan would restore him to them whole.

Backwardly tolerant, Faustus was expelled
From the Third Reich in Nineteen Thirty-nine.
His exit caused the breaching of the Rhine,
Except for which the frontier might have held.
Five years unknown to enemy and friend
He hid, appearing on the sixth to pose
In an American desert at war's end
Where, at his back, a dome of atoms rose.

Faust Globalized

Osman Durrani

Of the hundreds [of updatings] that could be mentioned, the briefest of references to examples from French, Portuguese, Spanish and Arabic will have to suffice. The French novelist and dramatist Philippe Raulet published *Jean Faust. Histoire d'un pacte* ('John Faust. History of a Pact') in 1987. Purporting to derive from a 'low German text from the late fifteenth century' (cover), this takes the form of a narrative interspersed with dramatic dialogues and diary entries attributed to Faust and Wagner and letters passed between many of their contemporaries. Faust is shown the wonders of the universe, but tires quickly of all the names of the planets and starsystems. His erotic adventures bring him little pleasure, and in the end Mephistopheles appears to regret having agreed to a twenty-four-year pact, as it gave his victim too much time to speculate on his fate (Raulet, 132, 245). The novel ends with Faust's death in the traditional manner, after his friends have quizzed him as to why he could not free himself from the pact. Fernando Pessoa's *Fausto. Tragédia Subjectiva* ('Faust. A Subjective Tragedy'), is an inordinately ambitious, unfinished torso, begun in 1908 when the author was twenty, and worked on from then until his death. Thousands of verses produced a posthumous package of 227 fragments, adding up to an enormous soliloquy that has been described as the tragedy of being oneself. Pessoa was, like Valéry, interested in Faust's intellectual frigidity, and his Faust is another solitary modern incapable of genuine emotion. In conversation with the great minds of the past, Christ, Buddha, Shakespeare and Goethe, he cannot devote himself to the present. His long, reflective monologues are placed beside short, emotionally vibrant exclamations by Maria, whom he claims to love, but in such a cerebral manner that he can only talk about rather than act out his love. He dies, as he has lived, in isolation. The author sums it up: 'The drama in its entirety represents the battle between the intellect and life, in which the intellect is always defeated' (Pessoa, 7). In 2000, the Swiss composer Xavier Dayer achieved a major award for his ballet project entitled *Sept Fragments de Faust* which was inspired by Pessoa's work.

A Faust novel by the Venezuelan author Francisco Herrera Luque, *La luna de Fausto* ('Faust's Moon'), first appeared in 1983. It takes as its point of departure a prophesy allegedly made by Faustus to Philip von Hutten, the adventurous brother of the Reformer Ulrich von Hutten. According to Faustus, the former's expedition to South America, intended to locate the legendary El Dorado, would go disastrously wrong, as indeed it did. This becomes the subject of a gripping novel in which German superstitions mingle with the cruelty of the conquistadors and the myth of El Dorado. The moving forces behind this fated expedition, of whose laborious progress Herrera Luque spares the reader few gory details, are the big businessmen of the day, notably the Welser banking concern and Emperor Charles V.

Fausts have been written in many parts of the world. André Dabezies lists and comments on several dozen little-known French, English and German novels, films, radio-plays and other spectacles dating from the 1950s. The Brazilian response is discussed by Rosenthal (Dabezies, 467–504; Rosenthal, 157–68). Non-European Fausts in Egypt were recently reviewed in a paper by Moustafa Maher. This reveals a perhaps surprising affinity between the German and European traditions and those circulating in the Arab world. When Goethe's play was translated into Arabic (Part I appeared in Egypt in 1929, accompanied by an introduction by Taha Hussein) it struck a chord and led to several subsequent adaptations. These include Taufiq al Hakim's *'Ahd esh Shaitan* ('Pact with Satan', 1938), influenced both by Gounod and Goethe, whom the author had read in French translation. Muhammad Farid Abu Hadid wrote a play called *'Abd esh Shaitan* ('Satan's Slave') in 1929 based on Goethe, whom he had read in English translation. Here Mephistopheles (Ahriman) has no difficult in seducing Faust (Toboz), if only because humans now enslave themselves to evil much more readily than they did in Goethe's time. As Satan's instrument, Toboz wreaks destruction in society, commerce, and politics. Toboz does eventually repent, but his conversion comes too late. More recent versions include Yussuf Wahbi's *Ash Shaitan* ('The Devil'), filmed as *Safir Gahannam* ('Journey to Hell'), and *Faust al gadid* ('The New Faust'), a radio play by Ahmad Bakathir, broadcast in 1987. Here, too, we find the familiar variety of approaches; Wahbi's Faust succumbs to Mephisto's promises and gains nothing, while Bakathir's, torn between the attractions of good and evil, recognises that he must work to save mankind and is able to break the pact and strive towards peace and love. Mephisto is powerless and Faust actually thanks him, in his dying moments, for showing him clearly what distinguishes good from evil (Maher, 437–50).

Works Cited

Peter Csobádi, Gernot Gruber, Jürgen Kühnel, Ulrich Müller, Oswald Panagl and Franz Viktor Spechtler (eds), *Europäische Mythen der Neuzeit: Faust und Don Juan. Gesammelte Vorträge des Salzburger Symposions 1992.* 2 volumes. Anif/Salzburg: Ursula Müller-Speiser, 1993.

André Dabezies, *Visages de Faust au XXe siècle.* Paris: Presses Universitaires de France, 1967.

Francisco Herrera Luque, *La luna de Fausto.* Santiago/Chile: Editorial Pomaire, 1983. Cited as *Ibid., Faustmond. La luna de Fausto.* Trans. by Claudia Sierich. Percha: R. S. Schulz, 1986.

Moustafa Maher, 'Die Rezeption des Faust-Stoffes in Ägypten und die vermittelnde Rolle des Theaters', in Csobádi, II, 437–50.

Fernando Pessoa, *Faust. Eine subjektive Tragödie. Fragmente und Entwürfe.* Translated and edited by Georg Rudolf Lind. Zurich: Ammann, 1990.

Philippe Raulet, *Jean Faust. Histoire d'un pacte.* Paris: Albin Michel, 1987.

Erwin Theodor Rosenthal, 'Gretchen ganz spesenfrei. Brasilianische Faustvisionen', in Boerner/Johnson, 157–68.

Faust Rock Opera

Paul M. Malone

From Concept Album to Rock Opera

Rudolf Volz holds a doctorate in mathematics from California's Clare-
mont Graduate University. In 1994, he set himself the task of 'packing
old, traditional intellectual property in new and modern forms, in order to
revive it for the present and future.'[1] After three years' work, the result
was to set Part I of Goethe's drama, using the original text, into the idiom
of popular music, as *Faust: Die Rockoper* ('Faust: The Rock Opera').

The rock opera form has little connection with classical opera other
than the name. It arose at the end of the 1960s, in a convergence of rock
and theatre: in 1967, the so-called 'concept album' began to displace the
collection of singles after the Beatles released *Sgt. Pepper's Lonely Hearts
Club Band* and the Rolling Stones quickly replied with the darker *Their Satanic Majesties Request*. Meanwhile, other rock bands were creating ever
more theatrical forms for their concerts, be it the Grand Guignol-in-
spired antics of American Alice Cooper – which led to KISS and eventually to Twisted Sister – or in England, the art school-influenced dra-
matics of Genesis and flashy but classically-grounded musicianship of the
Nice and Yes. At the same time, the legitimate theatre was being invaded
by musicals devoted to a rock aesthetic rather than the old-fashioned
sounds of Tin Pan Alley: in 1967, *Hair* premiered off-Broadway, as did
Your Own Thing, a rock musical based on Shakespeare's *Twelfth Night*.
These stage shows, aided by dialogue, had a surer sense of plot than the
still disjointed concept albums, but their songs were written by outsiders
to rock culture and earned little respect from the rock critics, one of
whom labelled *Hair*'s creators 'the Francis the Talking Mule of rock'n'roll'
(Anon., 52).

1968 saw efforts to construct concept albums around actual plots, with
the Kings' nostalgic *Village Green Preservation Society* (which by 1974 had
spawned a triple-album sequel, *Preservation Acts I and II*) and the Pretty
Things' seminal *S. F. Sorrow*, a dystopian fantasy now acknowledged as the
first true rock opera. Inspired equally by the latter album and by eastern
mysticism, The Who's Peter Townshend created the classic *Tommy* in

---

[1] This and all subsequent quotations from Volz are taken from his website at
www.faust.cc in July 2003. All translations are by the author, ignoring the less
complete English versions on the same site.

1969. Like *S. F. Sorrow*, *Tommy* is really an oratorio or cantata rather than opera, and though its music is brilliant compared to its precursor, its plot is little clearer. The story, on the other hand, was the strong point of Tim Rice's and Andrew Lloyd Webber's hit album *Jesus Christ Superstar*, also released in 1969 as a 'rock opera.' More truly operatic in form, and with the advantage of a well-structured and well-known plot, *Superstar* became a stage success in 1971. *Tommy* was briefly staged as an all-star musical the following year, but remained incoherent despite Townshend's attempt to act as narrator. Only a year before Volz began his labours, Boston Rock Opera had been formed in Massachusetts to maintain the tradition, reviving *Jesus Christ Superstar* (2000) and *The Rocky Horror Show* (1997), and even attempting to stage *Sgt. Pepper's Lonely Hearts Club Band* in 1995.

Volz's choice of this medium for the popularisation of Goethe's *Faust* is thus quite fitting; though it seems curious that he claims, 'There are indeed several classical operas on this theme, but absolutely no popular materials in music and film.' Leaving aside the question of film, there are many rock songs about the devil, though relatively few of them could be labelled 'Faustian,' and Volz is clearly speaking narrowly of interpretations of Goethe. Besides 'Sympathy for the Devil,' one might also name Black Sabbath's 'N.I.B. (Basically),' in which Ozzy Osbourne pines for love: 'my name is Lucifer, please take my hand.' More often than not, however, in rock the devil appears as a cardboard villain at best – as in Alice Cooper's 1976 concept album *Alice Cooper Goes to Hell* – when not reduced to a metaphor for dissipated living or hard-hearted women. The occult trappings of so-called 'black metal,' 'death metal,' 'doom metal,' on the other hand, are usually couched in such nihilistic terms as to minimise the Faustian element of temptation.

The major exceptions to these generalisations have in fact been produced by figures peripheral to the rock scene: most notable of these is Randy Newman's *Faust*. Like most of Newman's output, his *Faust* has been praised but was not commercially successful, and perhaps because of this and its relatively late appearance in 1995 Volz overlooks it. Equally marginal, and arguably more deservedly so, is Paul Williams's music for Brian De Palma's 1974 horror-comedy film *Phantom of the Paradise*. Williams himself appears in the film as the evil record producer Swan, who steals the 'pop cantata' Faust from its composer, Winslow Leach, in order to plagiarise it for music to open his new concert venue, the 'Paradise'. Leach, framed for theft, escapes from prison to revenge himself, falls into a record-press and is horribly scarred, becoming the eponymous phantom; Swan turns out to be invulnerable, however, having sold his soul years ago for eternal youth and fame. The film attempts to satirise both rock opera and theatrical rock, but its confused mélange of elements from *Faust*, Gaston Leroux's *The Phantom of the Opera* and Oscar Wilde's *The Picture of Dorian Gray* descends into a final chaotic bloodbath. The signature rock ballad 'Faust' appears twice on the soundtrack, sung once as a piano-only 'demo' by William Finlay as Leach and again with full band backing by Williams. Most of the songs, however, are parodies of 1970s rock styles that fall far short of their targets. As a model for rock versions of *Faust* it sets an ominous precedent, but its association of the theme with both hard rock and theatrical rock does anticipate Volz's endeavours.

The Faust Rock Opera

On the website devoted to his adaptation of *Faust*, Volz first offers a conventional interpretation of the story, claiming that the theme is 'independent of historical period, since it deals with crossing the border between ignorance and knowledge, and the automatically associated question of good vs. evil.' Goethe's version marks the transition from the old Faust legend of a quest for earthly wealth to 'the drive for knowledge and wisdom in order to achieve [...] a religious path to God via knowledge of the world and the cosmos.'

Having invoked Goethe's authority, Volz makes a claim that 'The rock opera is true to Goethe's texts'– although he quickly qualifies this statement: 'However, it is confined to Part I, and many cuts have been made. The remaining texts have been reduced to songs by repeating some passages as a refrain.' The cuts are indeed substantial: gone are the so-called 'Eastern Walk,' Goethe's famulus Wagner, Mephisto's twitting of the visiting student, the scene in Auerbach's Cellar, and Gretchen's brother Valentin; so that, even more than in Gounod's opera, the plot rushes toward the tragic love story. Moreover, to compensate for the cutting, visual aids are employed:

> Between the songs there are spoken passages to make the plot clear. Sections that are difficult to understand from the text, such as the poisoning of Gretchen's mother, are clarified by mimed scenes and lively video inserts. (www.Faust.cc website)

Additional changes include the modernisation, often to humorous effect, of the play's milieu: Faust calls up the Earth Spirit on his computer; Mephisto gives Faust a lift on a bicycle and later in a miniature space shuttle made of CDs; the two plotters stay in contact by cellular phone; and the Walpurgis Night festivities include a robot and machine-gun wielding criminals.

Having claimed his participation in 'high culture,' Volz now also attempts to establish the 'street credibility' of his opera in terms of rock culture, clarifying his choice of musical genre as follows:

> The production takes the form of a contemporary rock concert. This is stylistically appropriate, because in recent years such diabolical variants as black metal and death metal have become popular. Mephisto is also a 'devilish fiddler,' who indeed sounds more like Jimi Hendrix than Pagganini [*sic*]. Even Faust sometimes plays electric guitar and enters into a duet with Mephisto [...] Not only the music, but also the lighting, videos and costumes correspond to those of a contemporary rock concert. (*Loc. cit.*)

As Volz points out, the black and white makeup worn by Mephisto (a role already associated with whiteface in the German theatrical tradition) is 'similar to the painted faces of the rock band KISS'– and in its design even more similar to those of such Scandinavian death metal rockers as King Diamond, former lead singer of Mercyful Fate, and the groups Emperor and Immortal. The similarity, however, is deceptive.

Volz describes the music for his *Faust* as heavily indebted to the British band Deep Purple and Germany's Scorpions. It is therefore mainly in the category of 1970s-style hard rock or heavy metal. In general, both of these musical genres – the latter is sometimes considered a subcategory of the former – are characterised by extreme volume, produced by screaming vocals, distorted electric guitar and heavy bass; an adherence to the basic musical form of the blues, including the pentatonic blues scale; and themes of youthful rebellion, generational conflict, and sexuality. Hard rock usually expresses these themes in a quotidian, naturalistic context, and in a major key; whereas heavy metal is more frequently played in a minor key and set against a backdrop of fantasy, science fiction, or Gothic horror, and thus more suitable for *Faust*. Heavy metal is also more likely than hard rock to be influenced by classical music.

The use of keyboards, and particularly the sound of the Hammond organ, in the score of *Faust* recalls Deep Purple, while the electric guitars make use of such well-tried effects as distortion, compression, phasing/flanging, the vibrato unit (also known as the 'tremolo arm' or 'whammy bar'), and the 'wah-wah' pedal (a foot-controlled band pass filter) with its Jimi Hendrix associations, in a manner common to both Deep Purple and Scorpions, as well as to many other bands of the period. In fact, Volz's statements to the contrary notwithstanding, the more contemporary sound of death metal, with its typical barrage of industrial-noise guitar chords, throat-wrenching guttural vocals and determinedly repulsive themes, as evidenced in songs like Deicide's 'Satan Spawn, Caco-Daemon' or Cannibal Corpse's 'Necropedophile,' is almost nowhere evident in this rock opera.

The relatively safe ground of old-fashioned rock facilitates Volz's essentially domesticating strategy of marrying popular music with high culture:

> The synthesis of classical theatre and rock music creates a new art form. In music such forms have already existed, e.g. in the [1970s German] rock group Novalis.
>
> Similar to the Hegelian principle of creating a synthesis from thesis and antithesis, an old classic theatre piece and a musical form are combined to produce a new product from these hitherto independent and contiguously situated elements.
>
> This synthesis reaches its climax in the song 'Du bleibst doch immer' ['You'll always be the one you are,' F 1806 ff.], which uses the same music as 'Born to be Wild.' At first glance it seems impossible that a classic text by Goethe could be reconciled with a classic motorcycle song. (*Loc. cit.*)

Perhaps not coincidentally, 'Born to be Wild,' the 1968 Steppenwolf hit penned by Mars Bonfire (né Dennis McCrohan), contains the phrase 'heavy metal thunder,' allegedly the first occurrence, and therefore often suggested as the origin, of the term in rock music (for varying degrees of credulity on this latter point see Christe, 10; Weinstein, 18–20; Stuessy (1994), 321). The seminal importance of 'Born to be Wild' within rock is indicated by the fact that the song, which quickly became a biker anthem, remains instantly recognisable over thirty years after its release, and has been covered, particularly in concert, by artists as diverse as American heavy metal bands the Blue Öyster Cult and Slayer, instrumental surf rock band The Ventures, southern rocker Duane Allman, British glam-rock band Slade, the Muppets' Miss Piggy (in duet with Ozzy Osbourne), the West German art-rock group Grobschnitt, and veteran East German rockers, Puhdys. This song's inclusion in the score of *Faust* – with appropriate authorisation from the composer and publisher – is therefore clearly a programmatic choice.

Volz's adaptation achieves a degree of intertextuality: at the same time as Mephisto assures Faust that he will stay as he is, the well-known music supplies the subtext of temptation, promising the aged scholar that he is, after all, destined to live life to the fullest! The original text is just as confusing at this point.

Many of the other songs in the adaptation fall into the same hard rock vein, so that the music for *Du bleibst doch immer* is not conspicuously different. Mephisto's *Tierischer als jedes Tier* ('Beastlier than any beast,' sung to the Lord in the prologue), *Das Böse* ('Evil,' in which Mephisto introduces himself to Faust), and *Kein Teufel wär* ('Were I not a devil,' expressing his frustration that Gretchen has given his first gift of jewels to the priest) are skilfully executed hard rock songs based on solid riffs – brief ostinatos originating in the blues, usually chord-based, that underpin most success-ful rock songs – as are Faust's opening monologue *Der Magie ergeben* ('Turned to magic') and his *Das Leben mir verhasst* ('Life hateful to me,' Faust's contemplation of suicide, conflating scenes before and after Mep-histo's appearance).

Faust's *Mondenschein* ('Moonlight,' a continuation of his opening mono-logue) takes the slower form of the so-called 'heavy ballad,' building from a simple acoustic guitar intro to the verse, in which Faust's lines alternate with an echoing electric guitar solo in classic call-and-response fashion (another legacy of the blues and ultimately of African music forms) be-fore the chorus brings in the bass guitar and drums to propel the song forward dynamically. Culminating in an orgasmic guitar solo with strong Ritchie Blackmore overtones, *Mondenschein* is a classic example of the hard rock combination of sonic bombast and unabashed emotionality.

Volz also uses generic differences within contemporary music to aid both plot and characterisation: 'While Faust's and Mephisto's songs vary from heavy metal to death metal [*sic*], Gretchen's songs are ordinary pop songs' [in the English translation on Volz's website, 'ordinary pop songs which you can hear on the radio at any time']. A key contrast is thus set up between the two main male characters – in fact, they are the only remain-ing male characters in this heavily reduced version of Goethe – and Gretchen, who is offhandedly relegated to the lesser sphere of 'pop,' recal-ling Robert Pattison's definition:

> Pop is the most contemptuous term among the rock cognoscenti. Pop is what the mass public buys. Pop is pap. [...] The adjectives used in rock criticism to define pop are *tired, formulaic, unoriginal, boring.* The Sex Pistols, Iggy Pop, the Fall – the groups and performers who have been scorned by the mass market – are the heroes of rock precisely because their work is the opposite of pop. For these heroes, pop is the dreary foil to their misunderstood genius, which straight culture mistakes for confusion or depravity. (Pattison, 190)

And in fact, although Gretchen's 'King in Thule' cannily combines folk-rock stylings with the dynamics of the heavy ballad, and her complaint about Mephisto's influence on Faust, *Heimlich Grauen* ('Nameless Terror'), is equally clever in delaying the entrance of the electric guitars until the final section to signal the Evil One's presence, she otherwise does not fare particularly well musically in comparison to the dynamic, if equally derivative, nature of the numbers given to Faust and Mephisto. When, for example, she finds the jewels in her closet to *Am Golde hängt doch alles* ('Everything depends on gold'), the combination of synthesised marimba and strings with syncopated pop-funk rhythm guitar straight out of a Falco disco tune creates an almost unbearably saccharine effect; while her duet with Faust, *Er liebt mich* ('He loves me'), perfectly reproduces that 'melodious but embarrassing scene' of which *Rolling Stone* had complained in *Jesus Christ Superstar* three decades before (though here, at least, one could argue that the mawkishness is dramaturgically justified). *Meine Ruh ist hin* ('My Peace is Gone'), meanwhile, which inspired *Lieder* by Schumann and Spohr, is turned into a rather dreary slow rock waltz with a slight country-pop flavour – somewhat reminiscent of early 1970s-era Olivia Newton-John – which a brief but blistering guitar solo in the last section fails to enliven. A similarly slow power ballad treatment of the opera's last real song, *Meine Mutter hab' ich umgebracht* ('I killed my mother'), is arguably the score's nadir, with heavy guitar chords bathetically underpinning the title phrase in the chorus, as if Gretchen's confession of murder is to be accompanied by the audience waving their cigarette lighters in the air.

Among the other rock styles in evidence in *Faust*, particularly noteworthy are the songs *Erdgeist* and *Walpurgis Nacht*. The former is sung by the Earth Spirit as an appropriately earthy rock boogie with requisite piano solo. This lively number combines elements of the Acid Queen's song from *Tommy* with an arrangement that would not be out of place in *The Rocky Horror Show* (to which Volz refers on his English website, but not in the German, where he merely claims that *Faust* has already become a 'cult musical'). The song performed by the Walpurgis Night revellers, on the other hand, aspires to *Rocky Horror*-style novelty but misses the mark, and oddly suppresses the slightly obscene references in the song about the apple tree, apparently because Goethe himself struck them out of his manuscript. Given the alleged intent to 'mirror old literary goods in the garment of modern rock and pop music' and the tameness of these references for a contemporary audience, leaving gaps in the lyrics of this song seems contradictory, and is apparently motivated by a combination of reverence for the original text – a reverence that nonetheless proves extremely flexible elsewhere in the adaptation – and perhaps a desire to keep the adaptation suitable for school groups (interestingly, the English-language-version of the song, available for download on the website, is abysmally translated but fills in the gaps in the text; presumably English-speaking audiences can take this sort of thing without flinching).

The derivative quality of much of the music in *Faust: Die Rockoper* should not be considered a serious flaw (even though one of the press reviews posted on the website contains what I presume is a typo: *Rock-Opfer* – 'victim of rock'); much of the music produced by rock writers and performers from the 1950s to the present exists in an ongoing intertextual dialogue that swings between homage and plagiarism. The digital sampling typical of rap and hip-hop is only the latest, automated manifestation of this dialogue. In fact, much of the opera's hard rock music is competent in its idiom, largely thanks to very skilful arrangements. It remains questionable, however, whether Volz's work lives up to its explicit claim to be faithful to Goethe's text – as opposed to the plot, at least in its barest outline – given the amount of cutting and transposition undertaken.

Volz's project has an additional dimension, moreover, through which he intends to trump all previous operatic and musical interpretations: not content with confining his work to the first part of Goethe's tragedy, Volz has gone on to adapt the second part of *Faust* (which Volz rather bizarrely describes as 'hardly known') into rock musical form as well. In addition to his original claim of fidelity, Volz now adds the further claim of historically unique completeness: 'This is the first adaptation of this theme into operatic form.'

This claim too is not entirely true: as we have seen, Boito's *Mefistofele* works sections of Part II into the plot, as do several other works; and Alfred Brüggeman in fact composed a trilogy of operas covering both parts of the tragedy in the early 1900s, although the third opera, *Faust and Helena, Faust's Redemption*, was never performed (Kelly, 104–6). Thus Volz's claim is also not utterly false either. In any case, *Faust II: Die Rock-oper* premièred in October 2002; like its precursor, it has been greatly abbreviated, but in contrast to Part I, the second part contains at least fragments of all the major scenes, and hence runs much longer than Part I. Moreover, although the influence of hard rock is still present, as in the Emperor's song *Gegenkaiser* ('Anti-Emperor', very much in the Deep Purple mould), it is now counterbalanced by explorations of the classical elements of Goethe's text through the medium of another musical form that rose to prominence in the early 1970s, so-called 'progressive rock' or 'art rock' in the style of Yes, Procul Harum, Renaissance or the above-named Novalis. Accordingly the sounds of the Hammond organ and the piano prevalent in Part I are now supplemented by a greater variety of synthesised sounds, including those of the stereotypical 1970s art-rock instrument, the Mellotron. Classical music itself also appears: the 'Promenade' from Mussorgsky's *Pictures at an Exhibition* (shades of Emerson, Lake and Palmer) appears as a fanfare for the Emperor, and Faust's death is marked by Chopin's 'Funeral March.' The music is more complex, freely mixing styles and giving the expanded cast greater opportunities for harmony, background vocals and choral work – and more interesting parts for women's voices (Helen, Ariel and Homunculus, among the named roles). Indeed, the singers, especially the women, are often hard pressed to rise to the challenge of the higher notes. Of particular interest is the Emperor's and Mephisto's *Es fehlt an Geld* ('Money is lacking'), which segues from Mussorgsky into a number of styles, ranging from 1950s-style syncopation to a driving funk bass rhythm to eerie free-form wash of synthesisers and back again. *Rechnung* ('Reckoning,' about Mephisto's invention of paper money), on the other hand, mimics the style of David Bowie; *Hier knie nieder* ('Here kneel down,' Faust's order to the watchman Lynkeus to submit to Helen's punishment) is based on a twangy Byrds-style arpeggiated guitar riff that somehow evokes Gerry and the Pacemakers' 1964 hit 'Ferry across the Mersey'; and *Grablegung* ('Burial') alternates Mephisto's rage at being cheated of his prey, growling and screaming over irregular Metallica-inspired power chords and thus coming as close as *Faust* ever does to true death metal, with the angelic choir backed by synthesiser – a juxtaposition that, no doubt coincidentally, recalls the contrast between the voices of the virtues and that of the devil in Hildegard of Bingen's mediaeval work *Ordo Virtutum*.

Both a greater degree of confidence and a larger budget are evident in the second part, and the recent appearance of a new song for Part I, *Grau ist alle Theorie* ('Gray is all theory,' from Mephisto's scene masquerading as Faust for the Student), on the *Faust* website, may well indicate that the first part is now being enlarged to take advantage of the increased resources. A Spanish-language touring company has now been formed, and an English-language version is available for download on the website; the existence of these versions, combined with the offer of limited free performance rights for educational institutions in English-speaking countries, indicates the scope of Volz's ambition for his interpretation.

Unfortunately, the English translations are not only incompetent but also suffer from the handicap of not scanning correctly to fit the music – and matters are not helped by the fact that many of the German cast are clearly uncomfortable singing in English. This may prove, however, to be only a minor obstacle in the dissemination of Rudolf Volz's *Faust: Die Rockoper*. As the conclusion of Part II demonstrates: 'Whoever aspires unweariedly/ is not beyond redeeming' (F 11936f.).

Works Cited

Anon, Review of the album *DisinHAIRited, Rolling Stone*, 21 February 1970, 52.

Ian Christe, *Sound of the Beast: The Complete Headbanging History of Heavy Metal*. New York: Harper, 2003.

James William Kelly, *The Faust Legend in Music*, PhD Dissertation, Northwestern University, 1960. Bibliography updated 1974. Detroit: Information Coordinators, 1976.

Robert Pattison, *The Triumph of Vulgarity: Rock Music in the Mirror of Romanticism*. New York: Oxford University Press, 1987.

Joe Stuessy, *Rock and Roll: Its History and Stylistic Development*. Englewood Cliffs/ NJ: Prentice Hall, 1990. Revised 1994, 2003.

Deena Weinstein, *Heavy Metal: A Cultural Sociology*. New York: Lexington, 1991.

Suggestions for Further Reading

The following list of books and articles is intended for those who would like to have further knowledge of the works used in this collection, or who want to explore other aspects of the Faust legend.

For a more complete bibliography (including works in foreign languages) consult E.M. Butler, *The Fortunes of Faust*, Cambridge, 1952; André Dabezies, *Visages de Faust au XXe siècle*, Paris, 1967; J.W. Smeed, *Faust in Literature*, Oxford, 1975; *Faust: Annäherung an einen Mythos*, eds. Frank Möbus, Friederike Schmidt-Möbus, and Gerd Unverfehrt, Göttingen, 1995; and Osman Durrani, *Faust: Icon of Modern Culture*, Mountfield, East Sussex, 2004.

General

Butler, E.M., *The Fortunes of Faust*, Cambridge, 1952.
Durrani, Osman, *Faust: Icon of Modern Culture*, Mountfield, East Sussex, 2004.
Faust: Sources, Works, Criticism, ed. Paul A. Bates, New York, 1969.
Faust Through Four Centuries. Retrospect and Analysis, ed. Peter Boerner and Sidney Johnson, Tübingen, 1989.
Hawkes, David, *Faust Myth: Religion and the Rise of Representation*, New York, 2007.
Haynes, Roslynn D., *From Faust to Strangelove: Representations of the Scientist in Western Literature*, Baltimore, 1994.
International Faust Studies: Adaptation, Reception, Translation, ed. Lorna Fitzsimmons, London, 2008.
Meek, Harold, *Johann Faust. The Man and the Myth*, London, 1930.
Mitchell, Michael, *Hidden Mutualities: Faustian Themes from Gnostic Origins to the Postcolonial*, Amsterdam, 2006.
Our Faust? Roots and Ramifications of a Modern German Myth, ed. Reinhold Grimm and Jost Hermand, Madison, 1987.
Palmer, Philip Mason and Robert Pattison More, *The Sources of the Faust Tradition From Simon Magus to Lessing*, New York, 1936 (reissued, 1965).
Smeed, J.W., *Faust in Literature*, Oxford, 1975.
Watt, Ian, *Myths of Modern Individualism: Faust, Don Quixote, Don Juan, Robinson Crusoe*, Cambridge, 1996.
Werres, Peter, James Campbell, and Peter Beicken, *Doctor Faustus: Archetypal Subtext at the Millennium*, ed. Armand E. Singer and Jürgen Schlunk, Morgantown, 1999.

The Early Faust Books

Baron, Frank, *Faustus on Trial. The Origins of Johann Spies's "Historia" in an Age of Witch Hunting*, Tübingen, 1992.
The English Faust Book, ed. John Henry Jones, Cambridge, 1994.
The Historie of the Damnable Life and Deserved Death of Doctor John Faustus, ed. William Rose, New York, 1925 (reissued, Notre Dame, 1963).
Jantz, Harold, "An Elizabethan Statement on the Origin of the German Faust Book, With a Note on Marlowe's Sources," *Journal of English and German Philology*, 51 (1952), 137–153.
Knellwolf, Christa, *Faustus and the Promises of the New Science: From the Chapbooks to Harlequin Doctor Faustus, c. 1580–1730*, Aldershot, forthcoming.

Christopher Marlowe's *Doctor Faustus*

Cole, Douglas, *Christopher Marlowe and the Renaissance of Tragedy*, Westport, 1995.
Dollimore, Jonathan, "*Dr. Faustus* (c. 1589–92): Subversion Through Transgression," *Radical Tragedy*, Durham, 2004, 109–119.
Empson, William, *Faustus and the Censor. The English Faust-book and Marlowe's Doctor Faustus*, ed. John Henry Jones, Oxford, 1987.
Leech, Clifford, *Marlowe: A Collection of Critical Essays*, Englewood Cliffs, N.J., 1964.
Marlowe, Christopher, *Doctor Faustus*, ed. David Scott Kastan, New York, 2005.
– *Doctor Faustus*, ed. David Wootton, Indianapolis, 2005.
– *Doctor Faustus, 1604–1616*, ed. W. W. Greg, Oxford, 1950.

Puppet Plays and Ballads

The Old German Puppet Play of Doctor Faust, ed. and tr. T. C. H. Hedderwick, London, 1887.
In addition to the large number of German Faust ballads, published at various times, numerous English versions exist, as in the following:
The Roxburghe Ballads, ed. Joseph Woodfall Ebsworth, Hertford, 1888, Vol. VI, part 3, 703–705.
The Shirburn Ballads, 1585–1616, ed. Andrew Clark, Oxford, 1907, 72–75.

Goethe's *Faust*

Atkins, Stuart, *Goethe's Faust. A Literary Analysis*, Cambridge, 1958.
Binswanger, Hans Christoph, *Money and Magic: A Critique of the Modern Economy in the Light of Goethe's Faust*, tr. J. E. Harrison, Chicago, 1994.
Bohm, Arnd, *Goethe's Faust and European Epic*, Rochester, 2007.
Brown, Jane K., *Goethe's Faust: The German Tragedy*, Ithaca, 1986.
Companion to Goethe's Faust: Parts I and II, ed. Paul Bishop, Rochester, 2006.
Interpreting Goethe's Faust Today, ed. Jane K. Brown et al., Columbia, S.C., 1994.

Our Faust? *Roots and Ramifications of a Modern German Myth,* ed. Reinhold Grimm and Jost Hermand, Madison, 1987.

Pelikan, Jaroslav, *Faust the Theologian,* New Haven, 1995.

Prokhoris, Sabine, *The Witch's Kitchen: Freud, Faust, and the Transference,* Ithaca, 1995.

Van der Laan, James M., *Seeking Meaning for Goethe's Faust,* London, 2007.

Faust in Music

Albright, Daniel, *Berlioz's Semi-Operas: Roméo et Juliette and La damnation de Faust,* Rochester, 2001.

Barricelli, Jean-Pierre, "Faust and the Music of Evil," *Journal of European Studies,* 13 (1983), 1–26.

Berlioz, Hector, *Memoirs,* ed. and tr. David Cairns, New York, 1969.

Chamness, Nancy O., *The Libretto as Literature:* Doktor Faust *by Ferruccio Busoni,* New York, 2001.

Green, Marcia, "Faustian Modulations: Boito and Pynchon," *Ars Lyrica* 6 (1992), 55–61.

Grim, William, *The Faust Legend in Music and Literature,* Lewiston, 1988–92.

Kelly, James William, *The Faust Legend in Music,* Evanston, 1960.

Larkin, David, "A Tale of Two *Fausts:* An Examination of Reciprocal Influence in the Responses of Liszt and Wagner to Goethe's *Faust," Music and Literature in German Romanticism,* ed. Siobhán Donovan and Robin Elliott, Rochester, 2004, 87–104.

Schulz, Max F., *"Die Frau Ohne Schatten*: A Feminist Faust," *Ars Lyrica* 6 (1992), 41–47.

Faust in the 20th and 21st Centuries

Blackall, Eric A., "'What the devil?!' – Twentieth-Century Fausts," *Faust Through Four Centuries. Retrospect and Analysis,* ed. Peter Boerner and Sidney Johnson, Tübingen, 1989, 197–212.

Cobley, Evelyn, *Temptations of Faust: The Logic of Fascism and Postmodern Archaeologies,* Toronto, 2002.

Durrani, Osman, *Faust: Icon of Modern Culture,* Mountfield, East Sussex, 2004.

Grimstad, Kirsten J., *The Modern Revival of Gnosticism and Thomas Mann's* Doktor Faustus, Rochester, 2002.

Hamlin, Cyrus, "Faust in Performance: Peter Stein's Production of Goethe's *Faust,* Parts 1 and 2," *Theater* 32.1 (2002), 116–136.

Hawkes, David, *Faust Myth: Religion and the Rise of Representation,* New York, 2007.

Hedges, Inez, *Framing Faust: 20th Century Cultural Struggles,* Carbondale, 2005.

International Faust Studies: Adaptation, Reception, Translation, ed. Lorna Fitzsimmons, London, 2008.

Knust, Herbert, "From Faust to Oppenheimer: The Scientist's Pact with the Devil," *Journal of European Studies,* 13 (1983), 122–141.

Mamet, David, *Faustus*, New York, 2004.

Mitchell, Michael, *Hidden Mutualities: Faustian Themes from Gnostic Origins to the Post-colonial*, Amsterdam, 2006.

Pfaff, Lucie, *The Devil in Thomas Mann's "Doktor Faustus" and Paul Valéry's "Mon Faust*," Bern, 1976.

Weinberg, Kurt, *The Figure of Faust in Valéry and Goethe*, Princeton, 1976.

Index